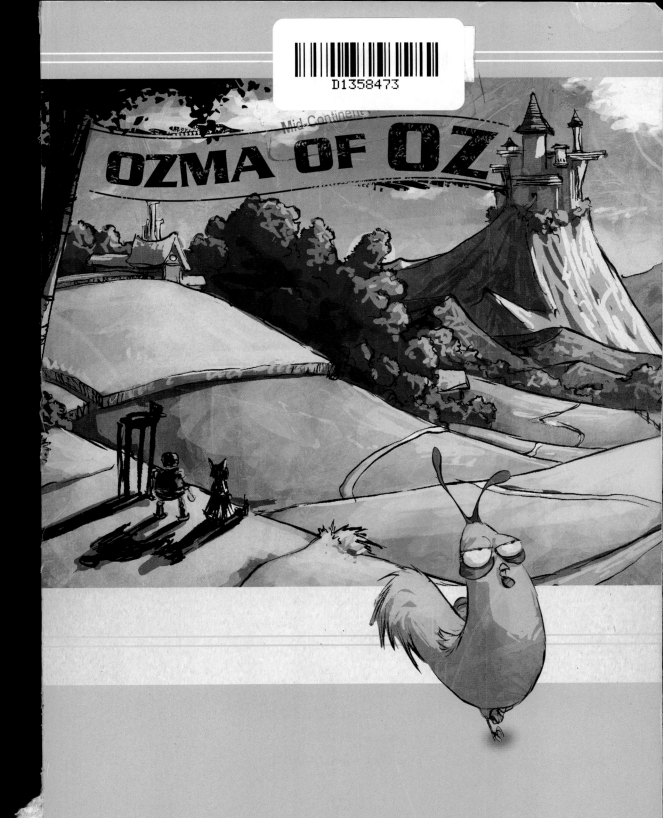

OZ: OZMA OF OZ. Contains material originally published in magazine form as OZMA OF OZ #1-8. First printing 2014. ISBN# 978-0-7851-9108-7. Published by MARVEL WORLDWIDE, INC., a subsidiary of MARVEL ENTERTAINMENT, LLC. OFFICE OF PUBLICATION: 135 West 50th Street, New York, NY 10020. Copyright © 2013 and 2014 Marvel Characters, Inc. All rights reserved. All characters featured in this issue and the distinctive names and likenesses thereof, and all related indicia are trademarks of Marvel Characters, Inc. No similarity between any of the names, characters, persons, and/or institutions in this magazine with those of any living or dead person or institution is intended, and any such similarity which may exist is purely coincidental. **Printed in the U.S.A.** ALAN FINE, EVP - Office of the President, Marvel Worldwide, Inc. and EVP & CMO Marvel Characters B.V.; DAN BUCKLEY, Publisher & President - Print, Animation & Digital Divisions; JOE QUESADA, Chief Creative Officer; TOM BREVOORT, SVP of Publishing; DAVID BOGART, SVP of Operations & Procurement, Publishing; C.B. CEBULSKI, SVP of Creator & Content Development; DAVID GABRIEL, SVP Print, Sales & Marketing; JIM O'KEEFE, VP of Operations & Logistics; DAN CARR, Executive Director of Publishing Technology; SUSAN CRESPI, Editorial Operations Manager; ALEX MORALES, Publishing Operations Manager; STAN LEE, Chairman Emeritus. For information regarding advertising in Marvel Comics or on Marvel.com, please contact Niza Disla, Director of Marvel Partnerships, at ndisla@marvel.com. For Marvel subscription inquiries, please call 800-217-9158. **Manufactured between 4/4/2014 and 5/12/2014 by R.R. DONNELLEY, INC., SALEM, VA, USA.**

10 9 8 7 6 5 4 3 2 1

OZMA OF OZ

ADAPTED FROM THE NOVEL BY L. FRANK BAUM

Writer: **ERIC SHANOWER**
Artist: **SKOTTIE YOUNG**
Colorist: **JEAN-FRANCOIS BEAULIEU**
Letterer: **JEFF ECKLEBERRY**

Production: **DAMIEN LUCCHESE, TAYLOR ESPOSITO, MAYA GUTIERREZ & MANNY MEDEROS**
Assistant Editor: **MICHAEL HORWITZ**
Editors: **SANA AMANAT & NATE COSBY**

Collection Editor: **MARK D. BEAZLEY**
Associate Managing Editor: **ALEX STARBUCK**
Editor, Special Projects: **JENNIFER GRÜNWALD**
Senior Editor, Special Projects: **JEFF YOUNGQUIST**
SVP Print, Sales & Marketing: **DAVID GABRIEL**
Book Design: **ARLENE SO**

Editor in Chief: **AXEL ALONSO**
Chief Creative Officer: **JOE QUESADA**
Publisher: **DAN BUCKLEY**
Executive Producer: **ALAN FINE**

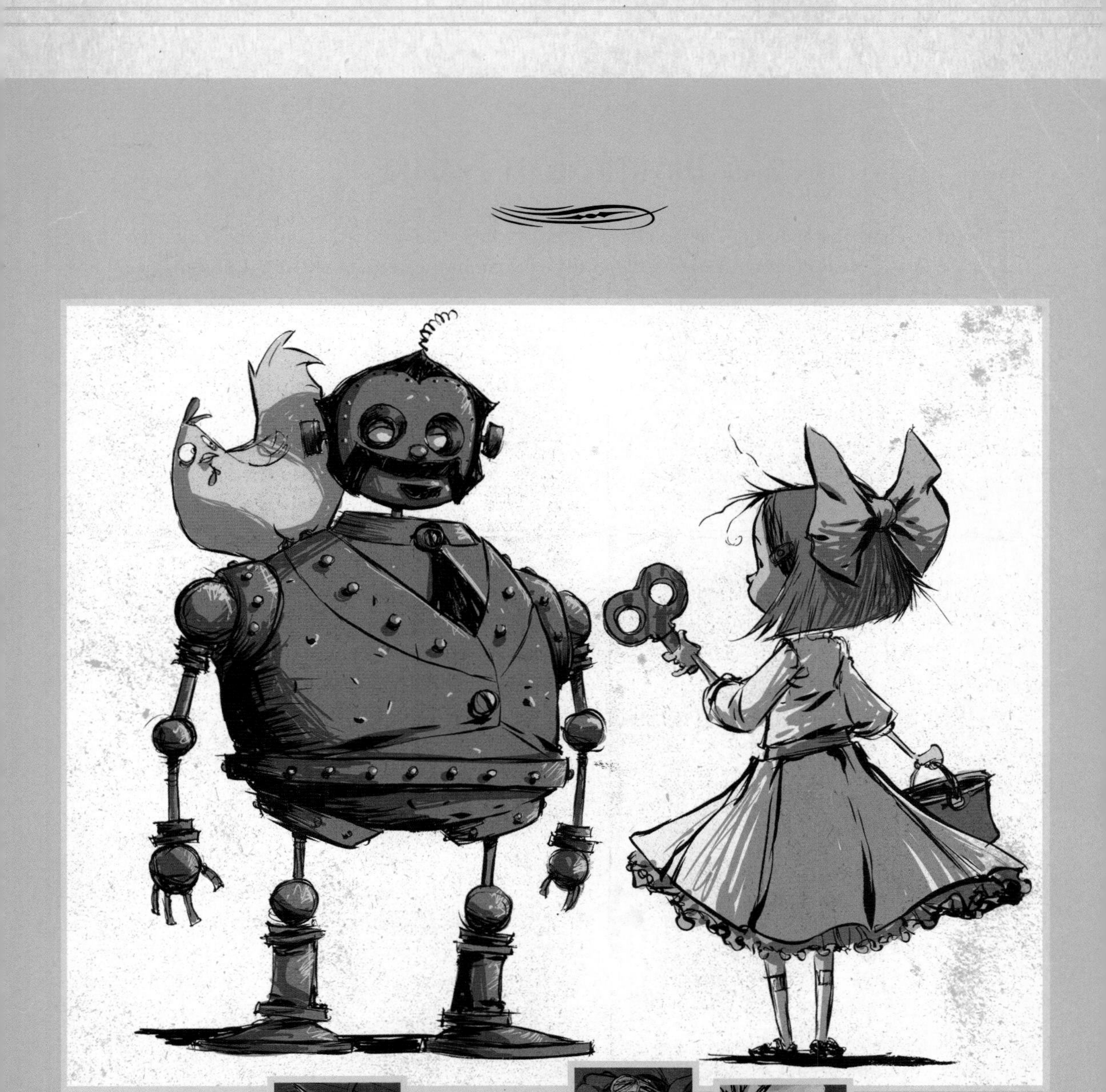
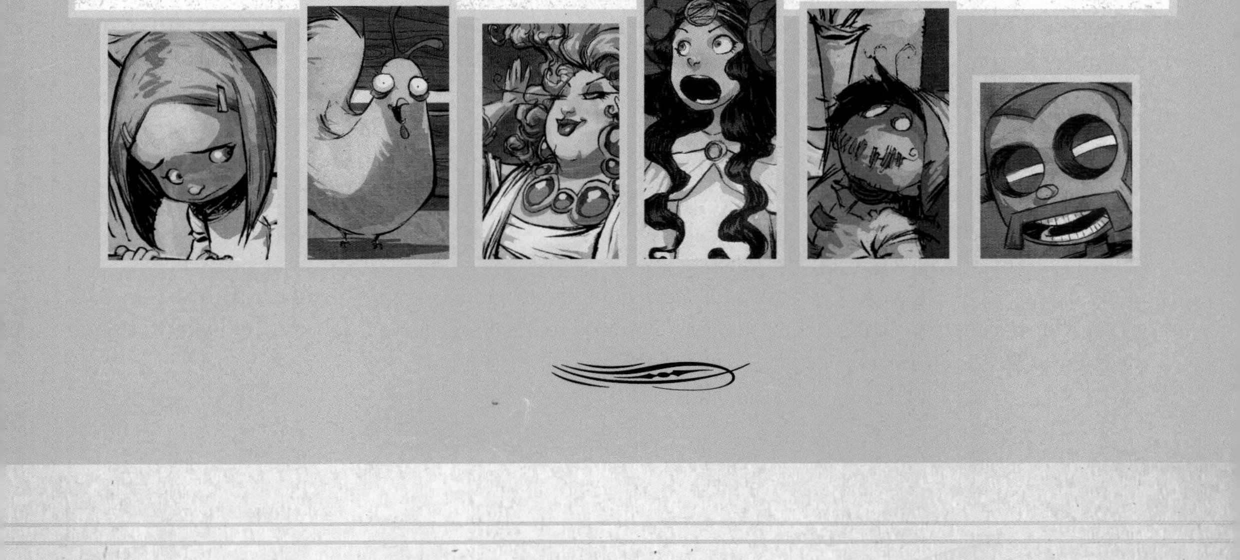

Dorothy Gale is Back

The main character of author L. Frank Baum's best-selling 1900 children's book, *The Wonderful Wizard of Oz*, was a Kansas farm girl named Dorothy who found herself in the strange and magical Land of Oz. Her goal was to return home. Baum's 1904 sequel, *The Marvelous Land of Oz,* barely mentioned Dorothy. Instead, the returning characters from the first book were Dorothy's Oz friends, the Scarecrow and the Tin Woodman. But readers demanded "more about Dorothy."

So in the third Oz book, *Ozma of Oz,* published in 1907, Dorothy Gale returned to Oz, and the Oz books officially became a series.

In *Ozma of Oz* L. Frank Baum could have mimicked the plot of *The Wonderful Wizard of Oz* by again giving his young heroine the goal of returning home. But Baum consciously tried to make each of his Oz stories unique. *Ozma of Oz* is tightly plotted and introduces many new characters destined to become mainstays of the Oz cast. When I read it first as a child, it immediately became my favorite Oz book. I know that I'm not alone in that experience.

Dorothy's main role in the story is as an ally to her new friend, Ozma, ruler of Oz. Ozma's goal is to free a group of slaves from another country by leading her army against the ruler of a third country. Much criticism has been leveled over the years at Ozma's foreign policy, which tends to be well intentioned but naïve. What her critics seem to forget is that Ozma is new to ruling a country. Her upbringing as a witch's servant was no fit preparation for dealing with affairs of state. She's a kid suddenly saddled with adult responsibility, still feeling her way as a monarch after her surprise discovery at the end of the previous Oz book. Some of her advisors have experience as rulers—the Tin Woodman, Glinda, the Scarecrow, and the Cowardly Lion. But youthful, inexperienced Ozma must largely rely on her own judgment. Yet even in the face of danger and her own mistakes Ozma never falters, as you'll see.

Ozma of Oz also features the return of the Cowardly Lion. Near the end of *The Wonderful Wizard of Oz* the Lion became King of Beasts. But from now on, he evidently takes up permanent residence in the Emerald City. He mentions his forest kingdom once in this story, but after that we never hear about it again.

The Scarecrow, the Tin Woodman, and the Sawhorse are back, too. Lots of other Oz characters from the first two books make appearances: Jack Pumpkinhead, the Woggle-bug, Jinjur, Jellia Jamb, even Boq the Munchkin—see if you can spot him.

But it wouldn't be an Oz book without plenty of new characters. Viewers of the 1985 Disney motion picture *Return to Oz* will recognize several of them in cartoonist Skottie Young's captivating new designs. Foremost are Billina the Yellow Hen, who doesn't stand for any nonsense, and Tik-tok, the copper Clockwork Man, who can do anything but actually live. The vain and self-absorbed Princess Langwidere with her cabinet of detachable heads also appeared in the movie *Return to Oz*—though there she was called Mombi, possibly because the play on words "languid air" was too obscure.

And here's the first appearance of the Nome King, the arch villain of the Oz books. Initially the Nome King doesn't seem like such a bad guy. Outwardly he's reasonable, even jolly. But like any good literary villain, the Nome King has deeper layers. And some of them are anything but reasonable. Many of the Nome King's justifications for his actions are as valid as any politician's, before or since. If you'd like an exercise in critical thinking, pay attention to the Nome King's debate with Dorothy about the King of Ev's long life.

Ozma of Oz has been adapted many times—to motion pictures, to the stage, to animation, to picture books, to comics art. I'd like to mention two instances.

First, L. Frank Baum, as he'd done with his previous Oz books, adapted *Ozma of Oz* into a stage musical. After several incarnations, the production finally reached the stage in 1913 as *The Tik-tok Man of Oz*, with music by Louis F. Gottschalk. The show played successfully in California and toured the Midwest, but never reached Broadway. Baum recycled much of the show's plot and many of its characters into his Oz book for 1914, *Tik-tok of Oz*.

Second, there was a previous Marvel Comics adaptation of *Ozma of Oz*. In 1975 Marvel Comics and DC Comics teamed up for the first time to publish *MGM's Marvelous Wizard of Oz*. It was an oversized comic book—in the format called a Treasury Edition—adapting the 1939 MGM movie adaptation of Baum's first Oz book. The art was penciled by John Buscema, who captured a close retelling of the movie, despite having seen it only once decades before. The script was by Roy Thomas, who also wrote the script for the follow-up, *The Marvelous Land of Oz* Treasury Edition, issued the next year by Marvel Comics alone. Its lush artwork by Alfredo Alcala was based on John R. Neill's original illustrations for the book, except in the depictions of the Scarecrow and the Tin Woodman, who resembled their MGM movie versions.

An advertisement in the *Marvelous Land* Treasury Edition announced *The Marvelous Ozma of Oz*, coming later in 1976, again with art by Alcala and script by Thomas. The completed project was a faithful adaptation of Baum's book, sprinkled with a handful of characters based on their MGM movie counterparts. This adherence to the MGM movie necessitated the Hungry Tiger walking on his hind legs to match the Cowardly Lion. As scripter Roy Thomas has noted elsewhere, the result was a bit odd-looking when the two characters pulled Ozma's chariot.

Back then, as I understand it, Marvel's legal department had determined that three Oz titles were in the public domain. The first two were *The Wonderful Wizard of Oz* and *The Marvelous Land of Oz*. But the third title wasn't Baum's third Oz book, *Ozma of Oz*, as had been assumed. It was actually *The New Wizard of Oz*, merely a retitling of *The Wonderful Wizard of Oz*. When Marvel realized that *Ozma of Oz* was still under copyright, rather than secure publication rights from Baum's heirs, they simply cancelled publication.

Today there's little chance of the first Marvel Comics adaptation of *Ozma of Oz* being published. While L. Frank Baum's *Ozma of Oz* has since entered public domain, the rights to the likenesses of the MGM movie characters would need to be secured again. An even greater hurdle to publication is the state of the artwork, assuming the art could be located. Photocopies of the art show that many word balloons—originally pasted onto Alcala's artwork—have fallen off. Restoration would be a major undertaking.

One fragment of the project, however, saw print. The front cover by John Romita—with coloring by yours truly—appeared on the back cover of a 1987 issue of *The Baum Bugle*, the journal of the International Wizard of Oz Club (whose web address is www.ozclub.org for those interested).

But now Marvel Comics presents a new comics version of *Ozma of Oz* for the enjoyment of all. So what are you waiting for? Turn the page and start enjoying Dorothy Gale's return.

Eric Shanower
July 2011

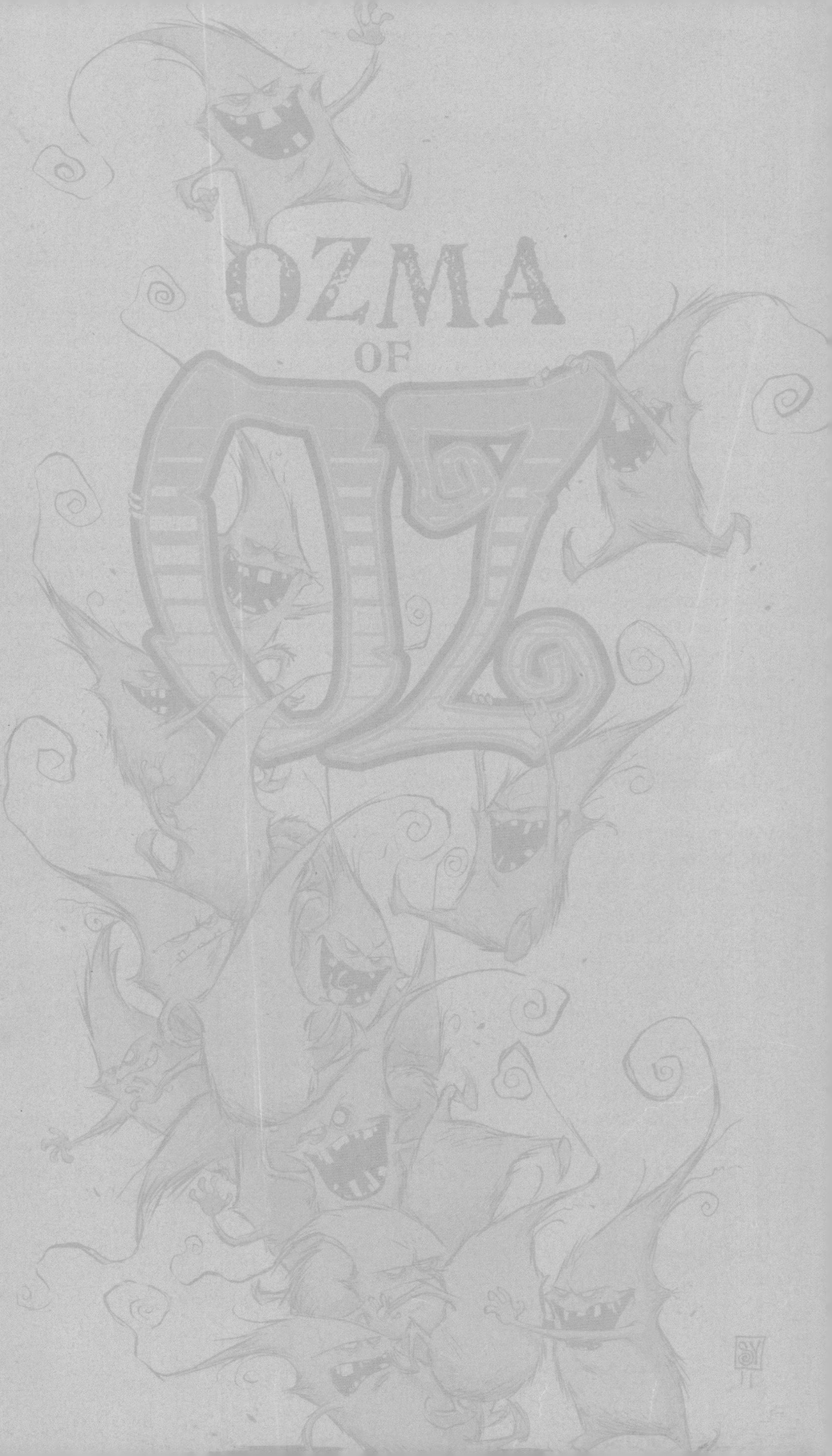
OZMA
OF
OZ

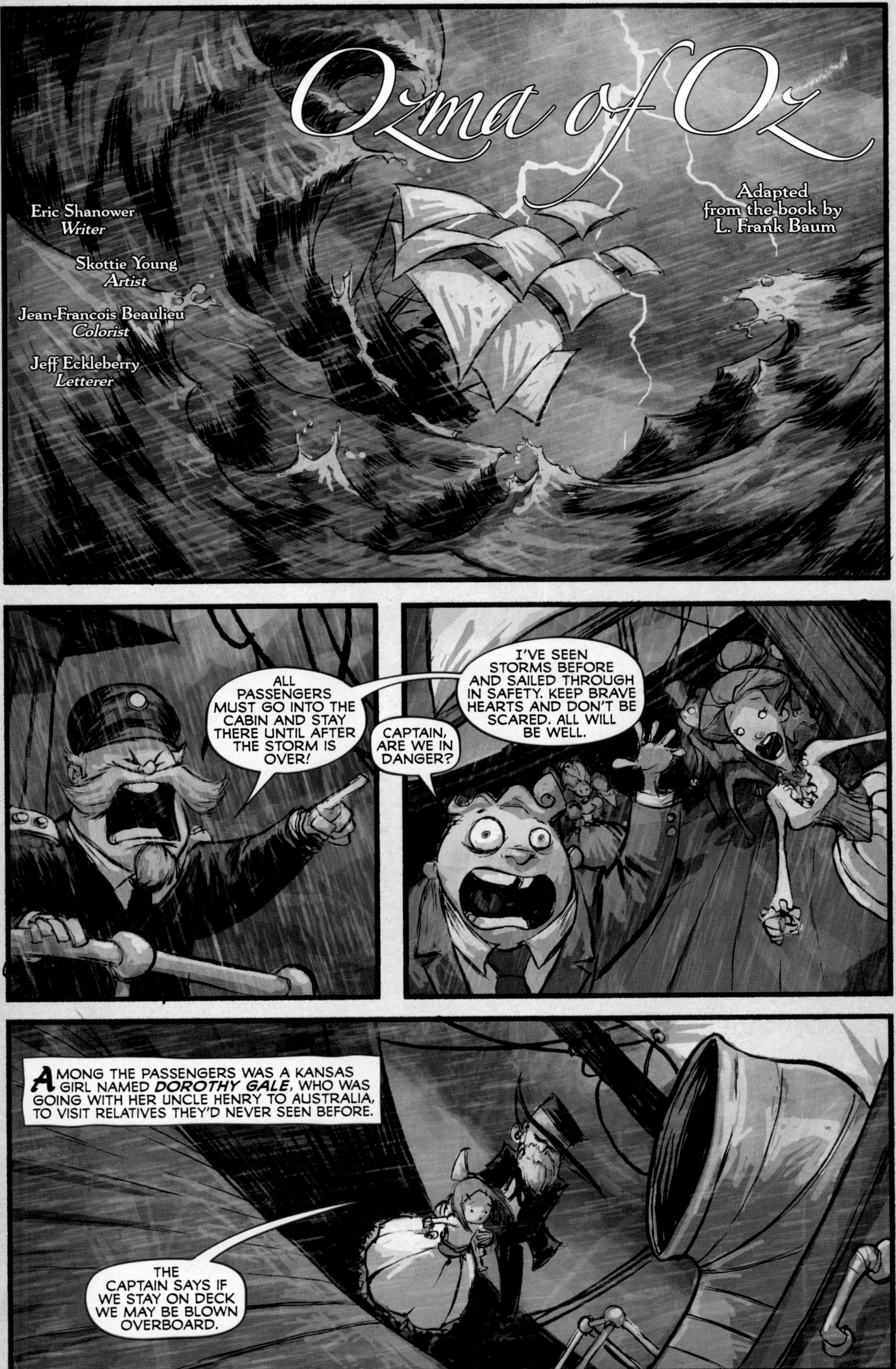

Ozma of Oz
Eric Shanower Writer
Skottie Young Artist
Jean-Francois Beaulieu Colorist
Jeff Eckleberry Letterer
Adapted from the book by L. Frank Baum
ALL PASSENGERS MUST GO INTO THE CABIN AND STAY THERE UNTIL AFTER THE STORM IS OVER!
CAPTAIN, ARE WE IN DANGER?
I'VE SEEN STORMS BEFORE AND SAILED THROUGH IN SAFETY. KEEP BRAVE HEARTS AND DON'T BE SCARED. ALL WILL BE WELL.
AMONG THE PASSENGERS WAS A KANSAS GIRL NAMED DOROTHY GALE, WHO WAS GOING WITH HER UNCLE HENRY TO AUSTRALIA, TO VISIT RELATIVES THEY'D NEVER SEEN BEFORE.
THE CAPTAIN SAYS IF WE STAY ON DECK WE MAY BE BLOWN OVERBOARD.

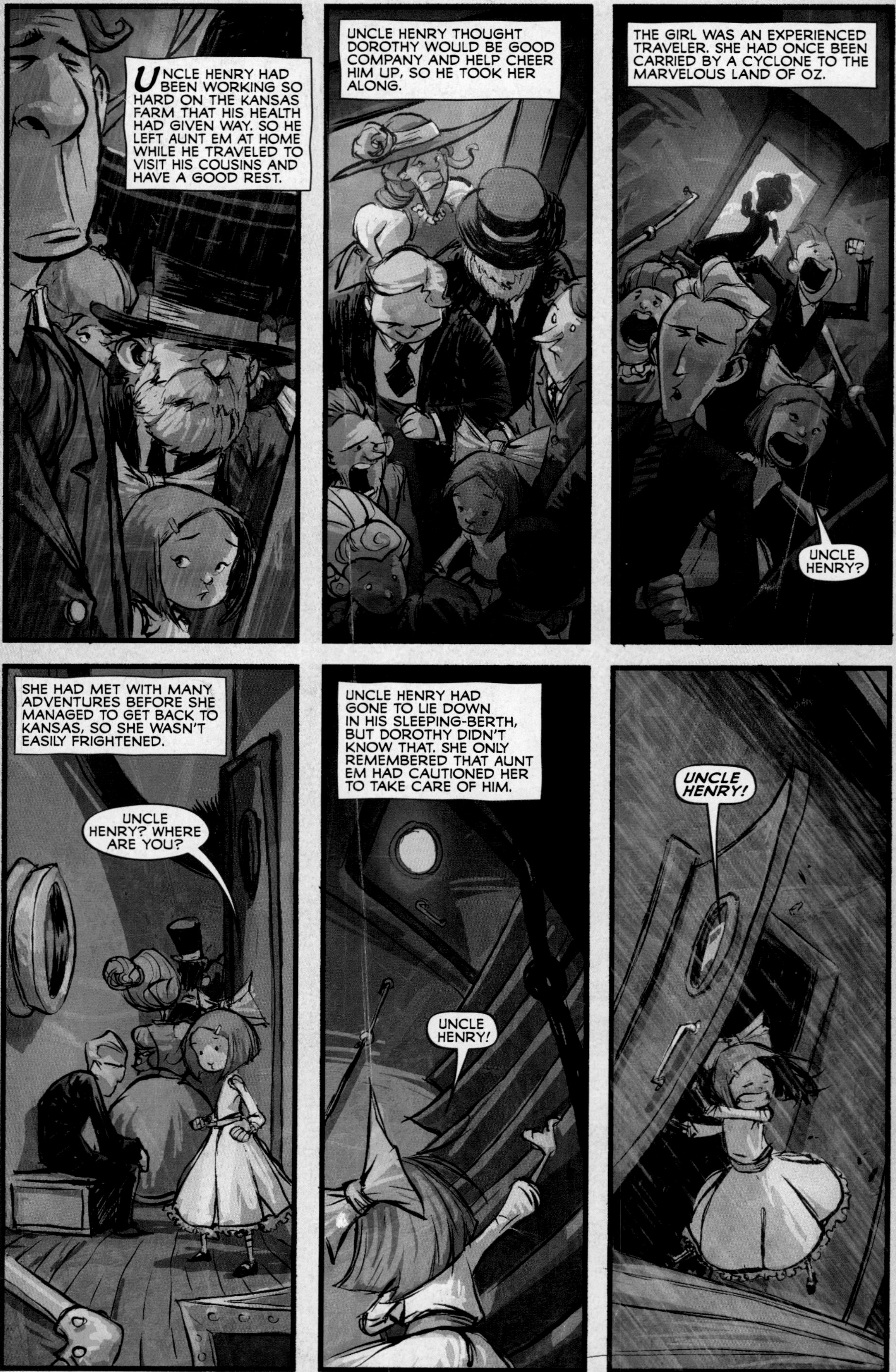
UNCLE HENRY HAD BEEN WORKING SO HARD ON THE KANSAS FARM THAT HIS HEALTH HAD GIVEN WAY. SO HE LEFT AUNT EM AT HOME WHILE HE TRAVELED TO VISIT HIS COUSINS AND HAVE A GOOD REST.
UNCLE HENRY THOUGHT DOROTHY WOULD BE GOOD COMPANY AND HELP CHEER HIM UP, SO HE TOOK HER ALONG.
THE GIRL WAS AN EXPERIENCED TRAVELER. SHE HAD ONCE BEEN CARRIED BY A CYCLONE TO THE MARVELOUS LAND OF OZ.
UNCLE HENRY?
SHE HAD MET WITH MANY ADVENTURES BEFORE SHE MANAGED TO GET BACK TO KANSAS, SO SHE WASN'T EASILY FRIGHTENED.
UNCLE HENRY? WHERE ARE YOU?
UNCLE HENRY HAD GONE TO LIE DOWN IN HIS SLEEPING-BERTH, BUT DOROTHY DIDN'T KNOW THAT. SHE ONLY REMEMBERED THAT AUNT EM HAD CAUTIONED HER TO TAKE CARE OF HIM.
UNCLE HENRY!
UNCLE HENRY!

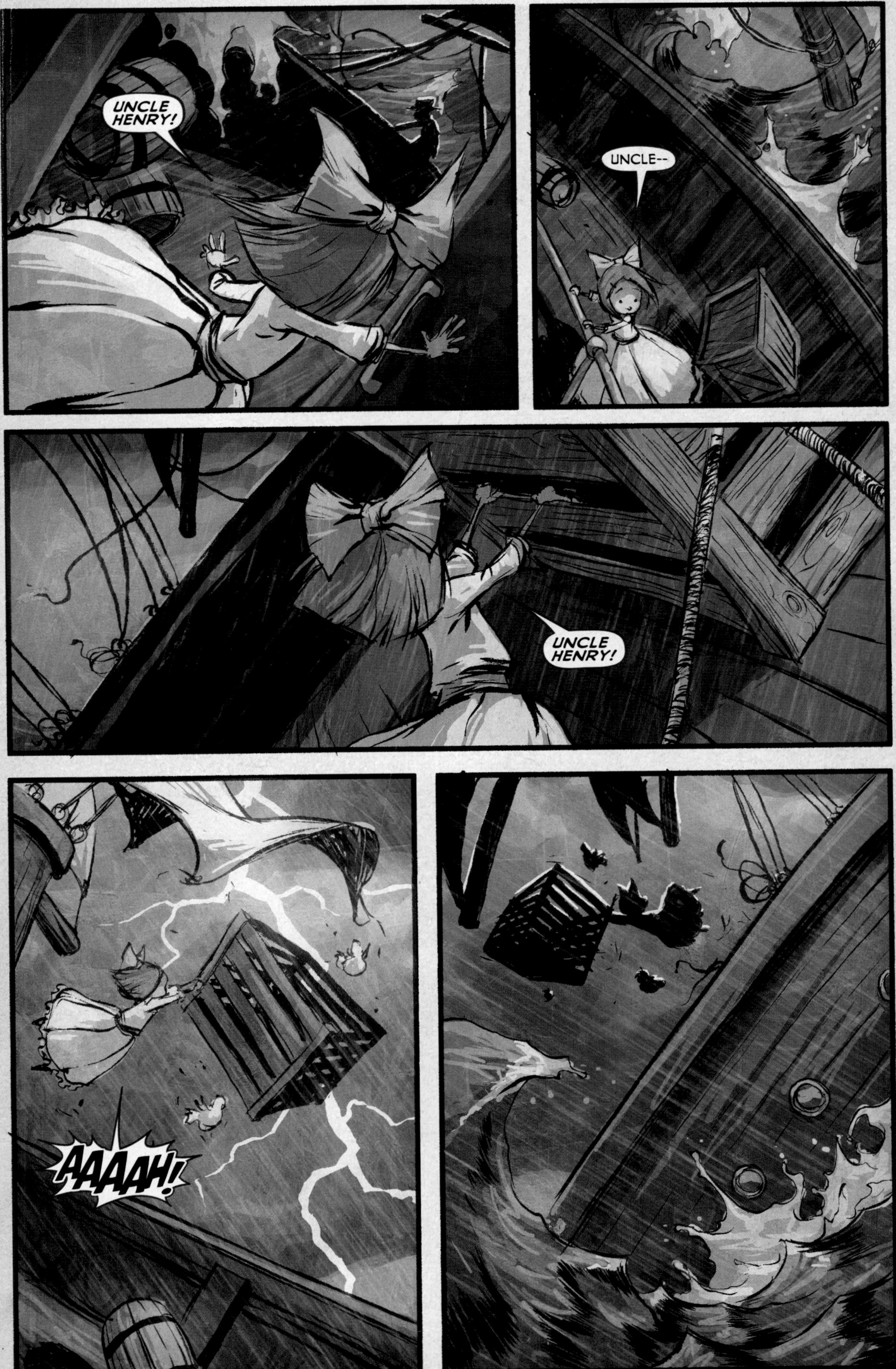
UNCLE HENRY!
UNCLE--
UNCLE HENRY!
AAAAH!

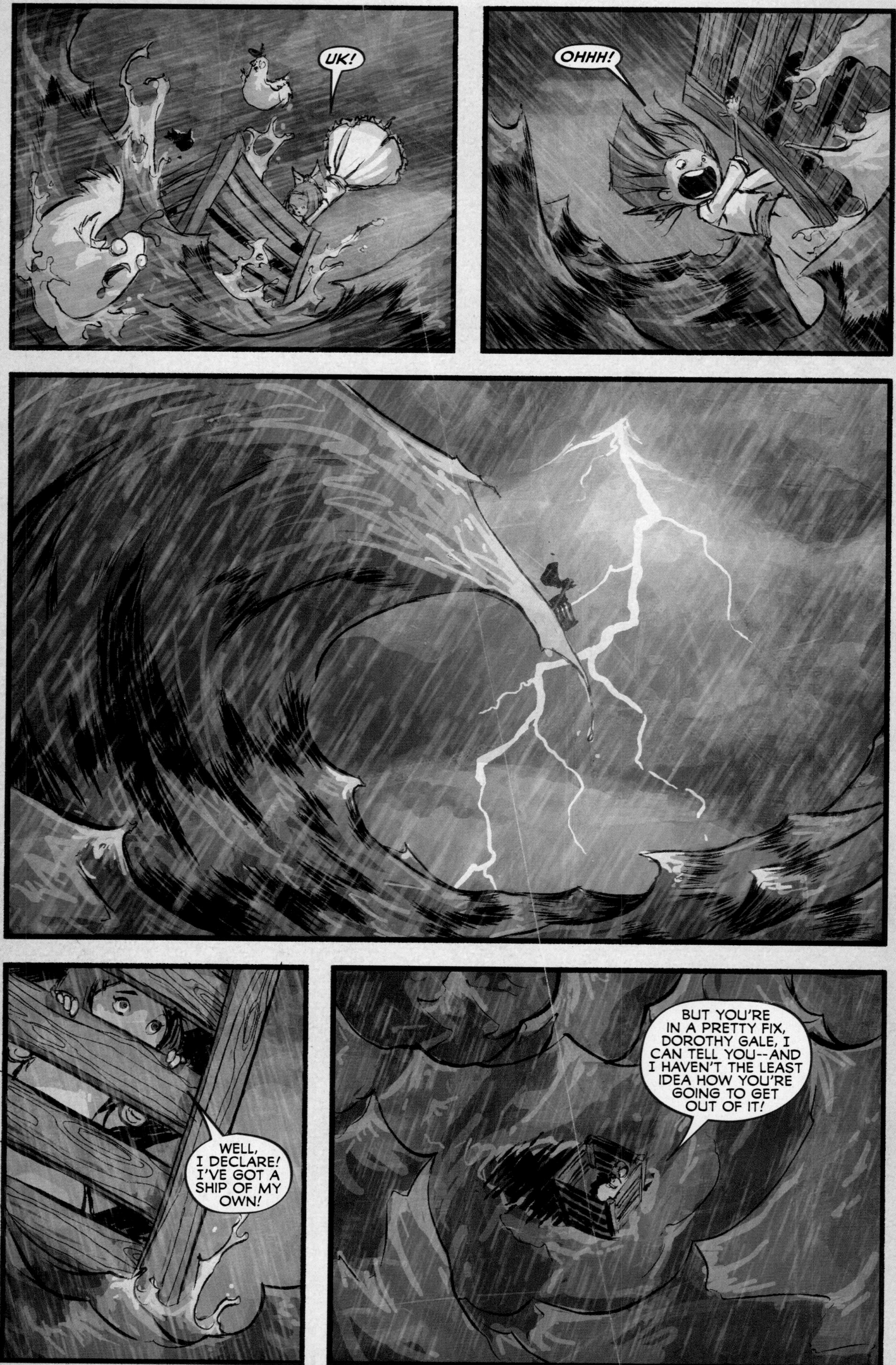
UK!
OHHH!
WELL, I DECLARE! I'VE GOT A SHIP OF MY OWN!
BUT YOU'RE IN A PRETTY FIX, DOROTHY GALE, I CAN TELL YOU--AND I HAVEN'T THE LEAST IDEA HOW YOU'RE GOING TO GET OUT OF IT!

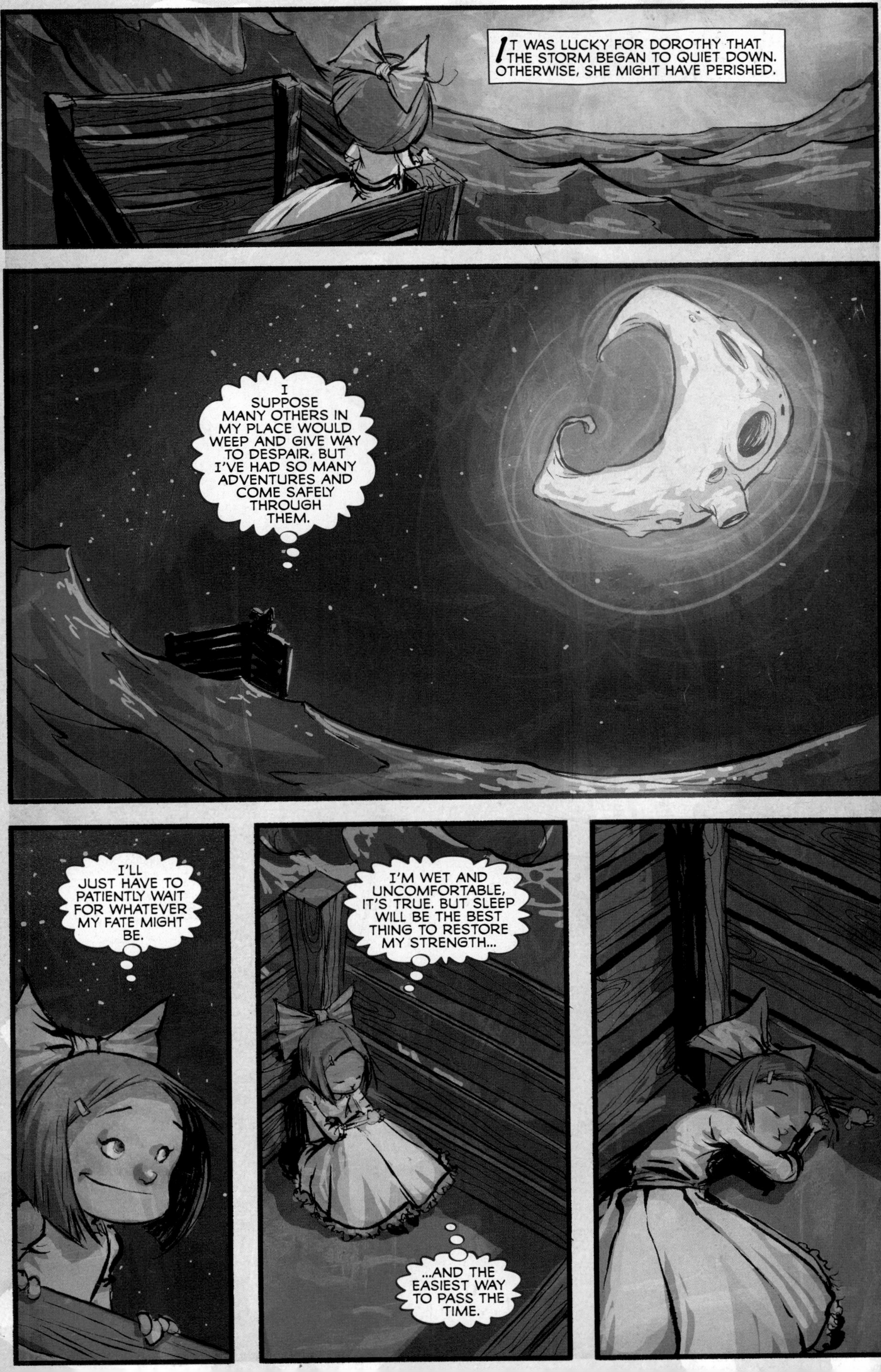
IT WAS LUCKY FOR DOROTHY THAT THE STORM BEGAN TO QUIET DOWN. OTHERWISE, SHE MIGHT HAVE PERISHED.
I SUPPOSE MANY OTHERS IN MY PLACE WOULD WEEP AND GIVE WAY TO DESPAIR. BUT I'VE HAD SO MANY ADVENTURES AND COME SAFELY THROUGH THEM.
I'LL JUST HAVE TO PATIENTLY WAIT FOR WHATEVER MY FATE MIGHT BE.
I'M WET AND UNCOMFORTABLE, IT'S TRUE. BUT SLEEP WILL BE THE BEST THING TO RESTORE MY STRENGTH...
...AND THE EASIEST WAY TO PASS THE TIME.

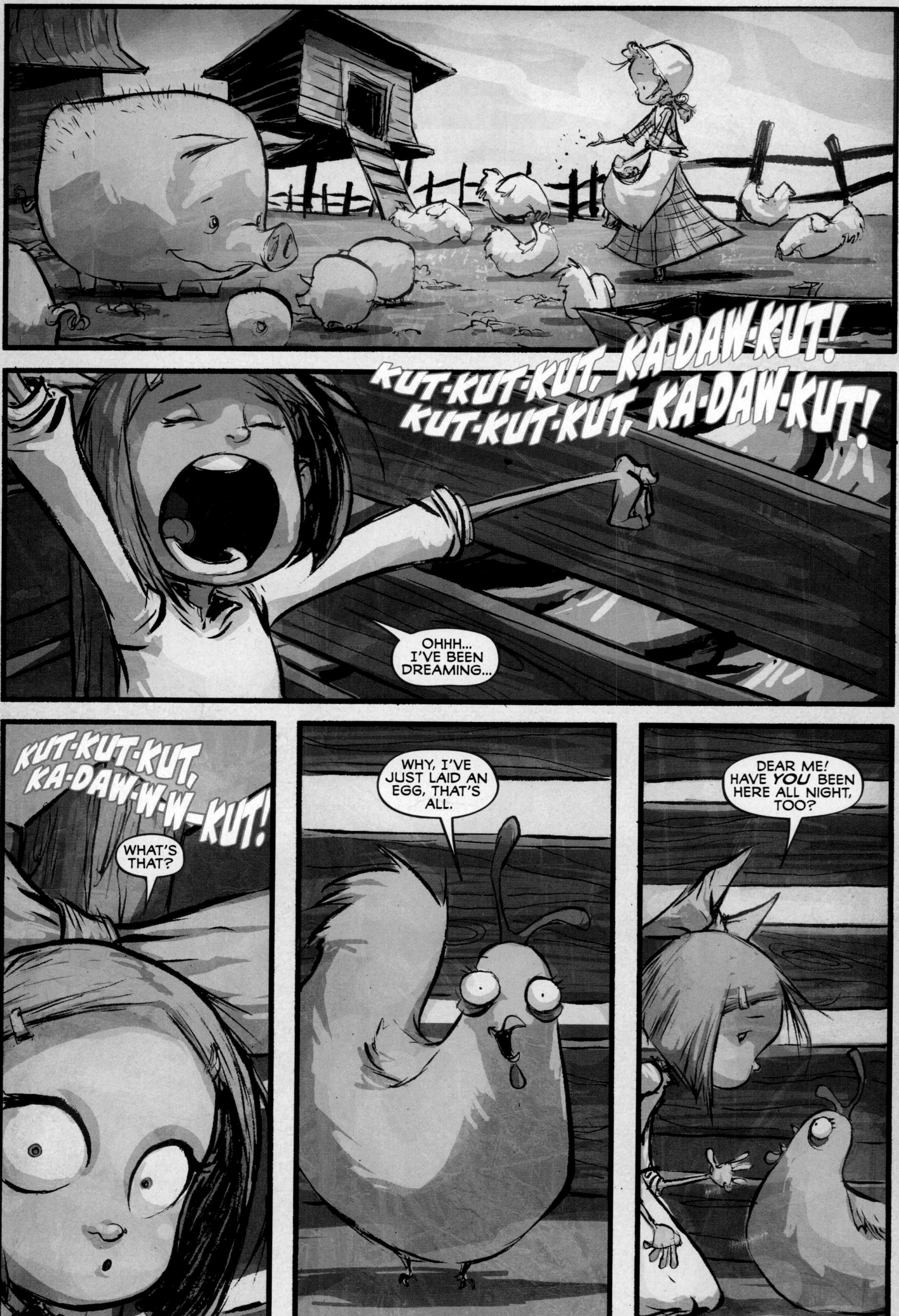
KUT-KUT-KUT, KA-DAW-KUT!
KUT-KUT-KUT, KA-DAW-KUT!
OHHH... I'VE BEEN DREAMING...
KUT-KUT-KUT, KA-DAW-W-W-KUT!
WHAT'S THAT?
WHY, I'VE JUST LAID AN EGG, THAT'S ALL.
DEAR ME! HAVE YOU BEEN HERE ALL NIGHT, TOO?

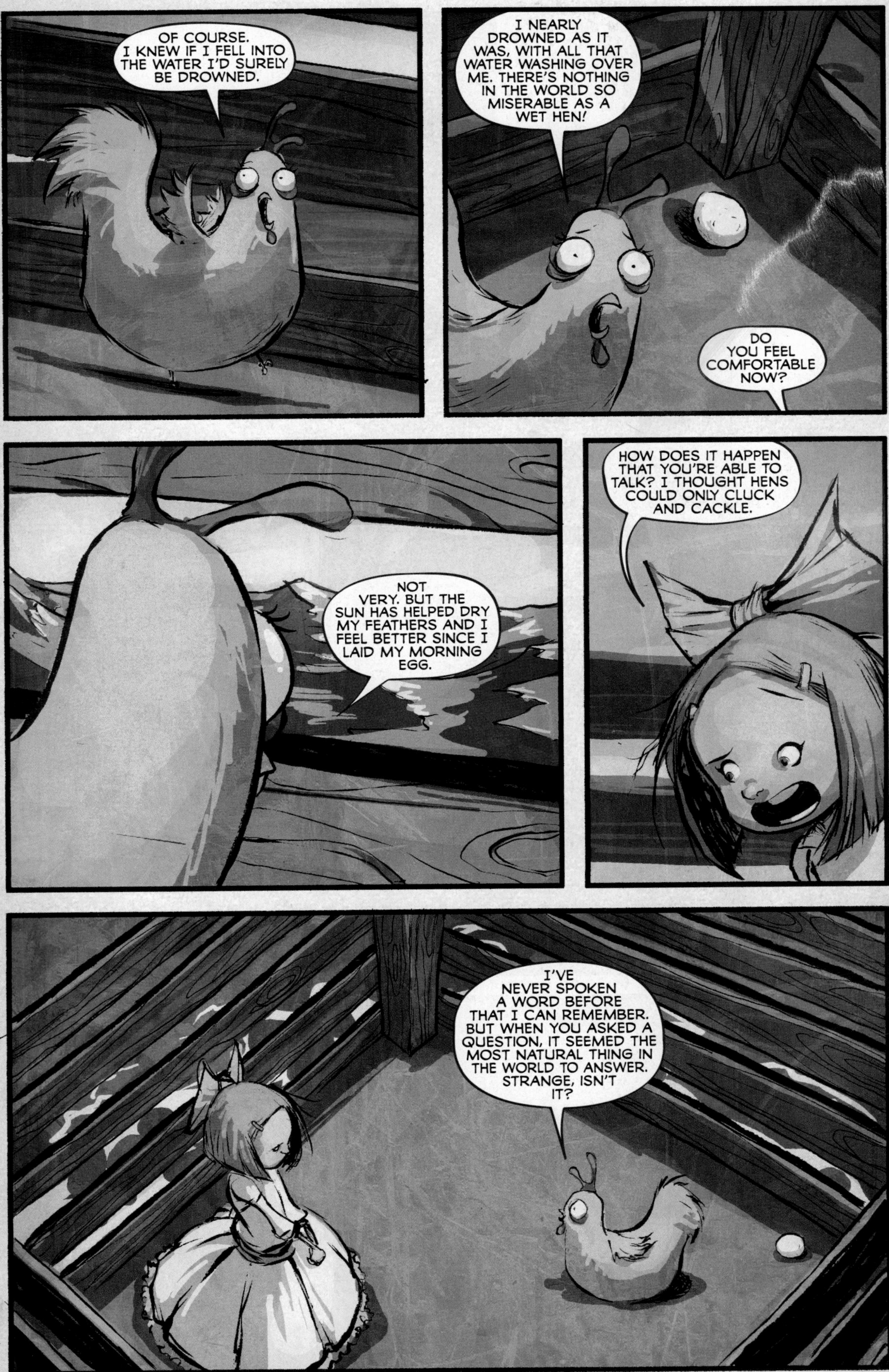

OF COURSE. I KNEW IF I FELL INTO THE WATER I'D SURELY BE DROWNED.
I NEARLY DROWNED AS IT WAS, WITH ALL THAT WATER WASHING OVER ME. THERE'S NOTHING IN THE WORLD SO MISERABLE AS A WET HEN!
DO YOU FEEL COMFORTABLE NOW?
NOT VERY. BUT THE SUN HAS HELPED DRY MY FEATHERS AND I FEEL BETTER SINCE I LAID MY MORNING EGG.
HOW DOES IT HAPPEN THAT YOU'RE ABLE TO TALK? I THOUGHT HENS COULD ONLY CLUCK AND CACKLE.
I'VE NEVER SPOKEN A WORD BEFORE THAT I CAN REMEMBER. BUT WHEN YOU ASKED A QUESTION, IT SEEMED THE MOST NATURAL THING IN THE WORLD TO ANSWER. STRANGE, ISN'T IT?

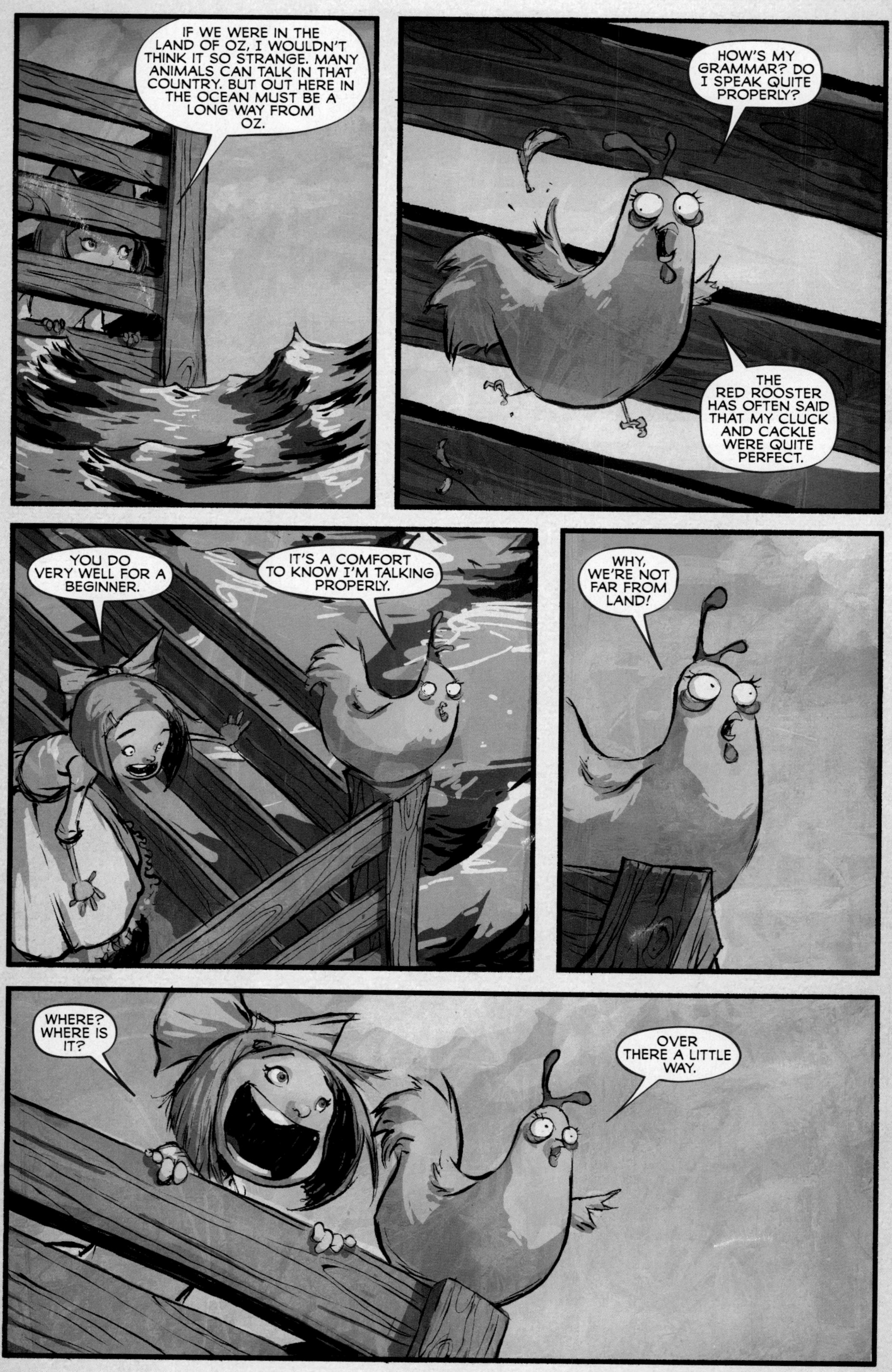
IF WE WERE IN THE LAND OF OZ, I WOULDN'T THINK IT SO STRANGE. MANY ANIMALS CAN TALK IN THAT COUNTRY. BUT OUT HERE IN THE OCEAN MUST BE A LONG WAY FROM OZ.
HOW'S MY GRAMMAR? DO I SPEAK QUITE PROPERLY?
THE RED ROOSTER HAS OFTEN SAID THAT MY CLUCK AND CACKLE WERE QUITE PERFECT.
YOU DO VERY WELL FOR A BEGINNER.
IT'S A COMFORT TO KNOW I'M TALKING PROPERLY.
WHY, WE'RE NOT FAR FROM LAND!
WHERE? WHERE IS IT?
OVER THERE A LITTLE WAY.

WE SEEM TO BE DRIFTING TOWARD IT. BEFORE NOON WE OUGHT TO FIND OURSELVES UPON DRY LAND AGAIN.

I HOPE WE'LL FIND SOMETHING TO EAT. IT'S LONG PAST BREAKFAST TIME.

YOU MAY AS WELL EAT THIS EGG.

I COULDN'T UNLESS IT WAS COOKED. DON'T YOU WANT TO HATCH IT?

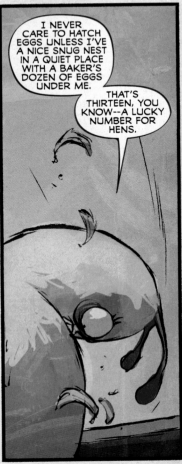

I NEVER CARE TO HATCH EGGS UNLESS I'VE A NICE SNUG NEST IN A QUIET PLACE WITH A BAKER'S DOZEN OF EGGS UNDER ME.

THAT'S THIRTEEN, YOU KNOW--A LUCKY NUMBER FOR HENS.

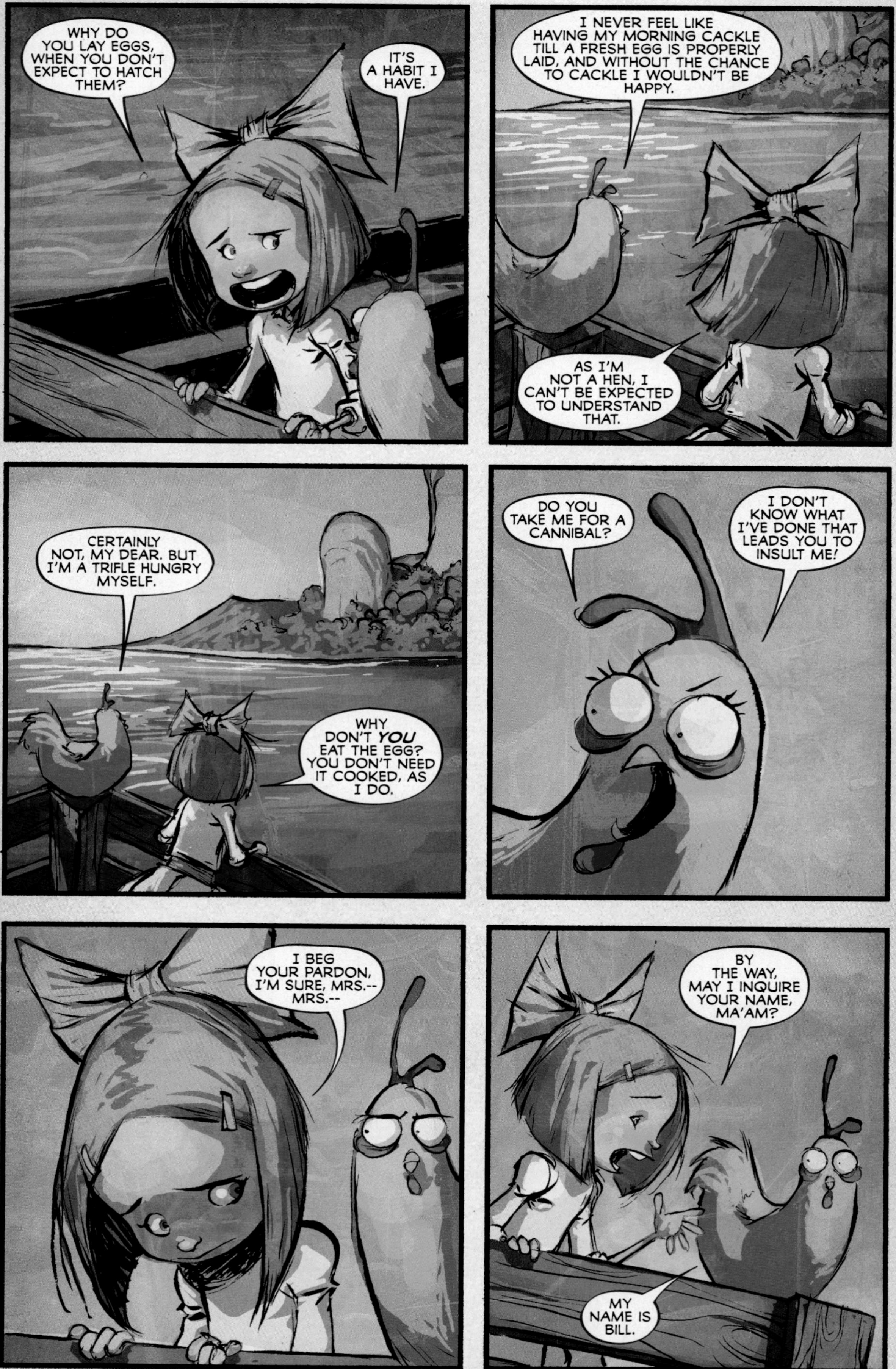
WHY DO YOU LAY EGGS, WHEN YOU DON'T EXPECT TO HATCH THEM?
IT'S A HABIT I HAVE.
I NEVER FEEL LIKE HAVING MY MORNING CACKLE TILL A FRESH EGG IS PROPERLY LAID, AND WITHOUT THE CHANCE TO CACKLE I WOULDN'T BE HAPPY.
AS I'M NOT A HEN, I CAN'T BE EXPECTED TO UNDERSTAND THAT.
CERTAINLY NOT, MY DEAR. BUT I'M A TRIFLE HUNGRY MYSELF.
WHY DON'T *YOU* EAT THE EGG? YOU DON'T NEED IT COOKED, AS I DO.
DO YOU TAKE ME FOR A CANNIBAL?
I DON'T KNOW WHAT I'VE DONE THAT LEADS YOU TO INSULT ME!
I BEG YOUR PARDON, I'M SURE, MRS.-- MRS.--
BY THE WAY, MAY I INQUIRE YOUR NAME, MA'AM?
MY NAME IS BILL.

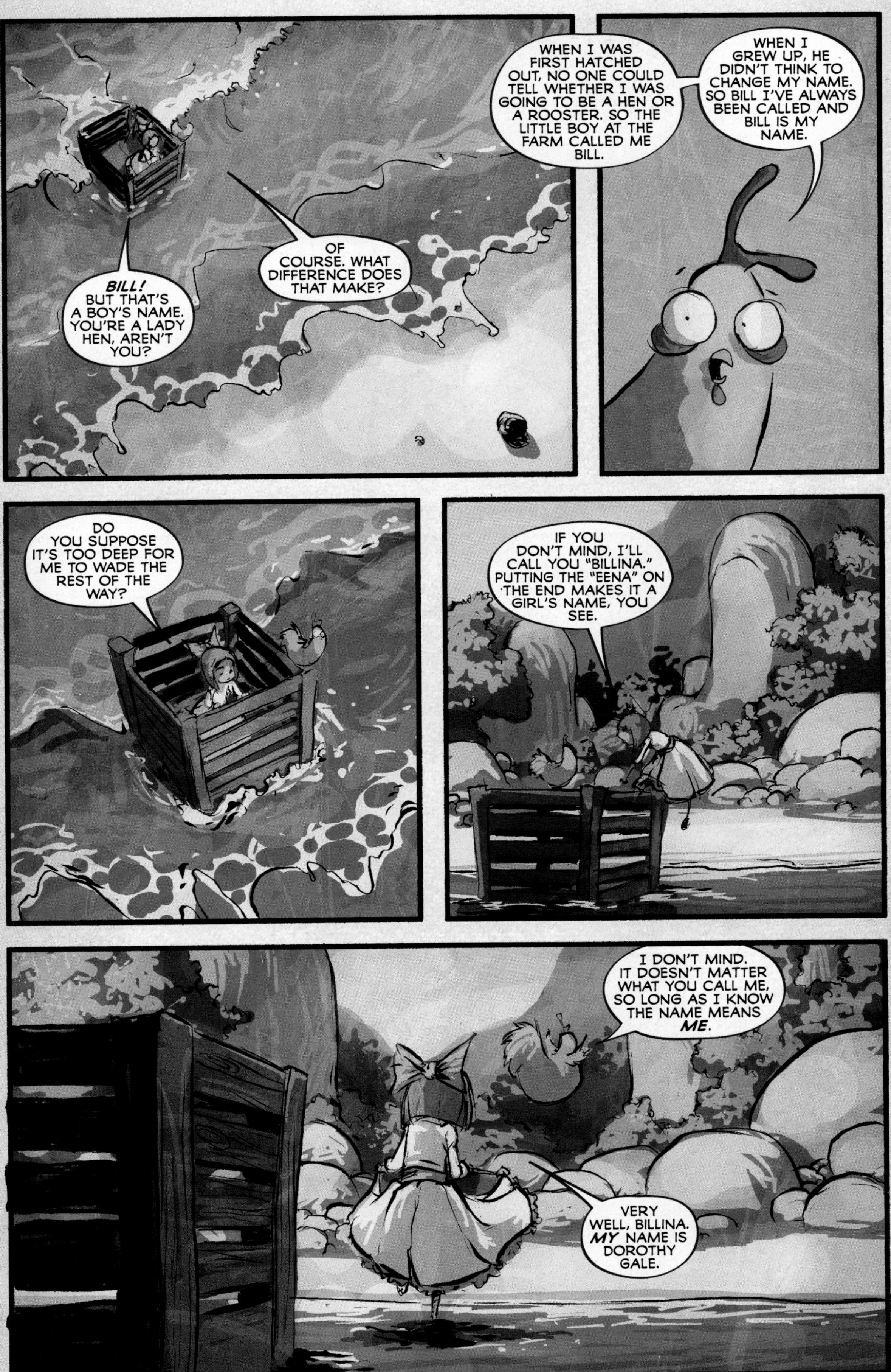
BILL! BUT THAT'S A BOY'S NAME. YOU'RE A LADY HEN, AREN'T YOU?
OF COURSE. WHAT DIFFERENCE DOES THAT MAKE?
WHEN I WAS FIRST HATCHED OUT, NO ONE COULD TELL WHETHER I WAS GOING TO BE A HEN OR A ROOSTER. SO THE LITTLE BOY AT THE FARM CALLED ME BILL.
WHEN I GREW UP, HE DIDN'T THINK TO CHANGE MY NAME. SO BILL I'VE ALWAYS BEEN CALLED AND BILL IS MY NAME.
DO YOU SUPPOSE IT'S TOO DEEP FOR ME TO WADE THE REST OF THE WAY?
IF YOU DON'T MIND, I'LL CALL YOU "BILLINA." PUTTING THE "EENA" ON THE END MAKES IT A GIRL'S NAME, YOU SEE.
I DON'T MIND. IT DOESN'T MATTER WHAT YOU CALL ME, SO LONG AS I KNOW THE NAME MEANS ME.
VERY WELL, BILLINA. MY NAME IS DOROTHY GALE.

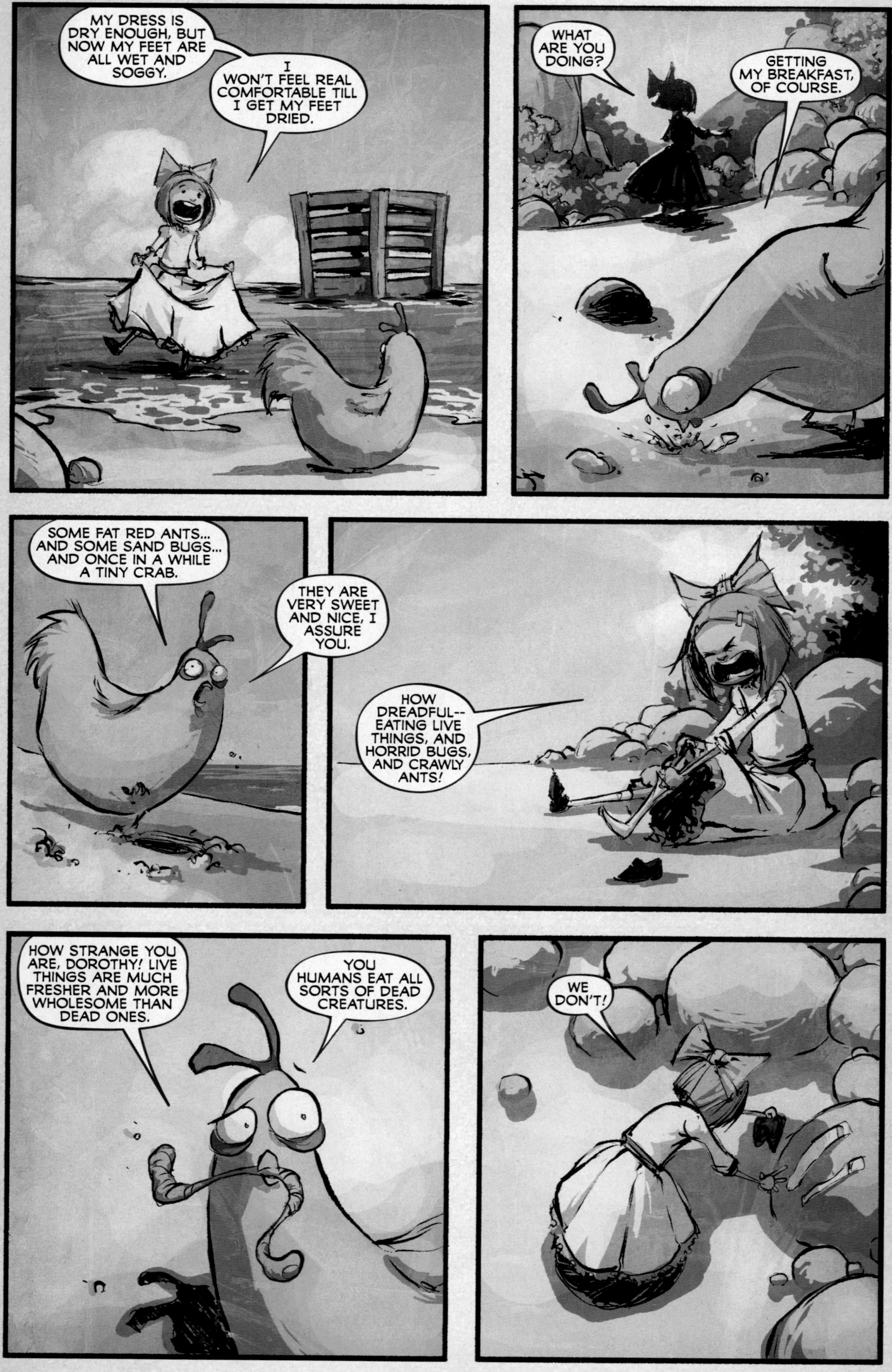
MY DRESS IS DRY ENOUGH, BUT NOW MY FEET ARE ALL WET AND SOGGY.
I WON'T FEEL REAL COMFORTABLE TILL I GET MY FEET DRIED.
WHAT ARE YOU DOING?
GETTING MY BREAKFAST, OF COURSE.
SOME FAT RED ANTS... AND SOME SAND BUGS... AND ONCE IN A WHILE A TINY CRAB.
THEY ARE VERY SWEET AND NICE, I ASSURE YOU.
HOW DREADFUL-- EATING LIVE THINGS, AND HORRID BUGS, AND CRAWLY ANTS!
HOW STRANGE YOU ARE, DOROTHY! LIVE THINGS ARE MUCH FRESHER AND MORE WHOLESOME THAN DEAD ONES.
YOU HUMANS EAT ALL SORTS OF DEAD CREATURES.
WE DON'T!

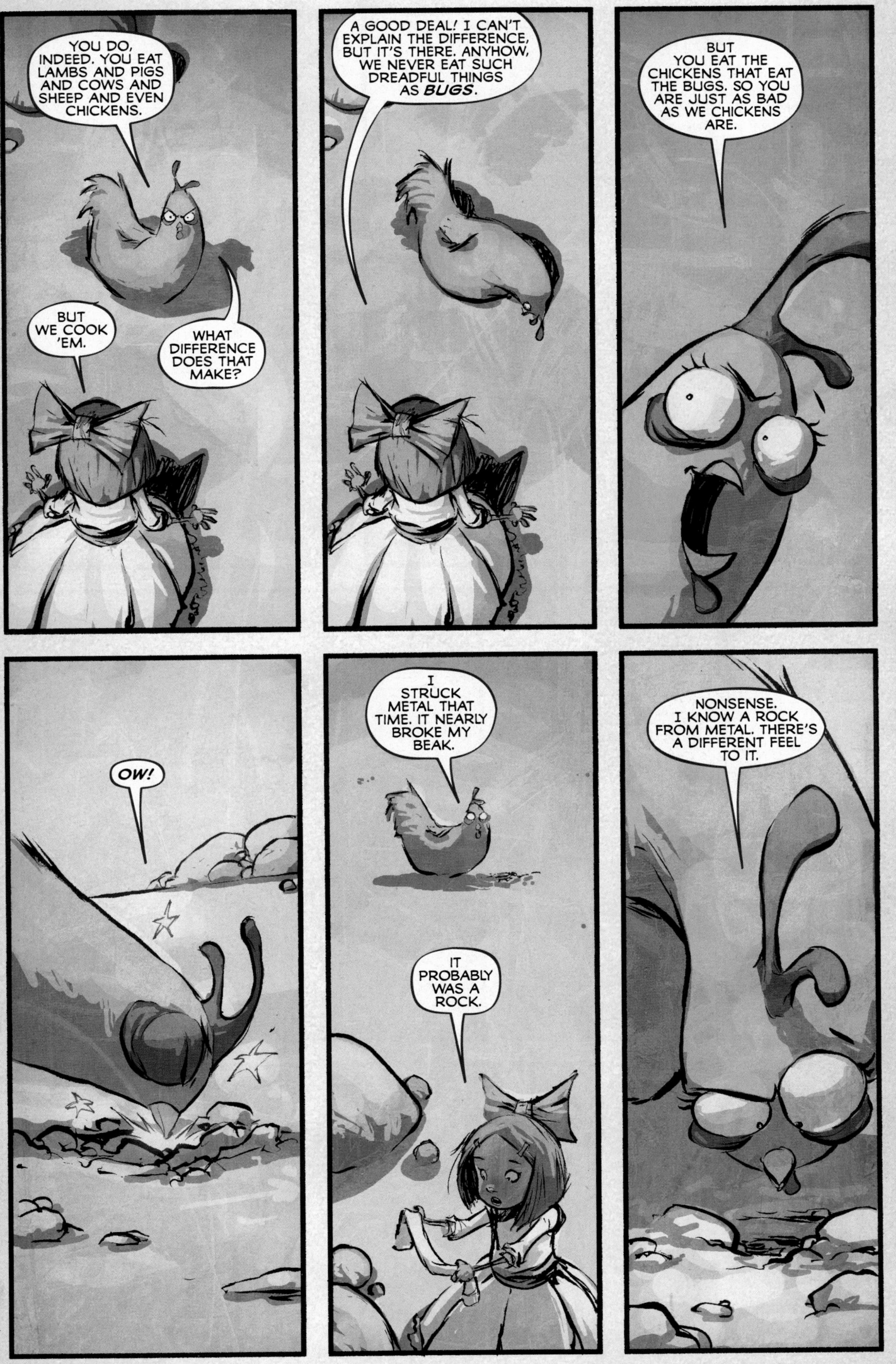
YOU DO, INDEED. YOU EAT LAMBS AND PIGS AND COWS AND SHEEP AND EVEN CHICKENS.
BUT WE COOK 'EM.
WHAT DIFFERENCE DOES THAT MAKE?
A GOOD DEAL! I CAN'T EXPLAIN THE DIFFERENCE, BUT IT'S THERE. ANYHOW, WE NEVER EAT SUCH DREADFUL THINGS AS *BUGS*.
BUT YOU EAT THE CHICKENS THAT EAT THE BUGS. SO YOU ARE JUST AS BAD AS WE CHICKENS ARE.
OW!
I STRUCK METAL THAT TIME. IT NEARLY BROKE MY BEAK.
IT PROBABLY WAS A ROCK.
NONSENSE. I KNOW A ROCK FROM METAL. THERE'S A DIFFERENT FEEL TO IT.

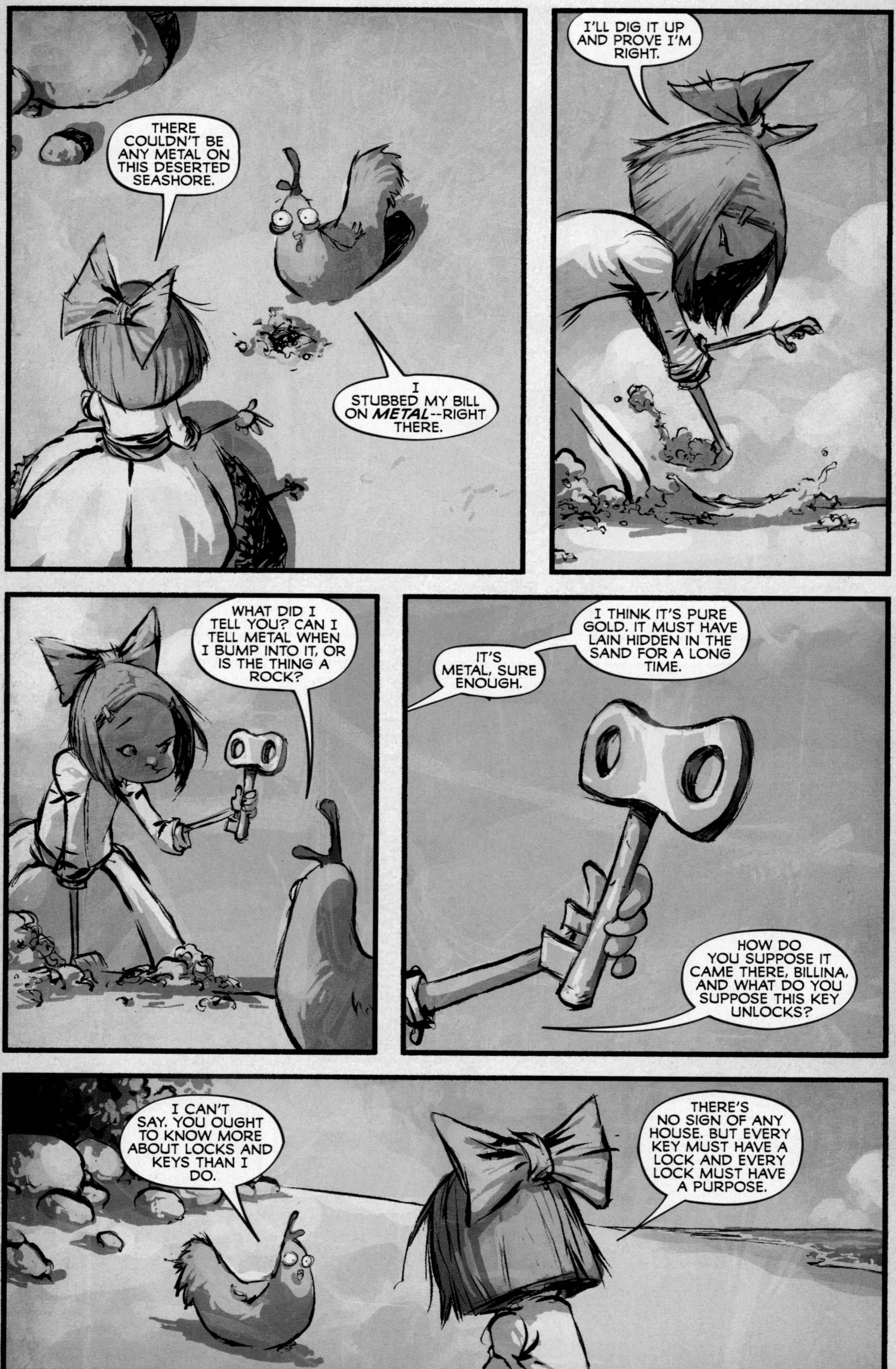
THERE COULDN'T BE ANY METAL ON THIS DESERTED SEASHORE.
I STUBBED MY BILL ON *METAL*--RIGHT THERE.
I'LL DIG IT UP AND PROVE I'M RIGHT.
WHAT DID I TELL YOU? CAN I TELL METAL WHEN I BUMP INTO IT, OR IS THE THING A ROCK?
IT'S METAL, SURE ENOUGH.
I THINK IT'S PURE GOLD. IT MUST HAVE LAIN HIDDEN IN THE SAND FOR A LONG TIME.
HOW DO YOU SUPPOSE IT CAME THERE, BILLINA, AND WHAT DO YOU SUPPOSE THIS KEY UNLOCKS?
I CAN'T SAY. YOU OUGHT TO KNOW MORE ABOUT LOCKS AND KEYS THAN I DO.
THERE'S NO SIGN OF ANY HOUSE. BUT EVERY KEY MUST HAVE A LOCK AND EVERY LOCK MUST HAVE A PURPOSE.

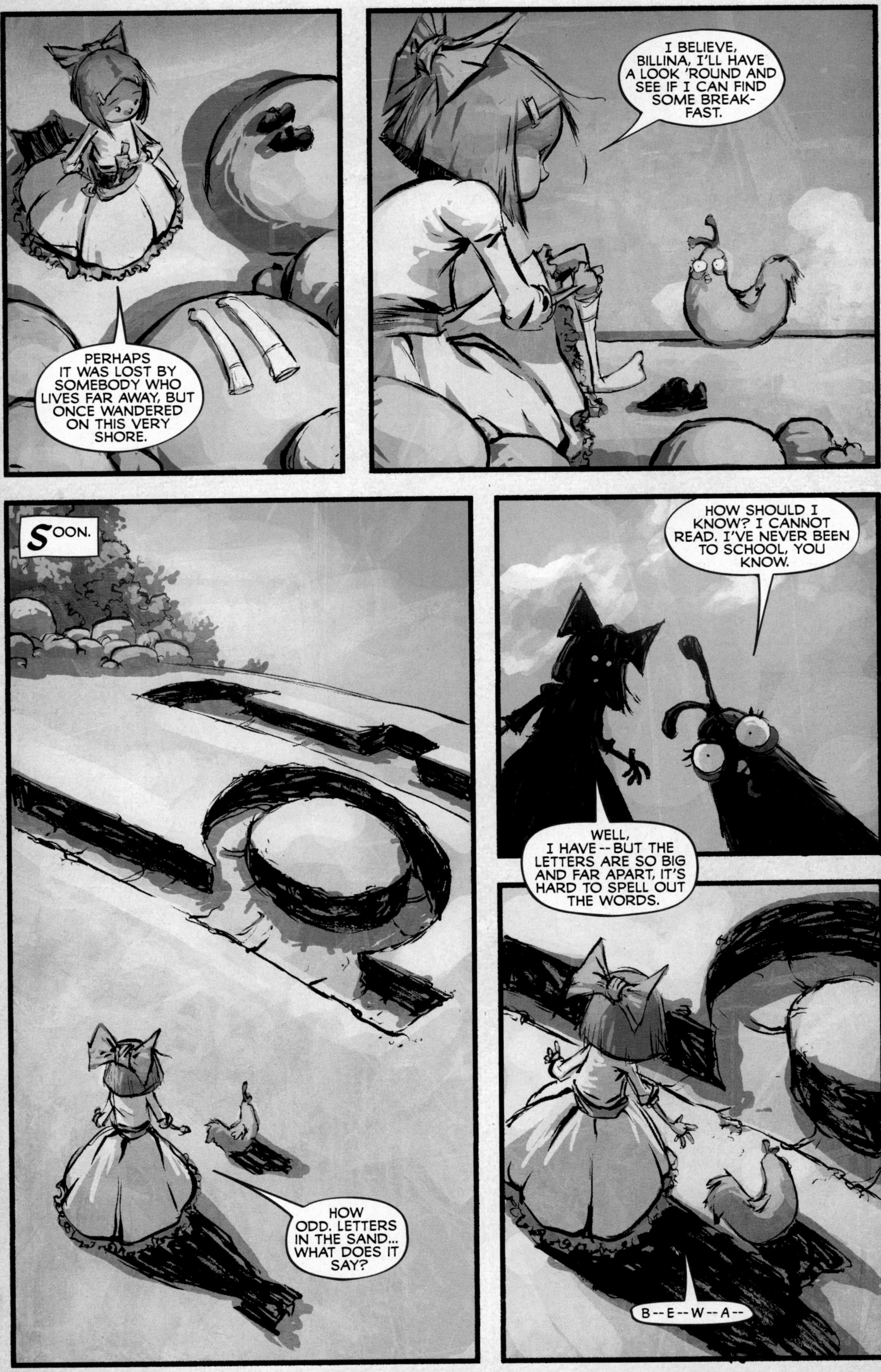
PERHAPS IT WAS LOST BY SOMEBODY WHO LIVES FAR AWAY, BUT ONCE WANDERED ON THIS VERY SHORE.
I BELIEVE, BILLINA, I'LL HAVE A LOOK 'ROUND AND SEE IF I CAN FIND SOME BREAK-FAST.
SOON.
HOW ODD. LETTERS IN THE SAND... WHAT DOES IT SAY?
HOW SHOULD I KNOW? I CANNOT READ. I'VE NEVER BEEN TO SCHOOL, YOU KNOW.
WELL, I HAVE -- BUT THE LETTERS ARE SO BIG AND FAR APART, IT'S HARD TO SPELL OUT THE WORDS.
B -- E -- W -- A --

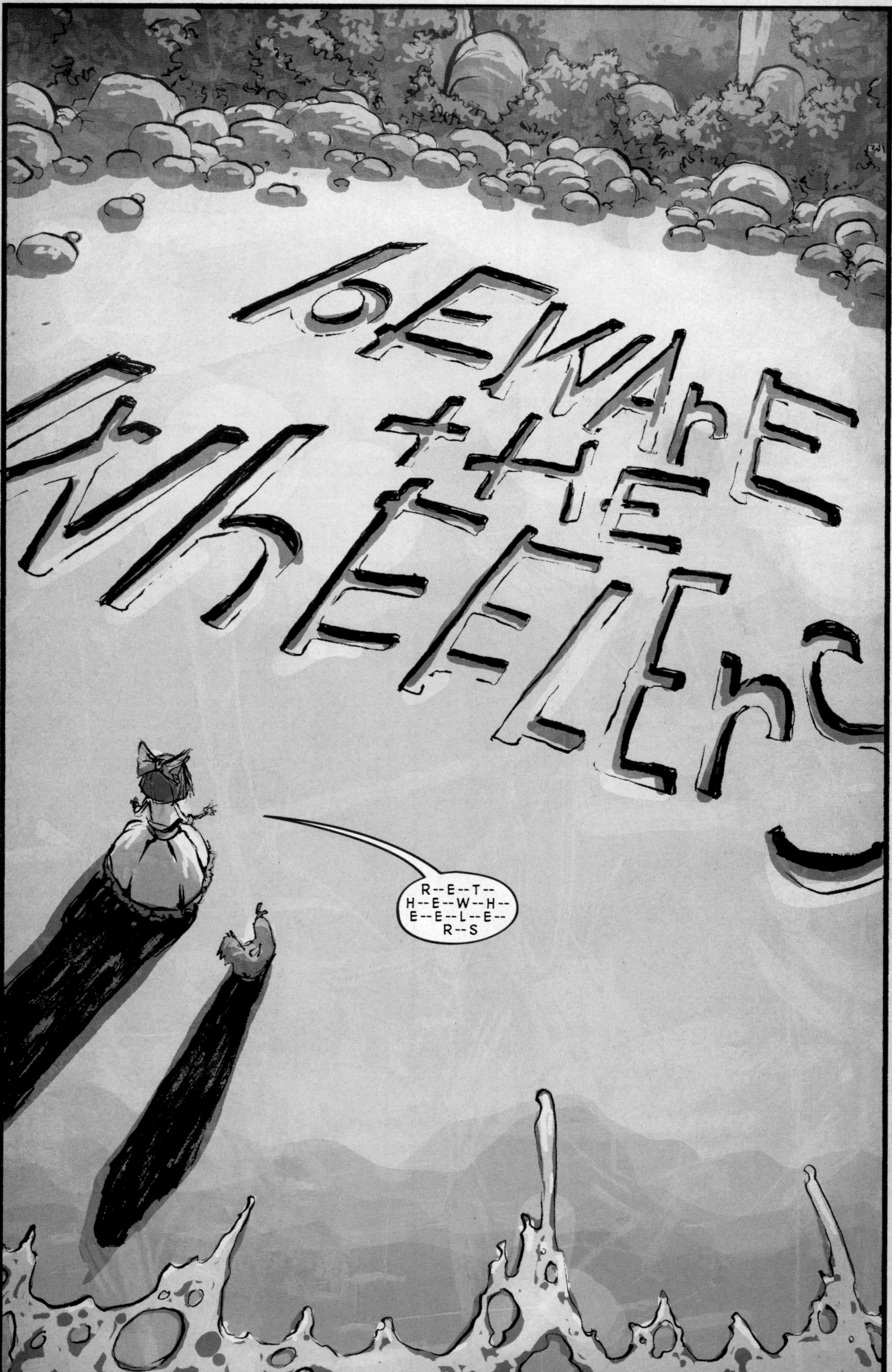
R--E--T--
H--E--W--H--
E--E--L--E--
R--S

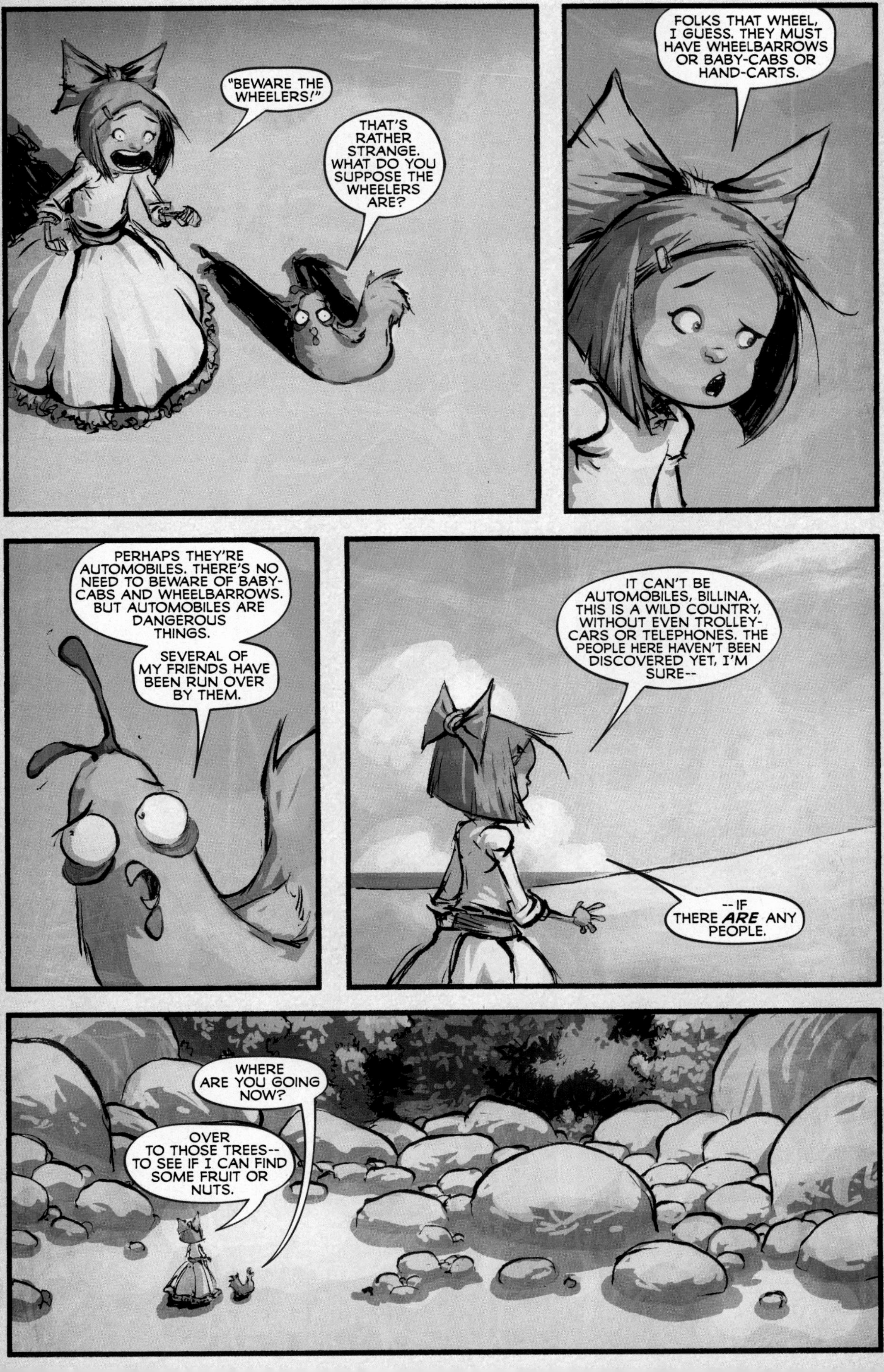
"BEWARE THE WHEELERS!"
THAT'S RATHER STRANGE. WHAT DO YOU SUPPOSE THE WHEELERS ARE?
FOLKS THAT WHEEL, I GUESS. THEY MUST HAVE WHEELBARROWS OR BABY-CABS OR HAND-CARTS.
PERHAPS THEY'RE AUTOMOBILES. THERE'S NO NEED TO BEWARE OF BABY-CABS AND WHEELBARROWS. BUT AUTOMOBILES ARE DANGEROUS THINGS.
SEVERAL OF MY FRIENDS HAVE BEEN RUN OVER BY THEM.
IT CAN'T BE AUTOMOBILES, BILLINA. THIS IS A WILD COUNTRY, WITHOUT EVEN TROLLEY-CARS OR TELEPHONES. THE PEOPLE HERE HAVEN'T BEEN DISCOVERED YET, I'M SURE--
--IF THERE ***ARE*** ANY PEOPLE.
WHERE ARE YOU GOING NOW?
OVER TO THOSE TREES-- TO SEE IF I CAN FIND SOME FRUIT OR NUTS.

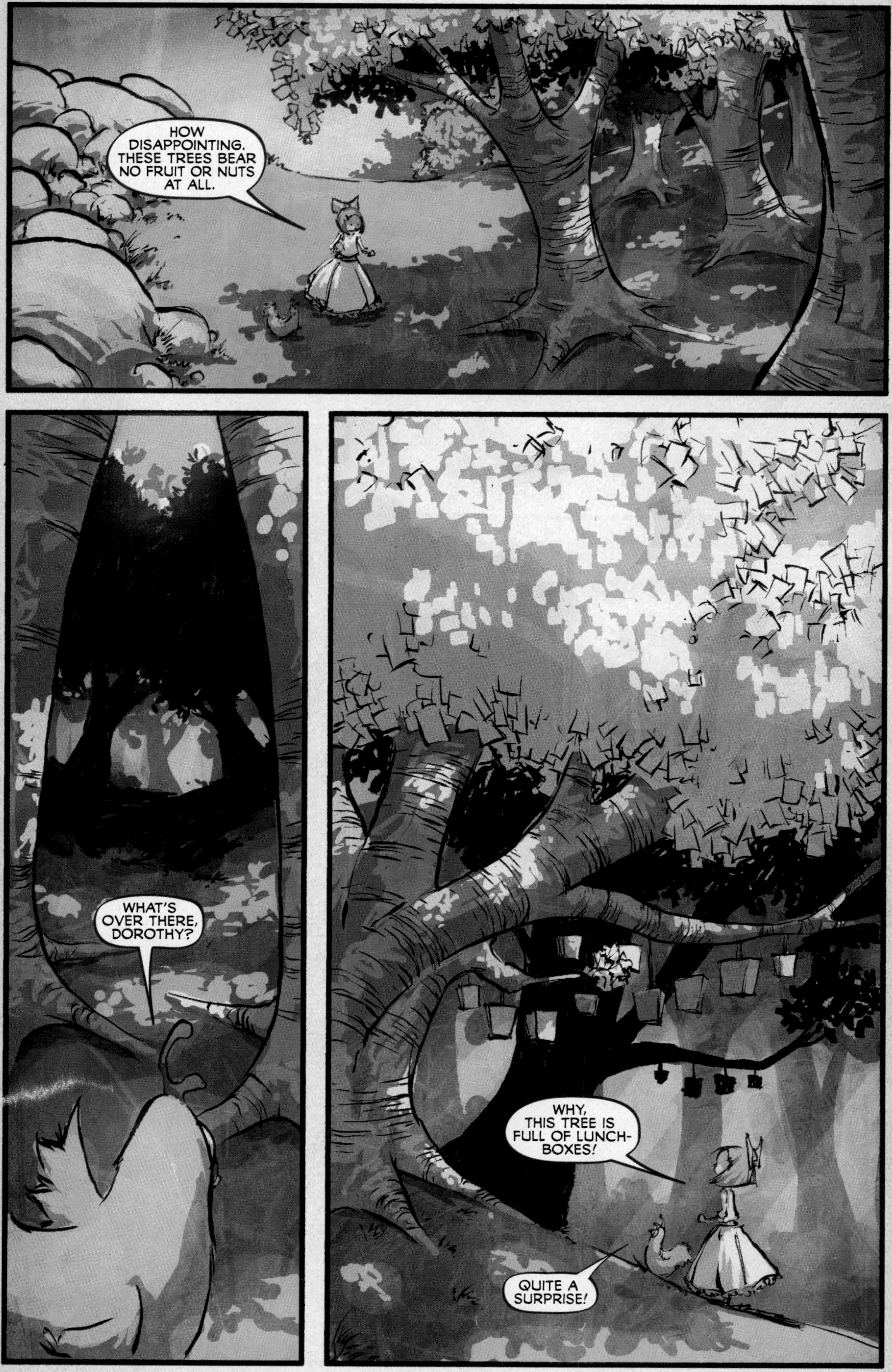
HOW DISAPPOINTING. THESE TREES BEAR NO FRUIT OR NUTS AT ALL.
WHAT'S OVER THERE, DOROTHY?
WHY, THIS TREE IS FULL OF LUNCH-BOXES!
QUITE A SURPRISE!

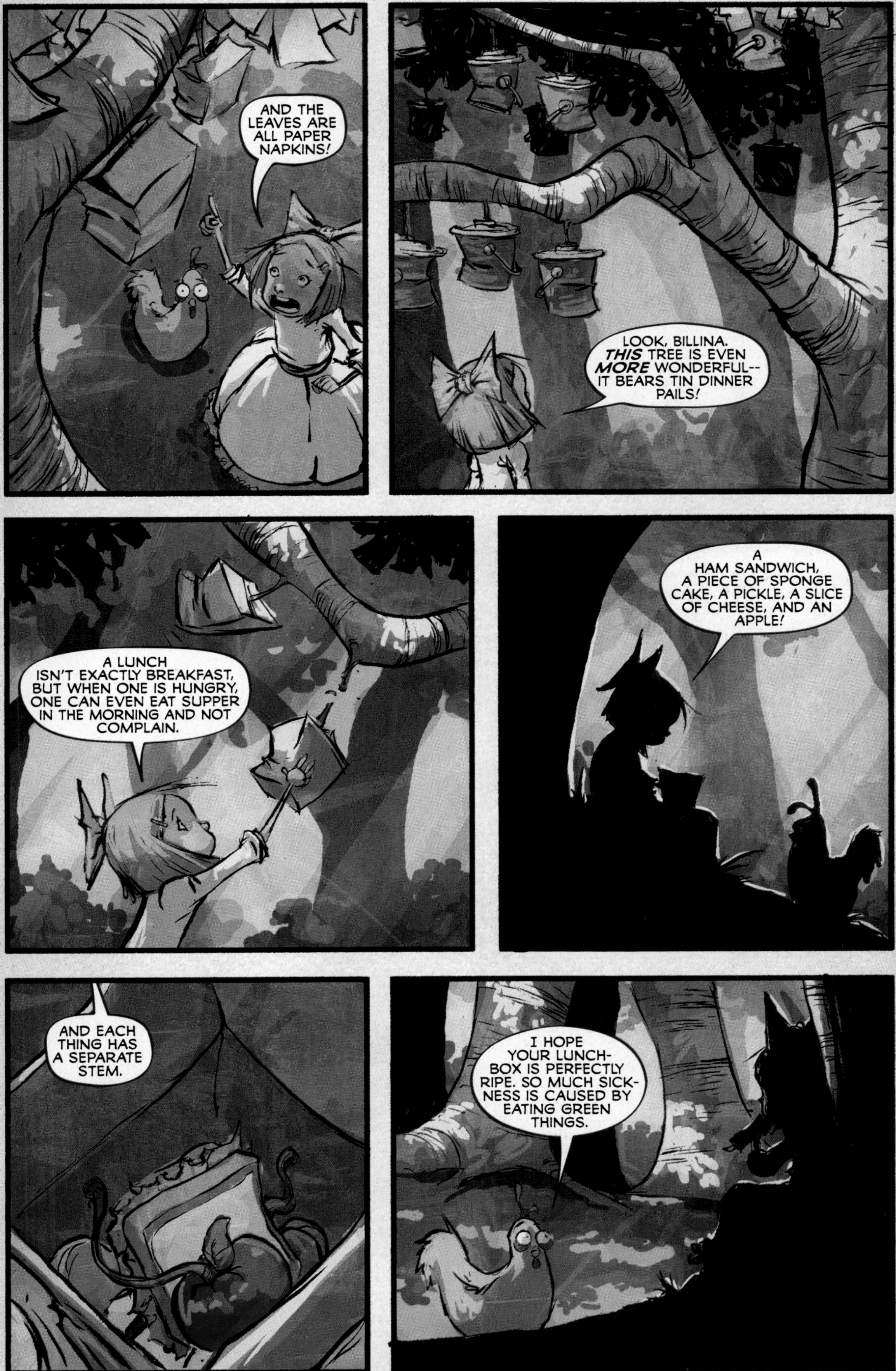
AND THE LEAVES ARE ALL PAPER NAPKINS!
LOOK, BILLINA. ***THIS*** TREE IS EVEN ***MORE*** WONDERFUL-- IT BEARS TIN DINNER PAILS!
A LUNCH ISN'T EXACTLY BREAKFAST, BUT WHEN ONE IS HUNGRY, ONE CAN EVEN EAT SUPPER IN THE MORNING AND NOT COMPLAIN.
A HAM SANDWICH, A PIECE OF SPONGE CAKE, A PICKLE, A SLICE OF CHEESE, AND AN APPLE!
AND EACH THING HAS A SEPARATE STEM.
I HOPE YOUR LUNCH-BOX IS PERFECTLY RIPE. SO MUCH SICK-NESS IS CAUSED BY EATING GREEN THINGS.

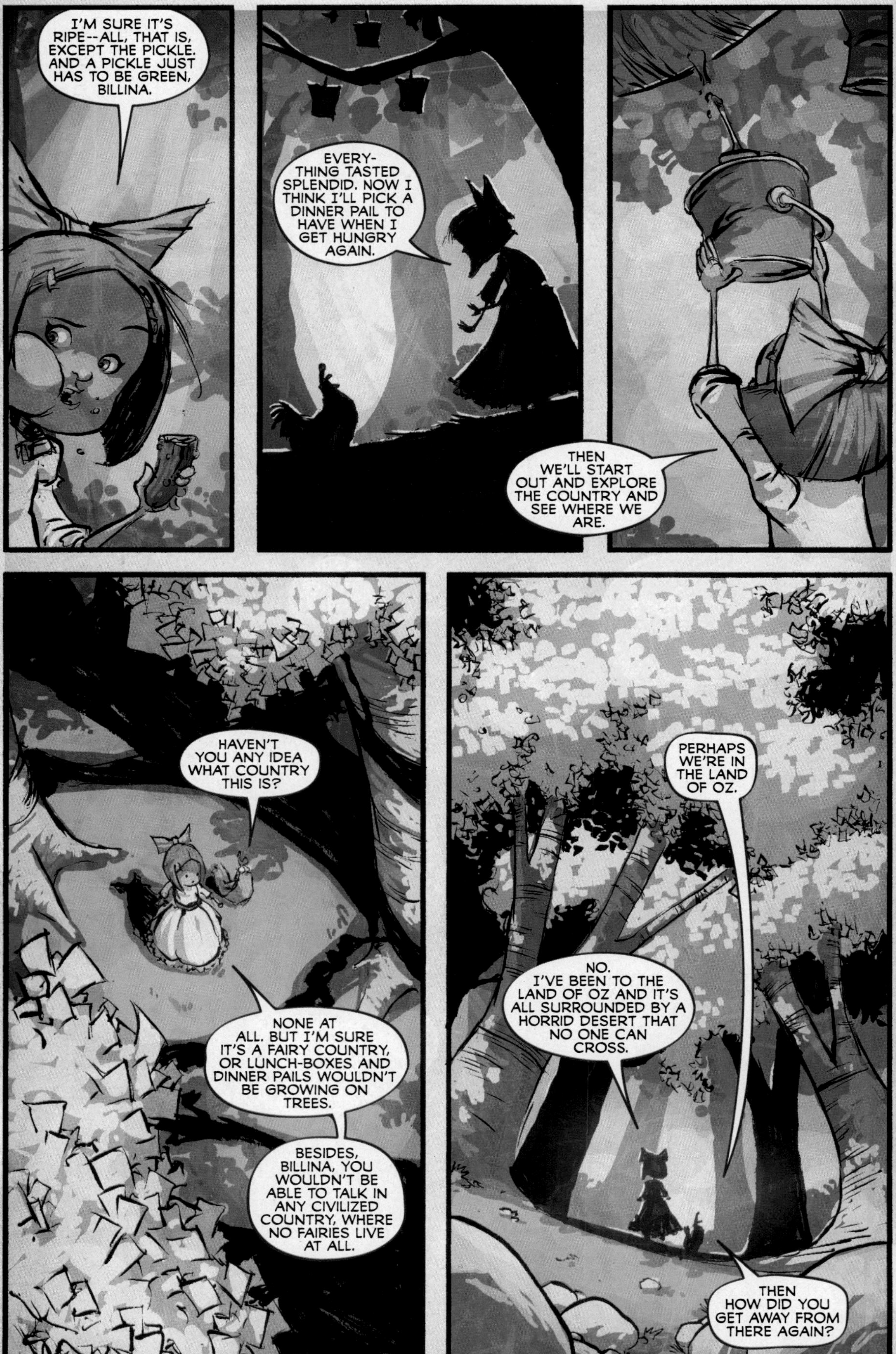
I'M SURE IT'S RIPE--ALL, THAT IS, EXCEPT THE PICKLE. AND A PICKLE JUST HAS TO BE GREEN, BILLINA.
EVERY-THING TASTED SPLENDID. NOW I THINK I'LL PICK A DINNER PAIL TO HAVE WHEN I GET HUNGRY AGAIN.
THEN WE'LL START OUT AND EXPLORE THE COUNTRY AND SEE WHERE WE ARE.
HAVEN'T YOU ANY IDEA WHAT COUNTRY THIS IS?
NONE AT ALL. BUT I'M SURE IT'S A FAIRY COUNTRY, OR LUNCH-BOXES AND DINNER PAILS WOULDN'T BE GROWING ON TREES.
BESIDES, BILLINA, YOU WOULDN'T BE ABLE TO TALK IN ANY CIVILIZED COUNTRY, WHERE NO FAIRIES LIVE AT ALL.
PERHAPS WE'RE IN THE LAND OF OZ.
NO. I'VE BEEN TO THE LAND OF OZ AND IT'S ALL SURROUNDED BY A HORRID DESERT THAT NO ONE CAN CROSS.
THEN HOW DID YOU GET AWAY FROM THERE AGAIN?

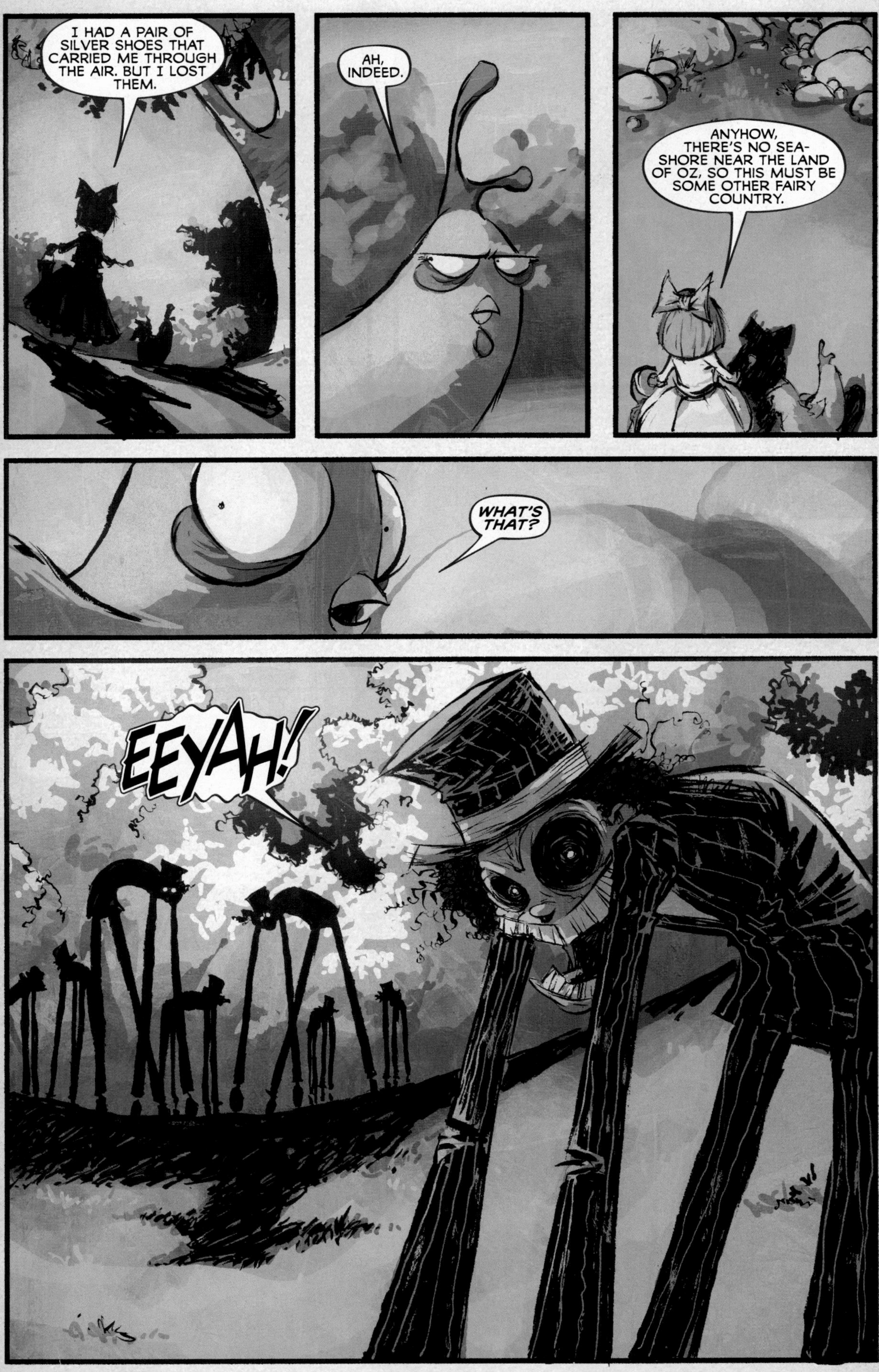
I HAD A PAIR OF SILVER SHOES THAT CARRIED ME THROUGH THE AIR. BUT I LOST THEM.
AH, INDEED.
ANYHOW, THERE'S NO SEA-SHORE NEAR THE LAND OF OZ, SO THIS MUST BE SOME OTHER FAIRY COUNTRY.
WHAT'S THAT?
EEYAH!

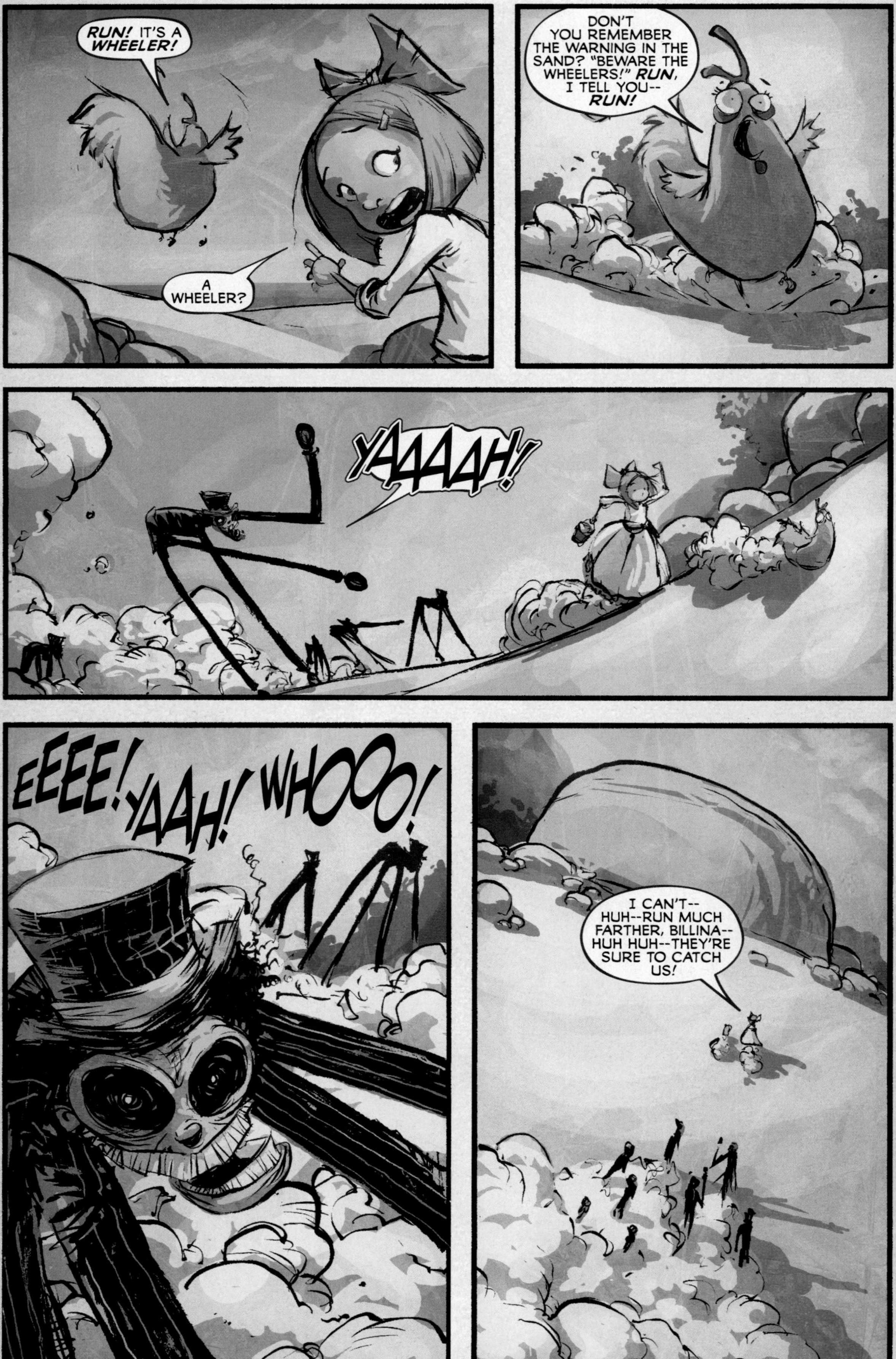

RUN! IT'S A WHEELER!
A WHEELER?
DON'T YOU REMEMBER THE WARNING IN THE SAND? "BEWARE THE WHEELERS!" RUN, I TELL YOU-- RUN!
YAAAAH!
EEEE!
YAAH!
WHOOO!
I CAN'T-- HUH--RUN MUCH FARTHER, BILLINA-- HUH HUH--THEY'RE SURE TO CATCH US!

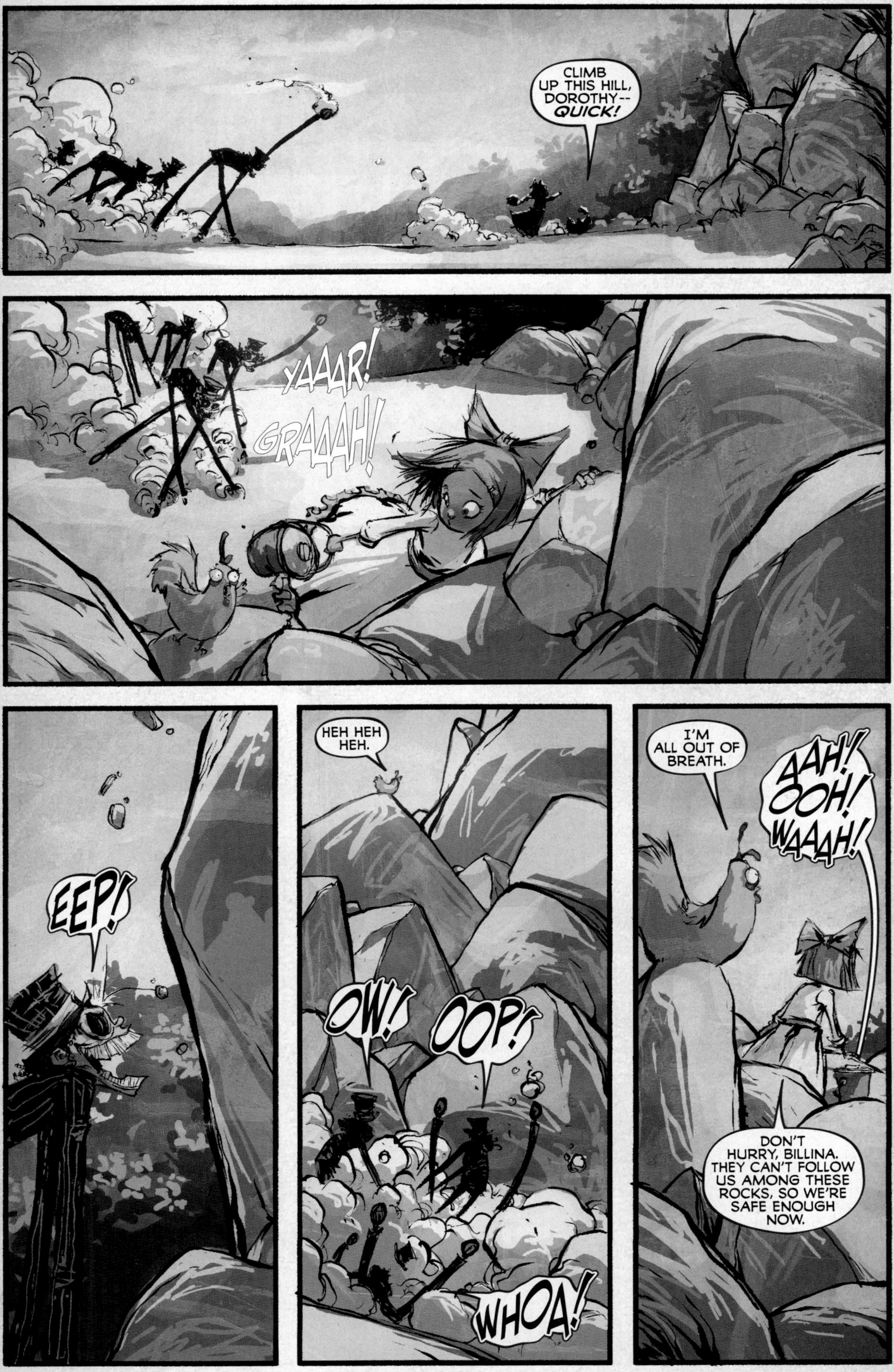
CLIMB UP THIS HILL, DOROTHY-- QUICK!
YAAAR!
GRAAAH!
EEP!
HEH HEH HEH.
OW!
OOP!
WHOA!
I'M ALL OUT OF BREATH.
AAH! OOH! WAAAH!
DON'T HURRY, BILLINA. THEY CAN'T FOLLOW US AMONG THESE ROCKS, SO WE'RE SAFE ENOUGH NOW.

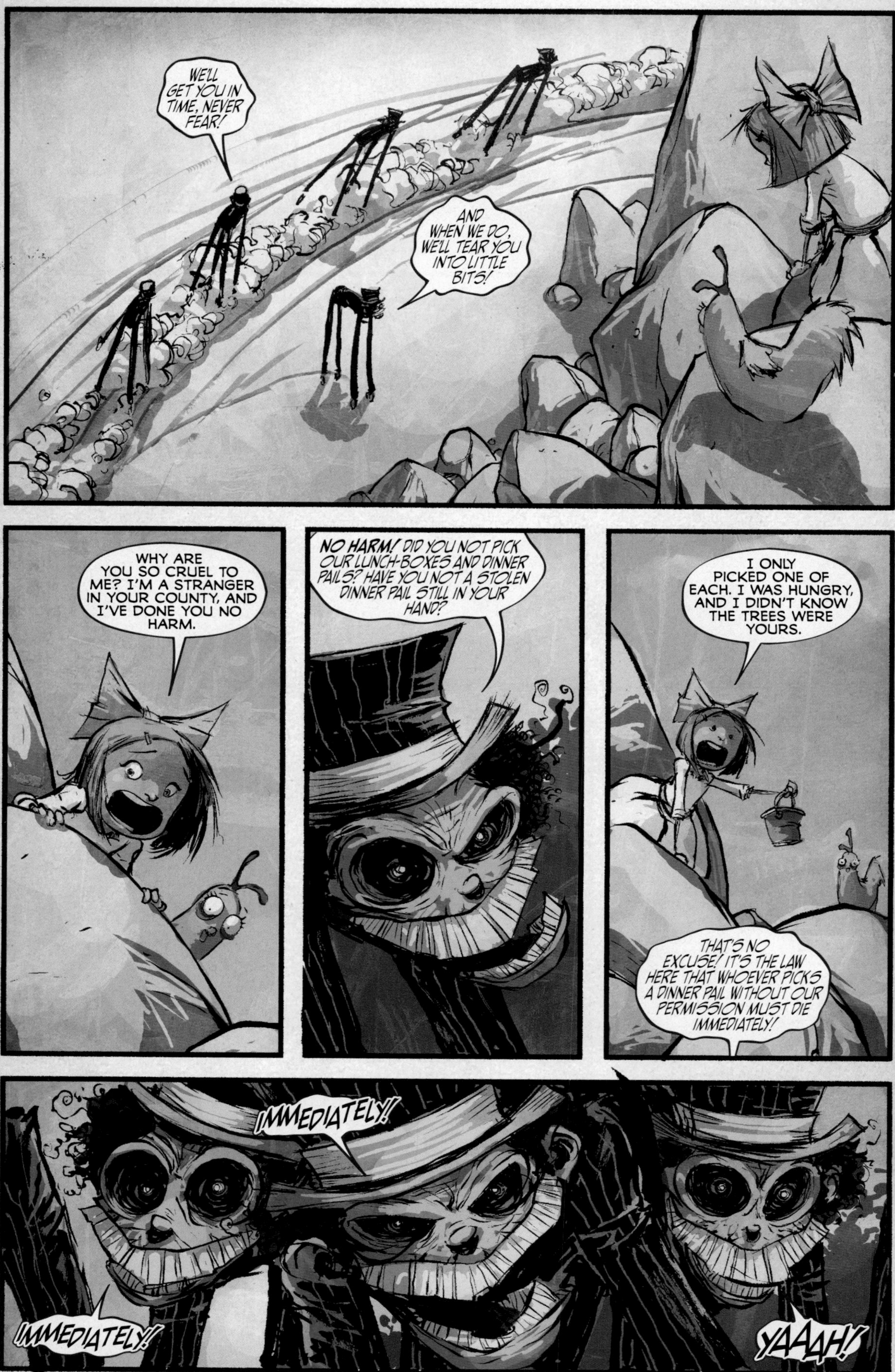
WE'LL GET YOU IN TIME, NEVER FEAR!
AND WHEN WE DO, WE'LL TEAR YOU INTO LITTLE BITS!
WHY ARE YOU SO CRUEL TO ME? I'M A STRANGER IN YOUR COUNTY, AND I'VE DONE YOU NO HARM.
NO HARM! DID YOU NOT PICK OUR LUNCH-BOXES AND DINNER PAILS? HAVE YOU NOT A STOLEN DINNER PAIL STILL IN YOUR HAND?
I ONLY PICKED ONE OF EACH. I WAS HUNGRY, AND I DIDN'T KNOW THE TREES WERE YOURS.
THAT'S NO EXCUSE! IT'S THE LAW HERE THAT WHOEVER PICKS A DINNER PAIL WITHOUT OUR PERMISSION MUST DIE IMMEDIATELY!
IMMEDIATELY!
IMMEDIATELY!
YAAAH!

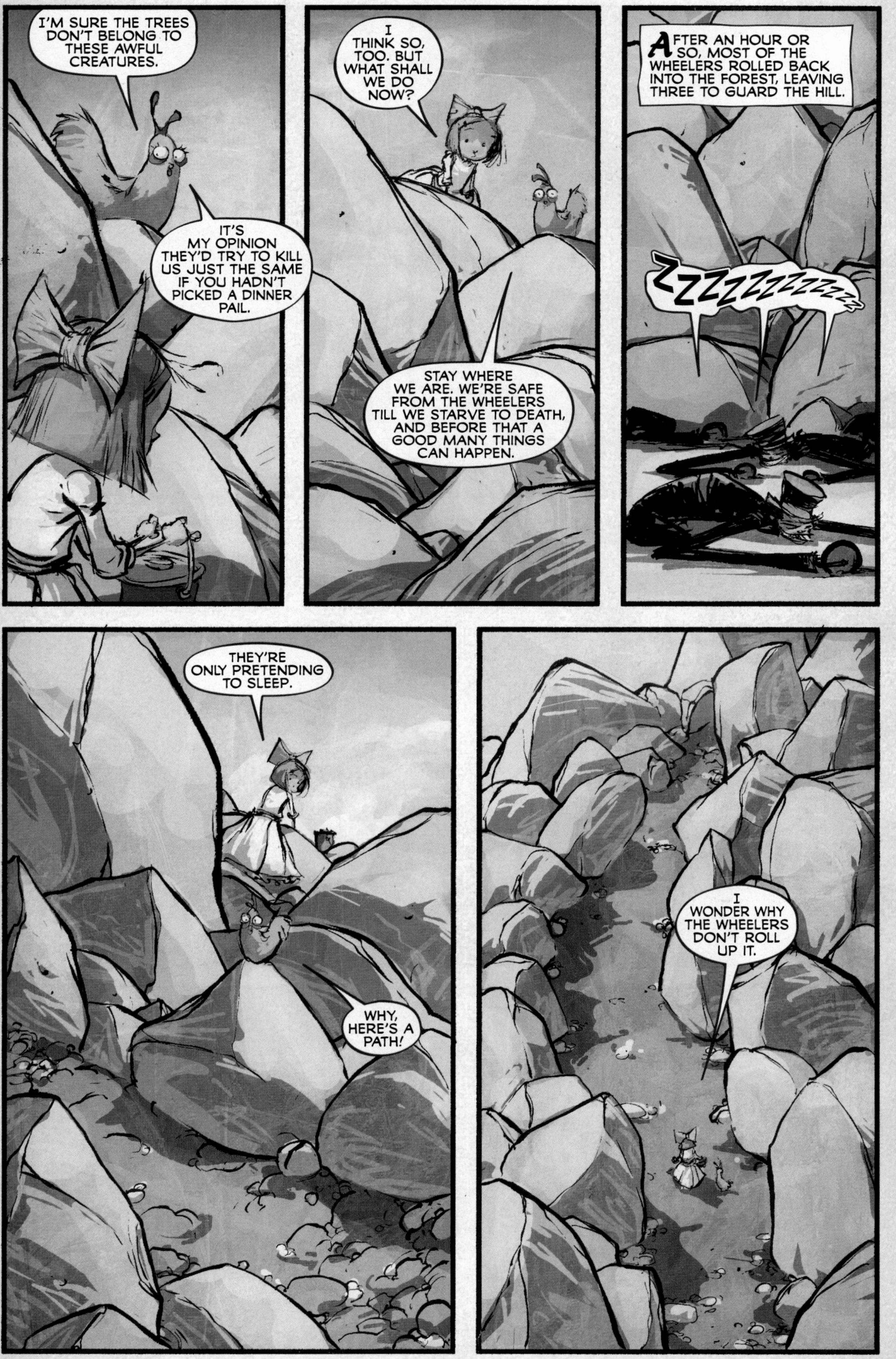
I'M SURE THE TREES DON'T BELONG TO THESE AWFUL CREATURES.
IT'S MY OPINION THEY'D TRY TO KILL US JUST THE SAME IF YOU HADN'T PICKED A DINNER PAIL.
I THINK SO, TOO. BUT WHAT SHALL WE DO NOW?
STAY WHERE WE ARE. WE'RE SAFE FROM THE WHEELERS TILL WE STARVE TO DEATH, AND BEFORE THAT A GOOD MANY THINGS CAN HAPPEN.
AFTER AN HOUR OR SO, MOST OF THE WHEELERS ROLLED BACK INTO THE FOREST, LEAVING THREE TO GUARD THE HILL.
ZZZZZZZZZZZZZZ
THEY'RE ONLY PRETENDING TO SLEEP.
WHY, HERE'S A PATH!
I WONDER WHY THE WHEELERS DON'T ROLL UP IT.

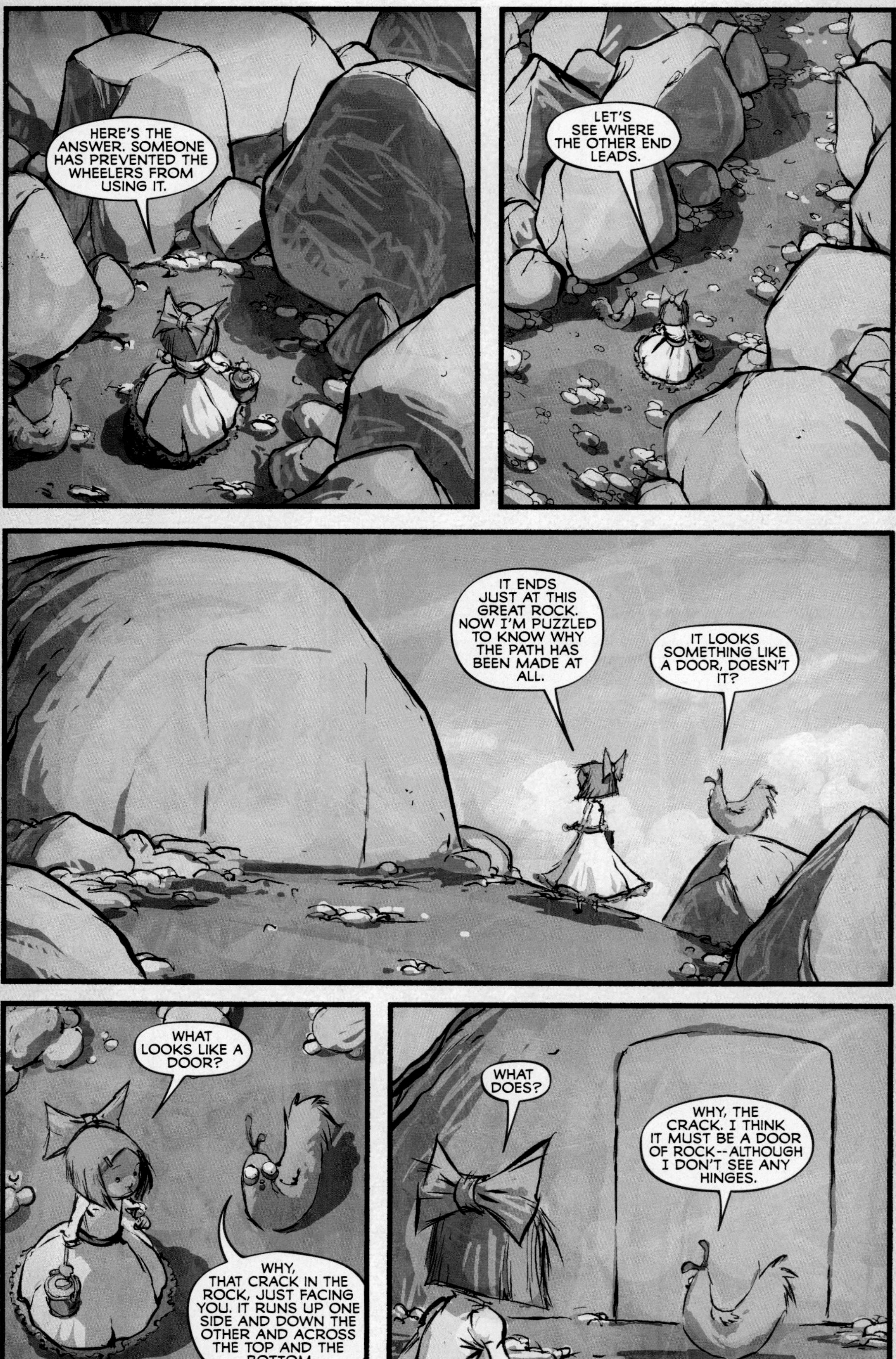
HERE'S THE ANSWER. SOMEONE HAS PREVENTED THE WHEELERS FROM USING IT.
LET'S SEE WHERE THE OTHER END LEADS.
IT ENDS JUST AT THIS GREAT ROCK. NOW I'M PUZZLED TO KNOW WHY THE PATH HAS BEEN MADE AT ALL.
IT LOOKS SOMETHING LIKE A DOOR, DOESN'T IT?
WHAT LOOKS LIKE A DOOR?
WHY, THAT CRACK IN THE ROCK, JUST FACING YOU. IT RUNS UP ONE SIDE AND DOWN THE OTHER AND ACROSS THE TOP AND THE BOTTOM.
WHAT DOES?
WHY, THE CRACK. I THINK IT MUST BE A DOOR OF ROCK--ALTHOUGH I DON'T SEE ANY HINGES.

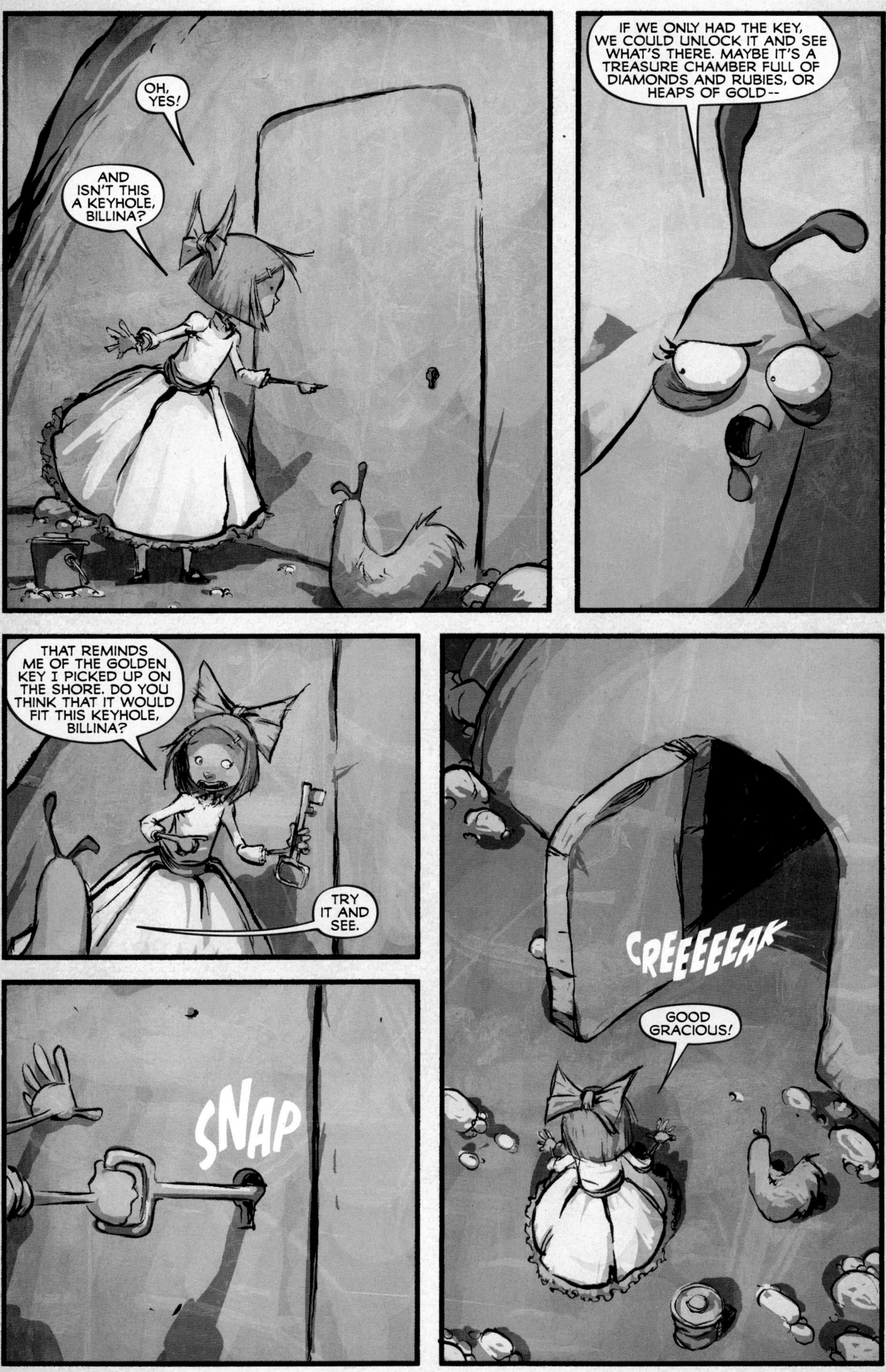
OH, YES!
AND ISN'T THIS A KEYHOLE, BILLINA?
IF WE ONLY HAD THE KEY, WE COULD UNLOCK IT AND SEE WHAT'S THERE. MAYBE IT'S A TREASURE CHAMBER FULL OF DIAMONDS AND RUBIES, OR HEAPS OF GOLD--
THAT REMINDS ME OF THE GOLDEN KEY I PICKED UP ON THE SHORE. DO YOU THINK THAT IT WOULD FIT THIS KEYHOLE, BILLINA?
TRY IT AND SEE.
SNAP
CREEEEEAK
GOOD GRACIOUS!

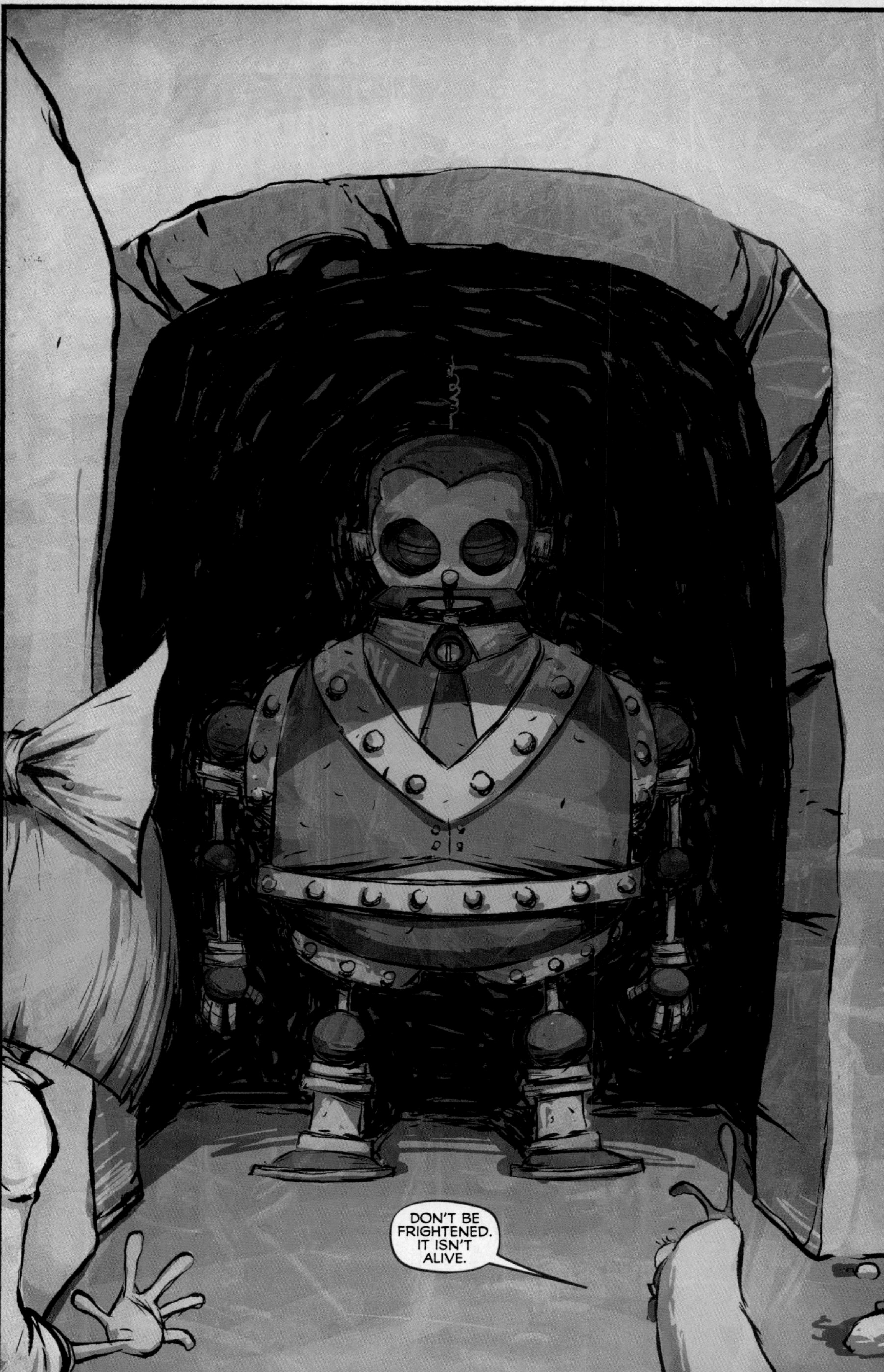
DON'T BE FRIGHTENED. IT ISN'T ALIVE.

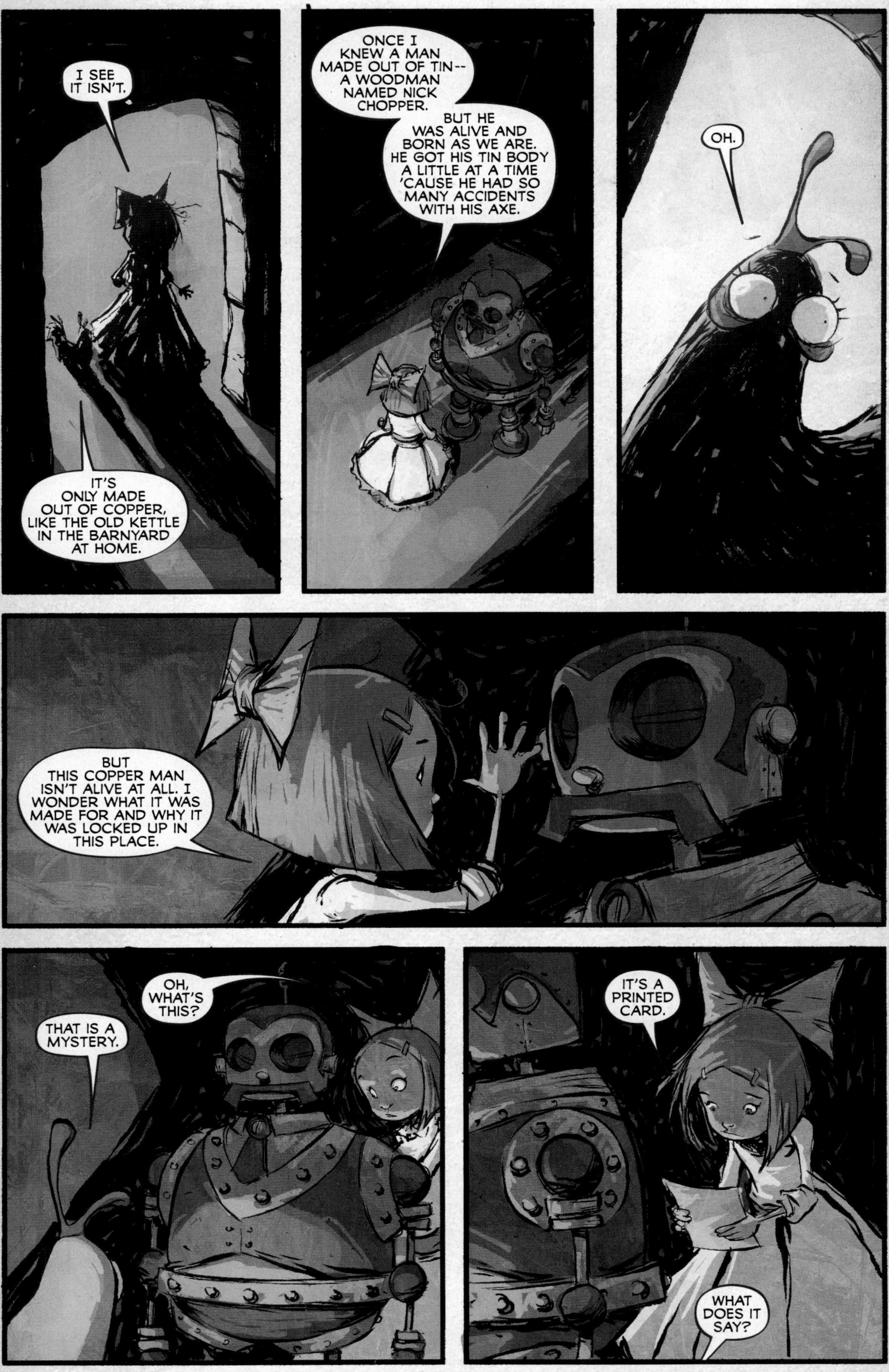
I SEE IT ISN'T.
IT'S ONLY MADE OUT OF COPPER, LIKE THE OLD KETTLE IN THE BARNYARD AT HOME.
ONCE I KNEW A MAN MADE OUT OF TIN-- A WOODMAN NAMED NICK CHOPPER.
BUT HE WAS ALIVE AND BORN AS WE ARE. HE GOT HIS TIN BODY A LITTLE AT A TIME 'CAUSE HE HAD SO MANY ACCIDENTS WITH HIS AXE.
OH.
BUT THIS COPPER MAN ISN'T ALIVE AT ALL. I WONDER WHAT IT WAS MADE FOR AND WHY IT WAS LOCKED UP IN THIS PLACE.
THAT IS A MYSTERY.
OH, WHAT'S THIS?
IT'S A PRINTED CARD.
WHAT DOES IT SAY?

DOROTHY
READ ALOUD:

SMITH & TINKER'S

Patent Double-Action, Extra-Responsive,
Thought-Creating, Perfect-Talking
MECHANICAL MAN
Fitted with our Special Clock-Work Attachment.

Thinks, Speaks, Acts, and Does Everything but Live.

Manufactured only at our Works at Evna, Land of Ev.
All infringements will be promptly Prosecuted according to Law.

HOW STRANGE! DO YOU THINK THAT'S ALL TRUE, MY DEAR?

I DON'T KNOW. LISTEN TO THIS, BILLINA.

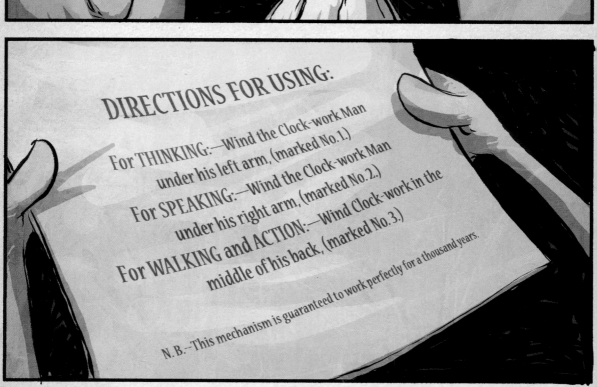

DIRECTIONS FOR USING:

For THINKING:—Wind the Clock-work Man under his left arm, (marked No. 1.)

For SPEAKING:—Wind the Clock-work Man under his right arm, (marked No. 2.)

For WALKING and ACTION:—Wind Clock-work in the middle of his back, (marked No. 3.)

N. B.—This mechanism is guaranteed to work perfectly for a thousand years.

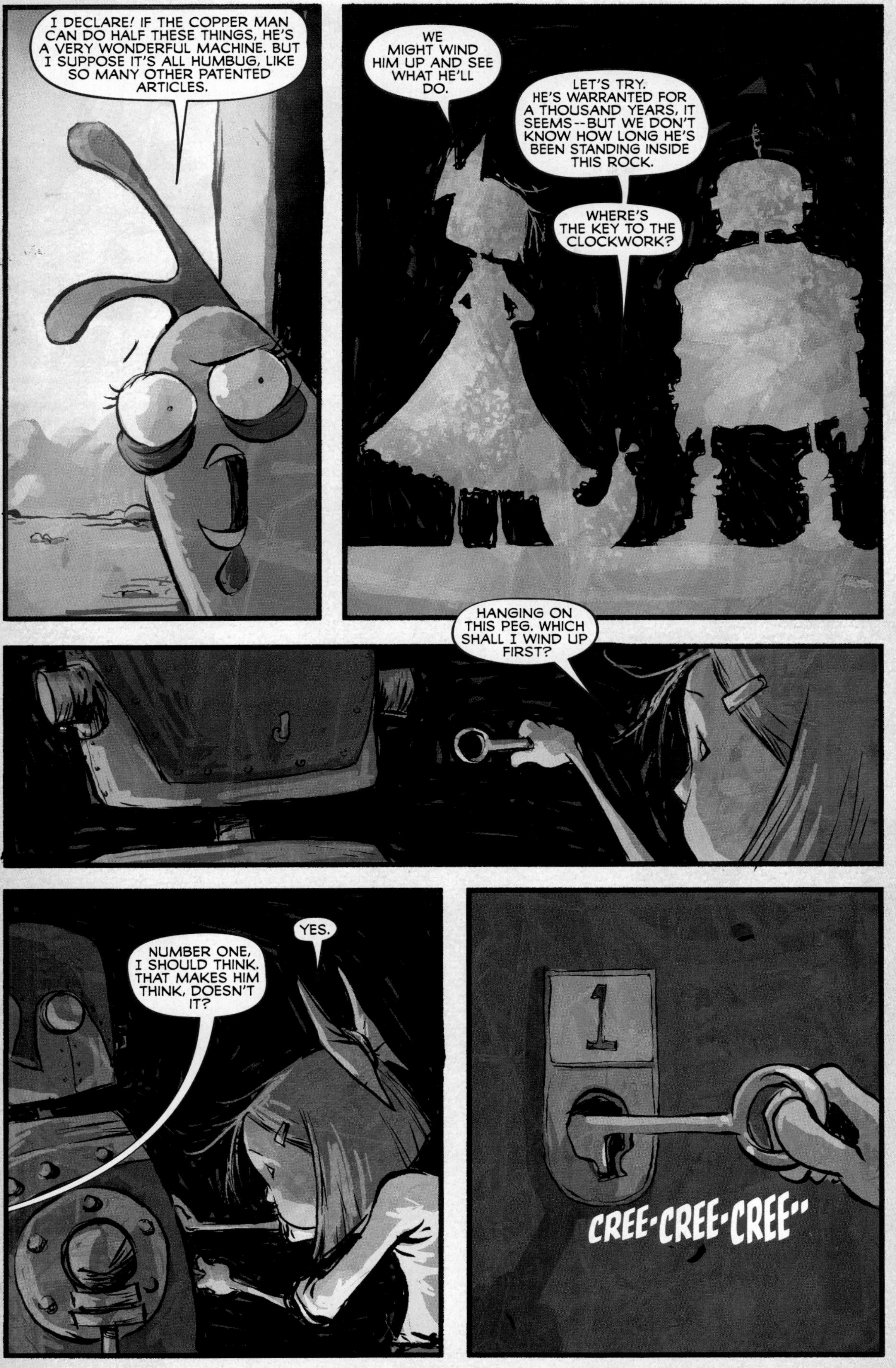
I DECLARE! IF THE COPPER MAN CAN DO HALF THESE THINGS, HE'S A VERY WONDERFUL MACHINE. BUT I SUPPOSE IT'S ALL HUMBUG, LIKE SO MANY OTHER PATENTED ARTICLES.
WE MIGHT WIND HIM UP AND SEE WHAT HE'LL DO.
LET'S TRY. HE'S WARRANTED FOR A THOUSAND YEARS, IT SEEMS--BUT WE DON'T KNOW HOW LONG HE'S BEEN STANDING INSIDE THIS ROCK.
WHERE'S THE KEY TO THE CLOCKWORK?
HANGING ON THIS PEG. WHICH SHALL I WIND UP FIRST?
NUMBER ONE, I SHOULD THINK. THAT MAKES HIM THINK, DOESN'T IT?
YES.
1
CREE-CREE-CREE--

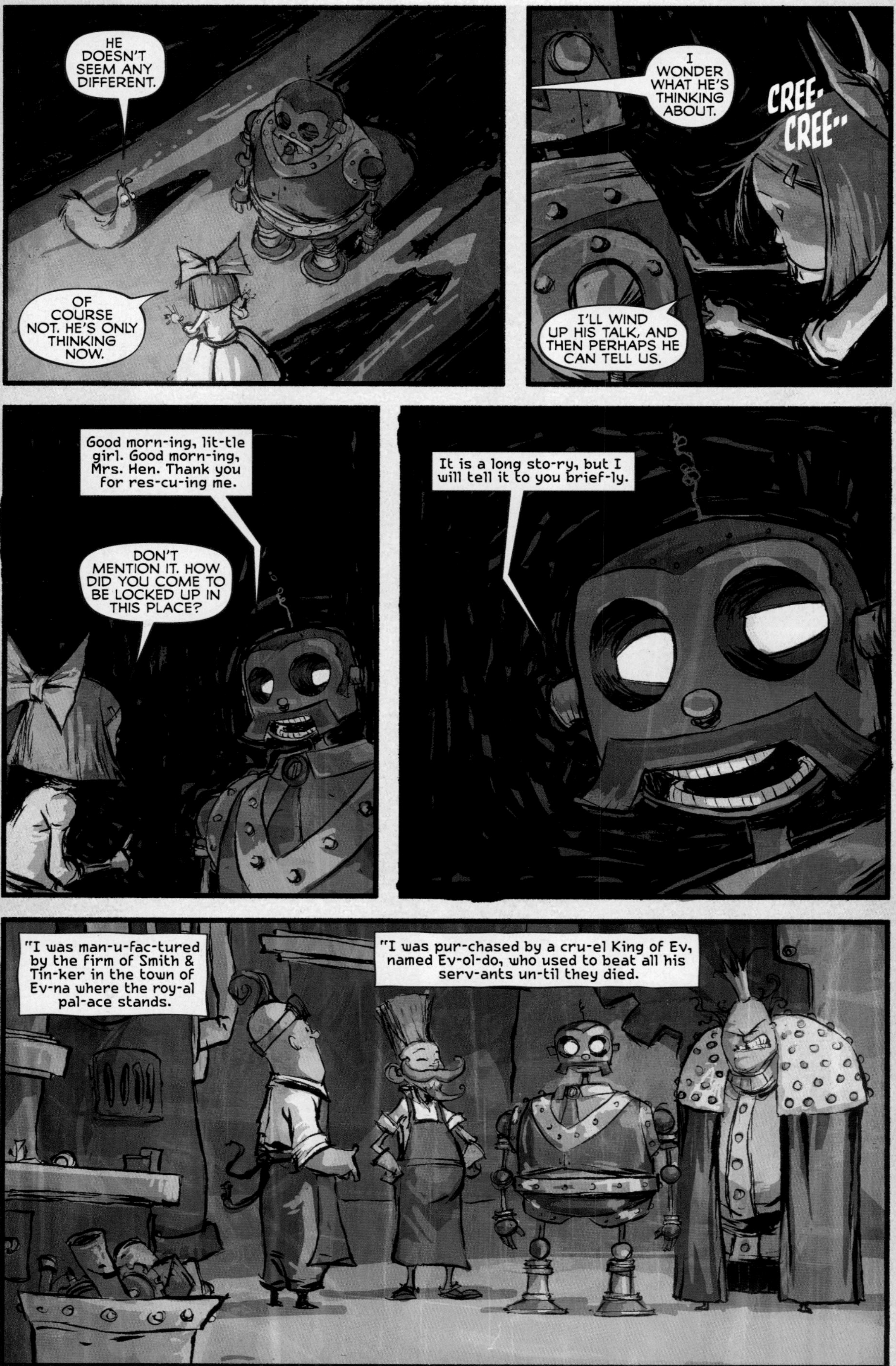
HE DOESN'T SEEM ANY DIFFERENT.
OF COURSE NOT. HE'S ONLY THINKING NOW.
I WONDER WHAT HE'S THINKING ABOUT.
CREE-CREE..
I'LL WIND UP HIS TALK, AND THEN PERHAPS HE CAN TELL US.
Good morn-ing, lit-tle girl. Good morn-ing, Mrs. Hen. Thank you for res-cu-ing me.
DON'T MENTION IT. HOW DID YOU COME TO BE LOCKED UP IN THIS PLACE?
It is a long sto-ry, but I will tell it to you brief-ly.
"I was man-u-fac-tured by the firm of Smith & Tin-ker in the town of Ev-na where the roy-al pal-ace stands.
"I was pur-chased by a cru-el King of Ev, named Ev-ol-do, who used to beat all his serv-ants un-til they died.

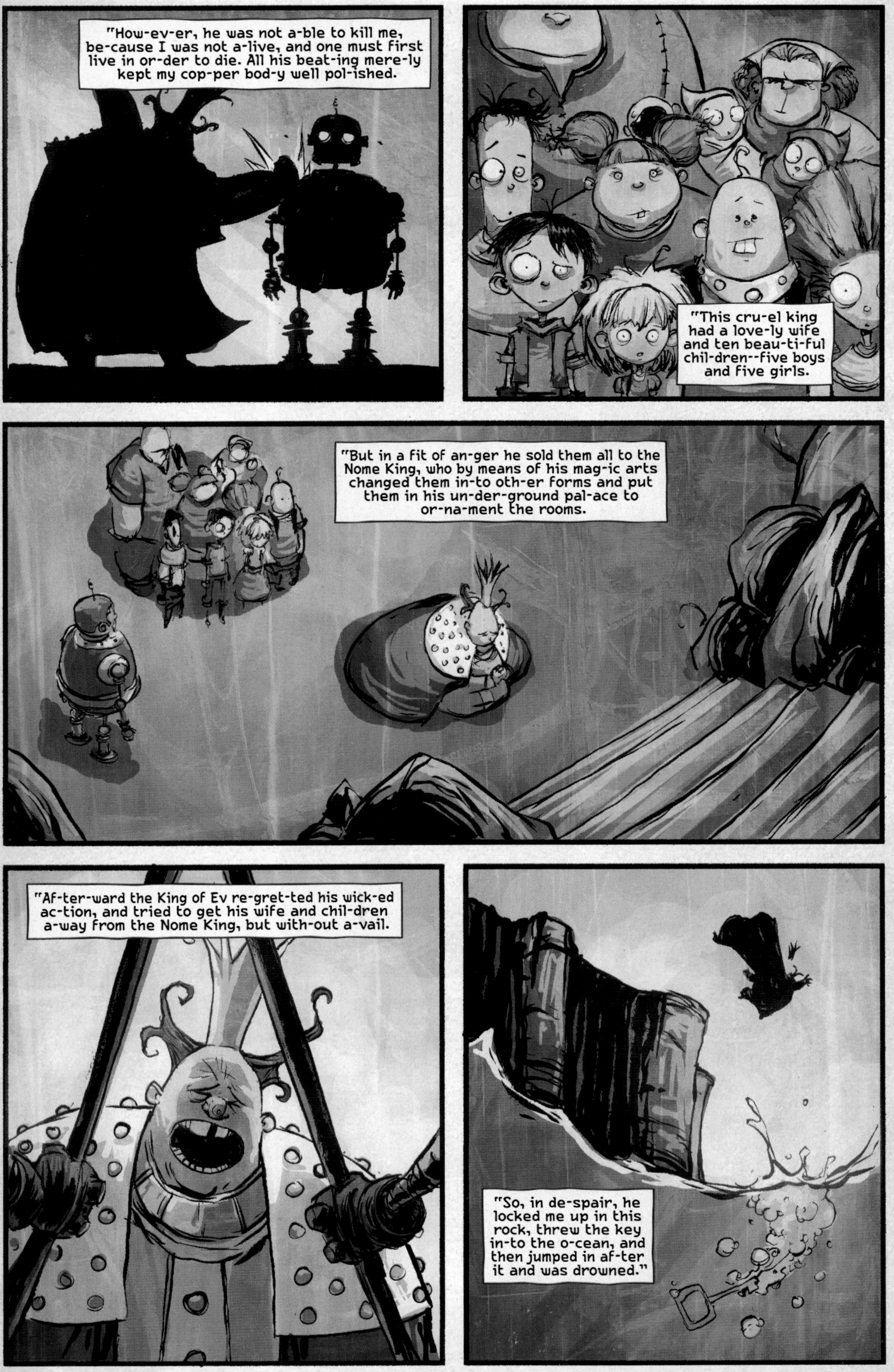
"How-ev-er, he was not a-ble to kill me, be-cause I was not a-live, and one must first live in or-der to die. All his beat-ing mere-ly kept my cop-per bod-y well pol-ished.
"This cru-el king had a love-ly wife and ten beau-ti-ful chil-dren--five boys and five girls.
"But in a fit of an-ger he sold them all to the Nome King, who by means of his mag-ic arts changed them in-to oth-er forms and put them in his un-der-ground pal-ace to or-na-ment the rooms.
"Af-ter-ward the King of Ev re-gret-ted his wick-ed ac-tion, and tried to get his wife and chil-dren a-way from the Nome King, but with-out a-vail.
"So, in de-spair, he locked me up in this rock, threw the key in-to the o-cean, and then jumped in af-ter it and was drowned."

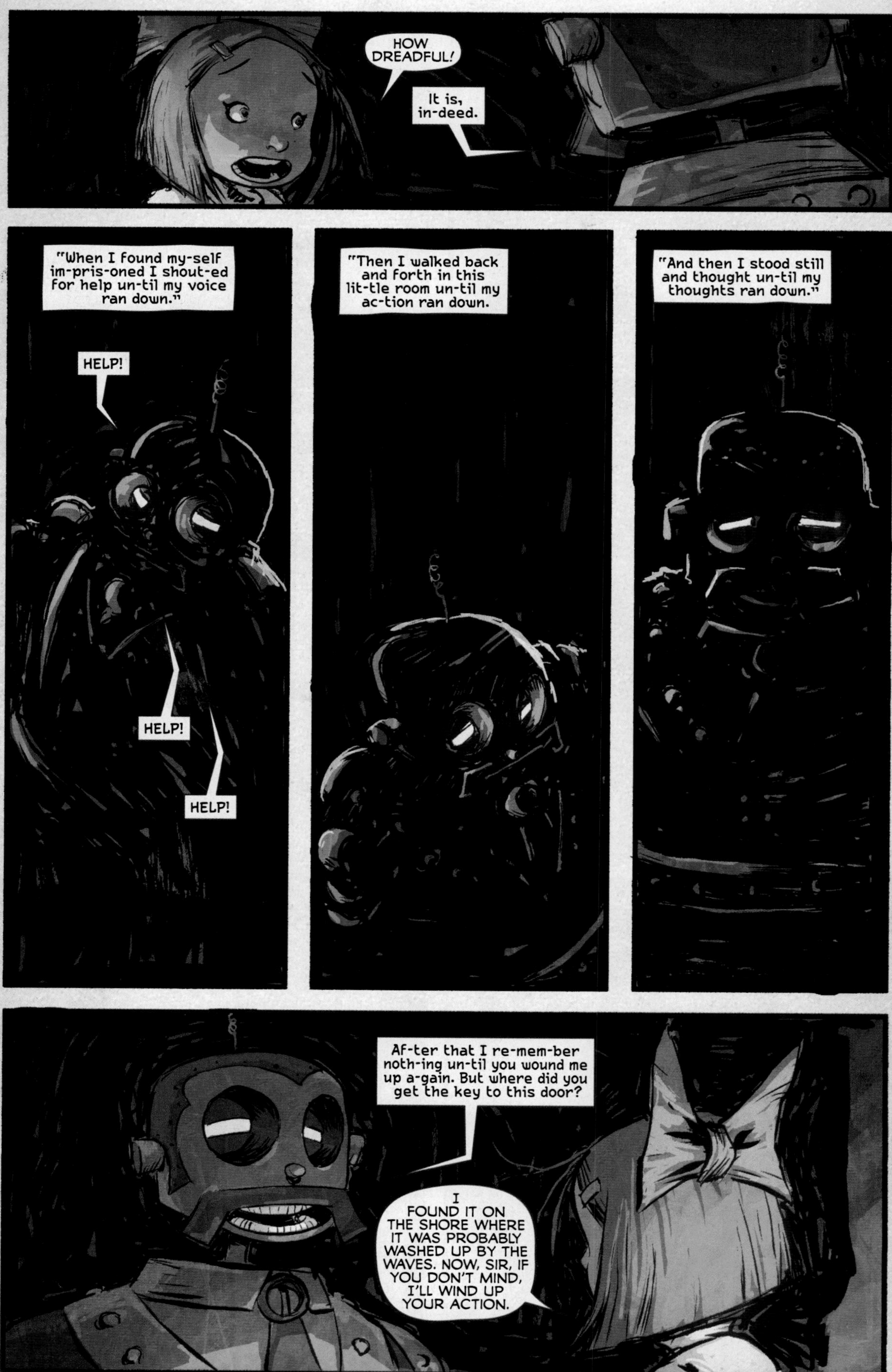

HOW DREADFUL!
It is, in-deed.
"When I found my-self im-pris-oned I shout-ed for help un-til my voice ran down."
HELP!
HELP!
HELP!
"Then I walked back and forth in this lit-tle room un-til my ac-tion ran down.
"And then I stood still and thought un-til my thoughts ran down."
Af-ter that I re-mem-ber noth-ing un-til you wound me up a-gain. But where did you get the key to this door?
I FOUND IT ON THE SHORE WHERE IT WAS PROBABLY WASHED UP BY THE WAVES. NOW, SIR, IF YOU DON'T MIND, I'LL WIND UP YOUR ACTION.

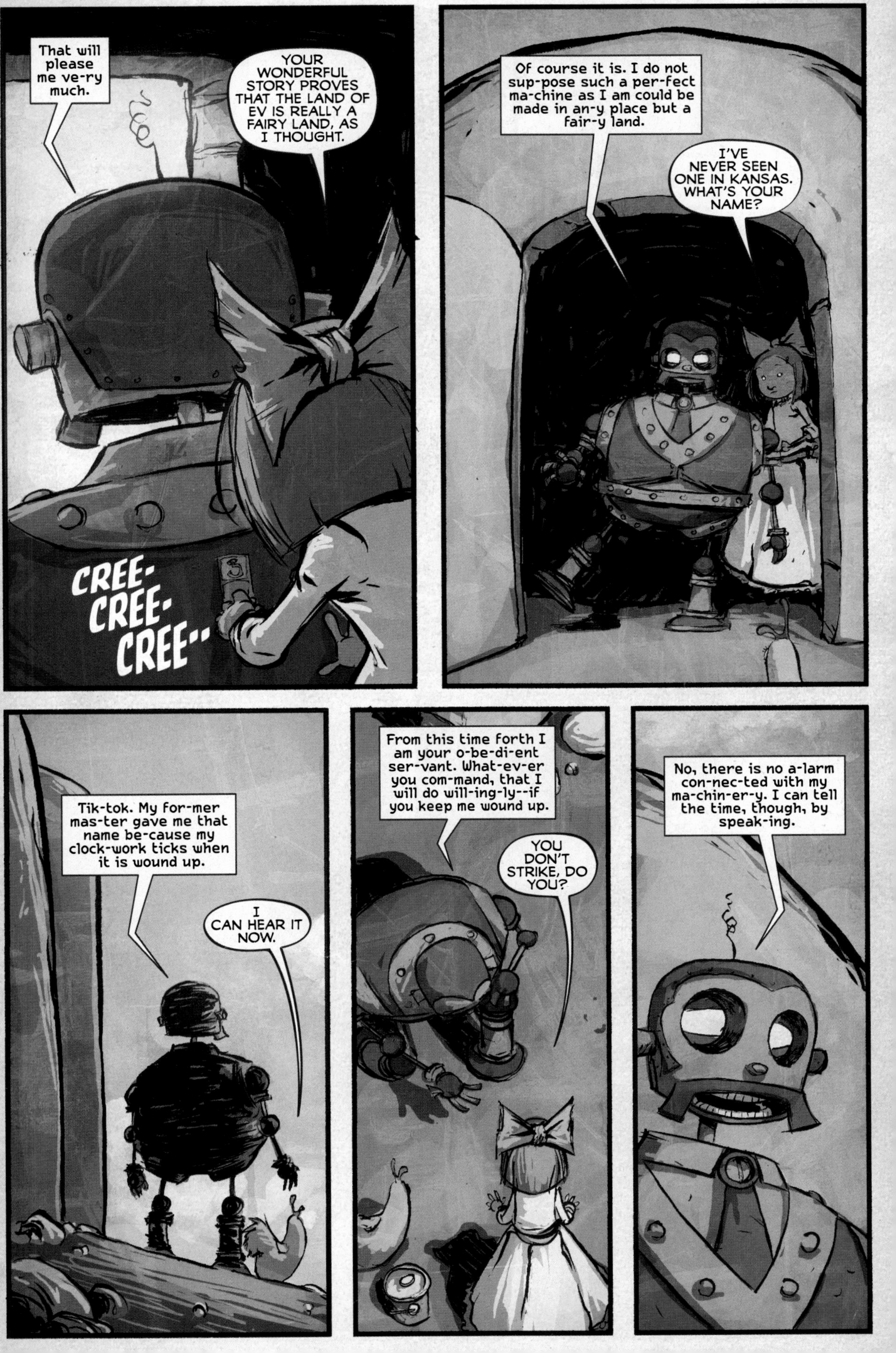
That will please me ve-ry much.
YOUR WONDERFUL STORY PROVES THAT THE LAND OF EV IS REALLY A FAIRY LAND, AS I THOUGHT.
CREE-
CREE-
CREE--
Of course it is. I do not sup-pose such a per-fect ma-chine as I am could be made in an-y place but a fair-y land.
I'VE NEVER SEEN ONE IN KANSAS. WHAT'S YOUR NAME?
Tik-tok. My for-mer mas-ter gave me that name be-cause my clock-work ticks when it is wound up.
I CAN HEAR IT NOW.
From this time forth I am your o-be-di-ent ser-vant. What-ev-er you com-mand, that I will do will-ing-ly--if you keep me wound up.
YOU DON'T STRIKE, DO YOU?
No, there is no a-larm con-nec-ted with my ma-chin-er-y. I can tell the time, though, by speak-ing.

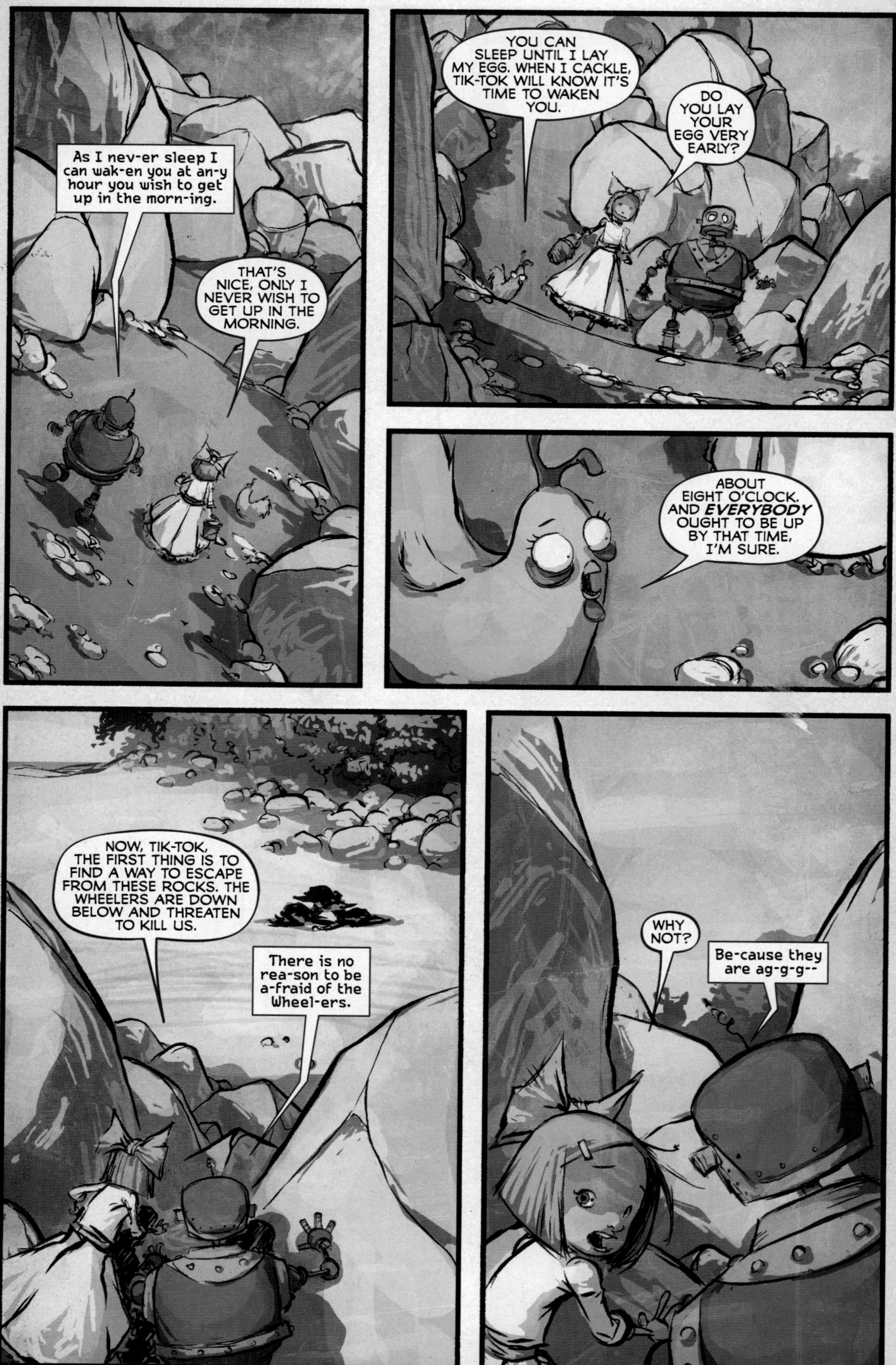
As I nev-er sleep I can wak-en you at an-y hour you wish to get up in the morn-ing.
THAT'S NICE, ONLY I NEVER WISH TO GET UP IN THE MORNING.
YOU CAN SLEEP UNTIL I LAY MY EGG. WHEN I CACKLE, TIK-TOK WILL KNOW IT'S TIME TO WAKEN YOU.
DO YOU LAY YOUR EGG VERY EARLY?
ABOUT EIGHT O'CLOCK. AND *EVERYBODY* OUGHT TO BE UP BY THAT TIME, I'M SURE.
NOW, TIK-TOK, THE FIRST THING IS TO FIND A WAY TO ESCAPE FROM THESE ROCKS. THE WHEELERS ARE DOWN BELOW AND THREATEN TO KILL US.
There is no rea-son to be a-fraid of the Wheel-ers.
WHY NOT?
Be-cause they are ag-g-g--

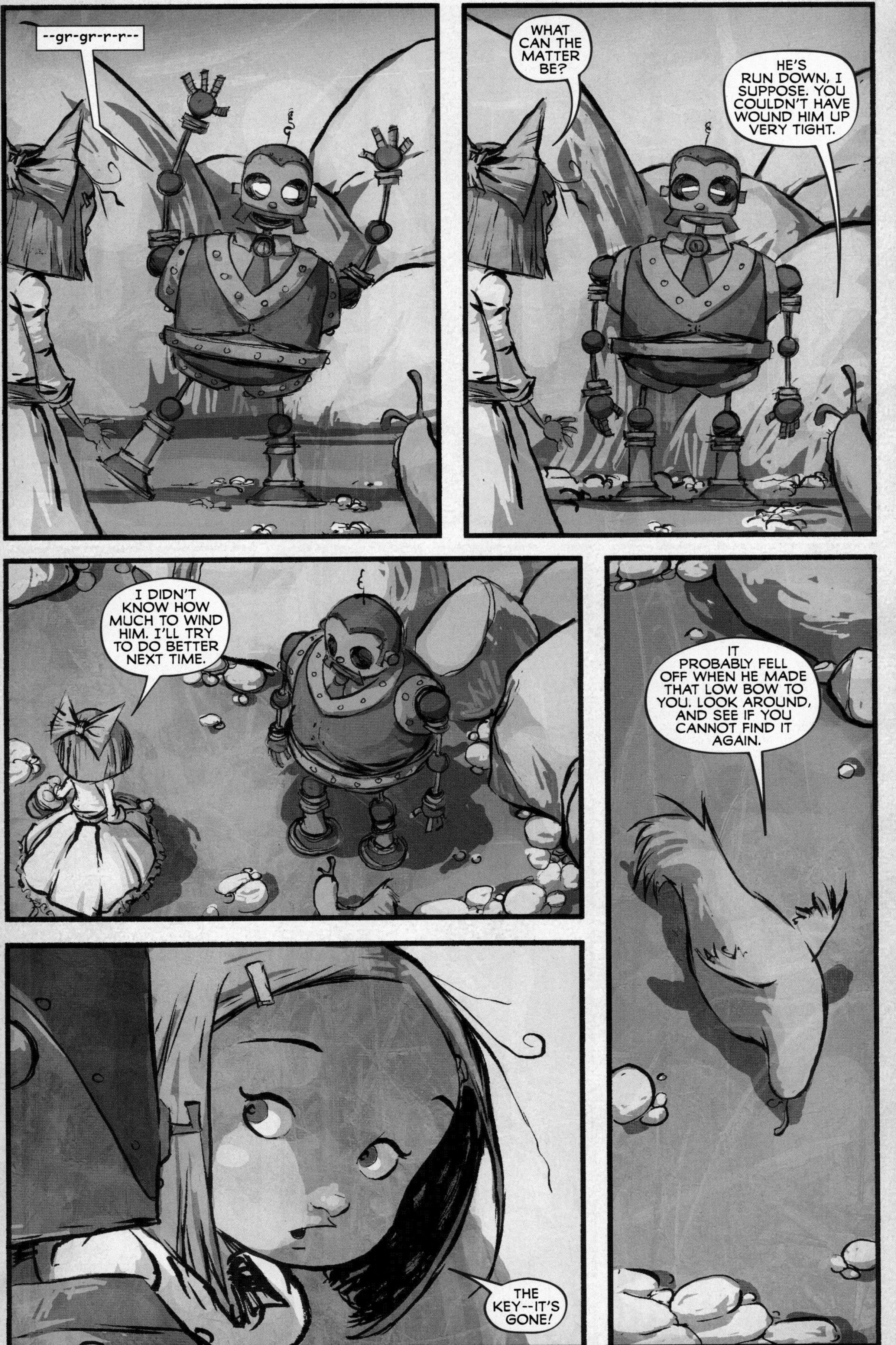
--gr-gr-r-r--
WHAT CAN THE MATTER BE?
HE'S RUN DOWN, I SUPPOSE. YOU COULDN'T HAVE WOUND HIM UP VERY TIGHT.
I DIDN'T KNOW HOW MUCH TO WIND HIM. I'LL TRY TO DO BETTER NEXT TIME.
IT PROBABLY FELL OFF WHEN HE MADE THAT LOW BOW TO YOU. LOOK AROUND, AND SEE IF YOU CANNOT FIND IT AGAIN.
THE KEY--IT'S GONE!

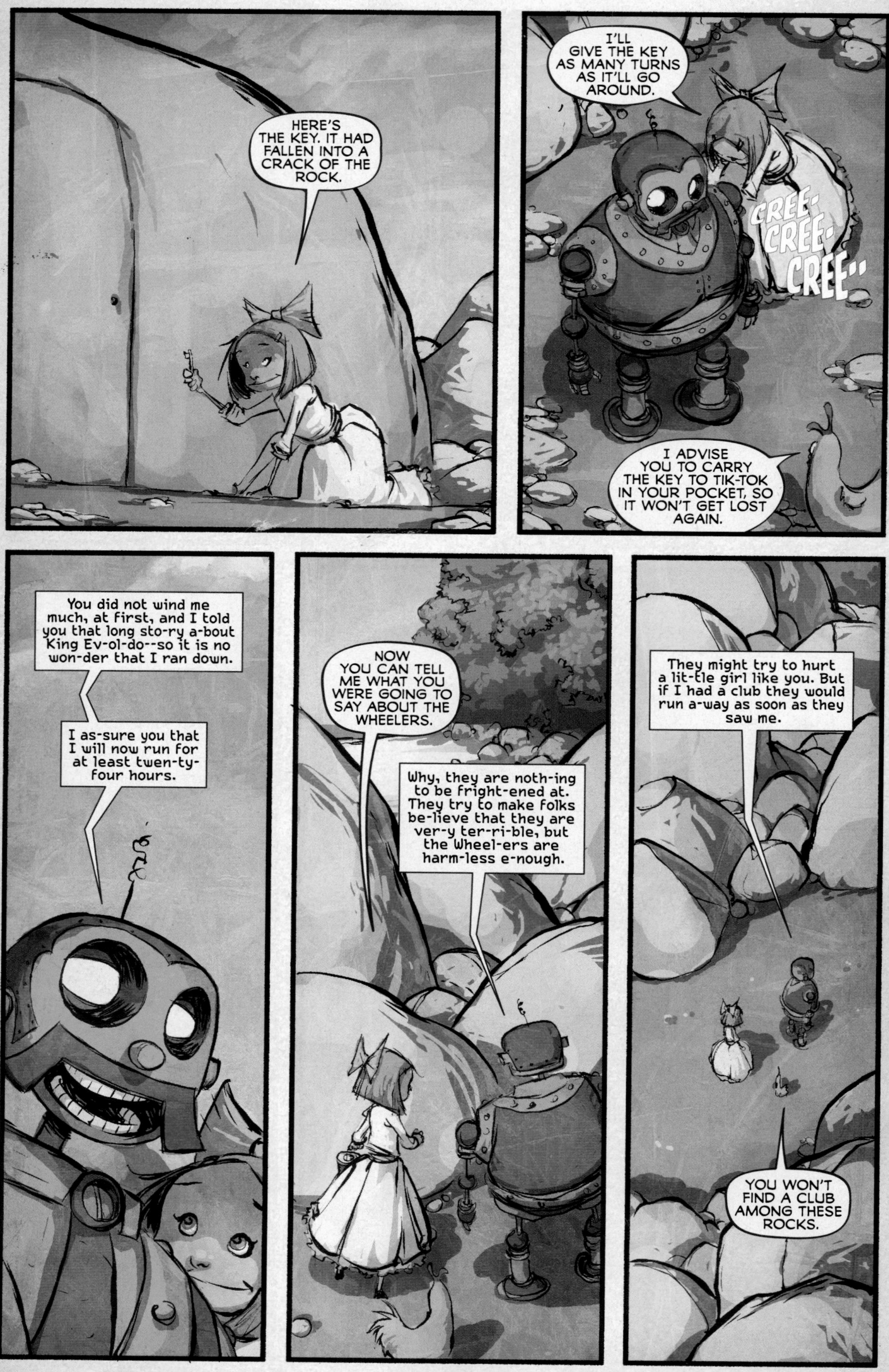
HERE'S THE KEY. IT HAD FALLEN INTO A CRACK OF THE ROCK.
I'LL GIVE THE KEY AS MANY TURNS AS IT'LL GO AROUND.
CREE-CREE-CREE..
I ADVISE YOU TO CARRY THE KEY TO TIK-TOK IN YOUR POCKET, SO IT WON'T GET LOST AGAIN.
You did not wind me much, at first, and I told you that long sto-ry a-bout King Ev-ol-do--so it is no won-der that I ran down.
I as-sure you that I will now run for at least twen-ty-four hours.
NOW YOU CAN TELL ME WHAT YOU WERE GOING TO SAY ABOUT THE WHEELERS.
Why, they are noth-ing to be fright-ened at. They try to make folks be-lieve that they are ver-y ter-ri-ble, but the Wheel-ers are harm-less e-nough.
They might try to hurt a lit-tle girl like you. But if I had a club they would run a-way as soon as they saw me.
YOU WON'T FIND A CLUB AMONG THESE ROCKS.

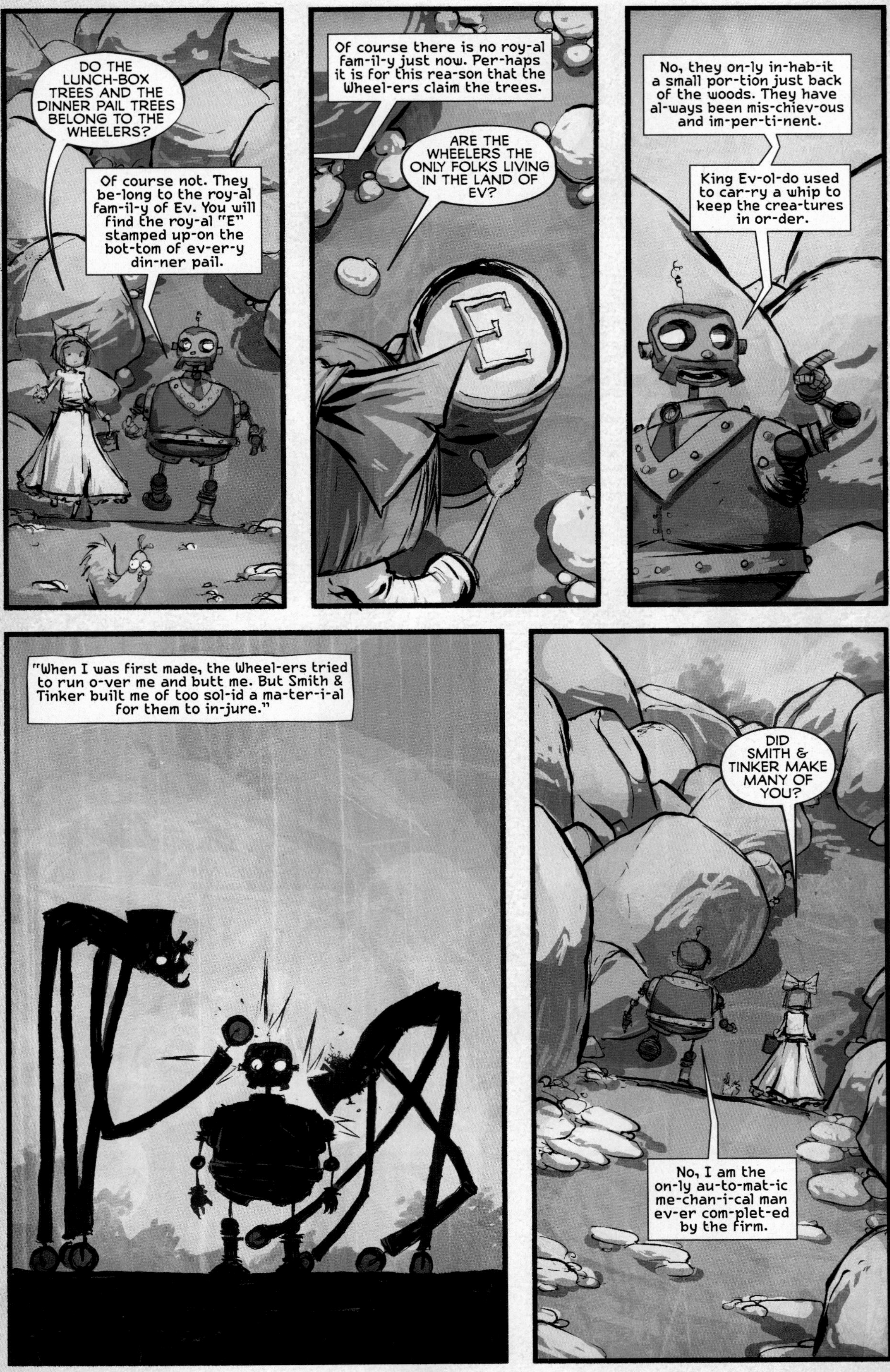
DO THE LUNCH-BOX TREES AND THE DINNER PAIL TREES BELONG TO THE WHEELERS?
Of course not. They be-long to the roy-al fam-il-y of Ev. You will find the roy-al "E" stamped up-on the bot-tom of ev-er-y din-ner pail.
Of course there is no roy-al fam-il-y just now. Per-haps it is for this rea-son that the Wheel-ers claim the trees.
ARE THE WHEELERS THE ONLY FOLKS LIVING IN THE LAND OF EV?
E
No, they on-ly in-hab-it a small por-tion just back of the woods. They have al-ways been mis-chiev-ous and im-per-ti-nent.
King Ev-ol-do used to car-ry a whip to keep the crea-tures in or-der.
"When I was first made, the Wheel-ers tried to run o-ver me and butt me. But Smith & Tinker built me of too sol-id a ma-ter-i-al for them to in-jure."
DID SMITH & TINKER MAKE MANY OF YOU?
No, I am the on-ly au-to-mat-ic me-chan-i-cal man ev-er com-plet-ed by the firm.

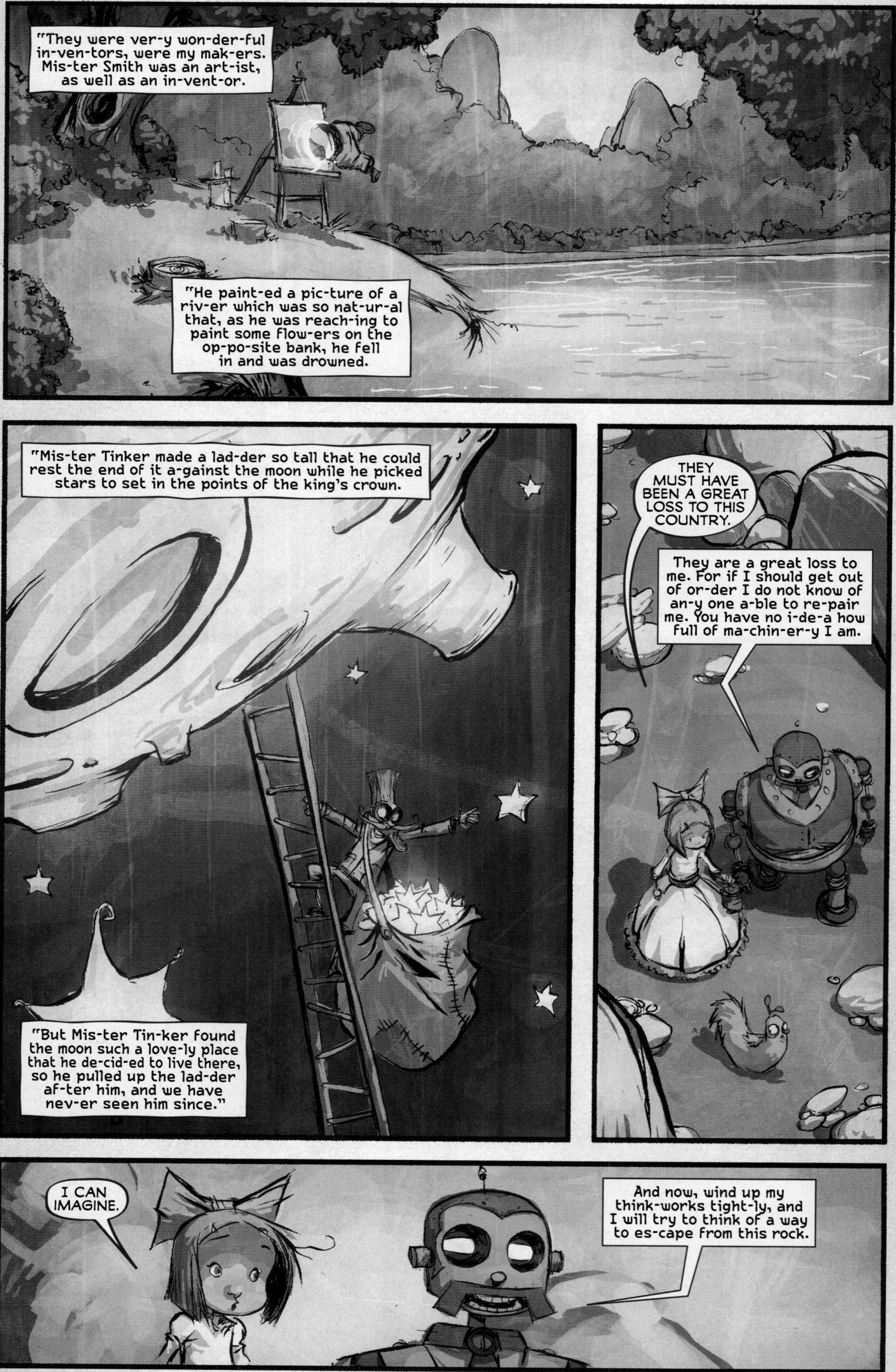
"They were ver-y won-der-ful in-ven-tors, were my mak-ers. Mis-ter Smith was an art-ist, as well as an in-vent-or.
"He paint-ed a pic-ture of a riv-er which was so nat-ur-al that, as he was reach-ing to paint some flow-ers on the op-po-site bank, he fell in and was drowned.
"Mis-ter Tinker made a lad-der so tall that he could rest the end of it a-gainst the moon while he picked stars to set in the points of the king's crown.
"But Mis-ter Tin-ker found the moon such a love-ly place that he de-cid-ed to live there, so he pulled up the lad-der af-ter him, and we have nev-er seen him since."
THEY MUST HAVE BEEN A GREAT LOSS TO THIS COUNTRY.
They are a great loss to me. For if I should get out of or-der I do not know of an-y one a-ble to re-pair me. You have no i-de-a how full of ma-chin-er-y I am.
I CAN IMAGINE.
And now, wind up my think-works tight-ly, and I will try to think of a way to es-cape from this rock.

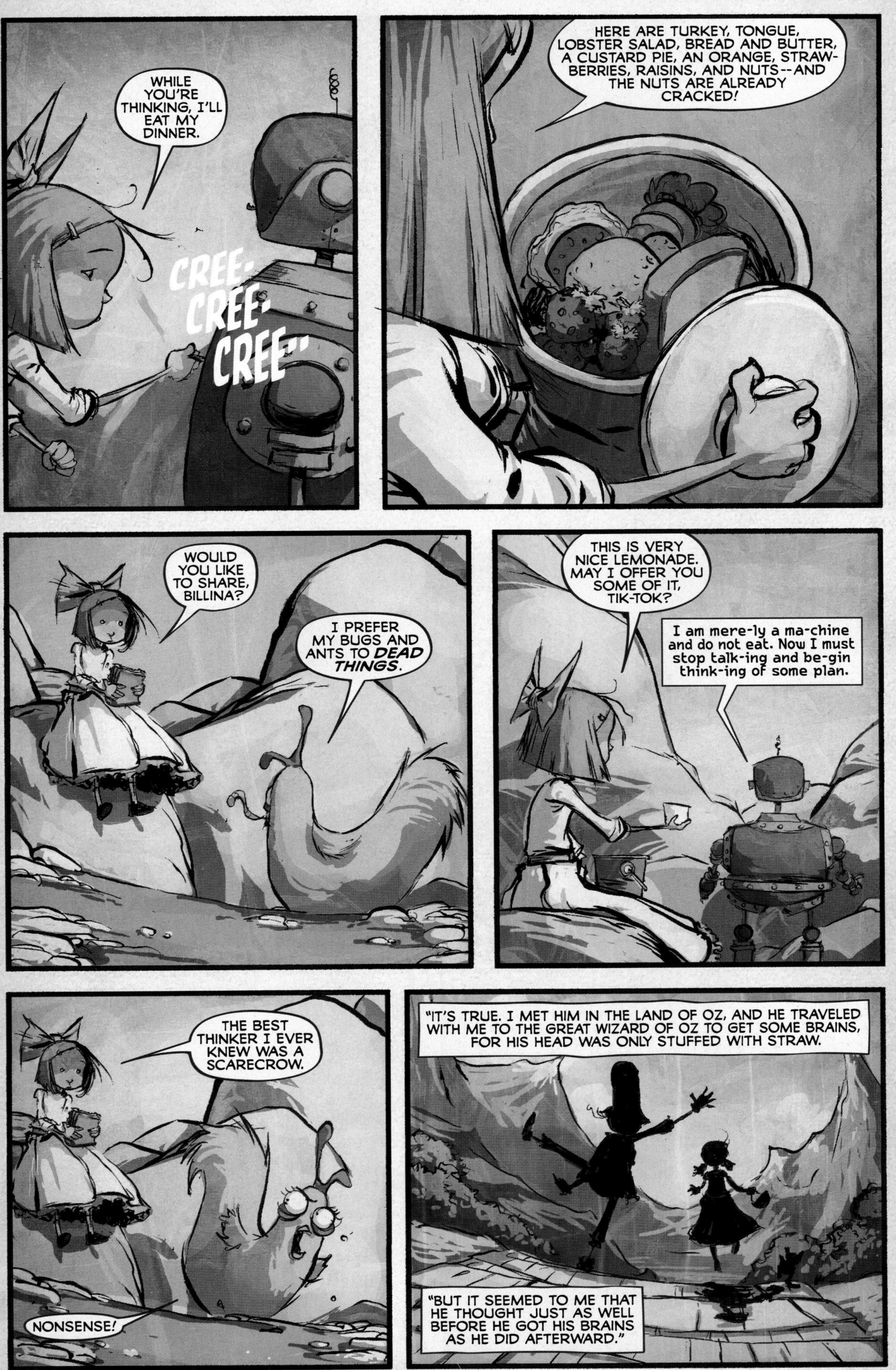
WHILE YOU'RE THINKING, I'LL EAT MY DINNER.
CREE-CREE-CREE...
HERE ARE TURKEY, TONGUE, LOBSTER SALAD, BREAD AND BUTTER, A CUSTARD PIE, AN ORANGE, STRAW-BERRIES, RAISINS, AND NUTS--AND THE NUTS ARE ALREADY CRACKED!
WOULD YOU LIKE TO SHARE, BILLINA?
I PREFER MY BUGS AND ANTS TO DEAD THINGS.
THIS IS VERY NICE LEMONADE. MAY I OFFER YOU SOME OF IT, TIK-TOK?
I am mere-ly a ma-chine and do not eat. Now I must stop talk-ing and be-gin think-ing of some plan.
THE BEST THINKER I EVER KNEW WAS A SCARECROW.
NONSENSE!
"IT'S TRUE. I MET HIM IN THE LAND OF OZ, AND HE TRAVELED WITH ME TO THE GREAT WIZARD OF OZ TO GET SOME BRAINS, FOR HIS HEAD WAS ONLY STUFFED WITH STRAW.
"BUT IT SEEMED TO ME THAT HE THOUGHT JUST AS WELL BEFORE HE GOT HIS BRAINS AS HE DID AFTERWARD."

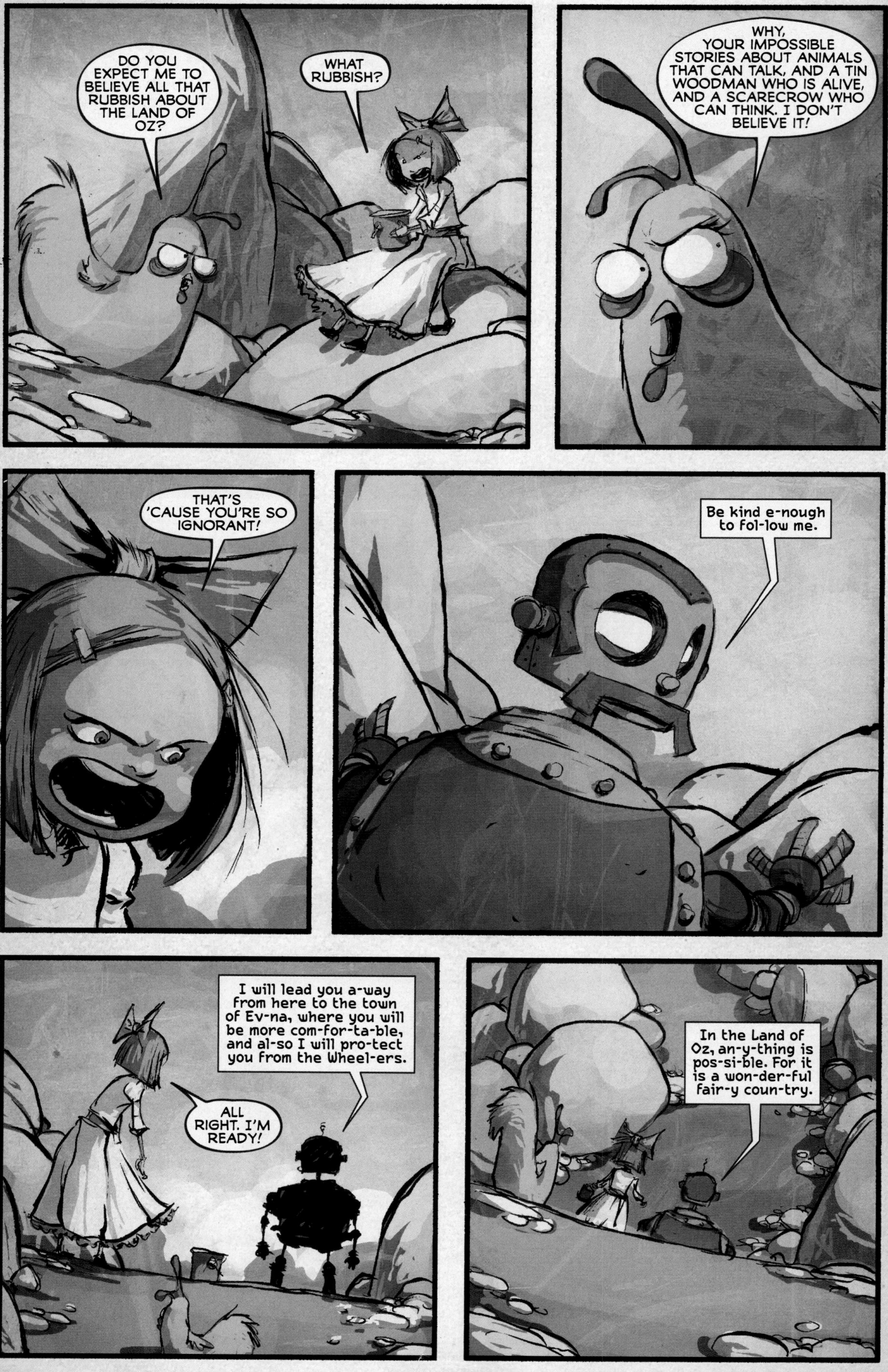
DO YOU EXPECT ME TO BELIEVE ALL THAT RUBBISH ABOUT THE LAND OF OZ?
WHAT RUBBISH?
WHY, YOUR IMPOSSIBLE STORIES ABOUT ANIMALS THAT CAN TALK, AND A TIN WOODMAN WHO IS ALIVE, AND A SCARECROW WHO CAN THINK. I DON'T BELIEVE IT!
THAT'S 'CAUSE YOU'RE SO IGNORANT!
Be kind e-nough to fol-low me.
I will lead you a-way from here to the town of Ev-na, where you will be more com-for-ta-ble, and al-so I will pro-tect you from the Wheel-ers.
ALL RIGHT. I'M READY!
In the Land of Oz, an-y-thing is pos-si-ble. For it is a won-der-ful fair-y coun-try.

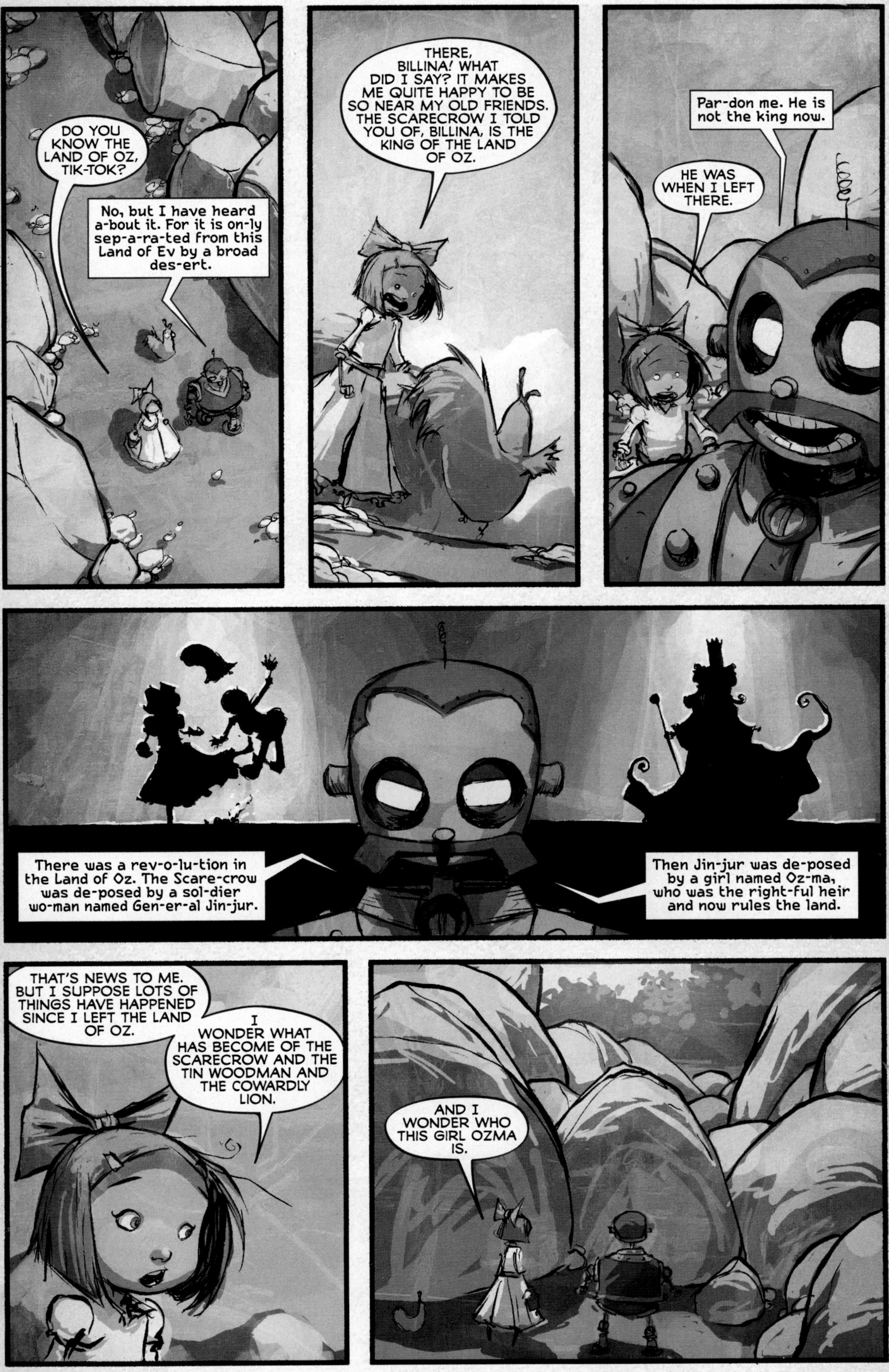
DO YOU KNOW THE LAND OF OZ, TIK-TOK?
No, but I have heard a-bout it. For it is on-ly sep-a-ra-ted from this Land of Ev by a broad des-ert.
THERE, BILLINA! WHAT DID I SAY? IT MAKES ME QUITE HAPPY TO BE SO NEAR MY OLD FRIENDS. THE SCARECROW I TOLD YOU OF, BILLINA, IS THE KING OF THE LAND OF OZ.
Par-don me. He is not the king now.
HE WAS WHEN I LEFT THERE.
There was a rev-o-lu-tion in the Land of Oz. The Scare-crow was de-posed by a sol-dier wo-man named Gen-er-al Jin-jur.
Then Jin-jur was de-posed by a girl named Oz-ma, who was the right-ful heir and now rules the land.
THAT'S NEWS TO ME. BUT I SUPPOSE LOTS OF THINGS HAVE HAPPENED SINCE I LEFT THE LAND OF OZ.
I WONDER WHAT HAS BECOME OF THE SCARECROW AND THE TIN WOODMAN AND THE COWARDLY LION.
AND I WONDER WHO THIS GIRL OZMA IS.

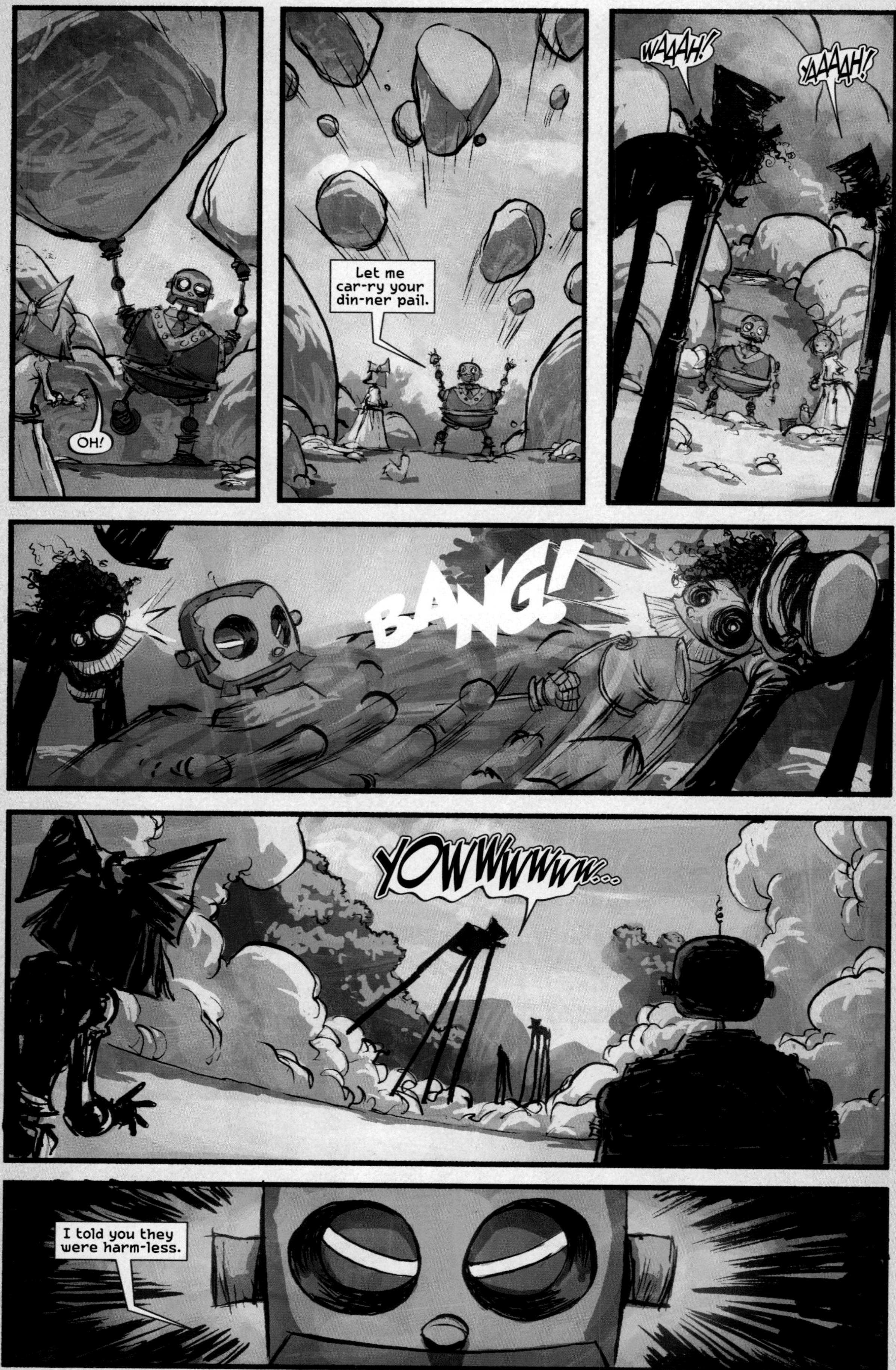
OH!
Let me car-ry your din-ner pail.
WAAAH!
YAAAAH!
BANG!
YOWWWWWW...
I told you they were harm-less.

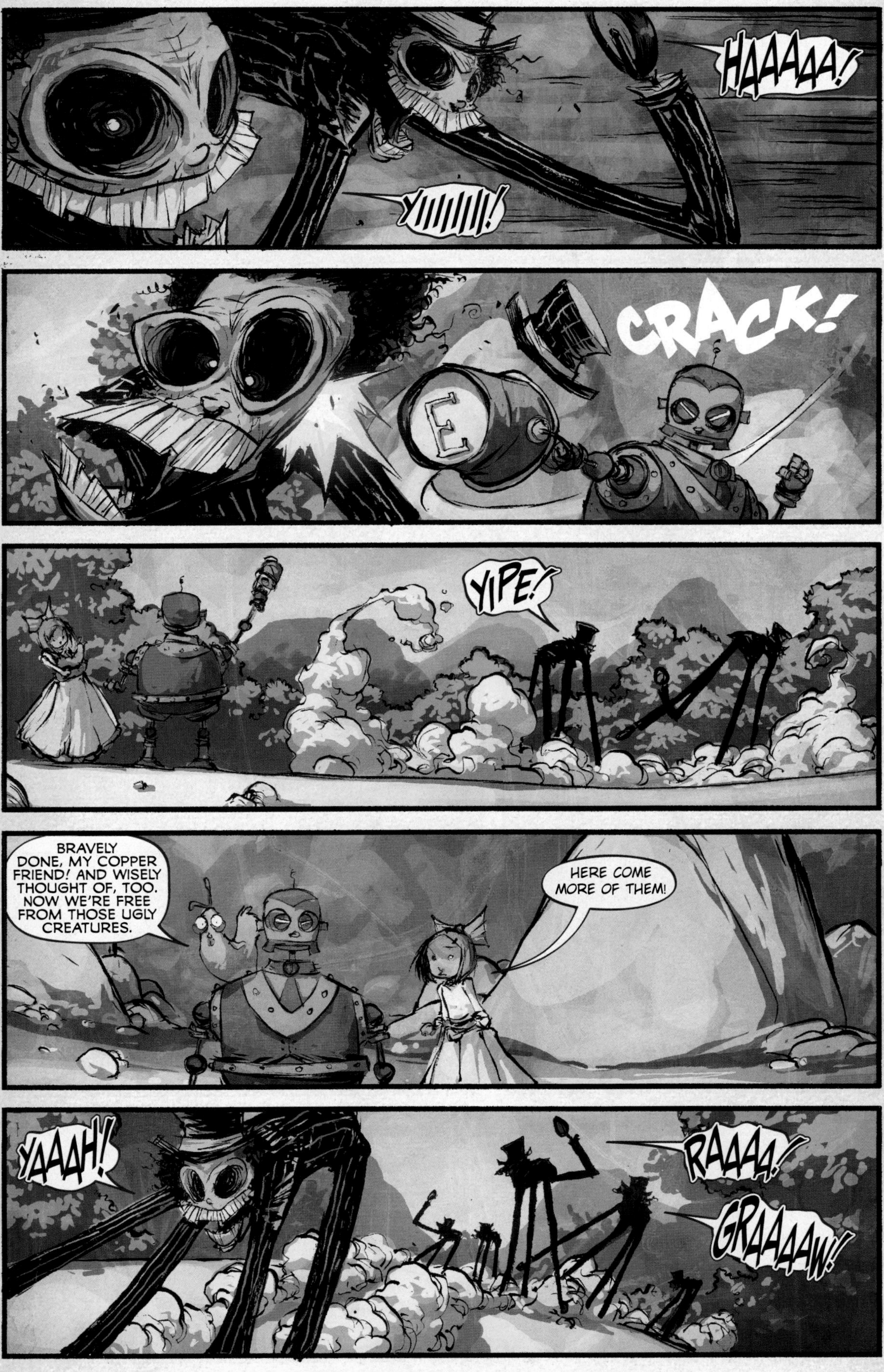
HAAAAA!
YIIIIIIII!
CRACK!
YIPE!
BRAVELY DONE, MY COPPER FRIEND! AND WISELY THOUGHT OF, TOO. NOW WE'RE FREE FROM THOSE UGLY CREATURES.
HERE COME MORE OF THEM!
YAAAH!
RAAAA!
GRAAAAW!

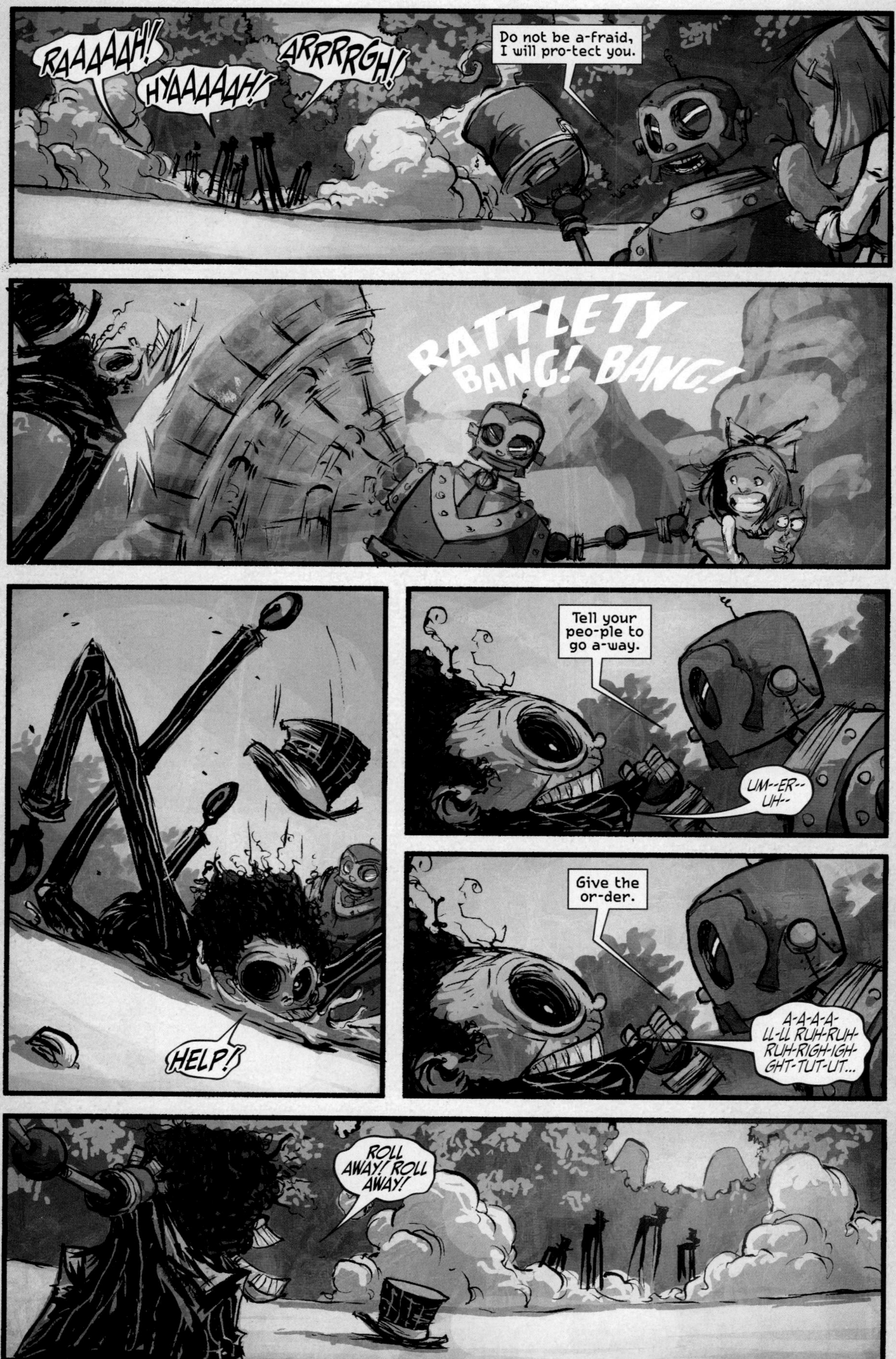
RAAAAAH!
HYAAAAAH!
ARRRRGH!
Do not be a-fraid, I will pro-tect you.
RATTLETY BANG! BANG!
HELP!
Tell your peo-ple to go a-way.
UM--ER--UH--
Give the or-der.
A-A-A-A-LL-LL RUH-RUH-RUH-RIGH-IGH-GHT-TUT-UT...
ROLL AWAY! ROLL AWAY!

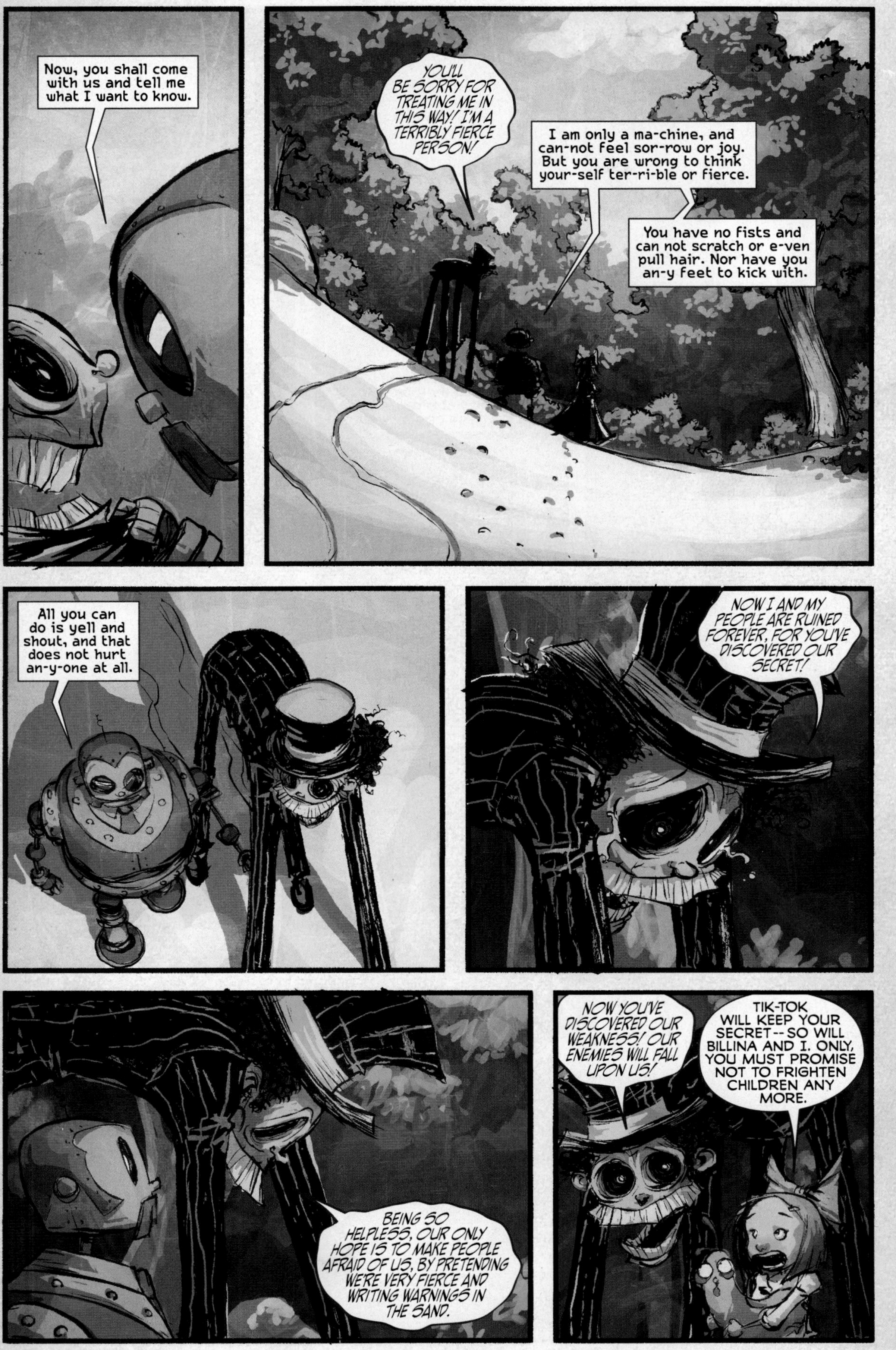

Now, you shall come with us and tell me what I want to know.
YOU'LL BE SORRY FOR TREATING ME IN THIS WAY! I'M A TERRIBLY FIERCE PERSON!
I am only a ma-chine, and can-not feel sor-row or joy. But you are wrong to think your-self ter-ri-ble or fierce.
You have no fists and can not scratch or e-ven pull hair. Nor have you an-y feet to kick with.
All you can do is yell and shout, and that does not hurt an-y-one at all.
NOW I AND MY PEOPLE ARE RUINED FOREVER, FOR YOU'VE DISCOVERED OUR SECRET!
BEING SO HELPLESS, OUR ONLY HOPE IS TO MAKE PEOPLE AFRAID OF US, BY PRETENDING WE'RE VERY FIERCE AND WRITING WARNINGS IN THE SAND.
NOW YOU'VE DISCOVERED OUR WEAKNESS! OUR ENEMIES WILL FALL UPON US!
TIK-TOK WILL KEEP YOUR SECRET -- SO WILL BILLINA AND I. ONLY, YOU MUST PROMISE NOT TO FRIGHTEN CHILDREN ANY MORE.

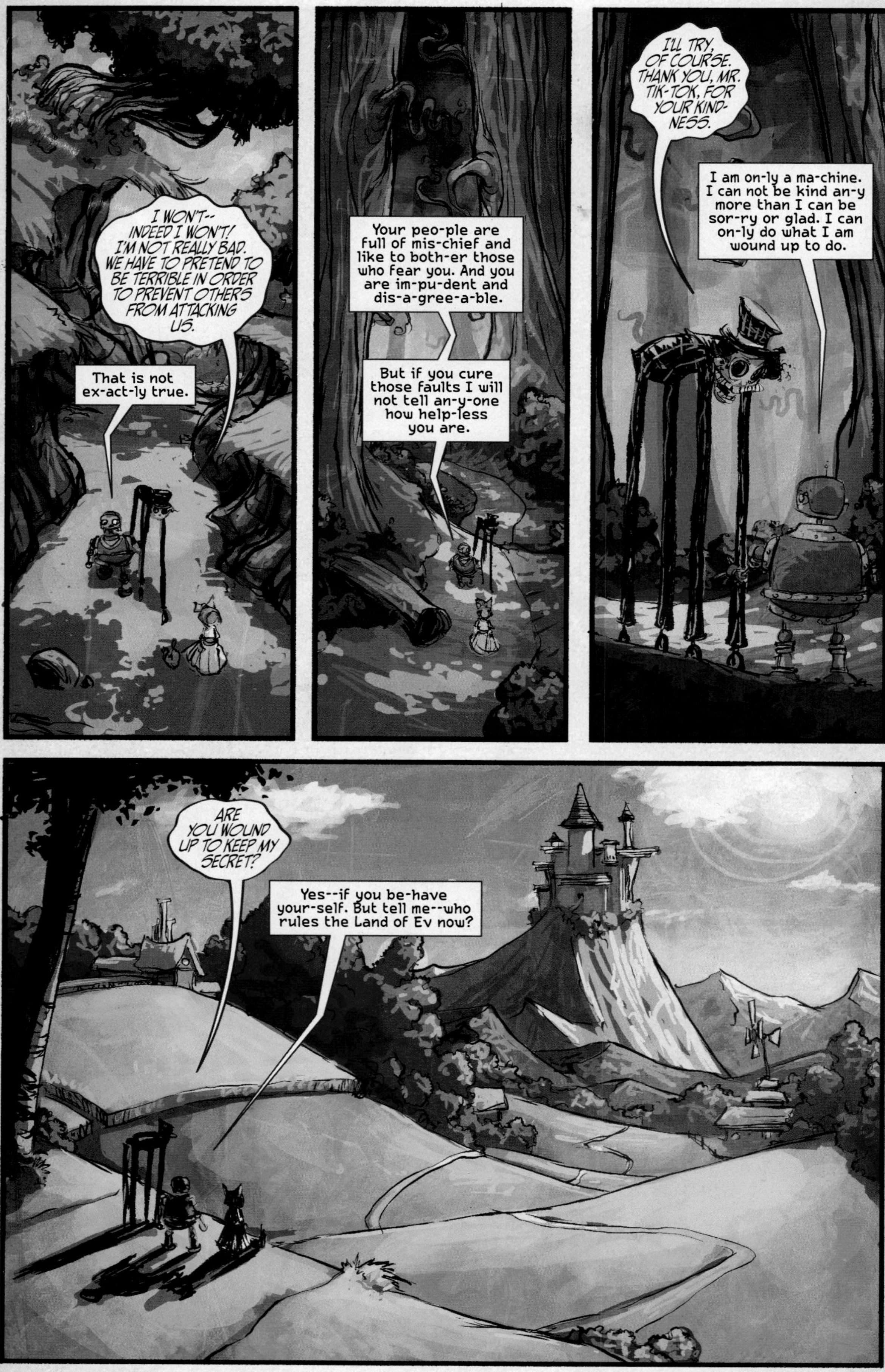
I WON'T--INDEED I WON'T! I'M NOT REALLY BAD. WE HAVE TO PRETEND TO BE TERRIBLE IN ORDER TO PREVENT OTHERS FROM ATTACKING US.
That is not ex-act-ly true.
Your peo-ple are full of mis-chief and like to both-er those who fear you. And you are im-pu-dent and dis-a-gree-a-ble.
But if you cure those faults I will not tell an-y-one how help-less you are.
I'LL TRY, OF COURSE. THANK YOU, MR. TIK-TOK, FOR YOUR KIND-NESS.
I am on-ly a ma-chine. I can not be kind an-y more than I can be sor-ry or glad. I can on-ly do what I am wound up to do.
ARE YOU WOUND UP TO KEEP MY SECRET?
Yes--if you be-have your-self. But tell me--who rules the Land of Ev now?

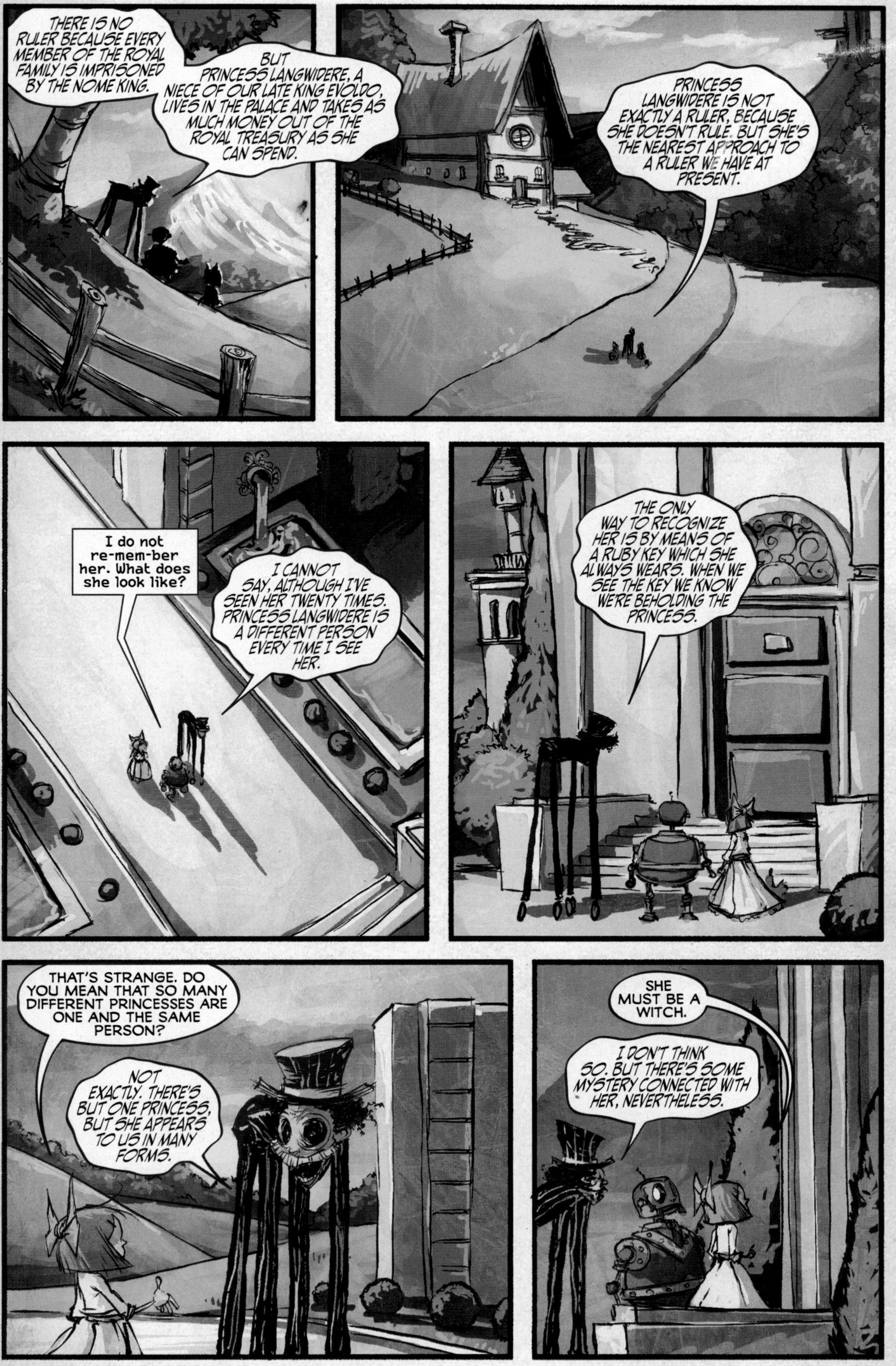
THERE IS NO RULER BECAUSE EVERY MEMBER OF THE ROYAL FAMILY IS IMPRISONED BY THE NOME KING.
BUT PRINCESS LANGWIDERE, A NIECE OF OUR LATE KING EVOLDO, LIVES IN THE PALACE AND TAKES AS MUCH MONEY OUT OF THE ROYAL TREASURY AS SHE CAN SPEND.
PRINCESS LANGWIDERE IS NOT EXACTLY A RULER, BECAUSE SHE DOESN'T RULE. BUT SHE'S THE NEAREST APPROACH TO A RULER WE HAVE AT PRESENT.
I do not re-mem-ber her. What does she look like?
I CANNOT SAY, ALTHOUGH I'VE SEEN HER TWENTY TIMES. PRINCESS LANGWIDERE IS A DIFFERENT PERSON EVERY TIME I SEE HER.
THE ONLY WAY TO RECOGNIZE HER IS BY MEANS OF A RUBY KEY WHICH SHE ALWAYS WEARS. WHEN WE SEE THE KEY WE KNOW WE'RE BEHOLDING THE PRINCESS.
THAT'S STRANGE. DO YOU MEAN THAT SO MANY DIFFERENT PRINCESSES ARE ONE AND THE SAME PERSON?
NOT EXACTLY. THERE'S BUT ONE PRINCESS, BUT SHE APPEARS TO US IN MANY FORMS.
SHE MUST BE A WITCH.
I DON'T THINK SO. BUT THERE'S SOME MYSTERY CONNECTED WITH HER, NEVERTHELESS.

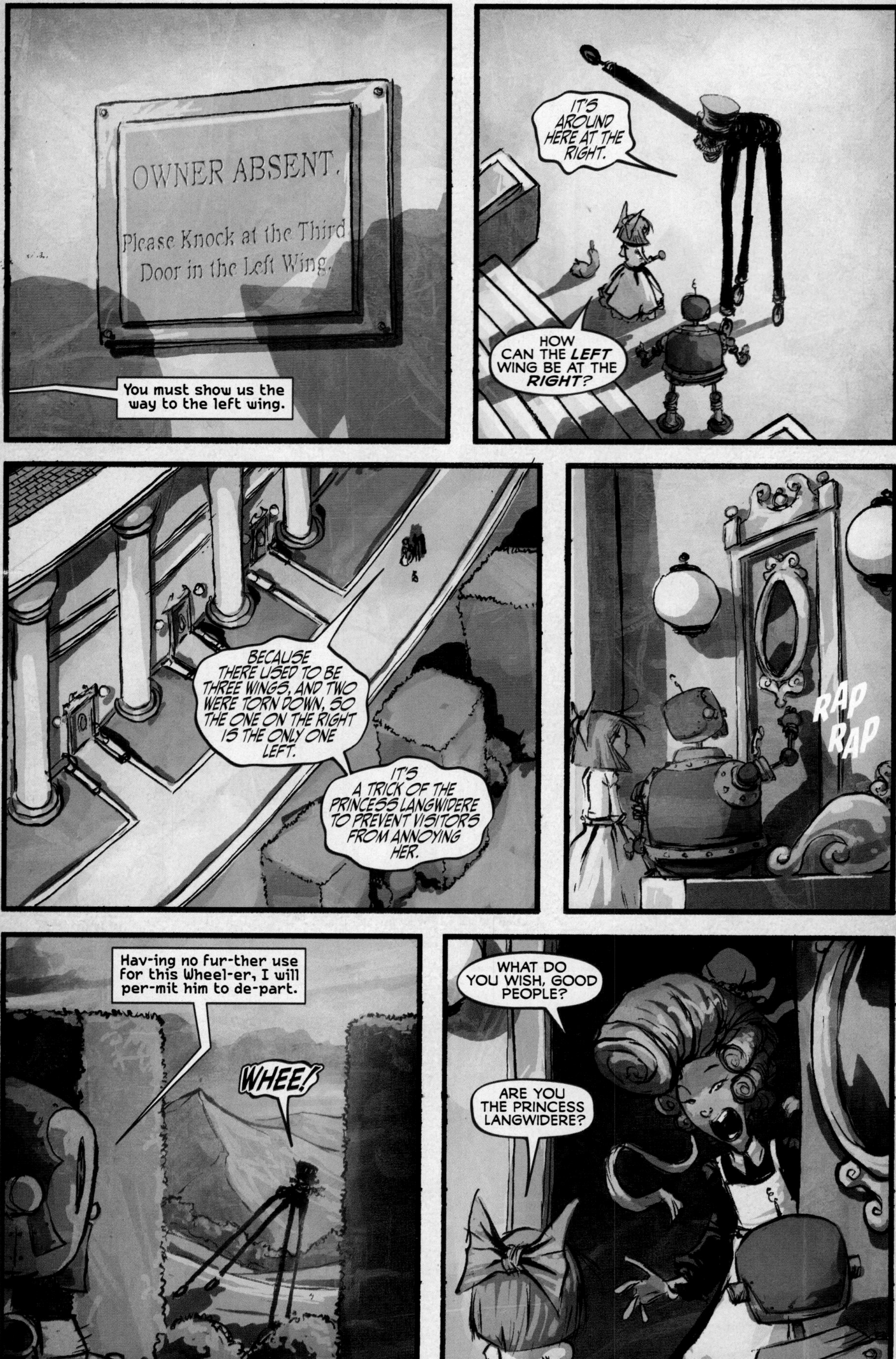
OWNER ABSENT.
Please Knock at the Third Door in the Left Wing.
You must show us the way to the left wing.
IT'S AROUND HERE AT THE RIGHT.
HOW CAN THE LEFT WING BE AT THE RIGHT?
BECAUSE THERE USED TO BE THREE WINGS, AND TWO WERE TORN DOWN, SO THE ONE ON THE RIGHT IS THE ONLY ONE LEFT.
IT'S A TRICK OF THE PRINCESS LANGWIDERE TO PREVENT VISITORS FROM ANNOYING HER.
RAP RAP
Hav-ing no fur-ther use for this Wheel-er, I will per-mit him to de-part.
WHEE!
WHAT DO YOU WISH, GOOD PEOPLE?
ARE YOU THE PRINCESS LANGWIDERE?

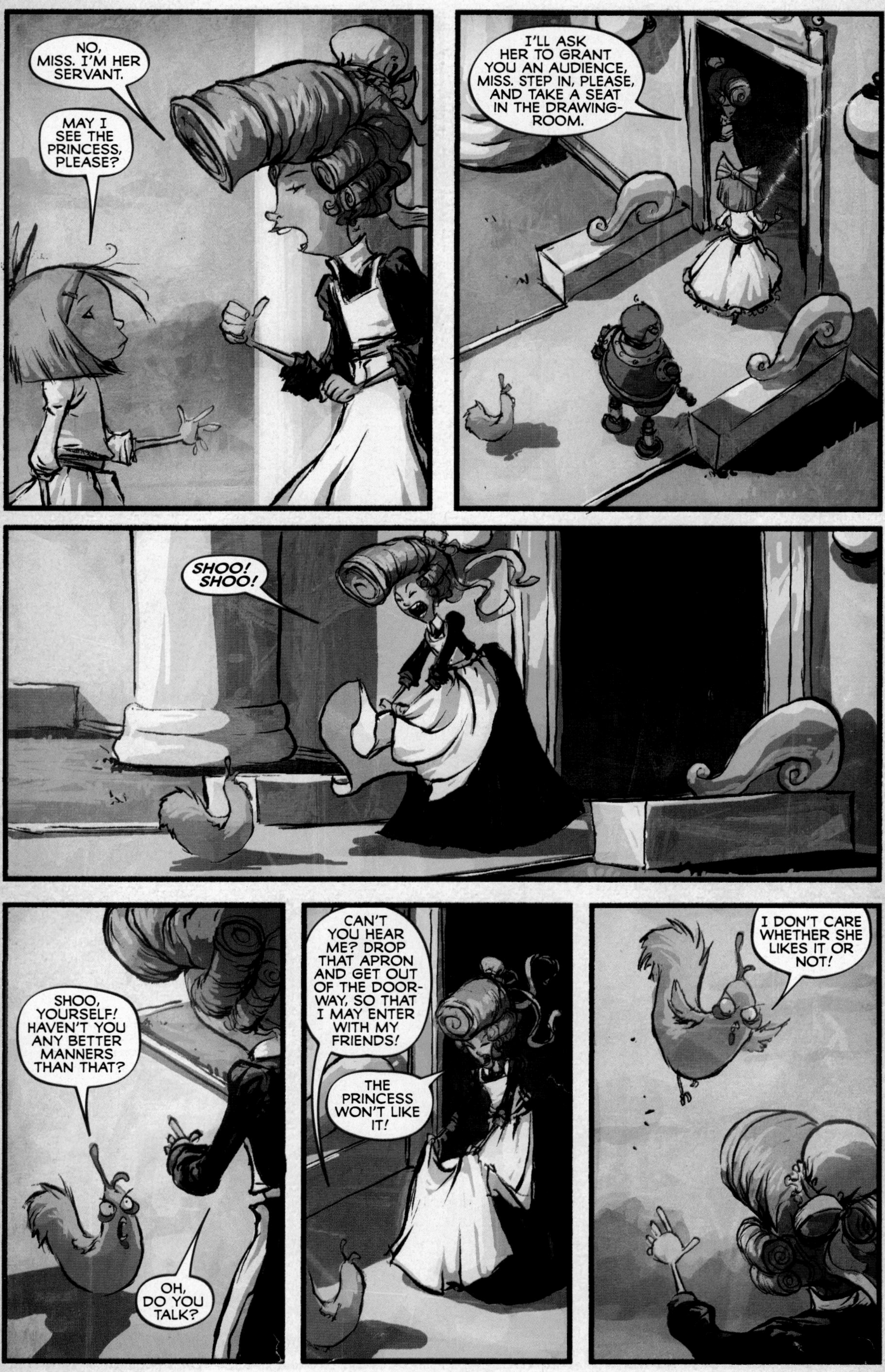
MAY I SEE THE PRINCESS, PLEASE?
NO, MISS. I'M HER SERVANT.
I'LL ASK HER TO GRANT YOU AN AUDIENCE, MISS. STEP IN, PLEASE, AND TAKE A SEAT IN THE DRAWING-ROOM.
SHOO! SHOO!
SHOO, YOURSELF! HAVEN'T YOU ANY BETTER MANNERS THAN THAT?
OH, DO YOU TALK?
CAN'T YOU HEAR ME? DROP THAT APRON AND GET OUT OF THE DOORWAY, SO THAT I MAY ENTER WITH MY FRIENDS!
THE PRINCESS WON'T LIKE IT!
I DON'T CARE WHETHER SHE LIKES IT OR NOT!

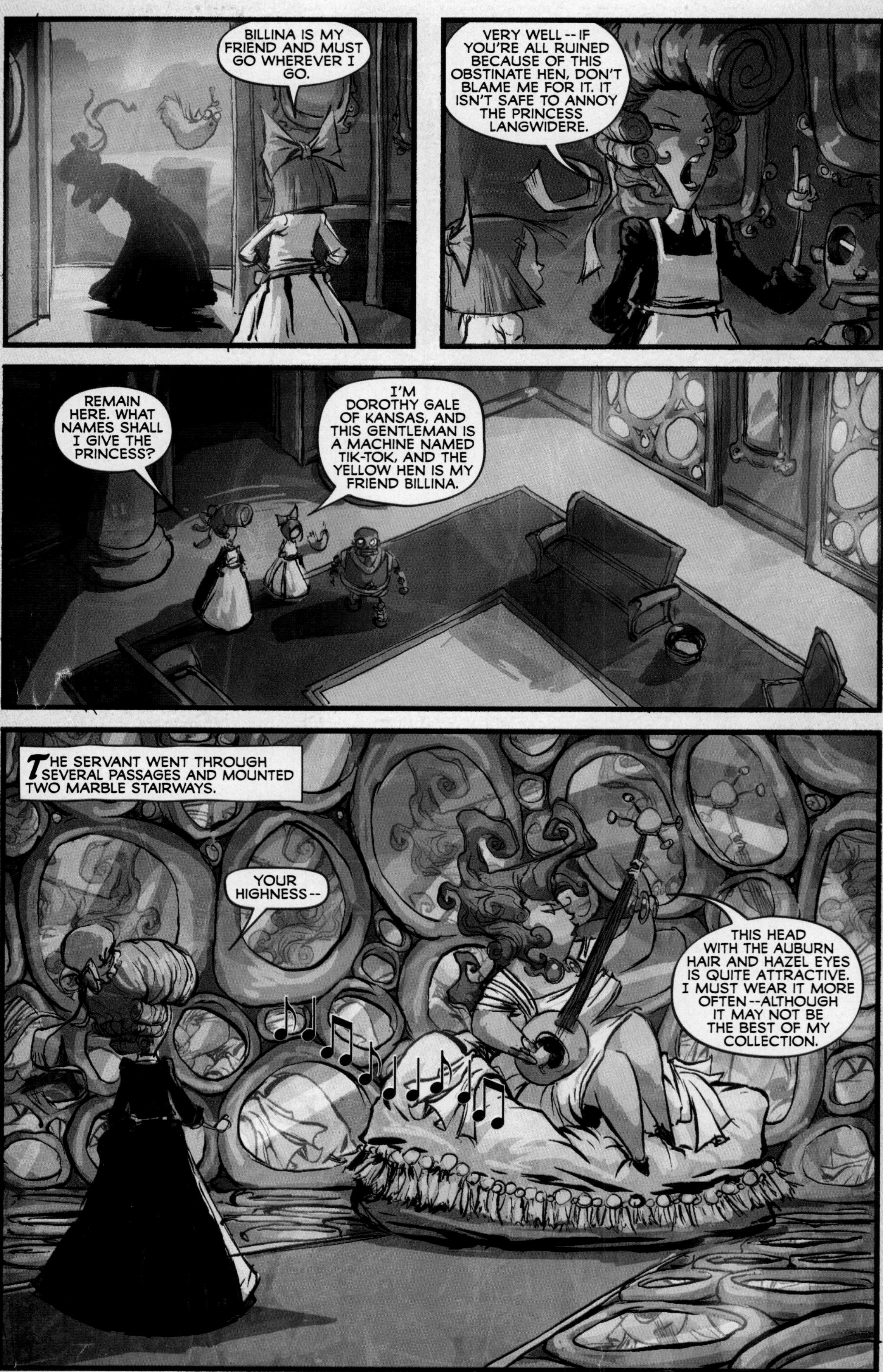
BILLINA IS MY FRIEND AND MUST GO WHEREVER I GO.
VERY WELL -- IF YOU'RE ALL RUINED BECAUSE OF THIS OBSTINATE HEN, DON'T BLAME ME FOR IT. IT ISN'T SAFE TO ANNOY THE PRINCESS LANGWIDERE.
REMAIN HERE. WHAT NAMES SHALL I GIVE THE PRINCESS?
I'M DOROTHY GALE OF KANSAS, AND THIS GENTLEMAN IS A MACHINE NAMED TIK-TOK, AND THE YELLOW HEN IS MY FRIEND BILLINA.
THE SERVANT WENT THROUGH SEVERAL PASSAGES AND MOUNTED TWO MARBLE STAIRWAYS.
YOUR HIGHNESS --
THIS HEAD WITH THE AUBURN HAIR AND HAZEL EYES IS QUITE ATTRACTIVE. I MUST WEAR IT MORE OFTEN -- ALTHOUGH IT MAY NOT BE THE BEST OF MY COLLECTION.

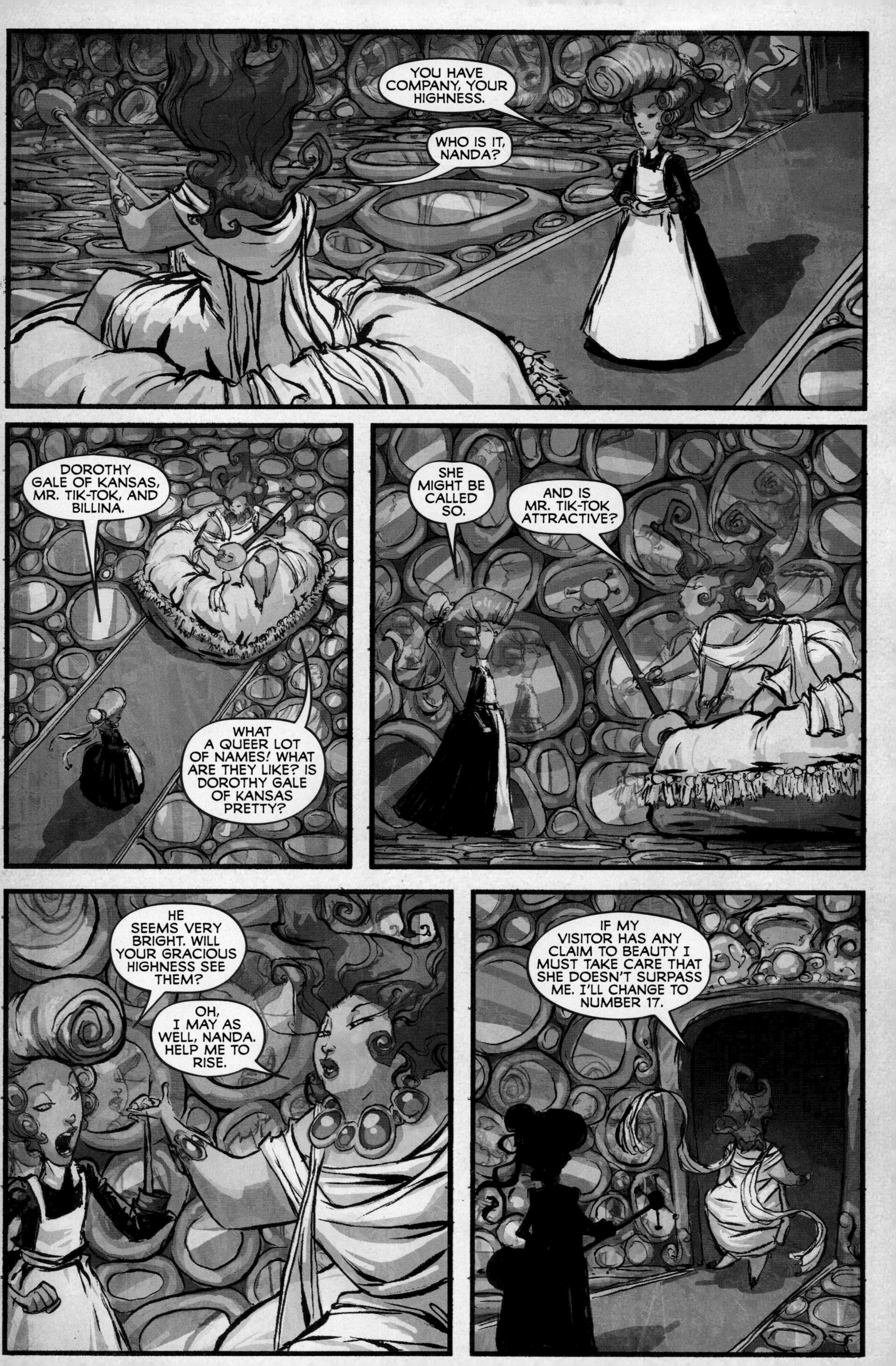
YOU HAVE COMPANY, YOUR HIGHNESS.
WHO IS IT, NANDA?
DOROTHY GALE OF KANSAS, MR. TIK-TOK, AND BILLINA.
WHAT A QUEER LOT OF NAMES! WHAT ARE THEY LIKE? IS DOROTHY GALE OF KANSAS PRETTY?
SHE MIGHT BE CALLED SO.
AND IS MR. TIK-TOK ATTRACTIVE?
HE SEEMS VERY BRIGHT. WILL YOUR GRACIOUS HIGHNESS SEE THEM?
OH, I MAY AS WELL, NANDA. HELP ME TO RISE.
IF MY VISITOR HAS ANY CLAIM TO BEAUTY I MUST TAKE CARE THAT SHE DOESN'T SURPASS ME. I'LL CHANGE TO NUMBER 17.

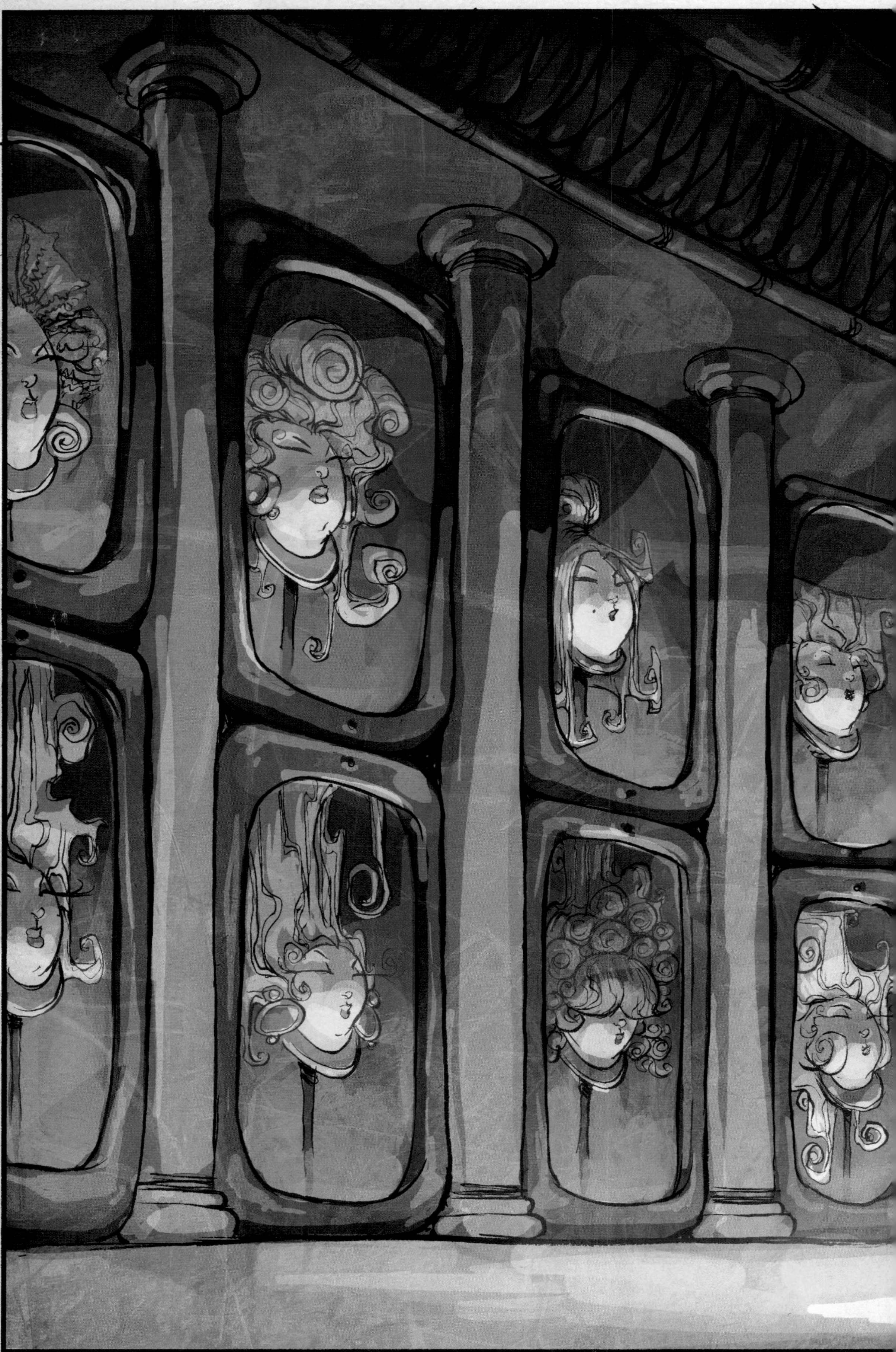

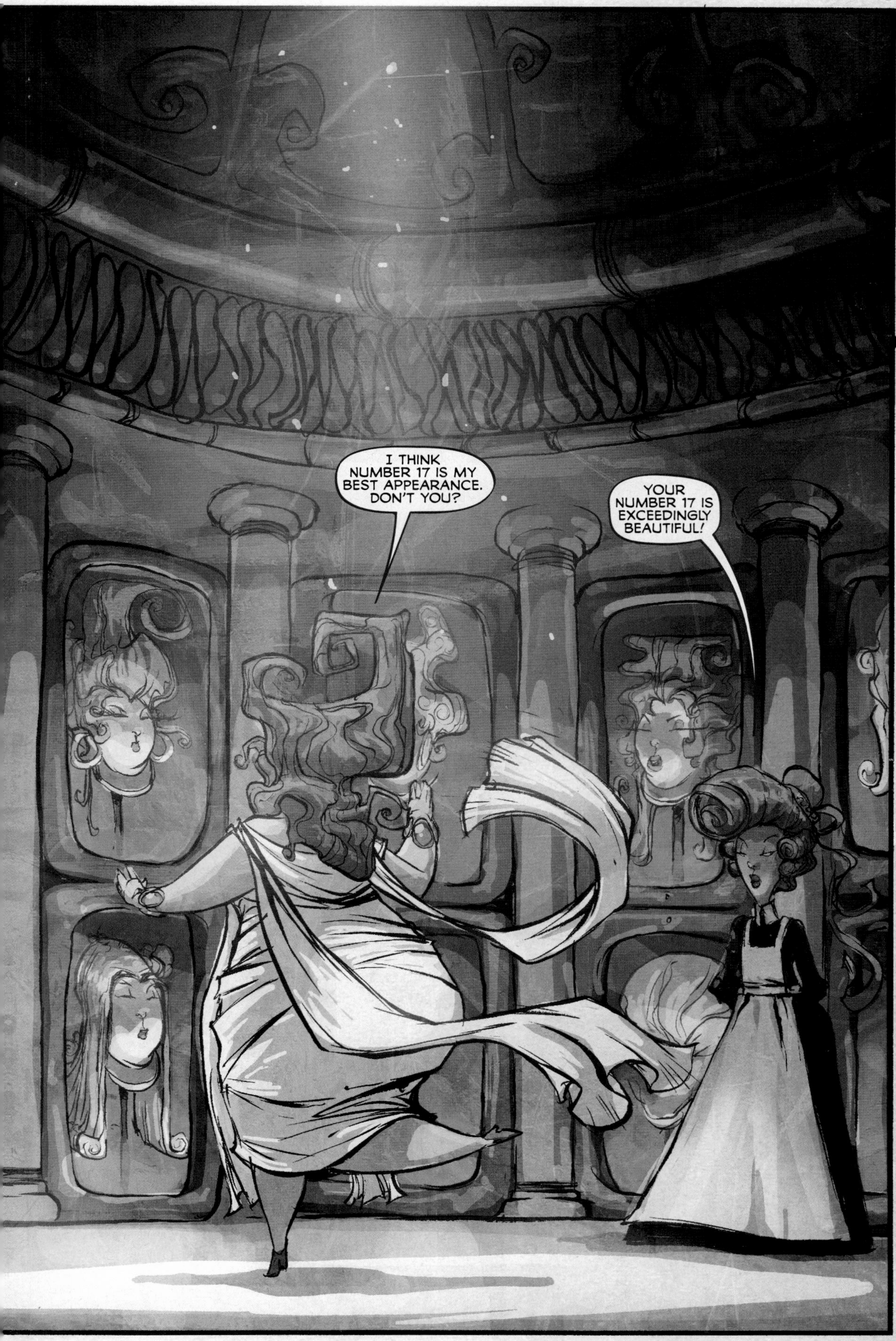
I THINK NUMBER 17 IS MY BEST APPEARANCE. DON'T YOU?
YOUR NUMBER 17 IS EXCEEDINGLY BEAUTIFUL!

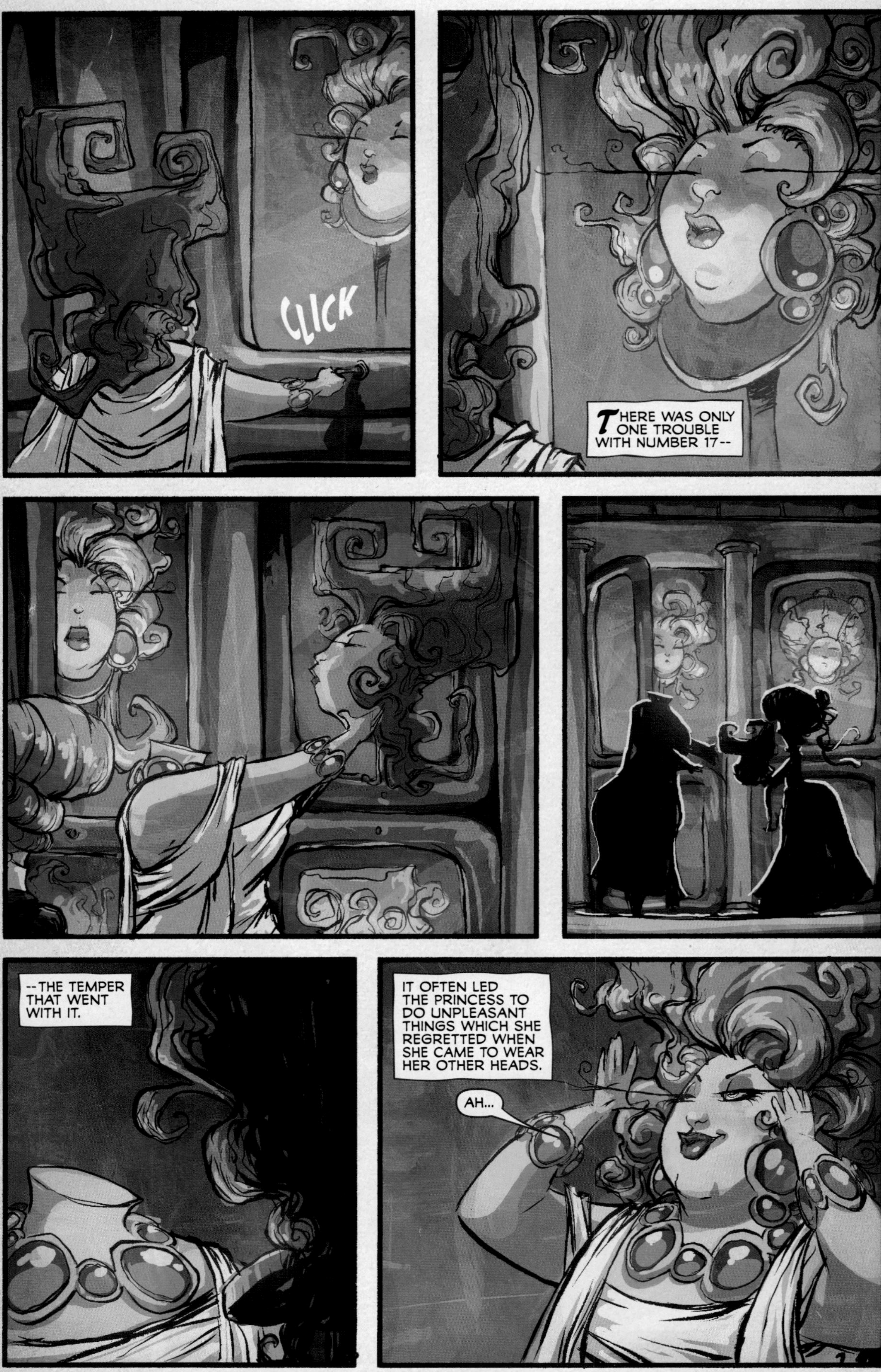

CLICK
THERE WAS ONLY ONE TROUBLE WITH NUMBER 17--
--THE TEMPER THAT WENT WITH IT.
IT OFTEN LED THE PRINCESS TO DO UNPLEASANT THINGS WHICH SHE REGRETTED WHEN SHE CAME TO WEAR HER OTHER HEADS.
AH...

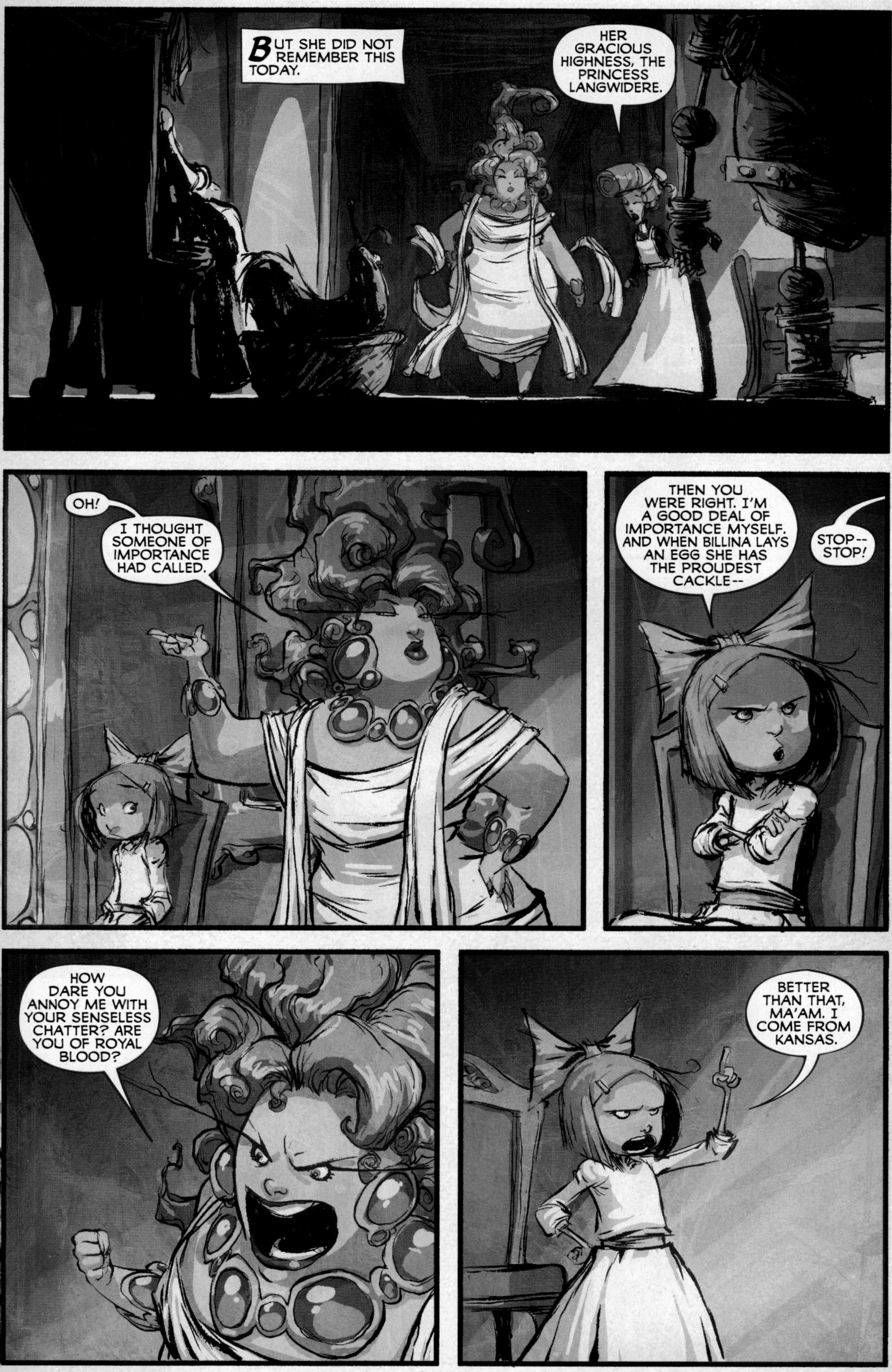
BUT SHE DID NOT REMEMBER THIS TODAY.
HER GRACIOUS HIGHNESS, THE PRINCESS LANGWIDERE.
OH!
I THOUGHT SOMEONE OF IMPORTANCE HAD CALLED.
THEN YOU WERE RIGHT. I'M A GOOD DEAL OF IMPORTANCE MYSELF. AND WHEN BILLINA LAYS AN EGG SHE HAS THE PROUDEST CACKLE--
STOP-- STOP!
HOW DARE YOU ANNOY ME WITH YOUR SENSELESS CHATTER? ARE YOU OF ROYAL BLOOD?
BETTER THAN THAT, MA'AM. I COME FROM KANSAS.

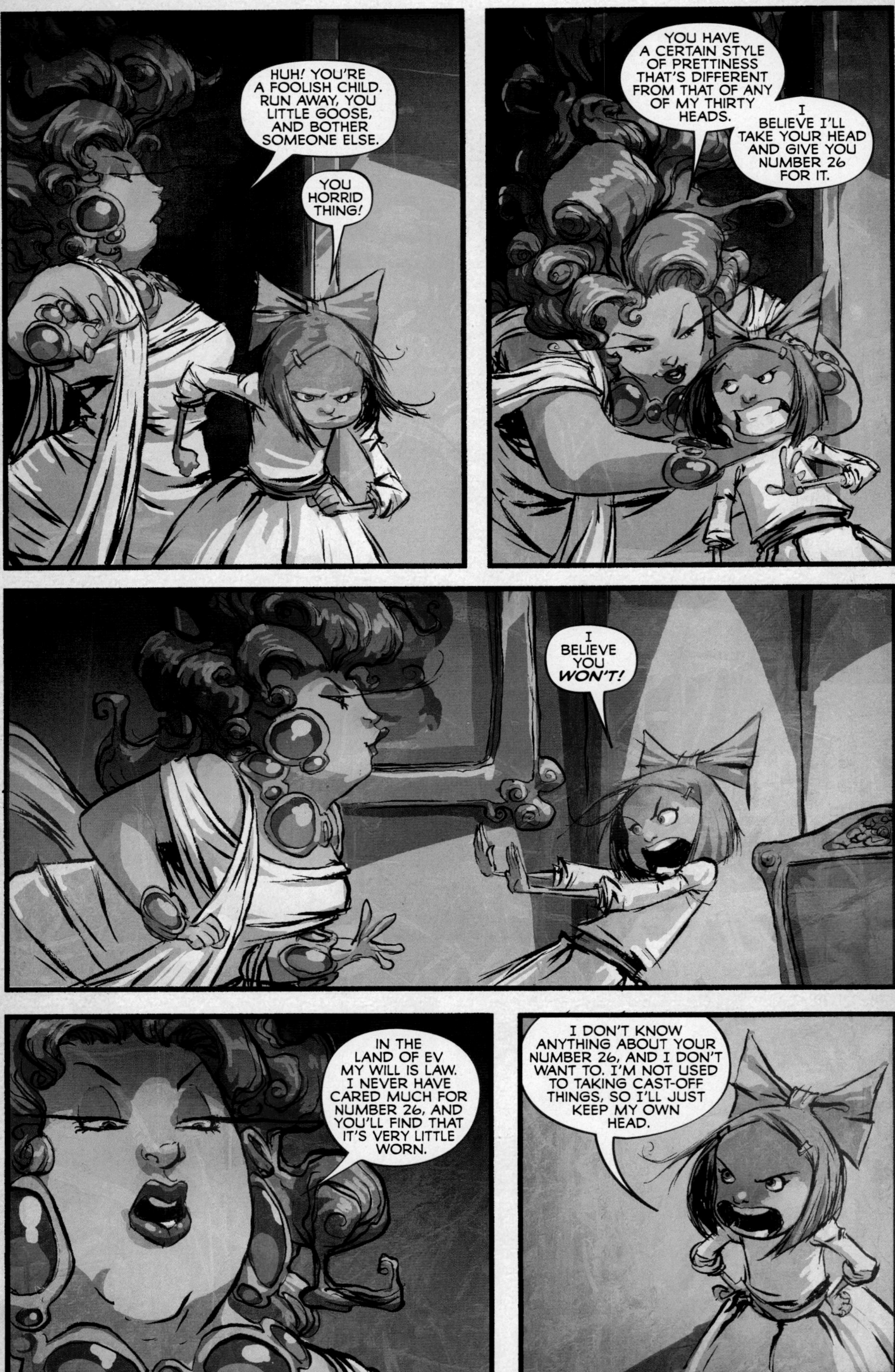
HUH! YOU'RE A FOOLISH CHILD. RUN AWAY, YOU LITTLE GOOSE, AND BOTHER SOMEONE ELSE.
YOU HORRID THING!
YOU HAVE A CERTAIN STYLE OF PRETTINESS THAT'S DIFFERENT FROM THAT OF ANY OF MY THIRTY HEADS.
I BELIEVE I'LL TAKE YOUR HEAD AND GIVE YOU NUMBER 26 FOR IT.
I BELIEVE YOU ***WON'T!***
IN THE LAND OF EV MY WILL IS LAW. I NEVER HAVE CARED MUCH FOR NUMBER 26, AND YOU'LL FIND THAT IT'S VERY LITTLE WORN.
I DON'T KNOW ANYTHING ABOUT YOUR NUMBER 26, AND I DON'T WANT TO. I'M NOT USED TO TAKING CAST-OFF THINGS, SO I'LL JUST KEEP MY OWN HEAD.

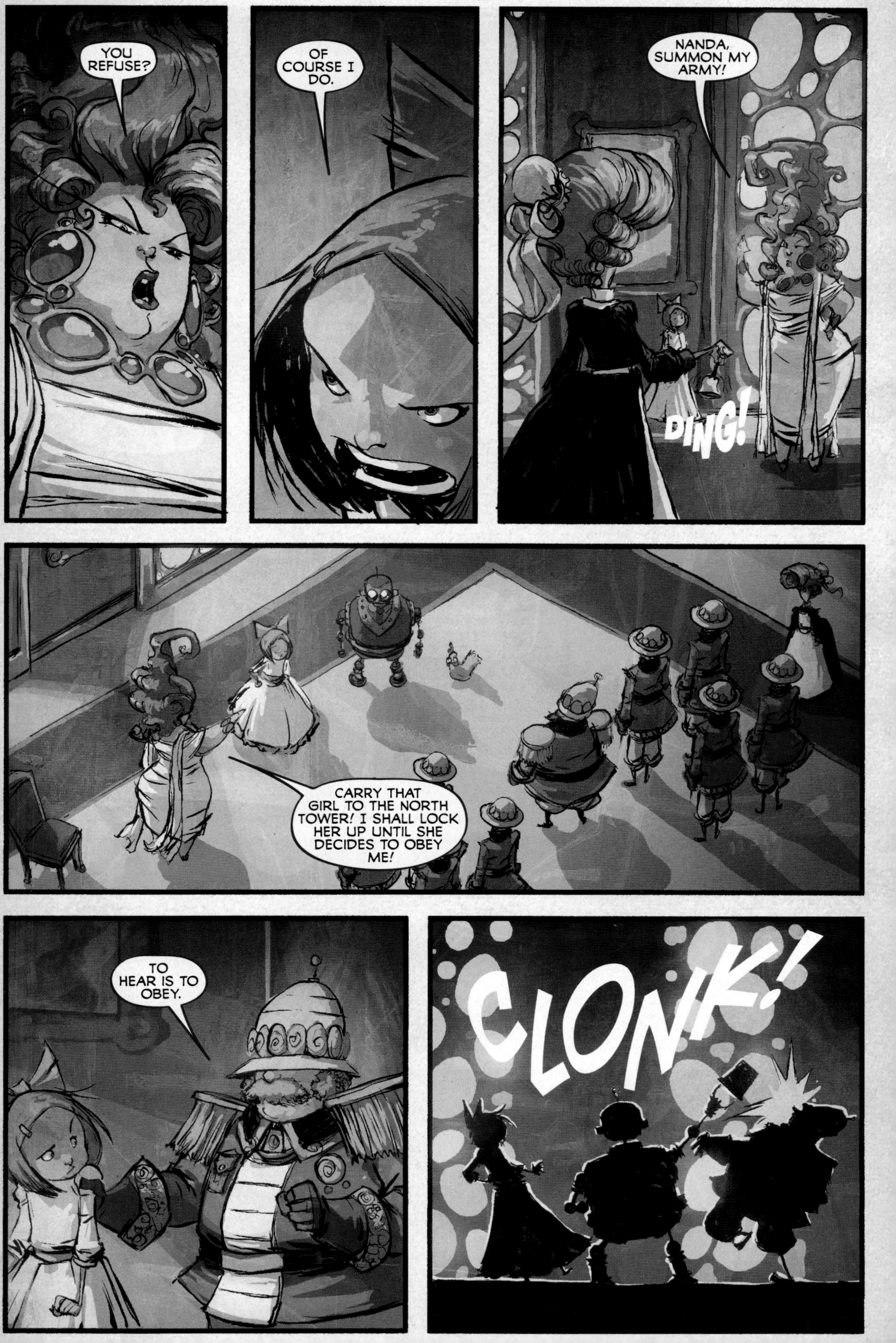
YOU REFUSE?
OF COURSE I DO.
NANDA, SUMMON MY ARMY!
DING!
CARRY THAT GIRL TO THE NORTH TOWER! I SHALL LOCK HER UP UNTIL SHE DECIDES TO OBEY ME!
TO HEAR IS TO OBEY.
CLONK!

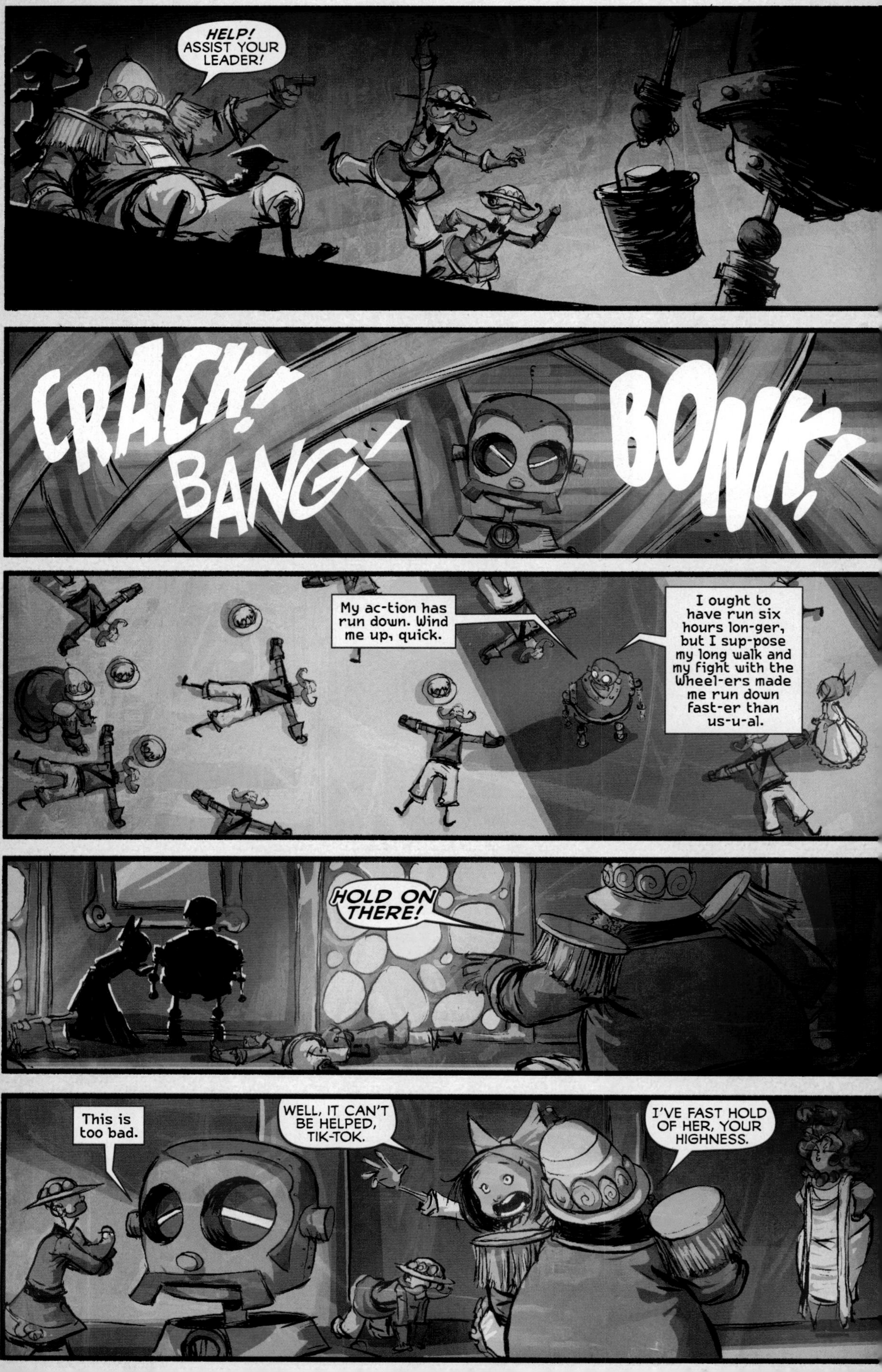
HELP! ASSIST YOUR LEADER!
CRACK!
BANG!
BONK!
My ac-tion has run down. Wind me up, quick.
I ought to have run six hours lon-ger, but I sup-pose my long walk and my fight with the Wheel-ers made me run down fast-er than us-u-al.
HOLD ON THERE!
This is too bad.
WELL, IT CAN'T BE HELPED, TIK-TOK.
I'VE FAST HOLD OF HER, YOUR HIGHNESS.

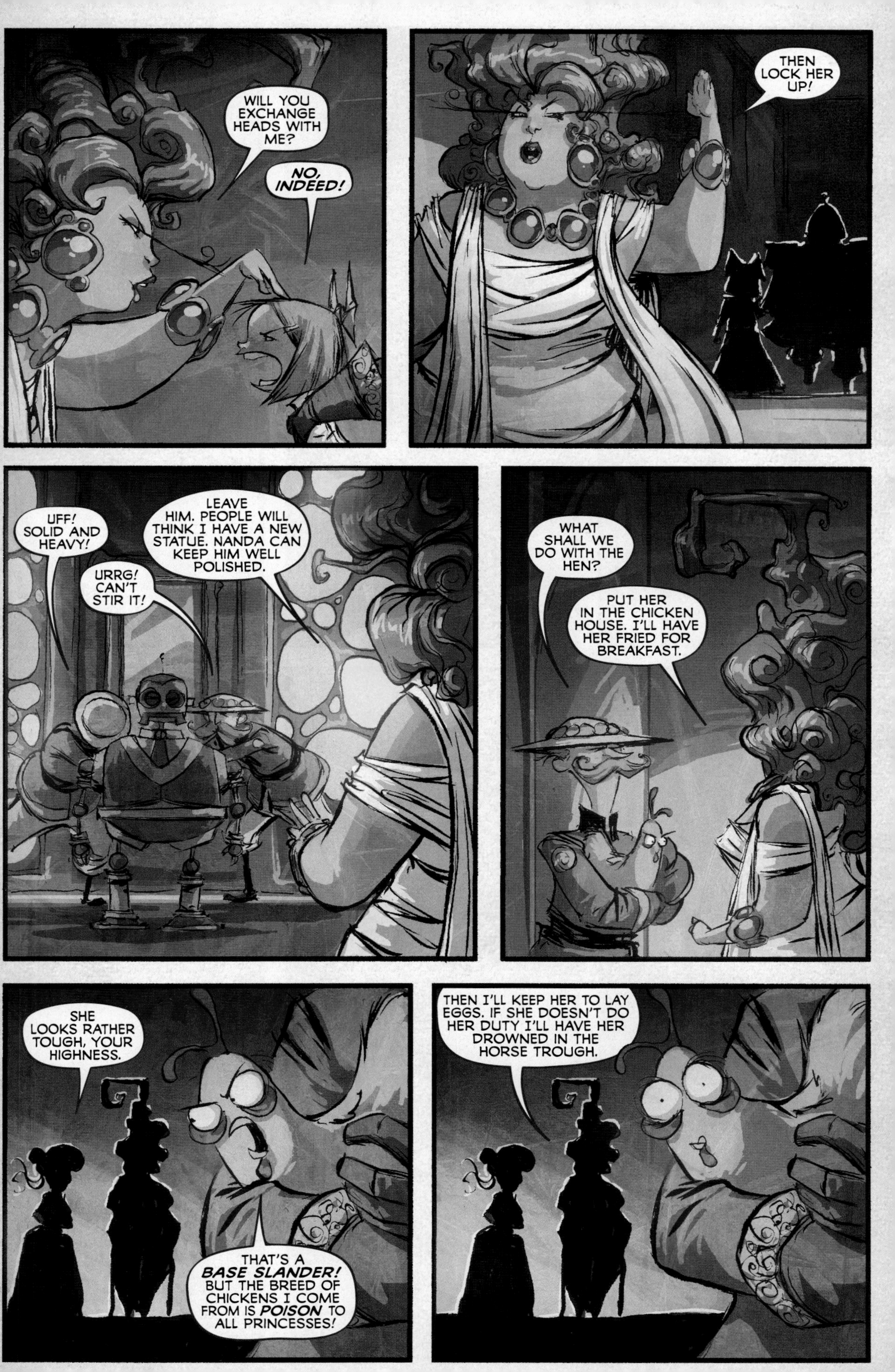
WILL YOU EXCHANGE HEADS WITH ME?
NO, INDEED!
THEN LOCK HER UP!
UFF! SOLID AND HEAVY!
LEAVE HIM. PEOPLE WILL THINK I HAVE A NEW STATUE. NANDA CAN KEEP HIM WELL POLISHED.
URRG! CAN'T STIR IT!
WHAT SHALL WE DO WITH THE HEN?
PUT HER IN THE CHICKEN HOUSE. I'LL HAVE HER FRIED FOR BREAKFAST.
SHE LOOKS RATHER TOUGH, YOUR HIGHNESS.
THAT'S A BASE SLANDER! BUT THE BREED OF CHICKENS I COME FROM IS POISON TO ALL PRINCESSES!
THEN I'LL KEEP HER TO LAY EGGS. IF SHE DOESN'T DO HER DUTY I'LL HAVE HER DROWNED IN THE HORSE TROUGH.

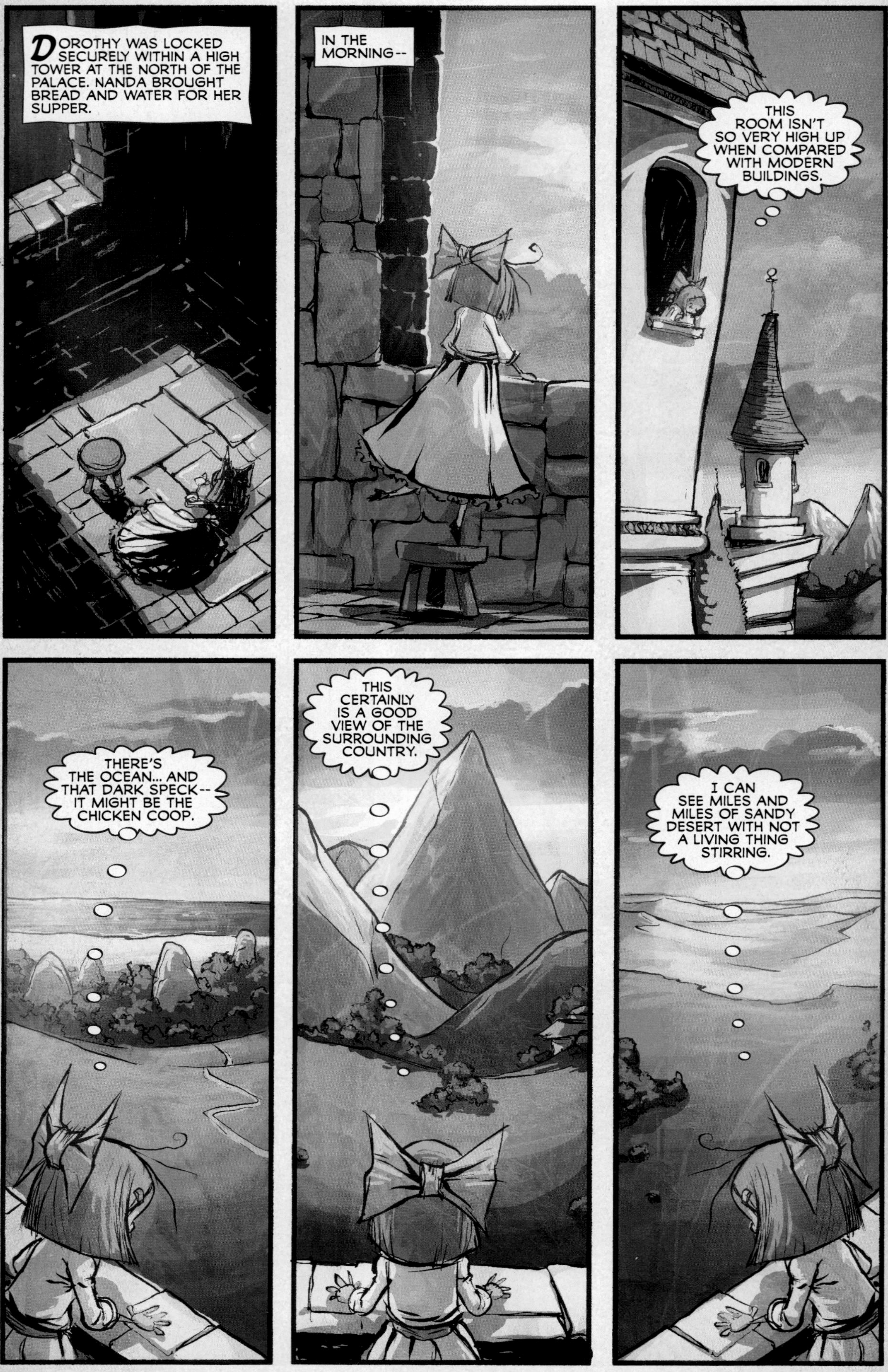
DOROTHY WAS LOCKED SECURELY WITHIN A HIGH TOWER AT THE NORTH OF THE PALACE. NANDA BROUGHT BREAD AND WATER FOR HER SUPPER.
IN THE MORNING--
THIS ROOM ISN'T SO VERY HIGH UP WHEN COMPARED WITH MODERN BUILDINGS.
THERE'S THE OCEAN... AND THAT DARK SPECK-- IT MIGHT BE THE CHICKEN COOP.
THIS CERTAINLY IS A GOOD VIEW OF THE SURROUNDING COUNTRY.
I CAN SEE MILES AND MILES OF SANDY DESERT WITH NOT A LIVING THING STIRRING.

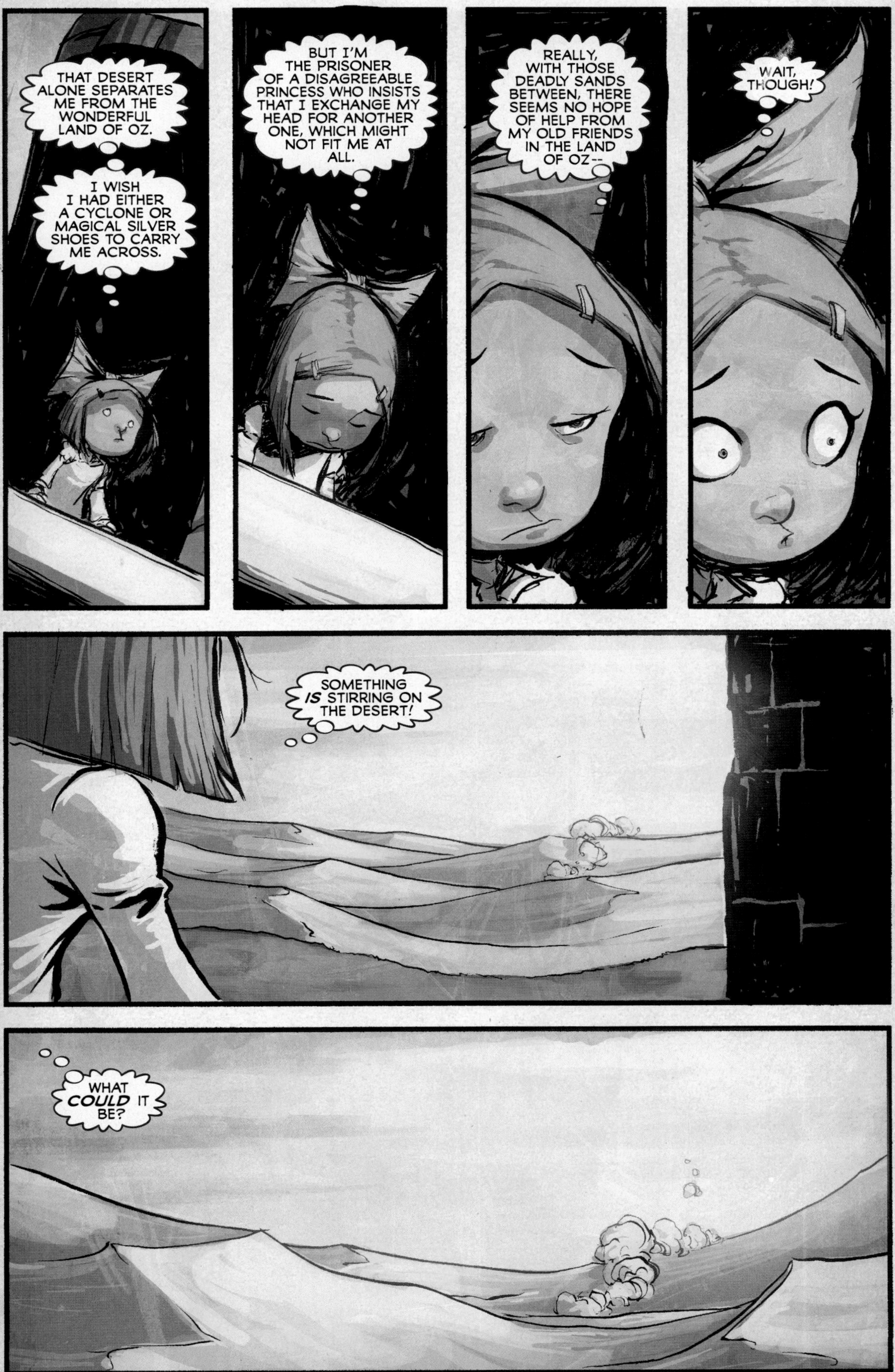
THAT DESERT ALONE SEPARATES ME FROM THE WONDERFUL LAND OF OZ.
I WISH I HAD EITHER A CYCLONE OR MAGICAL SILVER SHOES TO CARRY ME ACROSS.
BUT I'M THE PRISONER OF A DISAGREEABLE PRINCESS WHO INSISTS THAT I EXCHANGE MY HEAD FOR ANOTHER ONE, WHICH MIGHT NOT FIT ME AT ALL.
REALLY, WITH THOSE DEADLY SANDS BETWEEN, THERE SEEMS NO HOPE OF HELP FROM MY OLD FRIENDS IN THE LAND OF OZ--
WAIT, THOUGH!
SOMETHING *IS* STIRRING ON THE DESERT!
WHAT ***COULD*** IT BE?

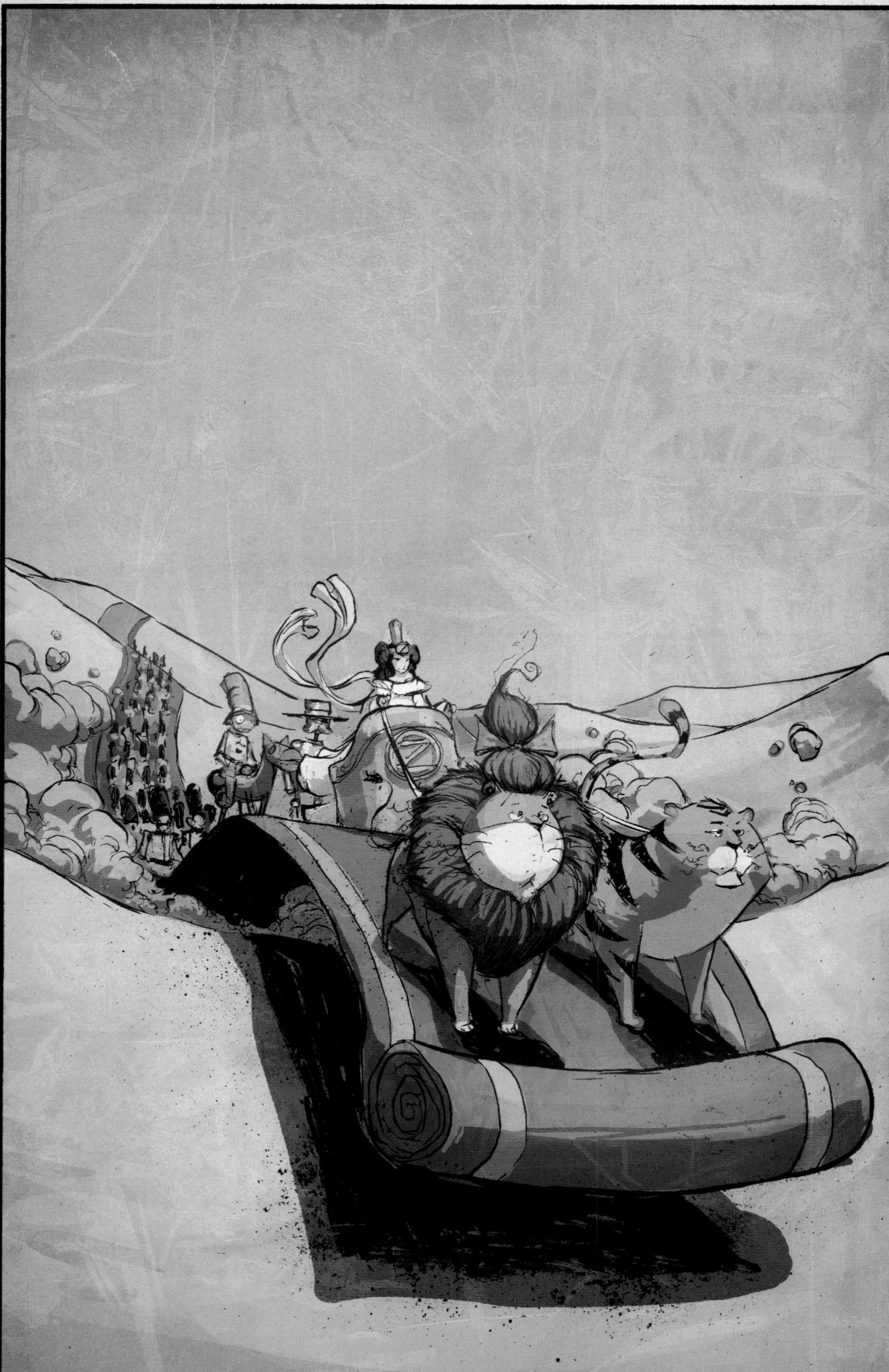

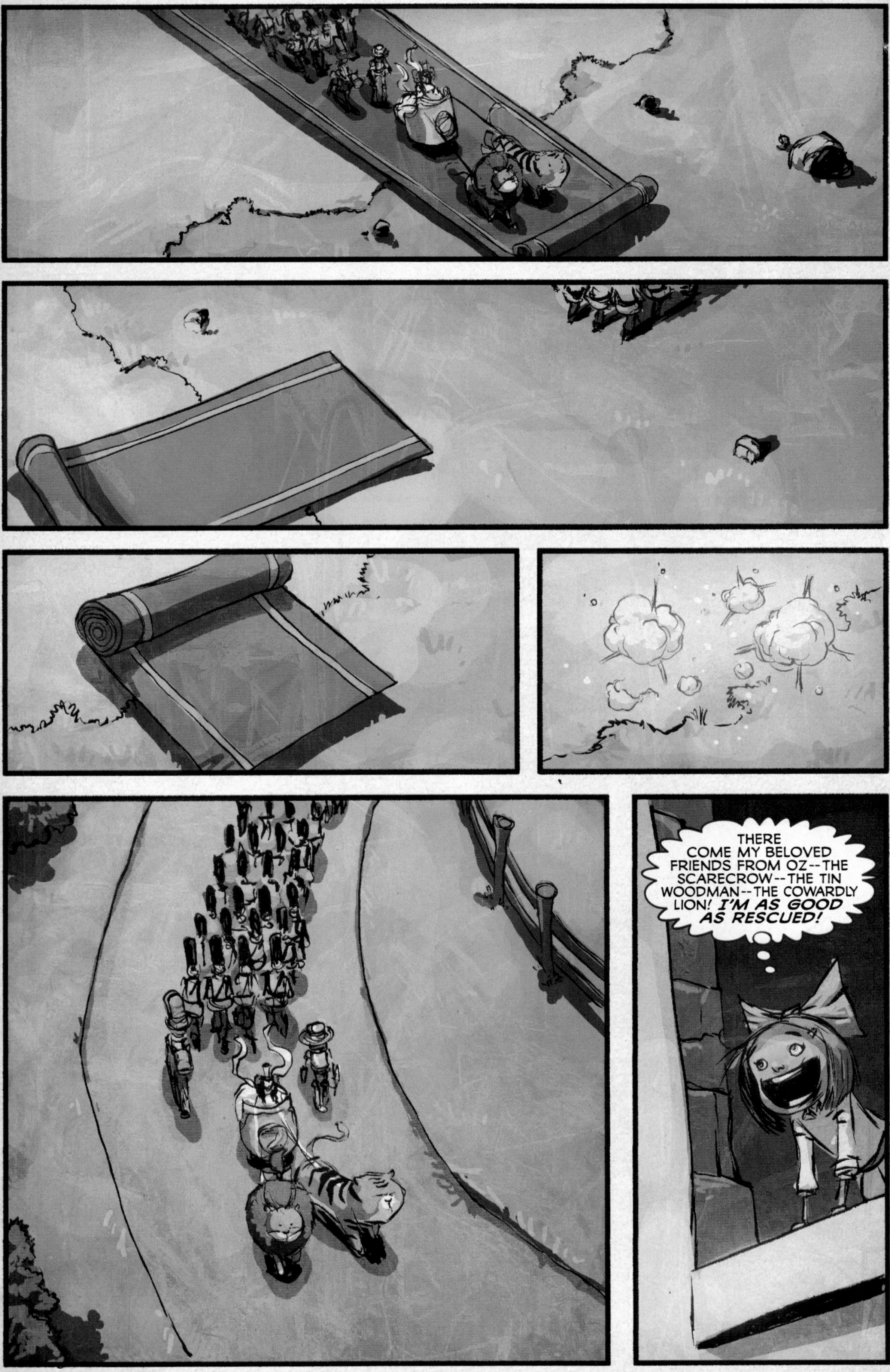
THERE COME MY BELOVED FRIENDS FROM OZ--THE SCARECROW--THE TIN WOODMAN--THE COWARDLY LION! *I'M AS GOOD AS RESCUED!*

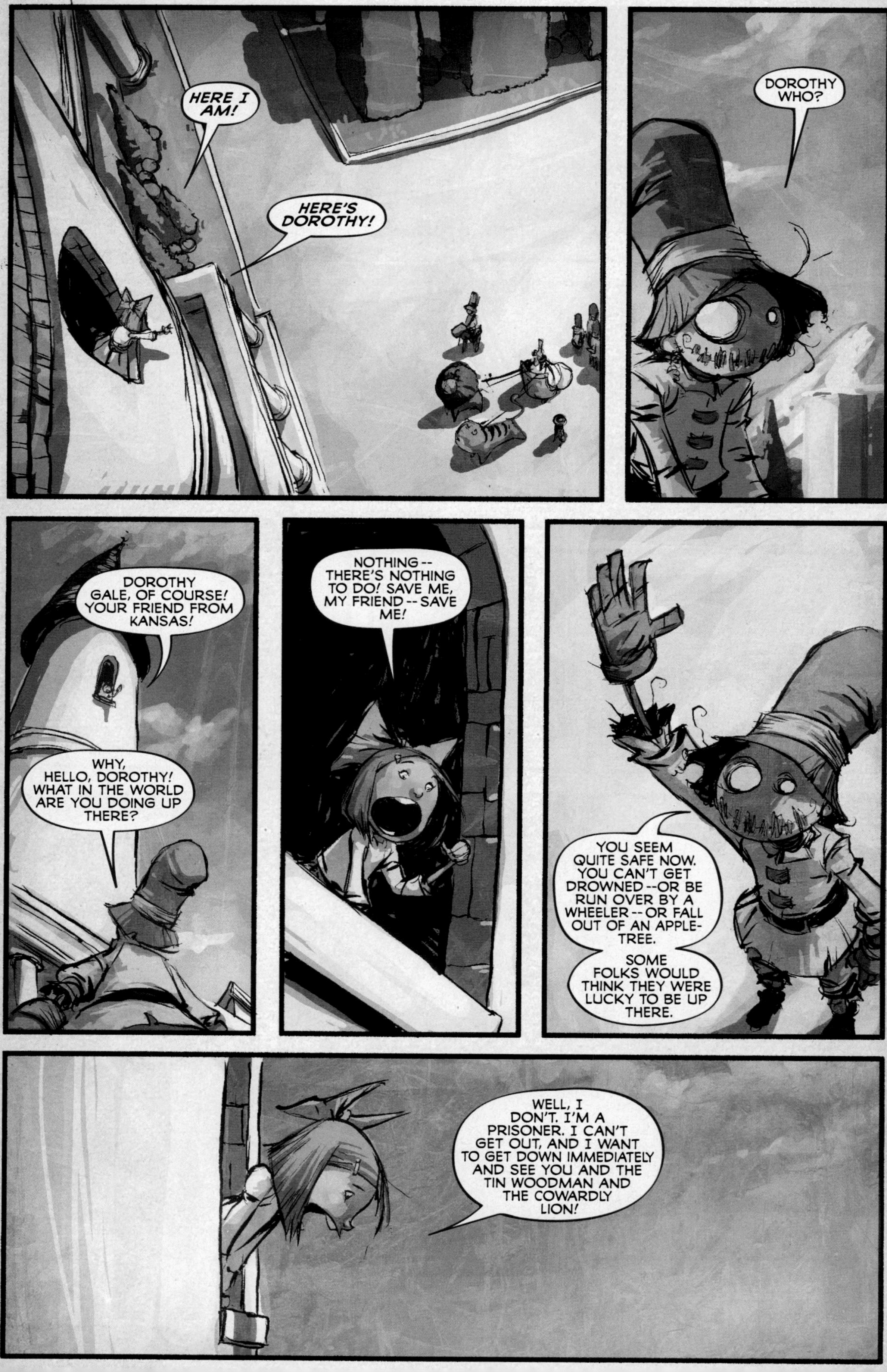
HERE I AM!
HERE'S DOROTHY!
DOROTHY WHO?
DOROTHY GALE, OF COURSE! YOUR FRIEND FROM KANSAS!
WHY, HELLO, DOROTHY! WHAT IN THE WORLD ARE YOU DOING UP THERE?
NOTHING -- THERE'S NOTHING TO DO! SAVE ME, MY FRIEND -- SAVE ME!
YOU SEEM QUITE SAFE NOW. YOU CAN'T GET DROWNED -- OR BE RUN OVER BY A WHEELER -- OR FALL OUT OF AN APPLE-TREE.
SOME FOLKS WOULD THINK THEY WERE LUCKY TO BE UP THERE.
WELL, I DON'T. I'M A PRISONER. I CAN'T GET OUT, AND I WANT TO GET DOWN IMMEDIATELY AND SEE YOU AND THE TIN WOODMAN AND THE COWARDLY LION!

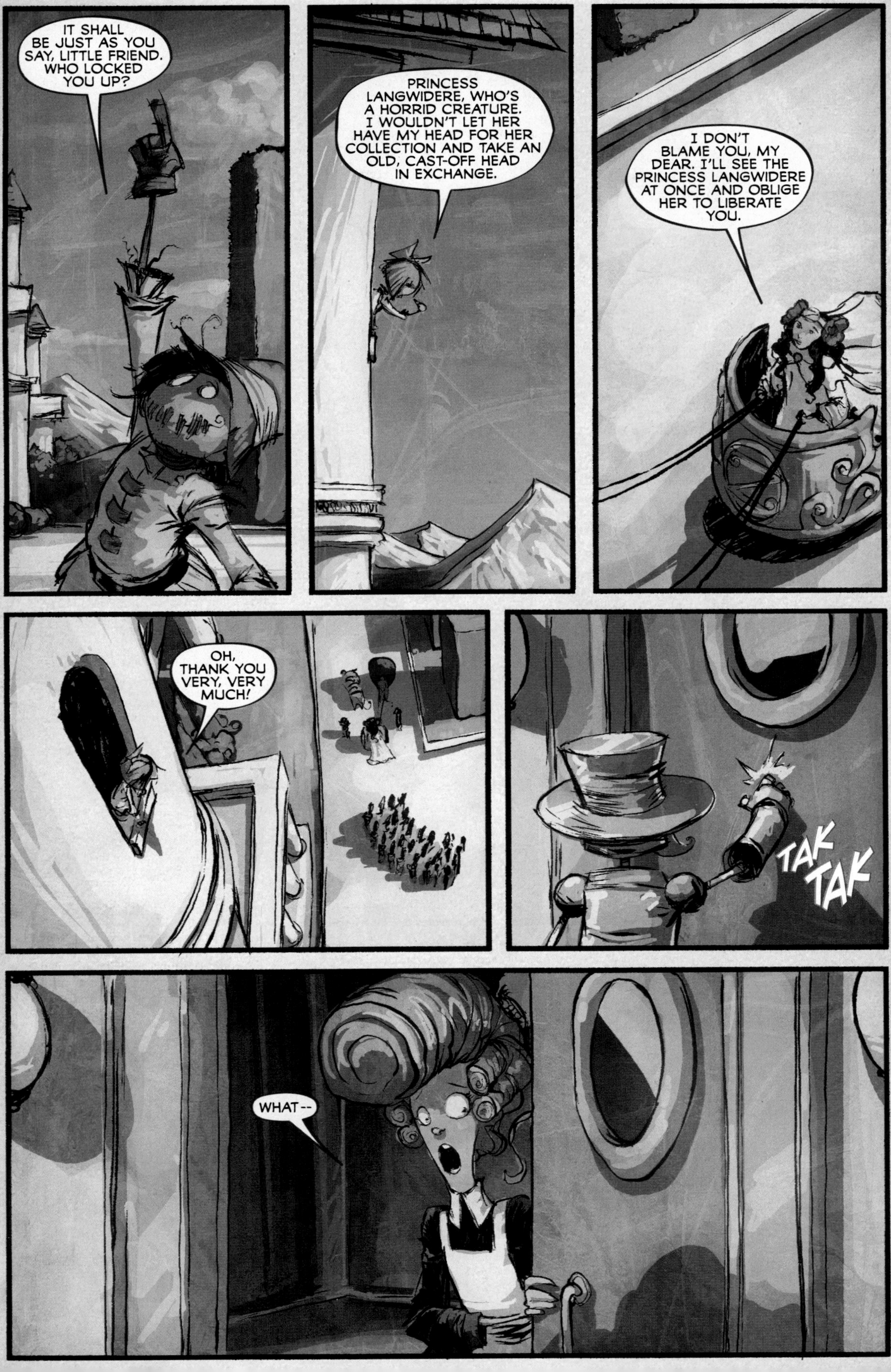
IT SHALL BE JUST AS YOU SAY, LITTLE FRIEND. WHO LOCKED YOU UP?
PRINCESS LANGWIDERE, WHO'S A HORRID CREATURE. I WOULDN'T LET HER HAVE MY HEAD FOR HER COLLECTION AND TAKE AN OLD, CAST-OFF HEAD IN EXCHANGE.
I DON'T BLAME YOU, MY DEAR. I'LL SEE THE PRINCESS LANGWIDERE AT ONCE AND OBLIGE HER TO LIBERATE YOU.
OH, THANK YOU VERY, VERY MUCH!
TAK TAK
WHAT--

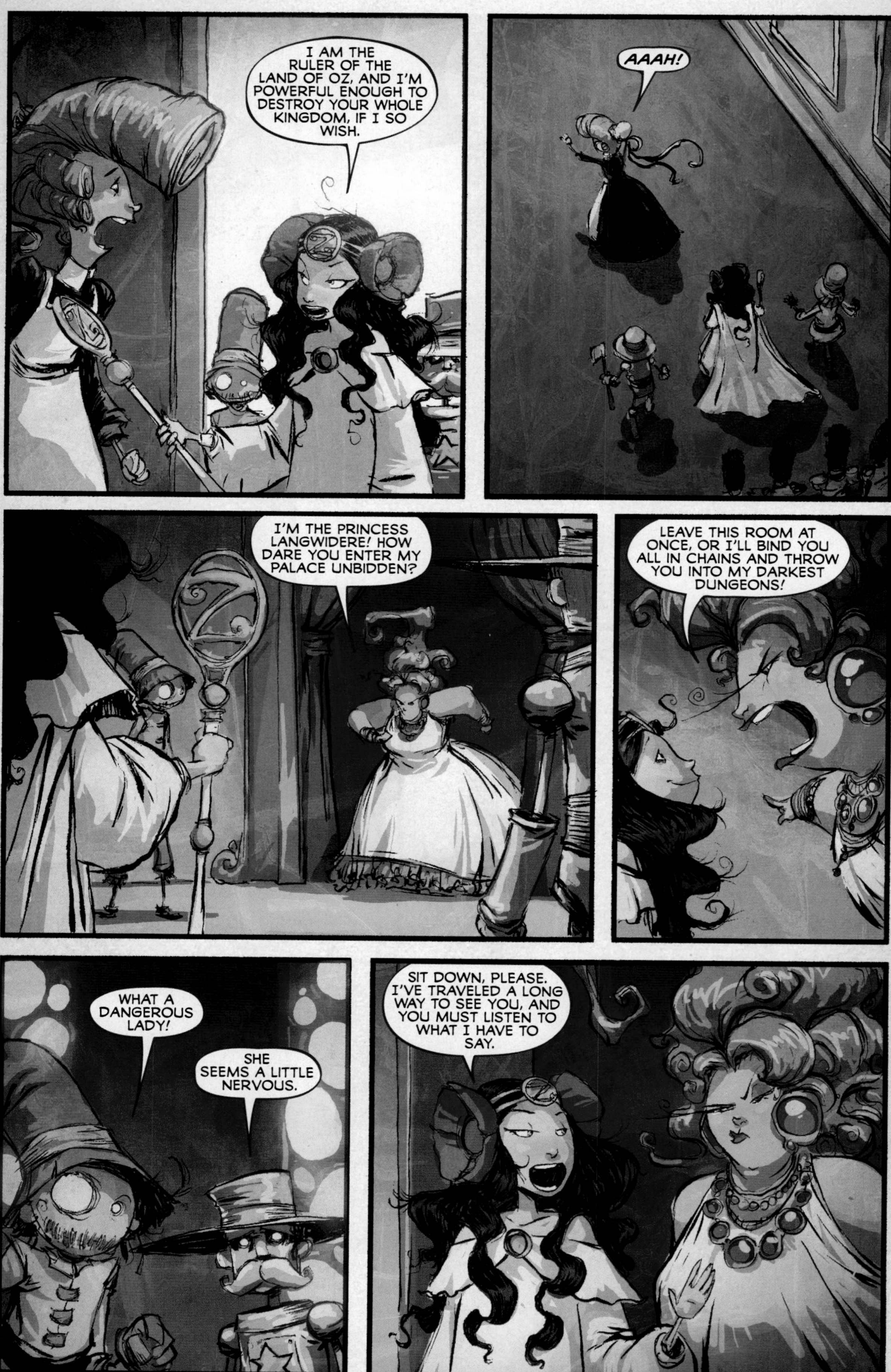
I AM THE RULER OF THE LAND OF OZ, AND I'M POWERFUL ENOUGH TO DESTROY YOUR WHOLE KINGDOM, IF I SO WISH.
AAAH!
I'M THE PRINCESS LANGWIDERE! HOW DARE YOU ENTER MY PALACE UNBIDDEN?
LEAVE THIS ROOM AT ONCE, OR I'LL BIND YOU ALL IN CHAINS AND THROW YOU INTO MY DARKEST DUNGEONS!
WHAT A DANGEROUS LADY!
SHE SEEMS A LITTLE NERVOUS.
SIT DOWN, PLEASE. I'VE TRAVELED A LONG WAY TO SEE YOU, AND YOU MUST LISTEN TO WHAT I HAVE TO SAY.

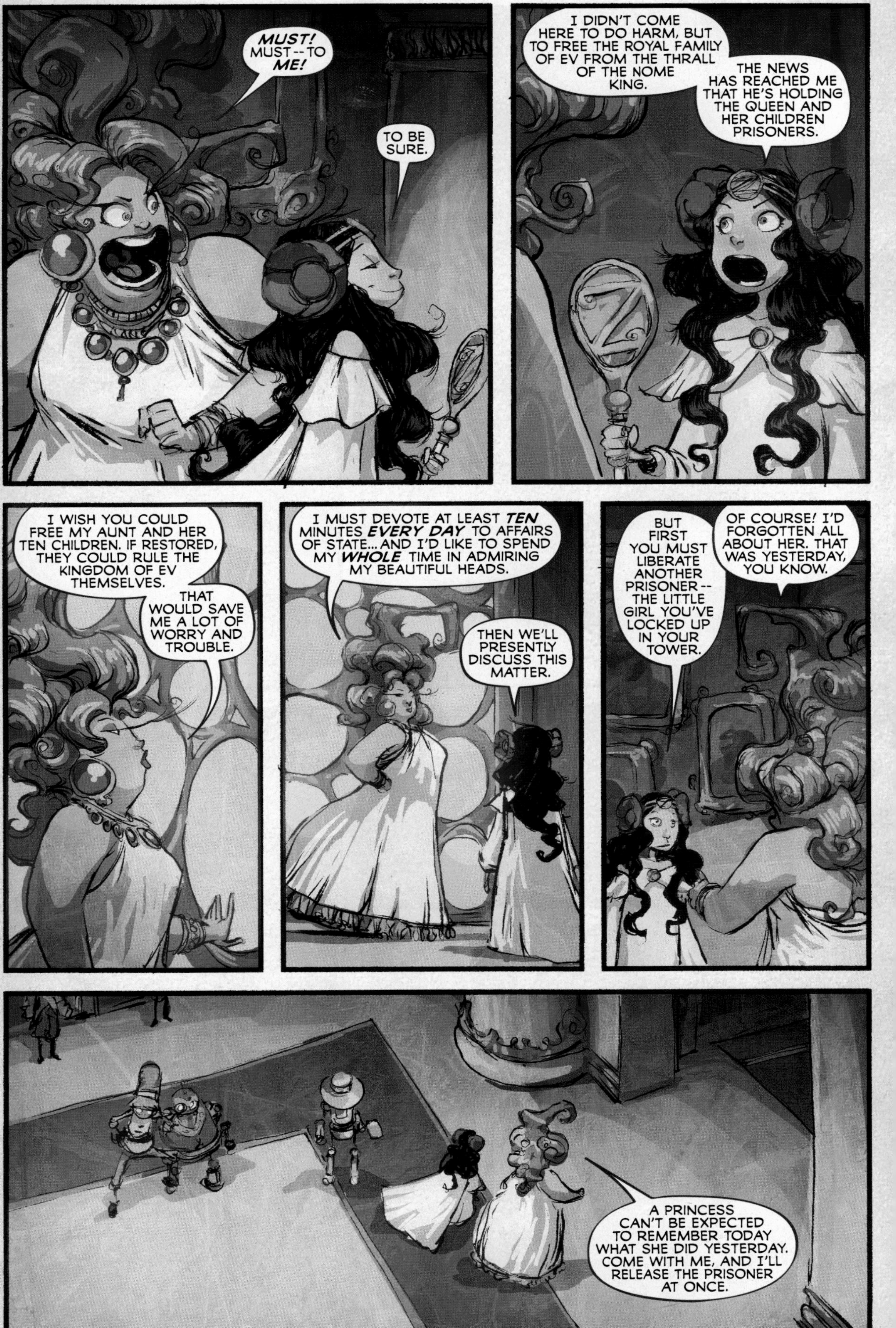
MUST! MUST--TO ME!
TO BE SURE.
I DIDN'T COME HERE TO DO HARM, BUT TO FREE THE ROYAL FAMILY OF EV FROM THE THRALL OF THE NOME KING.
THE NEWS HAS REACHED ME THAT HE'S HOLDING THE QUEEN AND HER CHILDREN PRISONERS.
I WISH YOU COULD FREE MY AUNT AND HER TEN CHILDREN. IF RESTORED, THEY COULD RULE THE KINGDOM OF EV THEMSELVES.
THAT WOULD SAVE ME A LOT OF WORRY AND TROUBLE.
I MUST DEVOTE AT LEAST TEN MINUTES EVERY DAY TO AFFAIRS OF STATE... AND I'D LIKE TO SPEND MY WHOLE TIME IN ADMIRING MY BEAUTIFUL HEADS.
THEN WE'LL PRESENTLY DISCUSS THIS MATTER.
BUT FIRST YOU MUST LIBERATE ANOTHER PRISONER-- THE LITTLE GIRL YOU'VE LOCKED UP IN YOUR TOWER.
OF COURSE! I'D FORGOTTEN ALL ABOUT HER. THAT WAS YESTERDAY, YOU KNOW.
A PRINCESS CAN'T BE EXPECTED TO REMEMBER TODAY WHAT SHE DID YESTERDAY. COME WITH ME, AND I'LL RELEASE THE PRISONER AT ONCE.

Get off my foot, please. You are scratch-ing my pol-ish.

OH, EXCUSE ME! ARE YOU ALIVE?

No. But I can think and speak and act when I am pro-per-ly wound up.

Just now my ac-tion is run down, and Dor-o-thy has the key.

DOROTHY WILL SOON BE FREE.

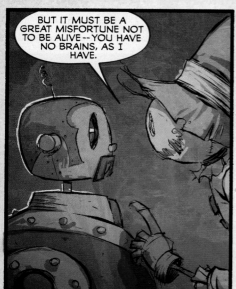

BUT IT MUST BE A GREAT MISFORTUNE NOT TO BE ALIVE -- YOU HAVE NO BRAINS, AS I HAVE.

Oh, yes, I have. I am fit-ted with Smith & Tin-ker's Im-proved Com-bi-na-tion Steel Brains.

What sort of brains are you fit-ted with?

I DON'T KNOW. THEY WERE GIVEN TO ME BY THE GREAT WIZARD OF OZ.

I DIDN'T GET A CHANCE TO EXAMINE THEM BEFORE HE PUT THEM IN, BUT THEY WORK SPLENDIDLY.

"YOU HAVE NO HEART, I SUPPOSE?"

"No."

"THEN I REGRET TO SAY THAT YOU'RE GREATLY INFERIOR TO THE SCARE-CROW AND MYSELF."

"HE HAS BRAINS, WHICH DON'T NEED TO BE WOUND UP, WHILE I HAVE AN EXCELLENT HEART THAT'S CONTINUALLY BEATING."

"I can-not help be-ing in-fer-i-or for I am a mere ma-chine. When I am wound up I go just as my ma-chin-er-y is made to go."

"You have no i-de-a how full of ma-chin-er-y I am."

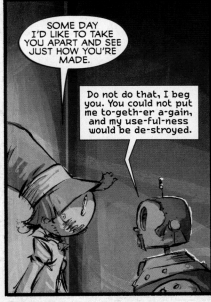

"SOME DAY I'D LIKE TO TAKE YOU APART AND SEE JUST HOW YOU'RE MADE."

"Do not do that, I beg you. You could not put me to-geth-er a-gain, and my use-ful-ness would be de-stroyed."

"OH! ARE YOU USEFUL? IN THAT CASE, I WON'T FOOL WITH YOUR INTERIOR. I'M A POOR MECHANIC AND MIGHT MIX YOU UP."

"Thank you."

JUST THEN.

"MY OLD COMRADES!"

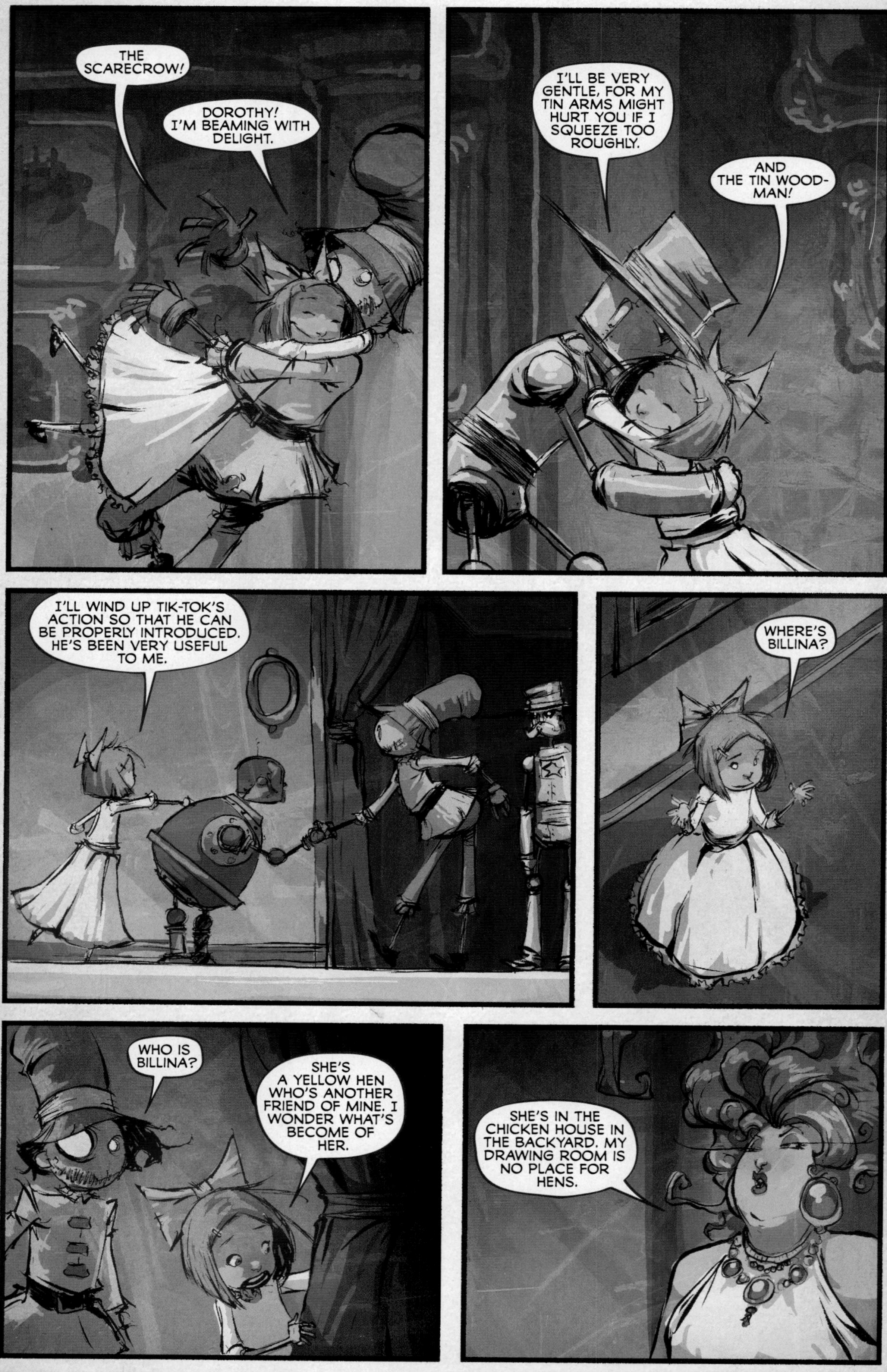
THE SCARECROW!
DOROTHY! I'M BEAMING WITH DELIGHT.
I'LL BE VERY GENTLE, FOR MY TIN ARMS MIGHT HURT YOU IF I SQUEEZE TOO ROUGHLY.
AND THE TIN WOOD-MAN!
I'LL WIND UP TIK-TOK'S ACTION SO THAT HE CAN BE PROPERLY INTRODUCED. HE'S BEEN VERY USEFUL TO ME.
WHERE'S BILLINA?
WHO IS BILLINA?
SHE'S A YELLOW HEN WHO'S ANOTHER FRIEND OF MINE. I WONDER WHAT'S BECOME OF HER.
SHE'S IN THE CHICKEN HOUSE IN THE BACKYARD. MY DRAWING ROOM IS NO PLACE FOR HENS.

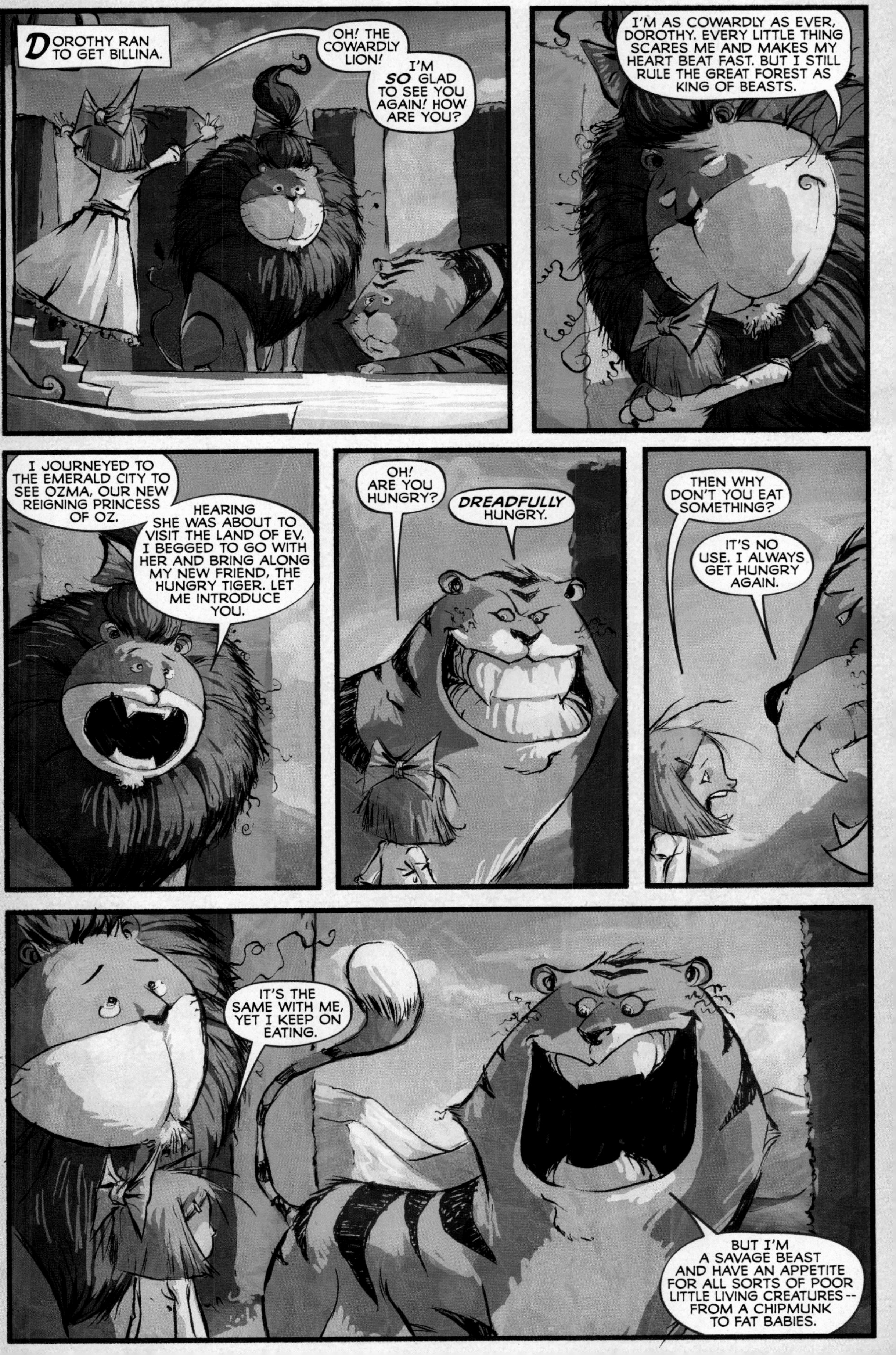
DOROTHY RAN TO GET BILLINA.
OH! THE COWARDLY LION!
I'M **SO** GLAD TO SEE YOU AGAIN! HOW ARE YOU?
I'M AS COWARDLY AS EVER, DOROTHY. EVERY LITTLE THING SCARES ME AND MAKES MY HEART BEAT FAST. BUT I STILL RULE THE GREAT FOREST AS KING OF BEASTS.
I JOURNEYED TO THE EMERALD CITY TO SEE OZMA, OUR NEW REIGNING PRINCESS OF OZ.
HEARING SHE WAS ABOUT TO VISIT THE LAND OF EV, I BEGGED TO GO WITH HER AND BRING ALONG MY NEW FRIEND, THE HUNGRY TIGER. LET ME INTRODUCE YOU.
OH! ARE YOU HUNGRY?
DREADFULLY HUNGRY.
THEN WHY DON'T YOU EAT SOMETHING?
IT'S NO USE. I ALWAYS GET HUNGRY AGAIN.
IT'S THE SAME WITH ME, YET I KEEP ON EATING.
BUT I'M A SAVAGE BEAST AND HAVE AN APPETITE FOR ALL SORTS OF POOR LITTLE LIVING CREATURES -- FROM A CHIPMUNK TO FAT BABIES.

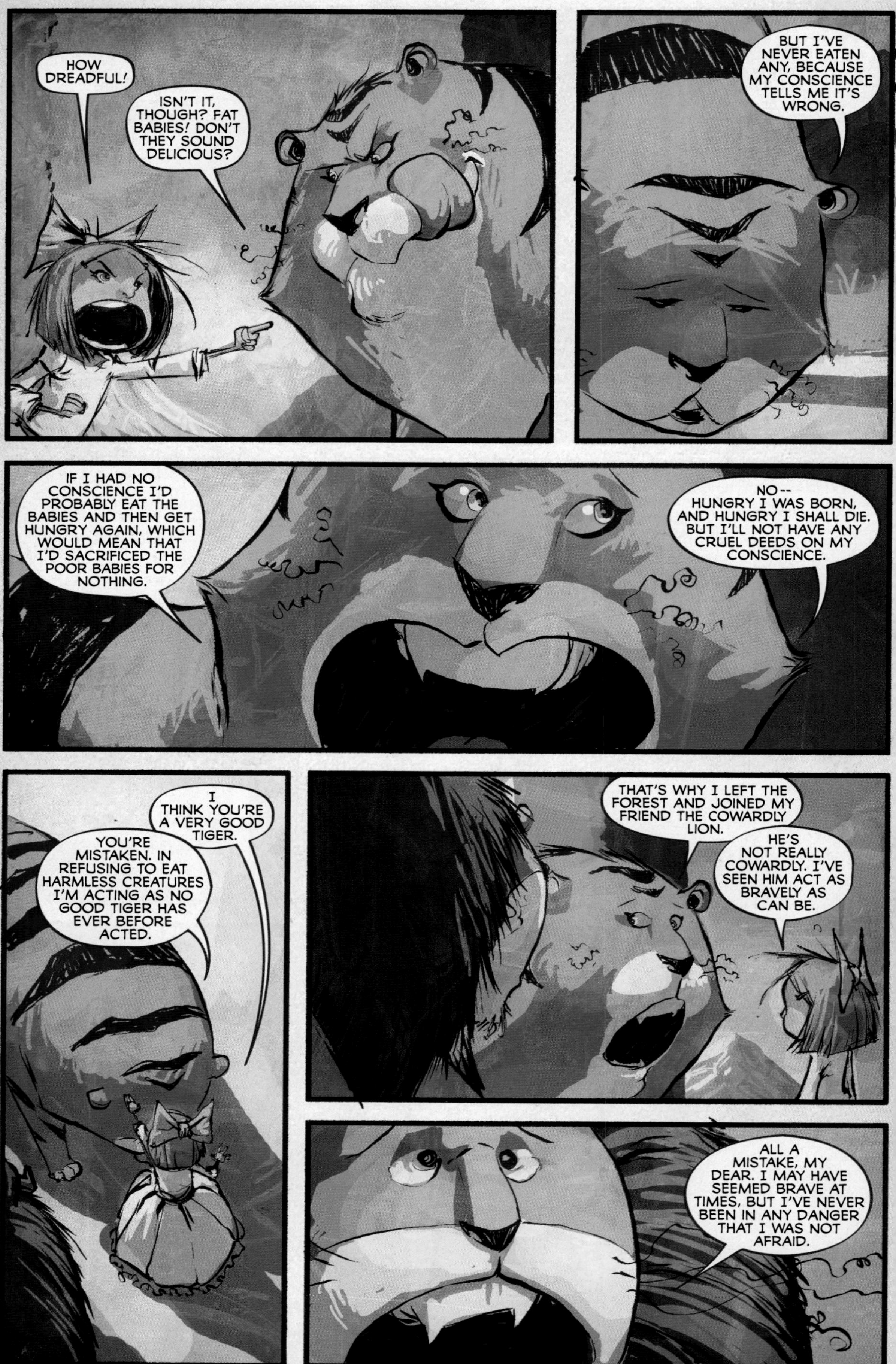
HOW DREADFUL!
ISN'T IT, THOUGH? FAT BABIES! DON'T THEY SOUND DELICIOUS?
BUT I'VE NEVER EATEN ANY, BECAUSE MY CONSCIENCE TELLS ME IT'S WRONG.
IF I HAD NO CONSCIENCE I'D PROBABLY EAT THE BABIES AND THEN GET HUNGRY AGAIN, WHICH WOULD MEAN THAT I'D SACRIFICED THE POOR BABIES FOR NOTHING.
NO-- HUNGRY I WAS BORN, AND HUNGRY I SHALL DIE. BUT I'LL NOT HAVE ANY CRUEL DEEDS ON MY CONSCIENCE.
I THINK YOU'RE A VERY GOOD TIGER.
YOU'RE MISTAKEN. IN REFUSING TO EAT HARMLESS CREATURES I'M ACTING AS NO GOOD TIGER HAS EVER BEFORE ACTED.
THAT'S WHY I LEFT THE FOREST AND JOINED MY FRIEND THE COWARDLY LION.
HE'S NOT REALLY COWARDLY. I'VE SEEN HIM ACT AS BRAVELY AS CAN BE.
ALL A MISTAKE, MY DEAR. I MAY HAVE SEEMED BRAVE AT TIMES, BUT I'VE NEVER BEEN IN ANY DANGER THAT I WAS NOT AFRAID.

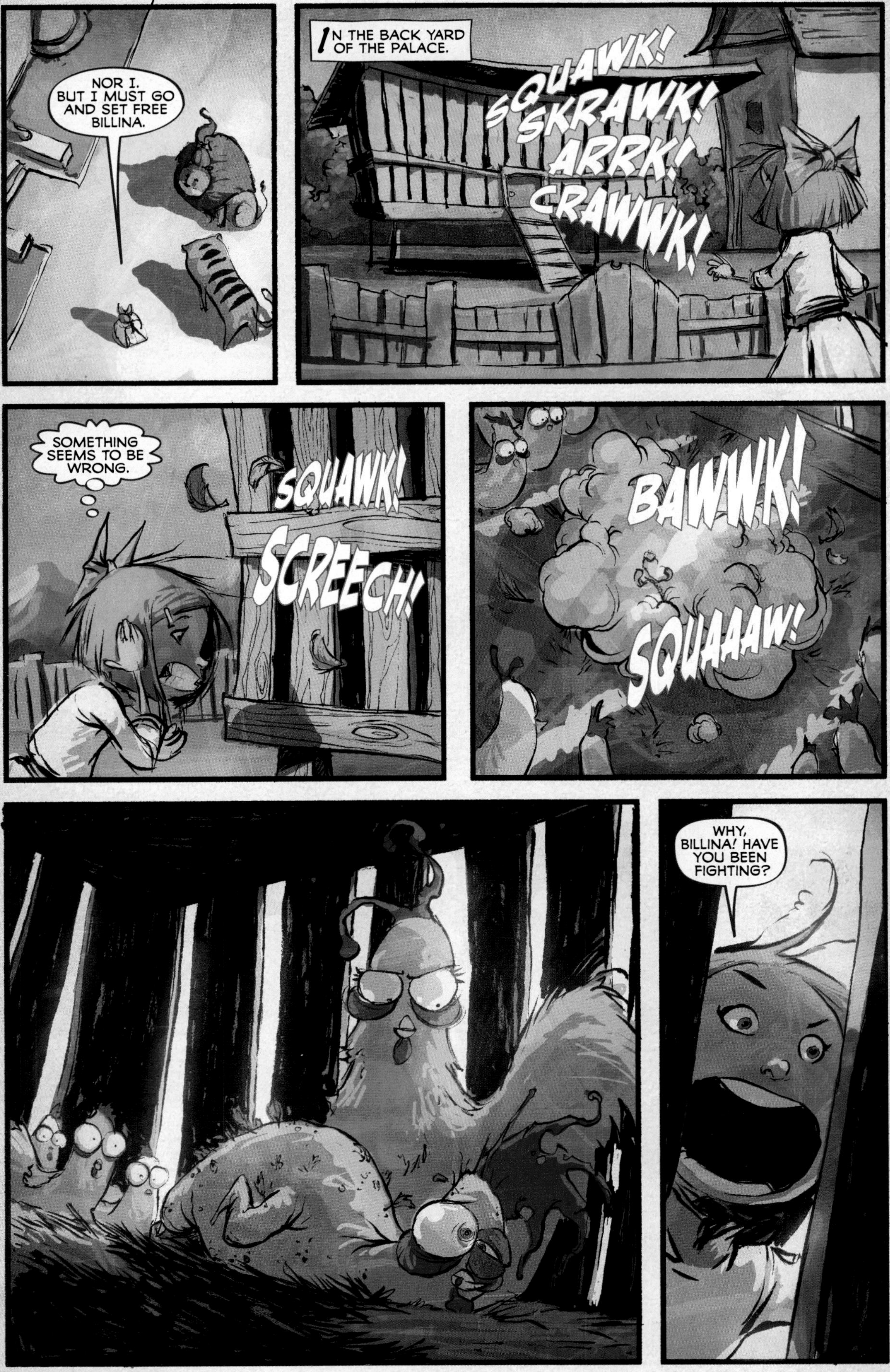
NOR I. BUT I MUST GO AND SET FREE BILLINA.
IN THE BACK YARD OF THE PALACE.
SQUAWK! SKRAWK! ARRK! CRAWWK!
SOMETHING SEEMS TO BE WRONG.
SQUAWK! SCREECH!
BAWWK! SQUAAAW!
WHY, BILLINA! HAVE YOU BEEN FIGHTING?

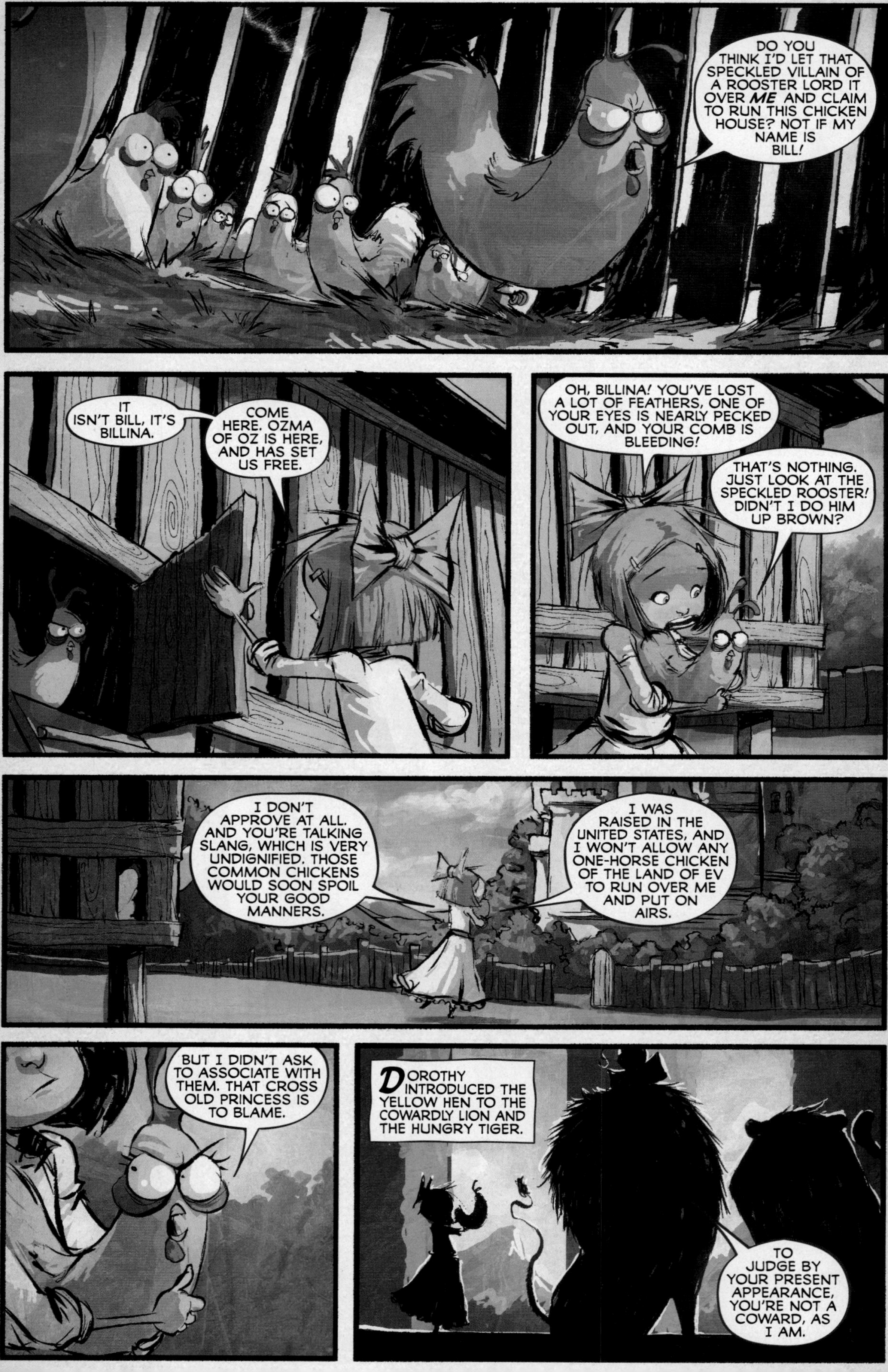
DO YOU THINK I'D LET THAT SPECKLED VILLAIN OF A ROOSTER LORD IT OVER ME AND CLAIM TO RUN THIS CHICKEN HOUSE? NOT IF MY NAME IS BILL!
IT ISN'T BILL, IT'S BILLINA.
COME HERE. OZMA OF OZ IS HERE, AND HAS SET US FREE.
OH, BILLINA! YOU'VE LOST A LOT OF FEATHERS, ONE OF YOUR EYES IS NEARLY PECKED OUT, AND YOUR COMB IS BLEEDING!
THAT'S NOTHING. JUST LOOK AT THE SPECKLED ROOSTER! DIDN'T I DO HIM UP BROWN?
I DON'T APPROVE AT ALL. AND YOU'RE TALKING SLANG, WHICH IS VERY UNDIGNIFIED. THOSE COMMON CHICKENS WOULD SOON SPOIL YOUR GOOD MANNERS.
I WAS RAISED IN THE UNITED STATES, AND I WON'T ALLOW ANY ONE-HORSE CHICKEN OF THE LAND OF EV TO RUN OVER ME AND PUT ON AIRS.
BUT I DIDN'T ASK TO ASSOCIATE WITH THEM. THAT CROSS OLD PRINCESS IS TO BLAME.
DOROTHY INTRODUCED THE YELLOW HEN TO THE COWARDLY LION AND THE HUNGRY TIGER.
TO JUDGE BY YOUR PRESENT APPEARANCE, YOU'RE NOT A COWARD, AS I AM.

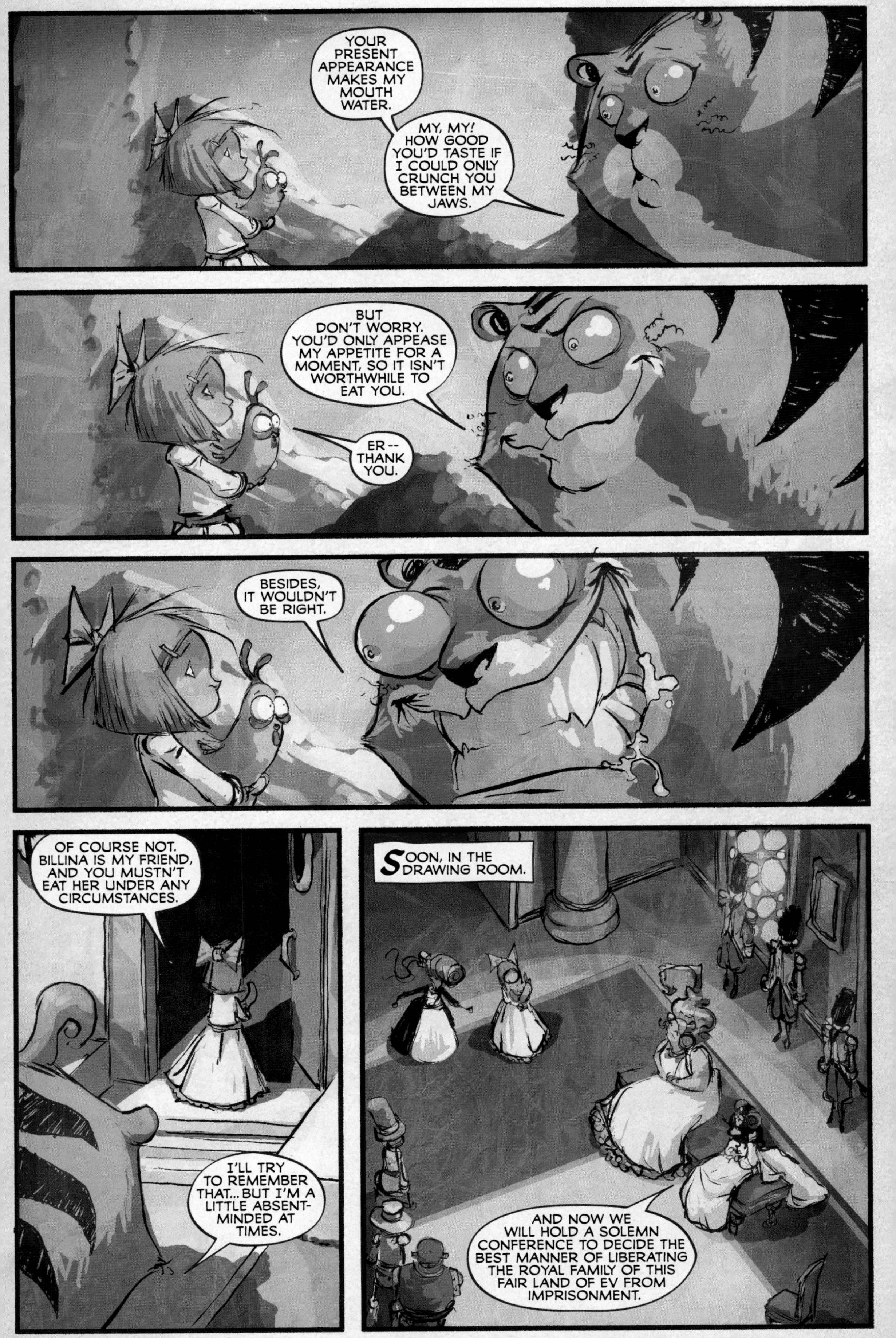
YOUR PRESENT APPEARANCE MAKES MY MOUTH WATER.
MY, MY! HOW GOOD YOU'D TASTE IF I COULD ONLY CRUNCH YOU BETWEEN MY JAWS.
BUT DON'T WORRY. YOU'D ONLY APPEASE MY APPETITE FOR A MOMENT, SO IT ISN'T WORTHWHILE TO EAT YOU.
ER -- THANK YOU.
BESIDES, IT WOULDN'T BE RIGHT.
OF COURSE NOT. BILLINA IS MY FRIEND, AND YOU MUSTN'T EAT HER UNDER ANY CIRCUMSTANCES.
I'LL TRY TO REMEMBER THAT... BUT I'M A LITTLE ABSENT-MINDED AT TIMES.
SOON, IN THE DRAWING ROOM.
AND NOW WE WILL HOLD A SOLEMN CONFERENCE TO DECIDE THE BEST MANNER OF LIBERATING THE ROYAL FAMILY OF THIS FAIR LAND OF EV FROM IMPRISONMENT.

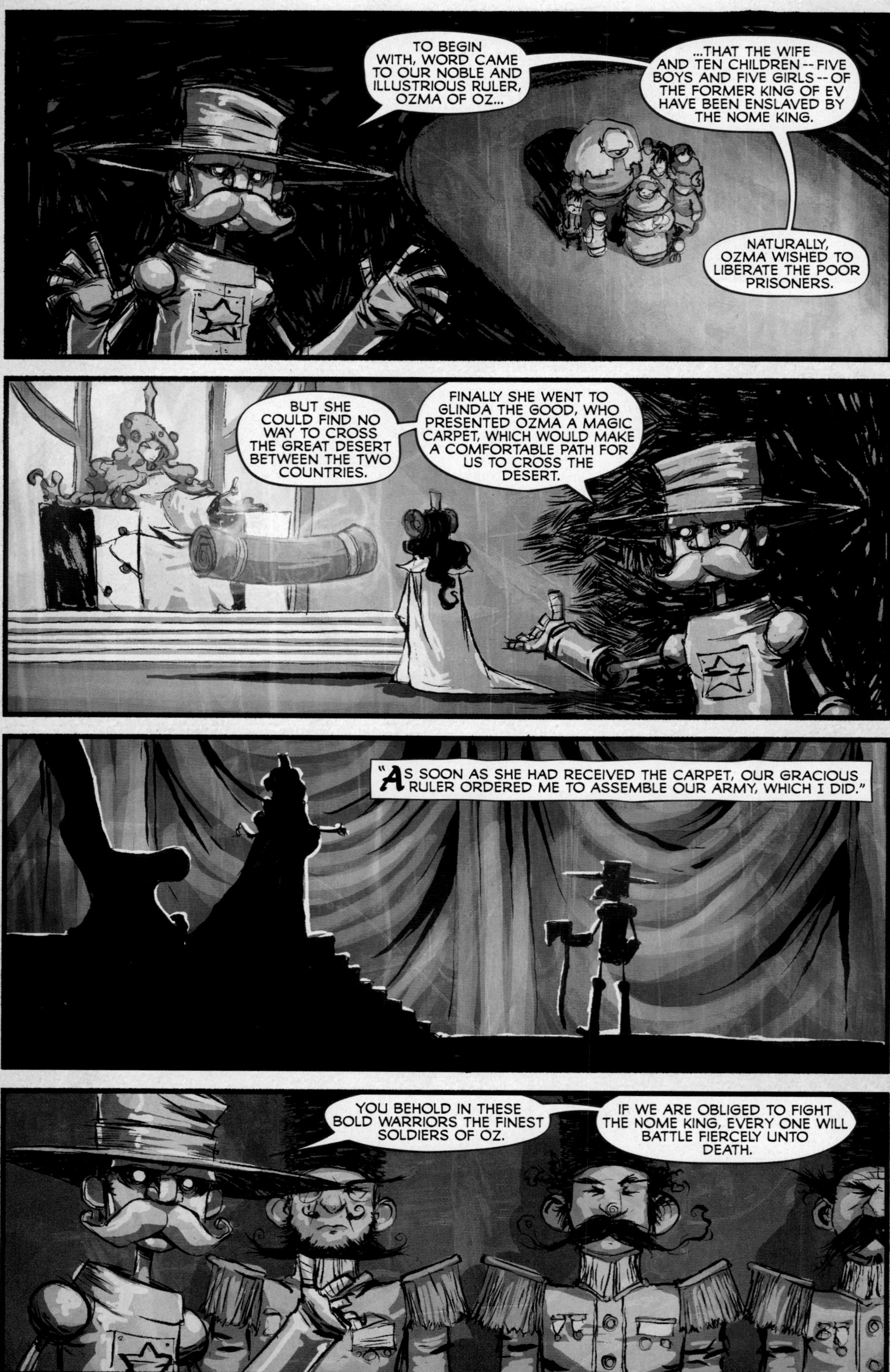
TO BEGIN WITH, WORD CAME TO OUR NOBLE AND ILLUSTRIOUS RULER, OZMA OF OZ...
...THAT THE WIFE AND TEN CHILDREN -- FIVE BOYS AND FIVE GIRLS -- OF THE FORMER KING OF EV HAVE BEEN ENSLAVED BY THE NOME KING.
NATURALLY, OZMA WISHED TO LIBERATE THE POOR PRISONERS.
BUT SHE COULD FIND NO WAY TO CROSS THE GREAT DESERT BETWEEN THE TWO COUNTRIES.
FINALLY SHE WENT TO GLINDA THE GOOD, WHO PRESENTED OZMA A MAGIC CARPET, WHICH WOULD MAKE A COMFORTABLE PATH FOR US TO CROSS THE DESERT.
"AS SOON AS SHE HAD RECEIVED THE CARPET, OUR GRACIOUS RULER ORDERED ME TO ASSEMBLE OUR ARMY, WHICH I DID."
YOU BEHOLD IN THESE BOLD WARRIORS THE FINEST SOLDIERS OF OZ.
IF WE ARE OBLIGED TO FIGHT THE NOME KING, EVERY ONE WILL BATTLE FIERCELY UNTO DEATH.

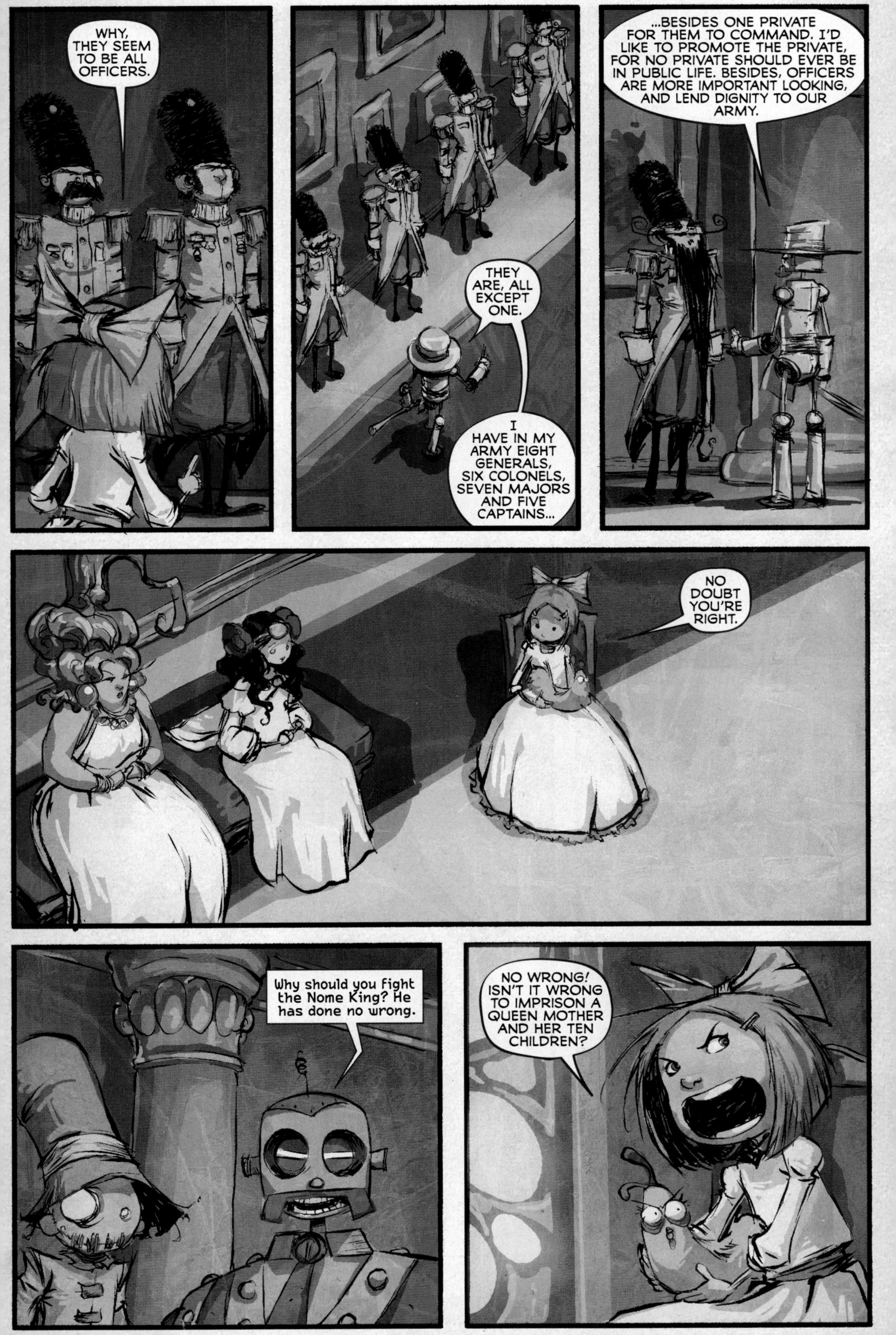
WHY, THEY SEEM TO BE ALL OFFICERS.
THEY ARE, ALL EXCEPT ONE.
I HAVE IN MY ARMY EIGHT GENERALS, SIX COLONELS, SEVEN MAJORS AND FIVE CAPTAINS...
...BESIDES ONE PRIVATE FOR THEM TO COMMAND. I'D LIKE TO PROMOTE THE PRIVATE, FOR NO PRIVATE SHOULD EVER BE IN PUBLIC LIFE. BESIDES, OFFICERS ARE MORE IMPORTANT LOOKING, AND LEND DIGNITY TO OUR ARMY.
NO DOUBT YOU'RE RIGHT.
Why should you fight the Nome King? He has done no wrong.
NO WRONG! ISN'T IT WRONG TO IMPRISON A QUEEN MOTHER AND HER TEN CHILDREN?

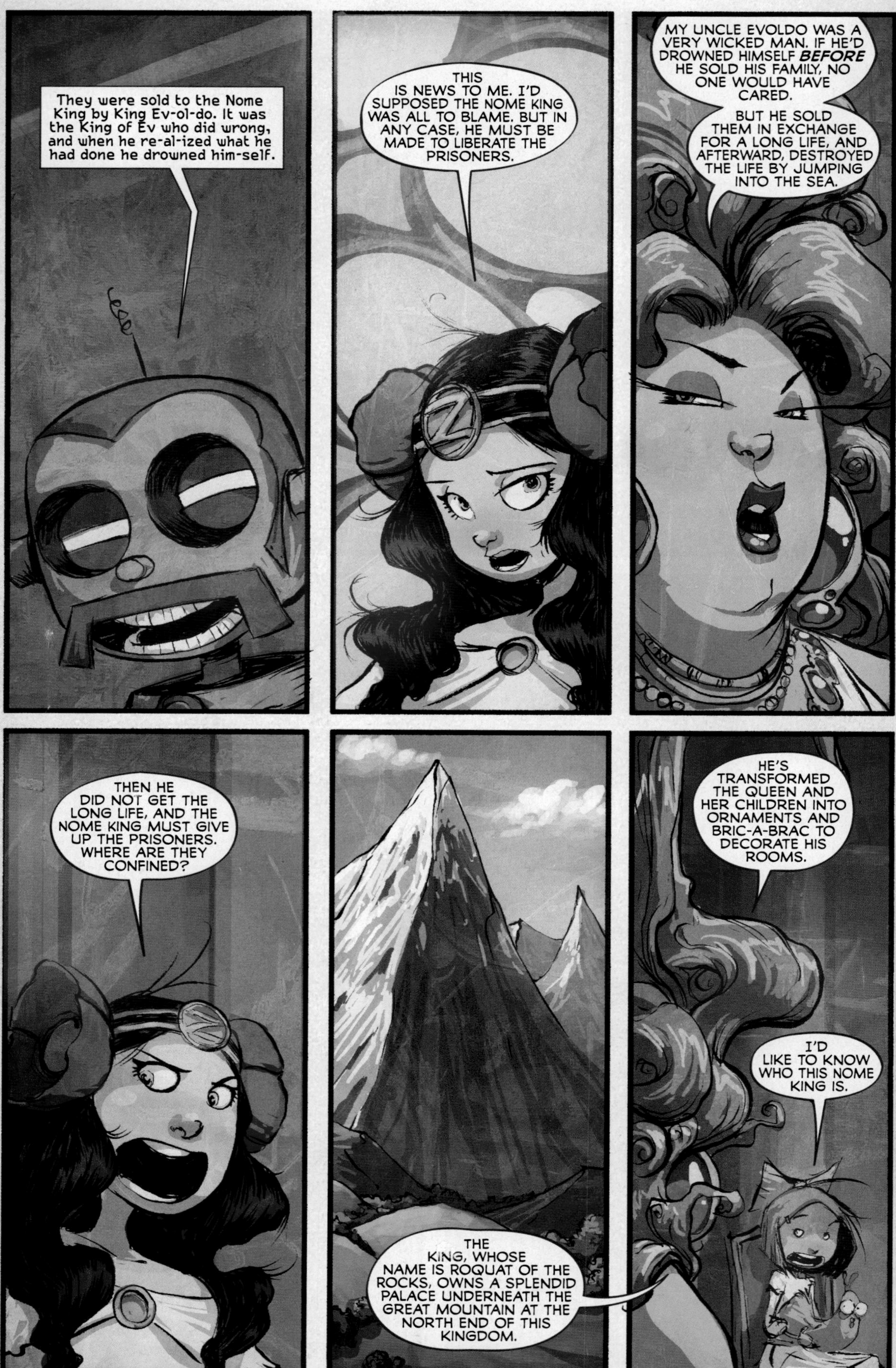

They were sold to the Nome King by King Ev-ol-do. It was the King of Ev who did wrong, and when he re-al-ized what he had done he drowned him-self.
THIS IS NEWS TO ME. I'D SUPPOSED THE NOME KING WAS ALL TO BLAME. BUT IN ANY CASE, HE MUST BE MADE TO LIBERATE THE PRISONERS.
MY UNCLE EVOLDO WAS A VERY WICKED MAN. IF HE'D DROWNED HIMSELF **BEFORE** HE SOLD HIS FAMILY, NO ONE WOULD HAVE CARED.
BUT HE SOLD THEM IN EXCHANGE FOR A LONG LIFE, AND AFTERWARD, DESTROYED THE LIFE BY JUMPING INTO THE SEA.
THEN HE DID NOT GET THE LONG LIFE, AND THE NOME KING MUST GIVE UP THE PRISONERS. WHERE ARE THEY CONFINED?
THE KING, WHOSE NAME IS ROQUAT OF THE ROCKS, OWNS A SPLENDID PALACE UNDERNEATH THE GREAT MOUNTAIN AT THE NORTH END OF THIS KINGDOM.
HE'S TRANSFORMED THE QUEEN AND HER CHILDREN INTO ORNAMENTS AND BRIC-A-BRAC TO DECORATE HIS ROOMS.
I'D LIKE TO KNOW WHO THIS NOME KING IS.

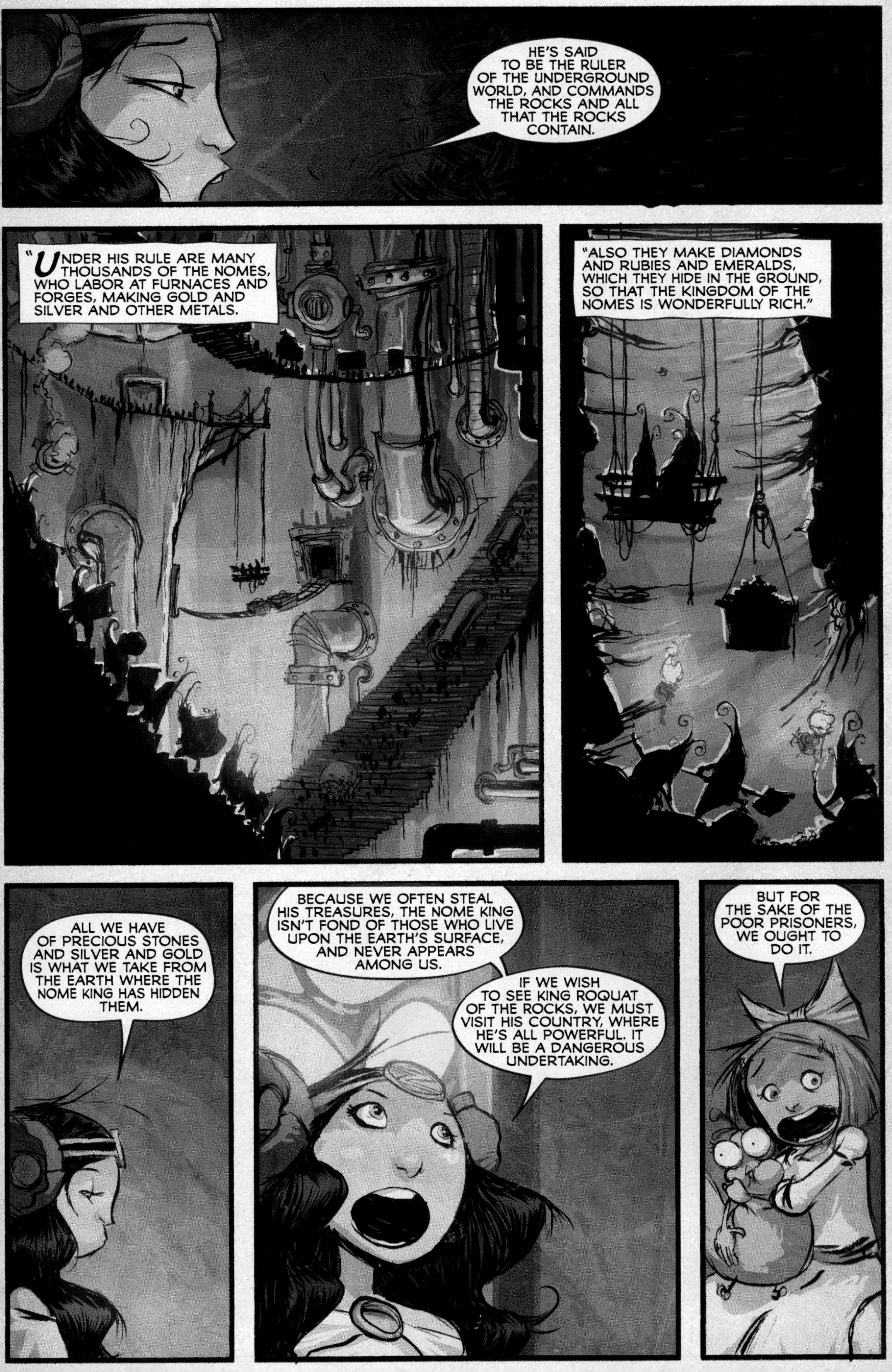
HE'S SAID TO BE THE RULER OF THE UNDERGROUND WORLD, AND COMMANDS THE ROCKS AND ALL THAT THE ROCKS CONTAIN.
"UNDER HIS RULE ARE MANY THOUSANDS OF THE NOMES, WHO LABOR AT FURNACES AND FORGES, MAKING GOLD AND SILVER AND OTHER METALS.
"ALSO THEY MAKE DIAMONDS AND RUBIES AND EMERALDS, WHICH THEY HIDE IN THE GROUND, SO THAT THE KINGDOM OF THE NOMES IS WONDERFULLY RICH."
ALL WE HAVE OF PRECIOUS STONES AND SILVER AND GOLD IS WHAT WE TAKE FROM THE EARTH WHERE THE NOME KING HAS HIDDEN THEM.
BECAUSE WE OFTEN STEAL HIS TREASURES, THE NOME KING ISN'T FOND OF THOSE WHO LIVE UPON THE EARTH'S SURFACE, AND NEVER APPEARS AMONG US.
IF WE WISH TO SEE KING ROQUAT OF THE ROCKS, WE MUST VISIT HIS COUNTRY, WHERE HE'S ALL POWERFUL. IT WILL BE A DANGEROUS UNDERTAKING.
BUT FOR THE SAKE OF THE POOR PRISONERS, WE OUGHT TO DO IT.

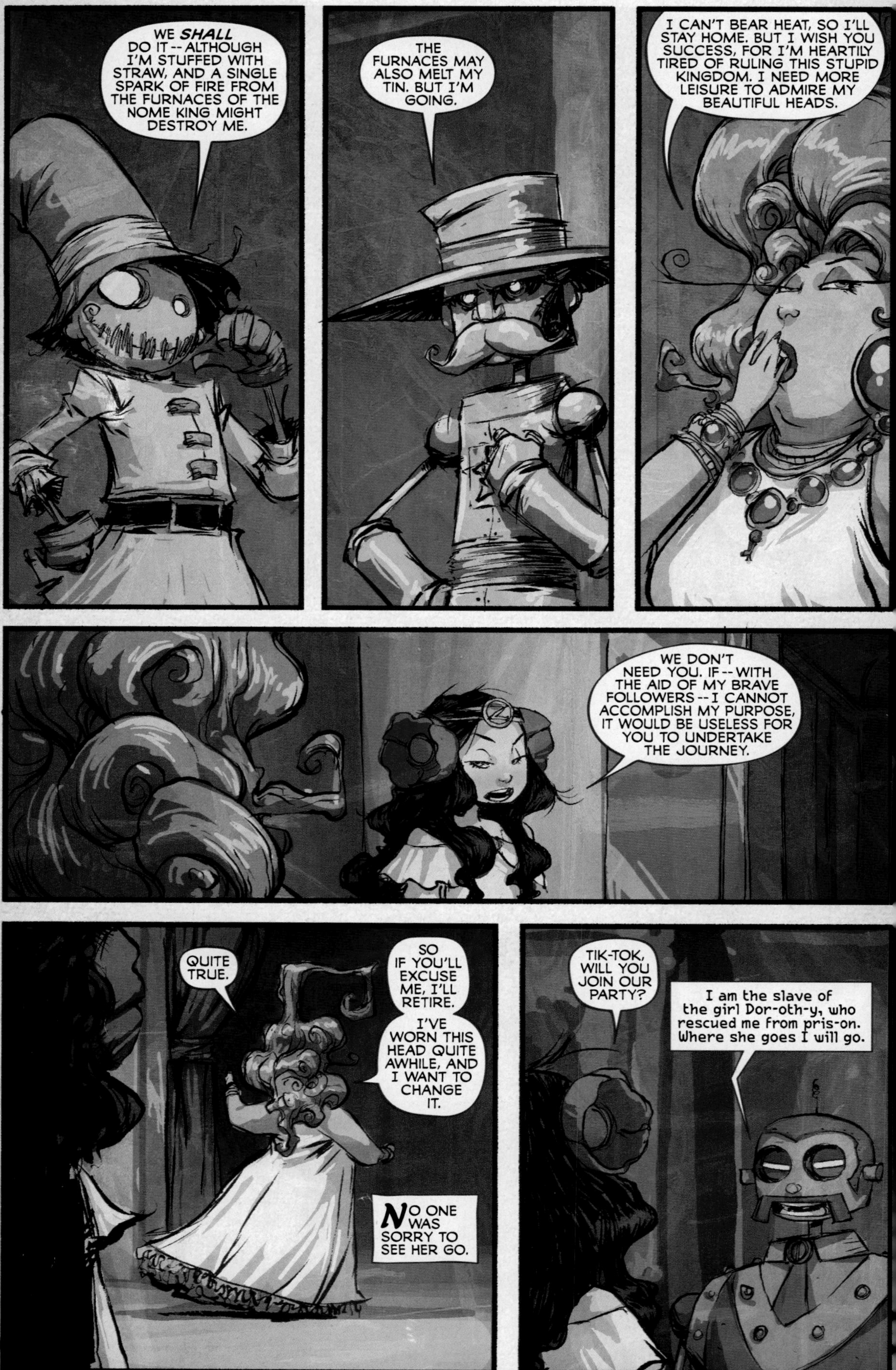
WE SHALL DO IT -- ALTHOUGH I'M STUFFED WITH STRAW, AND A SINGLE SPARK OF FIRE FROM THE FURNACES OF THE NOME KING MIGHT DESTROY ME.
THE FURNACES MAY ALSO MELT MY TIN. BUT I'M GOING.
I CAN'T BEAR HEAT, SO I'LL STAY HOME. BUT I WISH YOU SUCCESS, FOR I'M HEARTILY TIRED OF RULING THIS STUPID KINGDOM. I NEED MORE LEISURE TO ADMIRE MY BEAUTIFUL HEADS.
WE DON'T NEED YOU. IF -- WITH THE AID OF MY BRAVE FOLLOWERS -- I CANNOT ACCOMPLISH MY PURPOSE, IT WOULD BE USELESS FOR YOU TO UNDERTAKE THE JOURNEY.
QUITE TRUE.
SO IF YOU'LL EXCUSE ME, I'LL RETIRE.
I'VE WORN THIS HEAD QUITE AWHILE, AND I WANT TO CHANGE IT.
NO ONE WAS SORRY TO SEE HER GO.
TIK-TOK, WILL YOU JOIN OUR PARTY?
I am the slave of the girl Dor-oth-y, who rescued me from pris-on. Where she goes I will go.

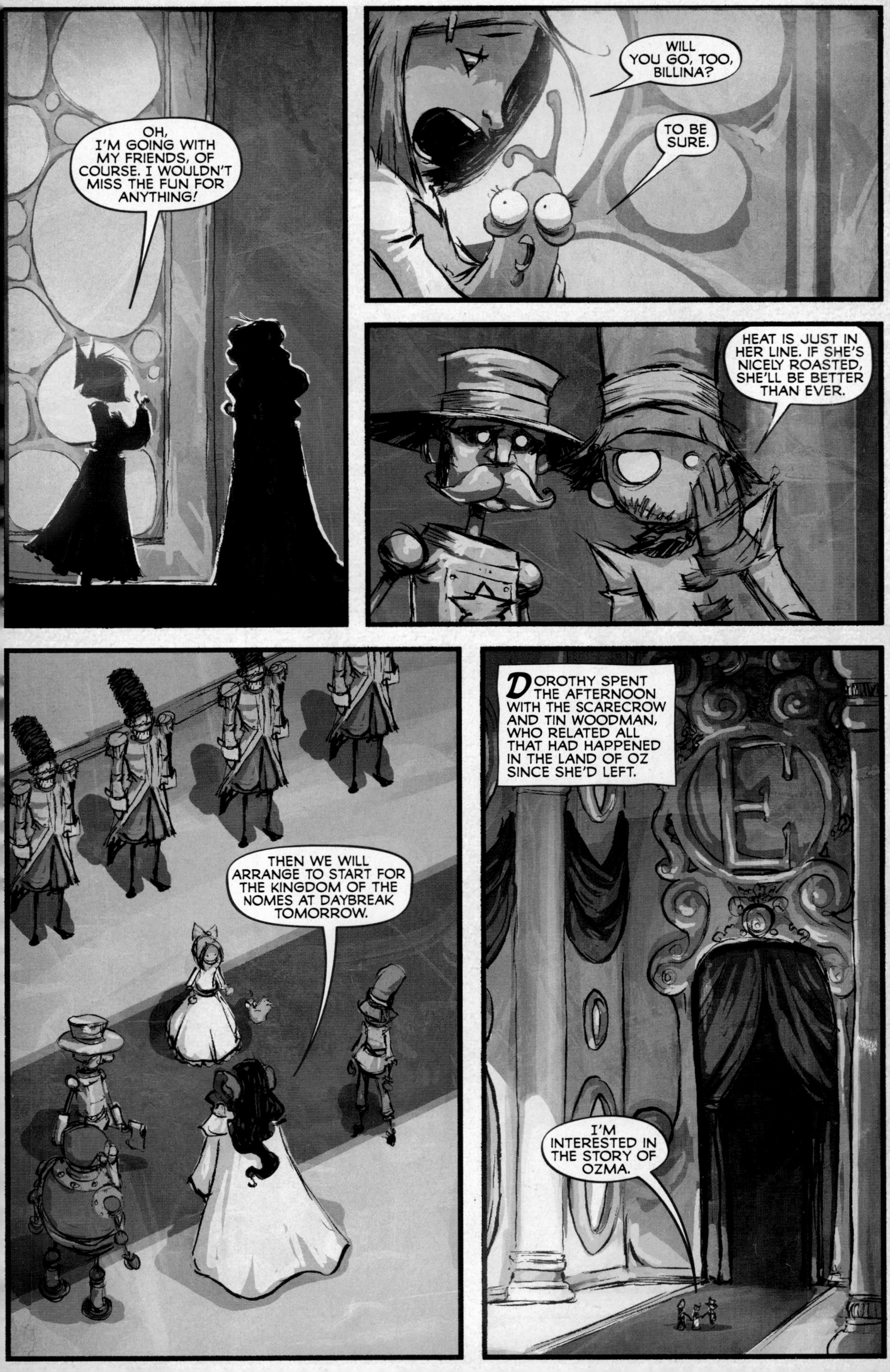
OH, I'M GOING WITH MY FRIENDS, OF COURSE. I WOULDN'T MISS THE FUN FOR ANYTHING!
WILL YOU GO, TOO, BILLINA?
TO BE SURE.
HEAT IS JUST IN HER LINE. IF SHE'S NICELY ROASTED, SHE'LL BE BETTER THAN EVER.
THEN WE WILL ARRANGE TO START FOR THE KINGDOM OF THE NOMES AT DAYBREAK TOMORROW.
DOROTHY SPENT THE AFTERNOON WITH THE SCARECROW AND TIN WOODMAN, WHO RELATED ALL THAT HAD HAPPENED IN THE LAND OF OZ SINCE SHE'D LEFT.
I'M INTERESTED IN THE STORY OF OZMA.

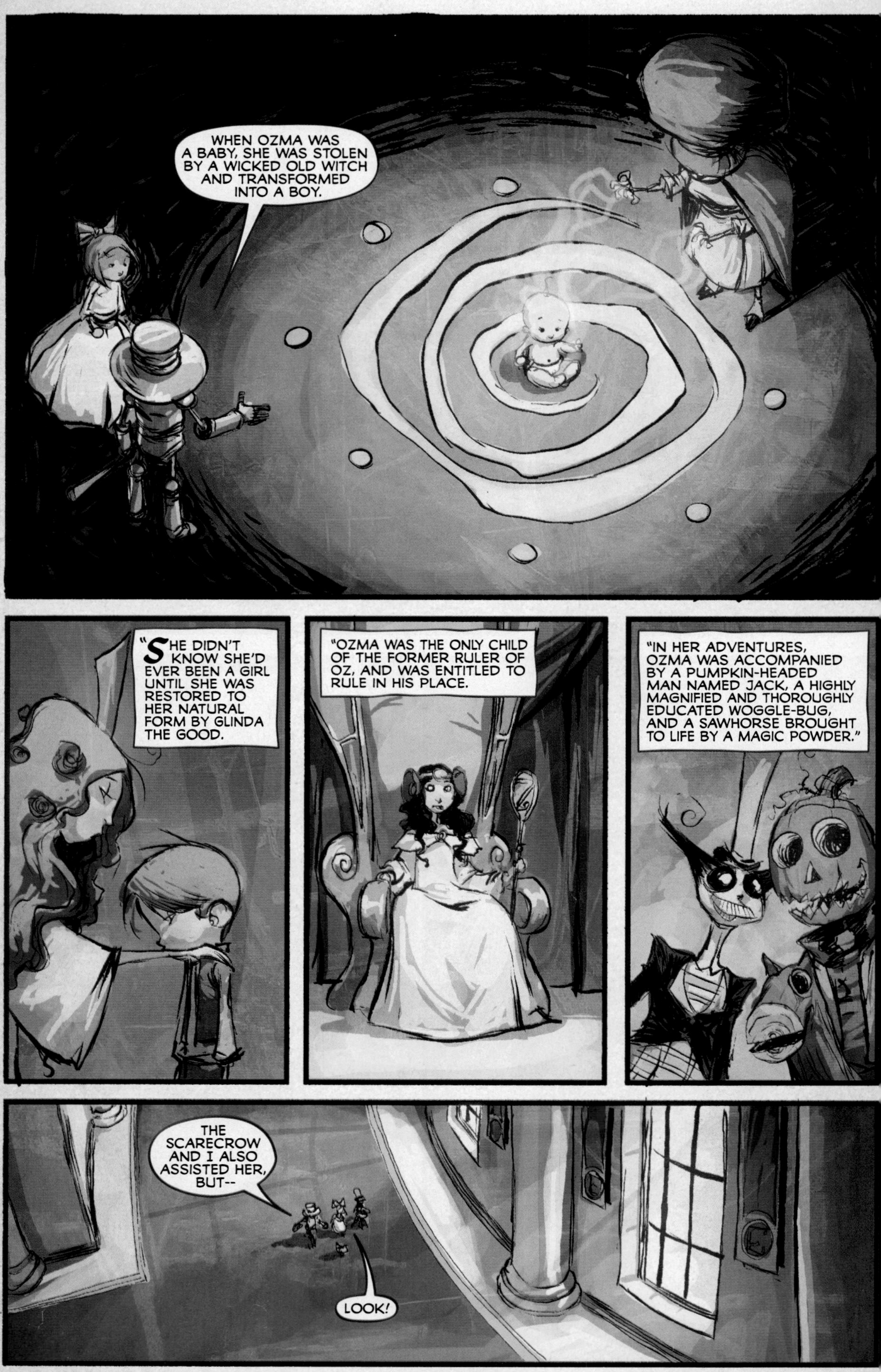
WHEN OZMA WAS A BABY, SHE WAS STOLEN BY A WICKED OLD WITCH AND TRANSFORMED INTO A BOY.
"SHE DIDN'T KNOW SHE'D EVER BEEN A GIRL UNTIL SHE WAS RESTORED TO HER NATURAL FORM BY GLINDA THE GOOD.
"OZMA WAS THE ONLY CHILD OF THE FORMER RULER OF OZ, AND WAS ENTITLED TO RULE IN HIS PLACE.
"IN HER ADVENTURES, OZMA WAS ACCOMPANIED BY A PUMPKIN-HEADED MAN NAMED JACK, A HIGHLY MAGNIFIED AND THOROUGHLY EDUCATED WOGGLE-BUG, AND A SAWHORSE BROUGHT TO LIFE BY A MAGIC POWDER."
THE SCARECROW AND I ALSO ASSISTED HER, BUT--
LOOK!

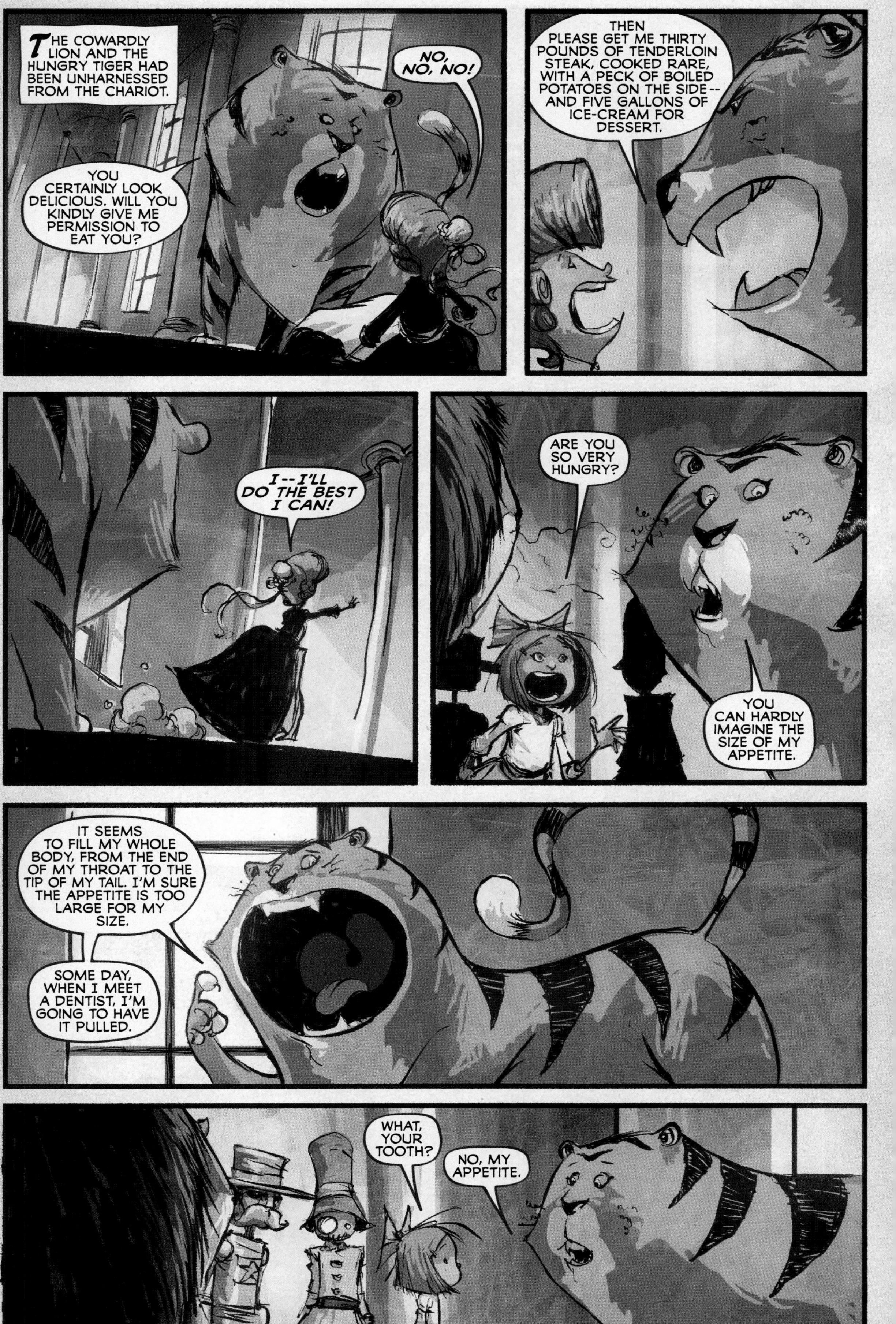
THE COWARDLY LION AND THE HUNGRY TIGER HAD BEEN UNHARNESSED FROM THE CHARIOT.
NO, NO, NO!
YOU CERTAINLY LOOK DELICIOUS. WILL YOU KINDLY GIVE ME PERMISSION TO EAT YOU?
THEN PLEASE GET ME THIRTY POUNDS OF TENDERLOIN STEAK, COOKED RARE, WITH A PECK OF BOILED POTATOES ON THE SIDE-- AND FIVE GALLONS OF ICE-CREAM FOR DESSERT.
I--I'LL DO THE BEST I CAN!
ARE YOU SO VERY HUNGRY?
YOU CAN HARDLY IMAGINE THE SIZE OF MY APPETITE.
IT SEEMS TO FILL MY WHOLE BODY, FROM THE END OF MY THROAT TO THE TIP OF MY TAIL. I'M SURE THE APPETITE IS TOO LARGE FOR MY SIZE.
SOME DAY, WHEN I MEET A DENTIST, I'M GOING TO HAVE IT PULLED.
WHAT, YOUR TOOTH?
NO, MY APPETITE.

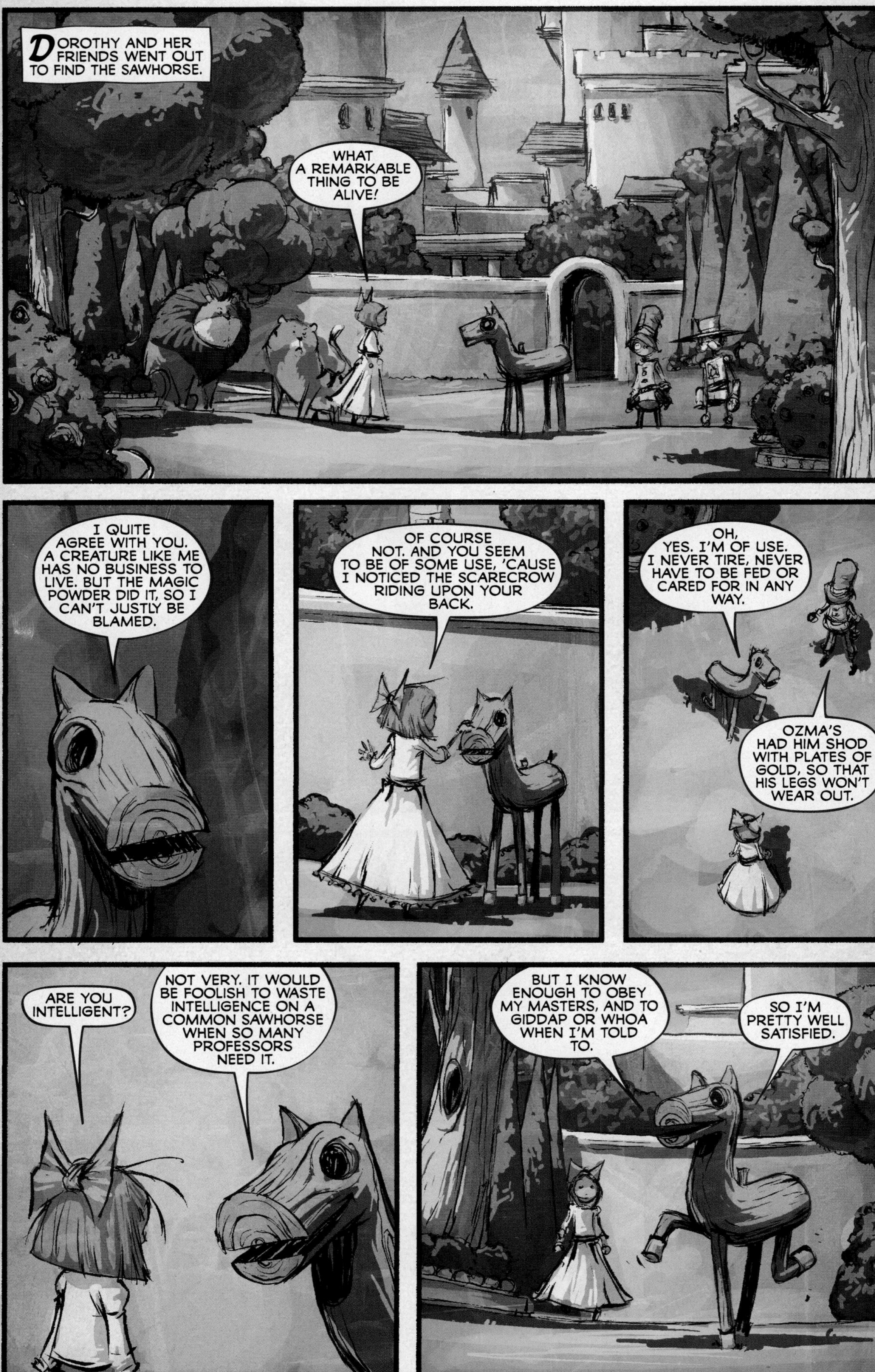

DOROTHY AND HER FRIENDS WENT OUT TO FIND THE SAWHORSE.
WHAT A REMARKABLE THING TO BE ALIVE!
I QUITE AGREE WITH YOU. A CREATURE LIKE ME HAS NO BUSINESS TO LIVE. BUT THE MAGIC POWDER DID IT, SO I CAN'T JUSTLY BE BLAMED.
OF COURSE NOT. AND YOU SEEM TO BE OF SOME USE, 'CAUSE I NOTICED THE SCARECROW RIDING UPON YOUR BACK.
OH, YES. I'M OF USE. I NEVER TIRE, NEVER HAVE TO BE FED OR CARED FOR IN ANY WAY.
OZMA'S HAD HIM SHOD WITH PLATES OF GOLD, SO THAT HIS LEGS WON'T WEAR OUT.
ARE YOU INTELLIGENT?
NOT VERY. IT WOULD BE FOOLISH TO WASTE INTELLIGENCE ON A COMMON SAWHORSE WHEN SO MANY PROFESSORS NEED IT.
BUT I KNOW ENOUGH TO OBEY MY MASTERS, AND TO GIDDAP OR WHOA WHEN I'M TOLD TO.
SO I'M PRETTY WELL SATISFIED.

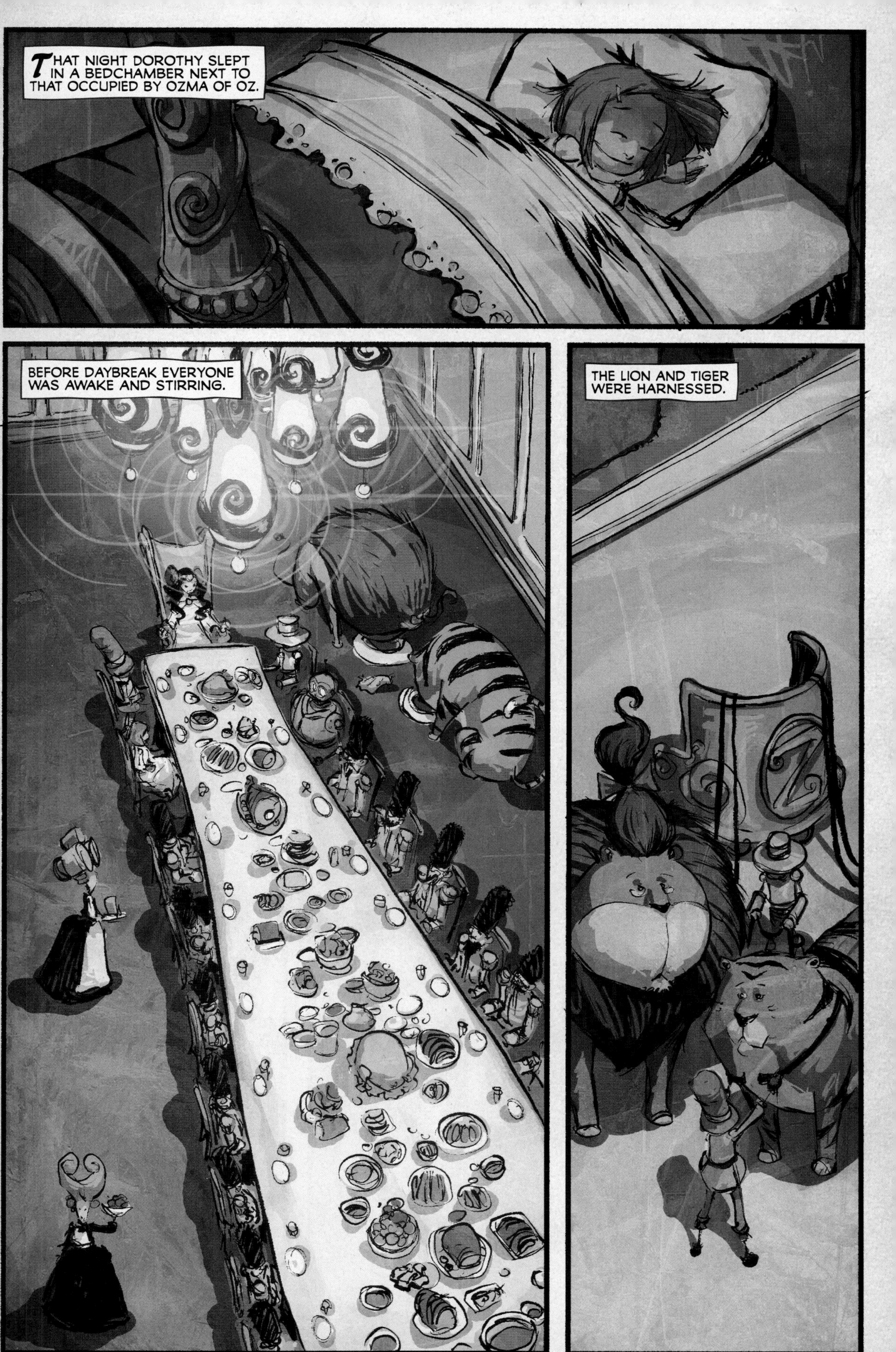
THAT NIGHT DOROTHY SLEPT IN A BEDCHAMBER NEXT TO THAT OCCUPIED BY OZMA OF OZ.
BEFORE DAYBREAK EVERYONE WAS AWAKE AND STIRRING.
THE LION AND TIGER WERE HARNESSED.

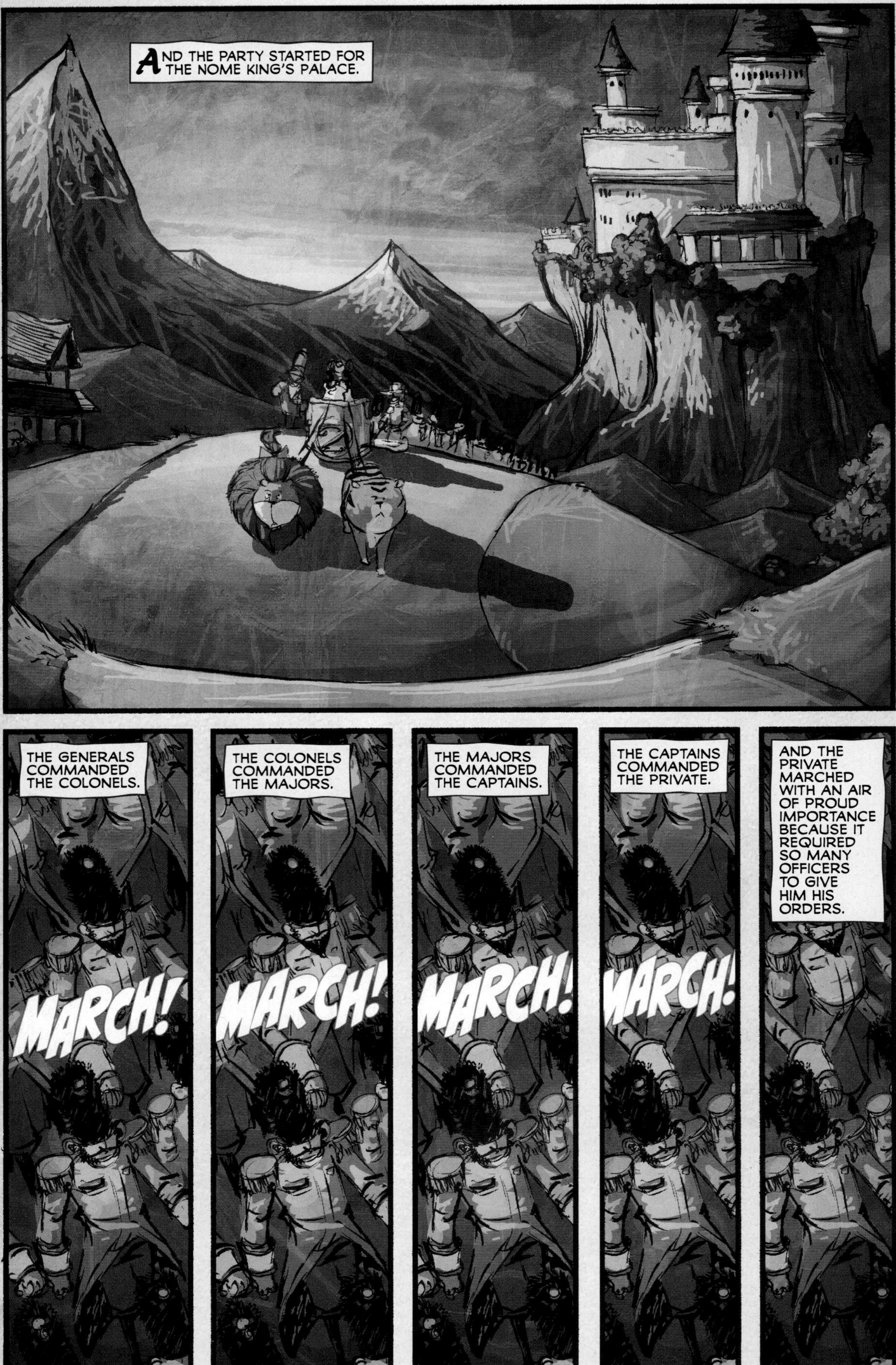
AND THE PARTY STARTED FOR THE NOME KING'S PALACE.
THE GENERALS COMMANDED THE COLONELS.
MARCH!
THE COLONELS COMMANDED THE MAJORS.
MARCH!
THE MAJORS COMMANDED THE CAPTAINS.
MARCH!
THE CAPTAINS COMMANDED THE PRIVATE.
MARCH!
AND THE PRIVATE MARCHED WITH AN AIR OF PROUD IMPORTANCE BECAUSE IT REQUIRED SO MANY OFFICERS TO GIVE HIM HIS ORDERS.

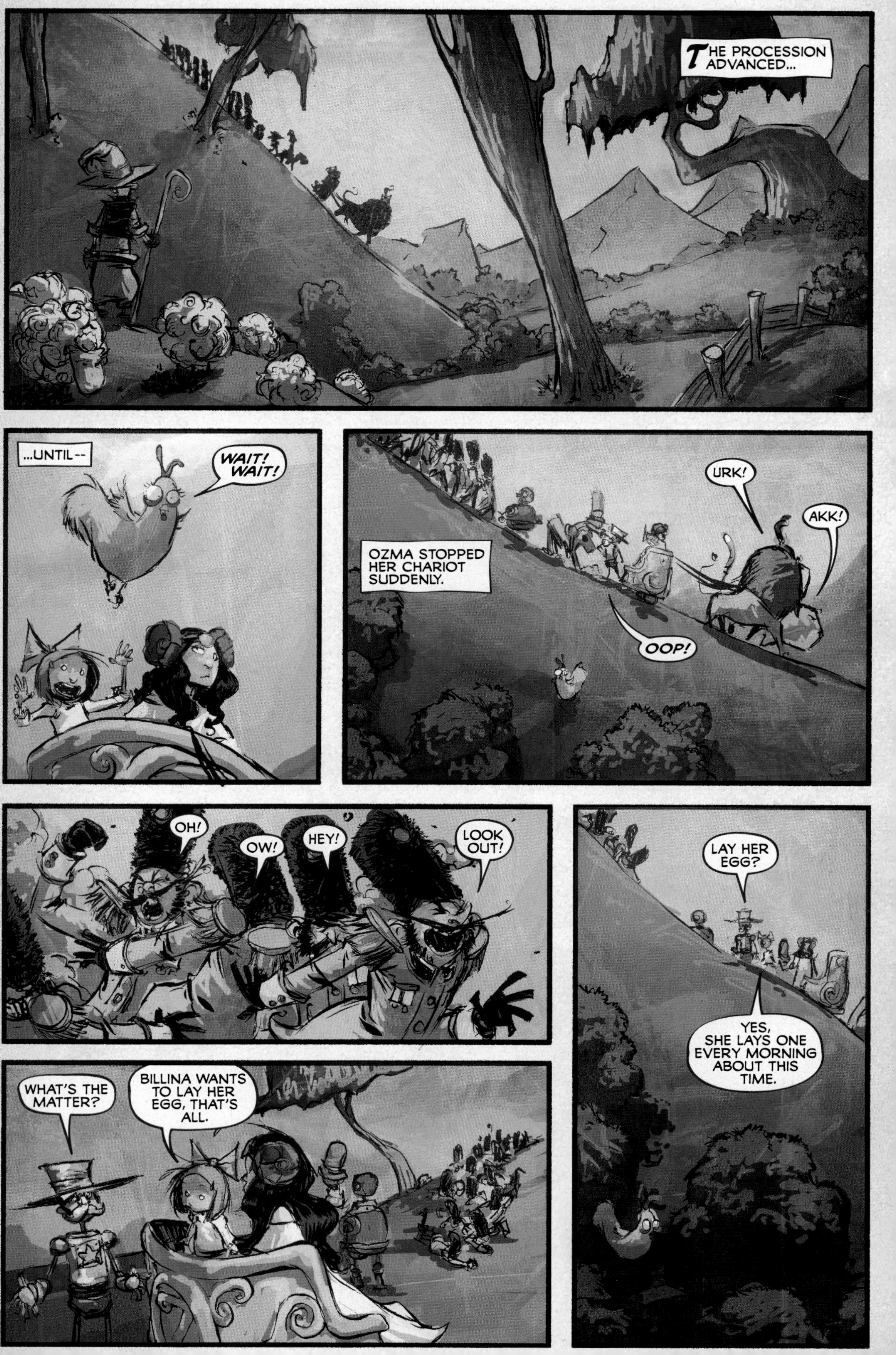
THE PROCESSION ADVANCED...
...UNTIL--
WAIT! WAIT!
OZMA STOPPED HER CHARIOT SUDDENLY.
URK!
AKK!
OOP!
OH!
OW!
HEY!
LOOK OUT!
WHAT'S THE MATTER?
BILLINA WANTS TO LAY HER EGG, THAT'S ALL.
LAY HER EGG?
YES, SHE LAYS ONE EVERY MORNING ABOUT THIS TIME.

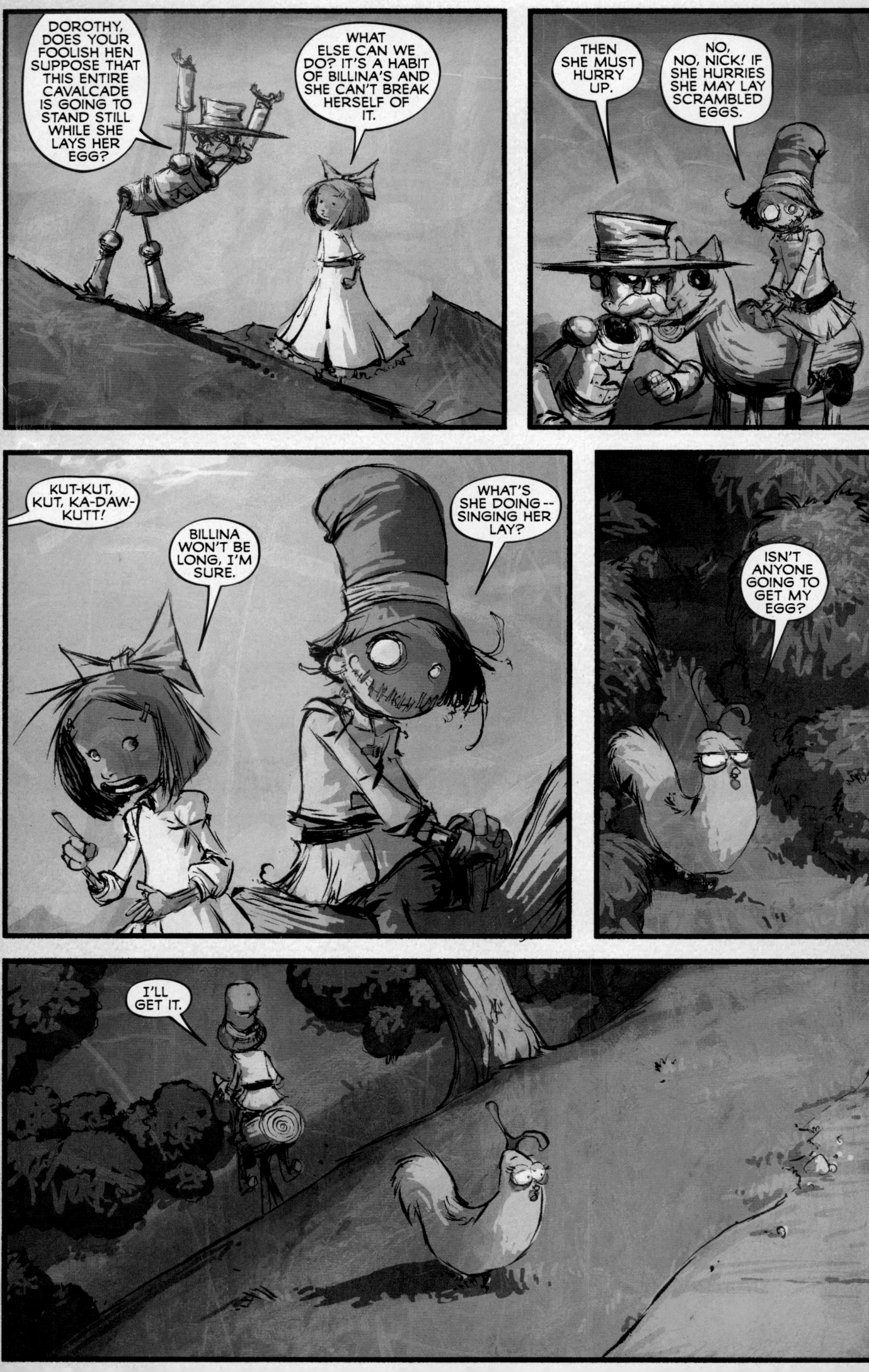
DOROTHY, DOES YOUR FOOLISH HEN SUPPOSE THAT THIS ENTIRE CAVALCADE IS GOING TO STAND STILL WHILE SHE LAYS HER EGG?
WHAT ELSE CAN WE DO? IT'S A HABIT OF BILLINA'S AND SHE CAN'T BREAK HERSELF OF IT.
THEN SHE MUST HURRY UP.
NO, NO, NICK! IF SHE HURRIES SHE MAY LAY SCRAMBLED EGGS.
KUT-KUT, KUT, KA-DAW-KUTT!
BILLINA WON'T BE LONG, I'M SURE.
WHAT'S SHE DOING -- SINGING HER LAY?
ISN'T ANYONE GOING TO GET MY EGG?
I'LL GET IT.

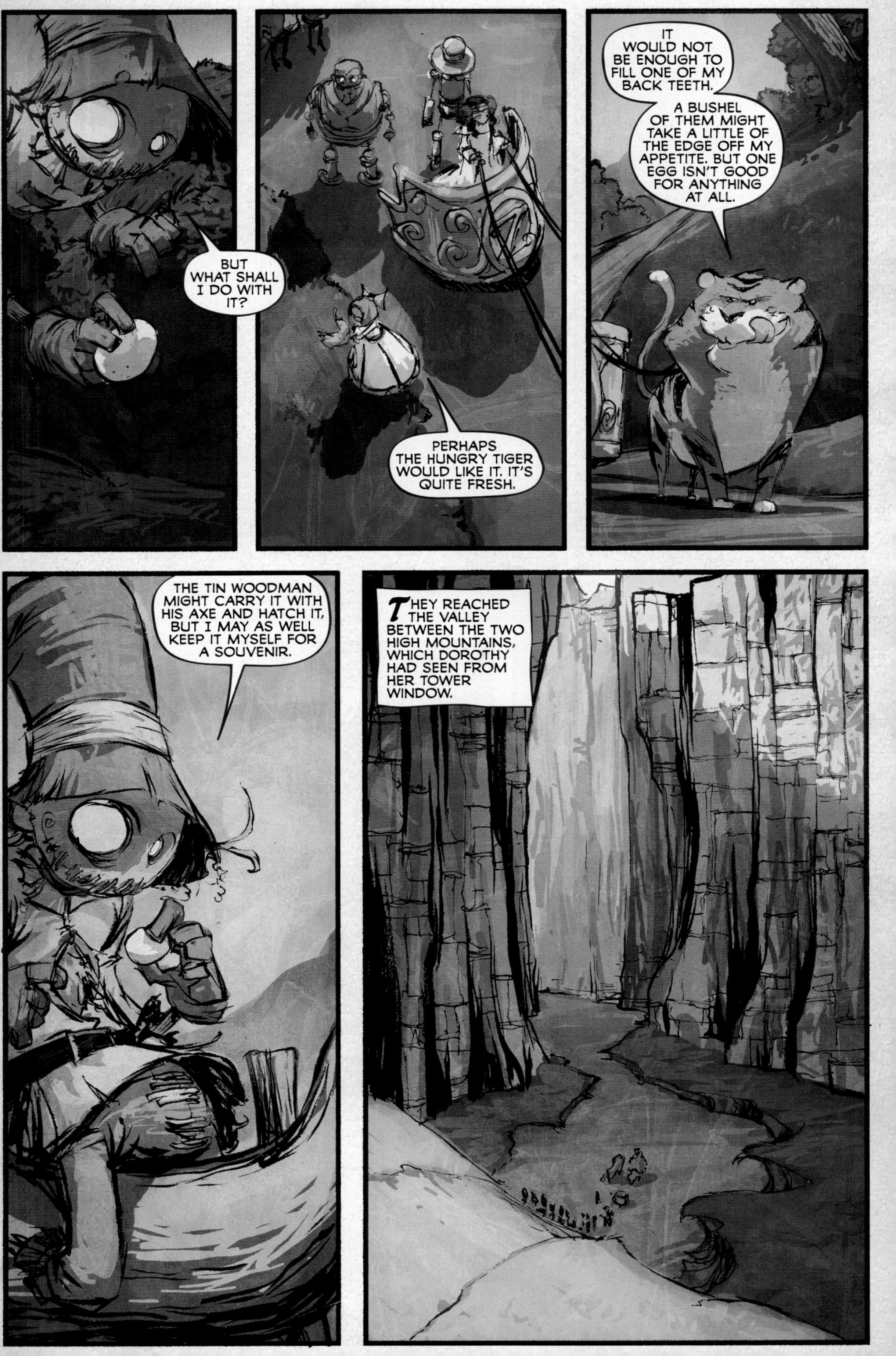
BUT WHAT SHALL I DO WITH IT?
PERHAPS THE HUNGRY TIGER WOULD LIKE IT. IT'S QUITE FRESH.
IT WOULD NOT BE ENOUGH TO FILL ONE OF MY BACK TEETH.
A BUSHEL OF THEM MIGHT TAKE A LITTLE OF THE EDGE OFF MY APPETITE. BUT ONE EGG ISN'T GOOD FOR ANYTHING AT ALL.
THE TIN WOODMAN MIGHT CARRY IT WITH HIS AXE AND HATCH IT, BUT I MAY AS WELL KEEP IT MYSELF FOR A SOUVENIR.
THEY REACHED THE VALLEY BETWEEN THE TWO HIGH MOUNTAINS, WHICH DOROTHY HAD SEEN FROM HER TOWER WINDOW.

THIS PATH IS BECOMING SO ROCKY, IT'S DIFFICULT FOR THE CHARIOT WHEELS TO PASS OVER.

SOON.

OZMA, THIS GULF IS TOO WIDE TO LEAP.

THE NOME KING'S PALACE IS SAID TO BE UNDERNEATH THE GREAT MOUNTAIN AT THE FAR END OF THIS VALLEY.

TO REACH IT, WE MUST VENTURE ON.

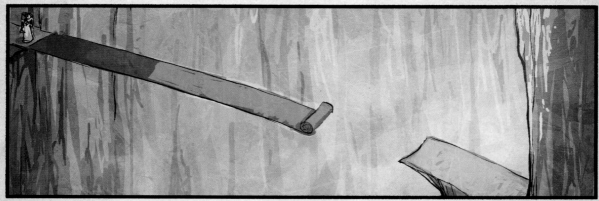

THIS IS EASY ENOUGH!

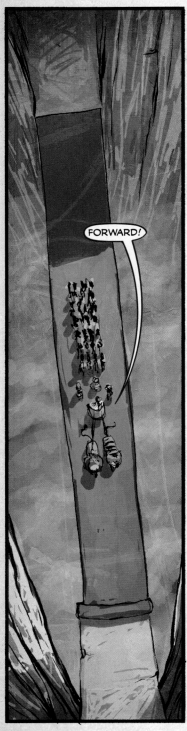

FORWARD!

*T*HEY CONTINUED ON.

Thump... Thump...

THUMP! THUMP!

WHAT IS THAT ECHOING SOUND?

It seems to grow loud-er as we ad-vance.

THUMP! THUMP!

THUMP!

OH!

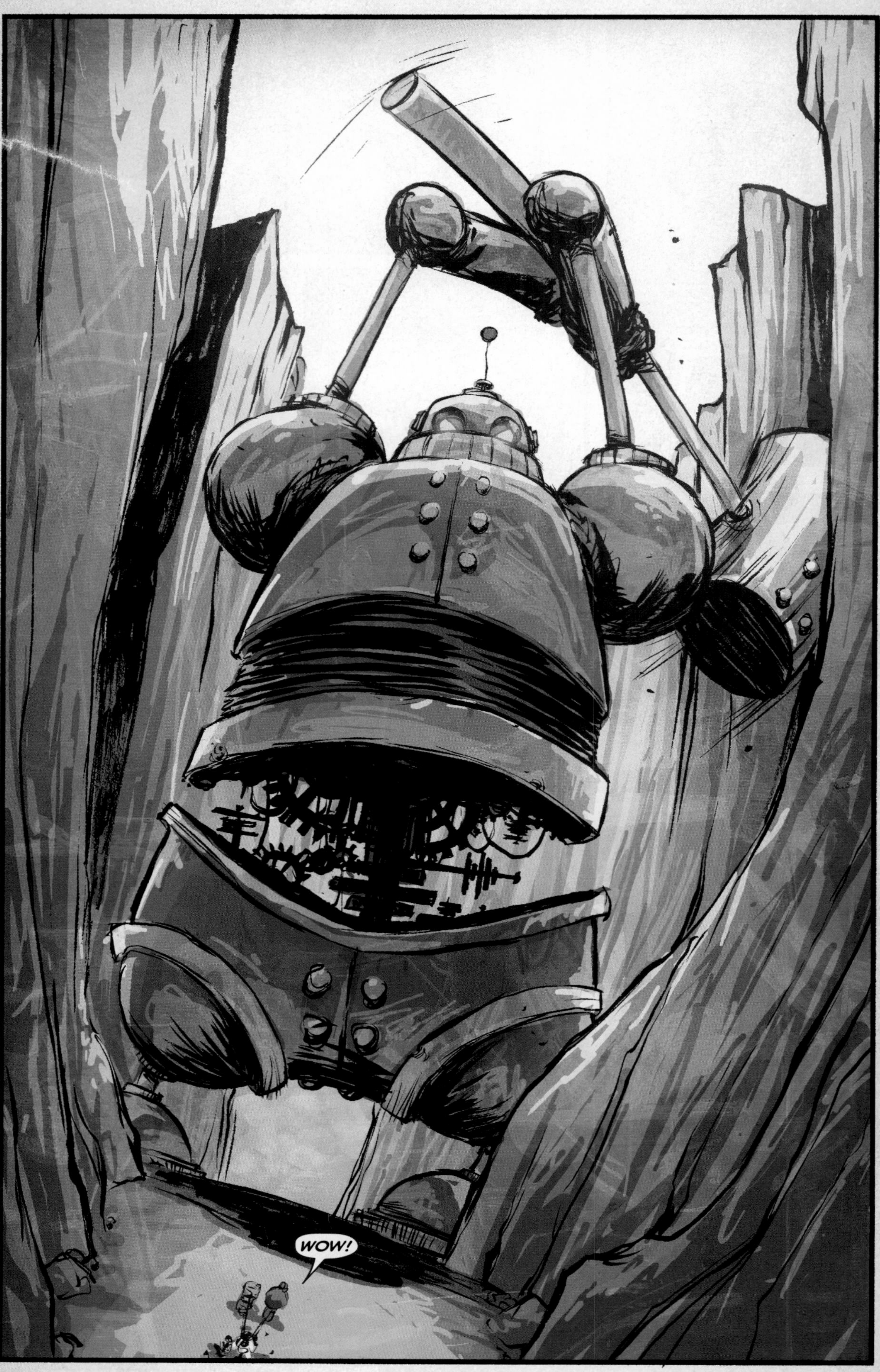
WOW!

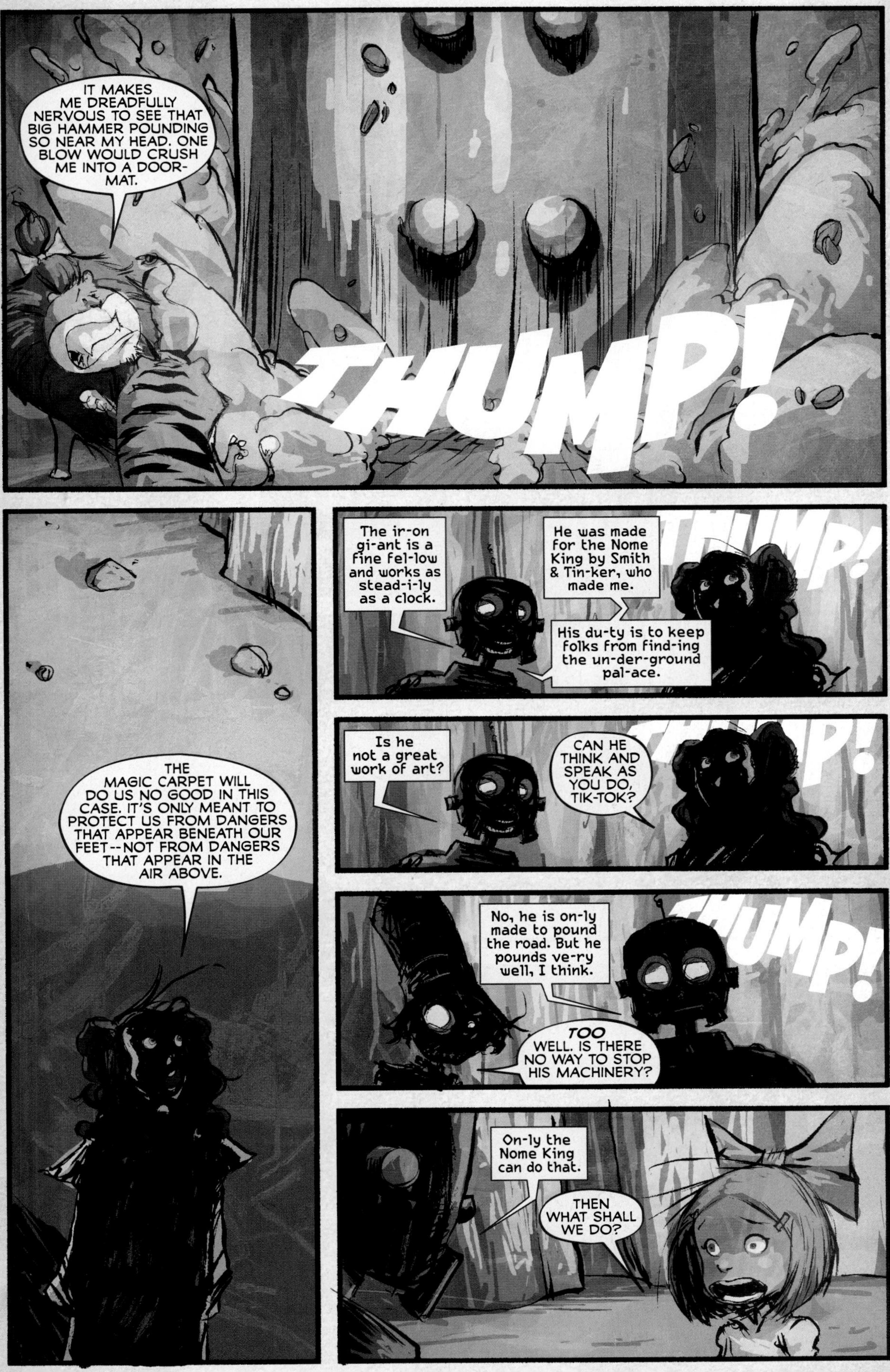
IT MAKES ME DREADFULLY NERVOUS TO SEE THAT BIG HAMMER POUNDING SO NEAR MY HEAD. ONE BLOW WOULD CRUSH ME INTO A DOOR-MAT.
THUMP!
THE MAGIC CARPET WILL DO US NO GOOD IN THIS CASE. IT'S ONLY MEANT TO PROTECT US FROM DANGERS THAT APPEAR BENEATH OUR FEET--NOT FROM DANGERS THAT APPEAR IN THE AIR ABOVE.
The ir-on gi-ant is a fine fel-low and works as stead-i-ly as a clock.
He was made for the Nome King by Smith & Tin-ker, who made me.
His du-ty is to keep folks from find-ing the un-der-ground pal-ace.
THUMP!
Is he not a great work of art?
CAN HE THINK AND SPEAK AS YOU DO, TIK-TOK?
THUMP!
No, he is on-ly made to pound the road. But he pounds ve-ry well, I think.
TOO WELL. IS THERE NO WAY TO STOP HIS MACHINERY?
THUMP!
On-ly the Nome King can do that.
THEN WHAT SHALL WE DO?

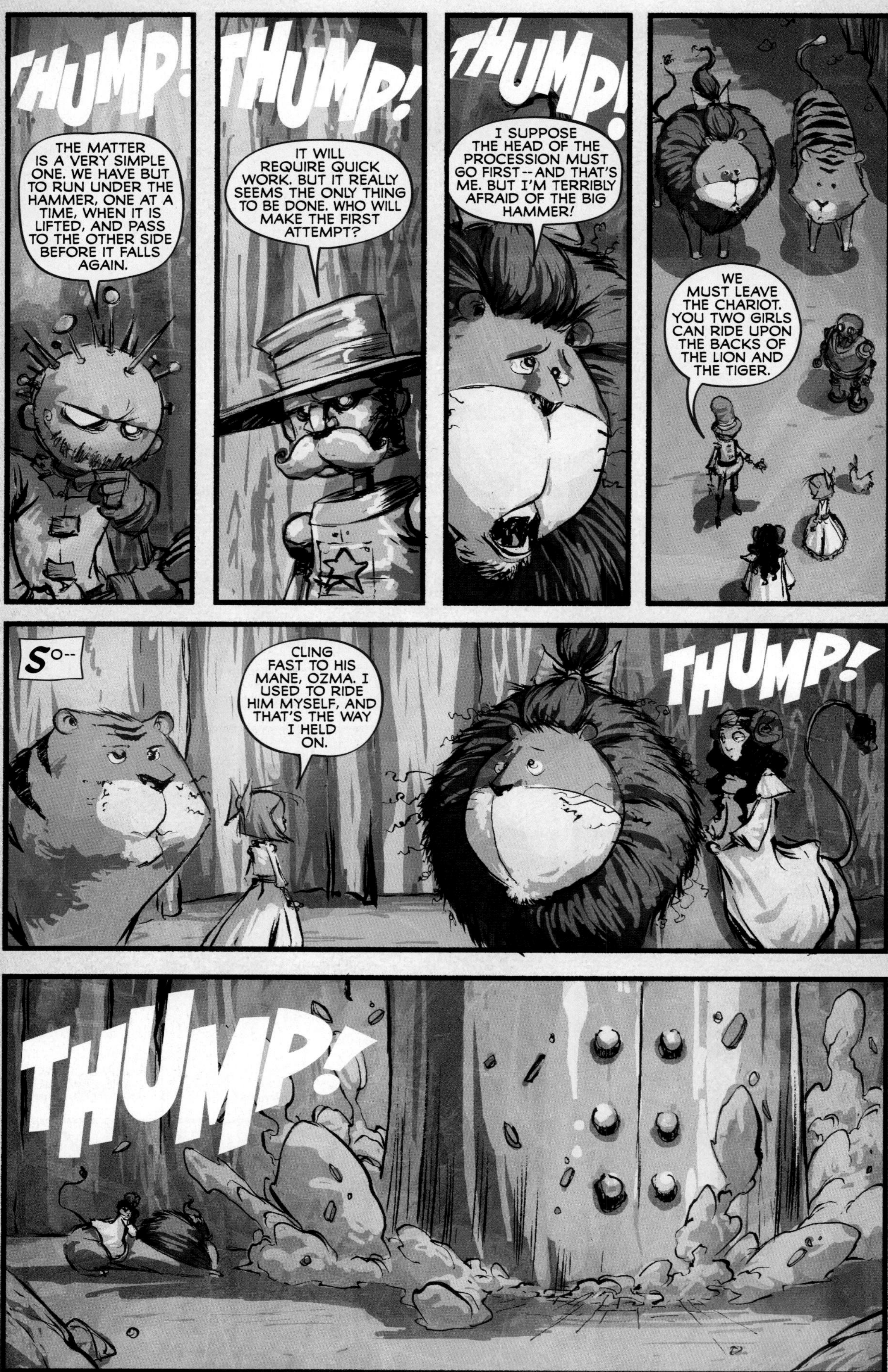
THUMP!
THE MATTER IS A VERY SIMPLE ONE. WE HAVE BUT TO RUN UNDER THE HAMMER, ONE AT A TIME, WHEN IT IS LIFTED, AND PASS TO THE OTHER SIDE BEFORE IT FALLS AGAIN.
THUMP!
IT WILL REQUIRE QUICK WORK. BUT IT REALLY SEEMS THE ONLY THING TO BE DONE. WHO WILL MAKE THE FIRST ATTEMPT?
THUMP!
I SUPPOSE THE HEAD OF THE PROCESSION MUST GO FIRST--AND THAT'S ME. BUT I'M TERRIBLY AFRAID OF THE BIG HAMMER!
WE MUST LEAVE THE CHARIOT. YOU TWO GIRLS CAN RIDE UPON THE BACKS OF THE LION AND THE TIGER.
SO--
CLING FAST TO HIS MANE, OZMA. I USED TO RIDE HIM MYSELF, AND THAT'S THE WAY I HELD ON.
THUMP!
THUMP!

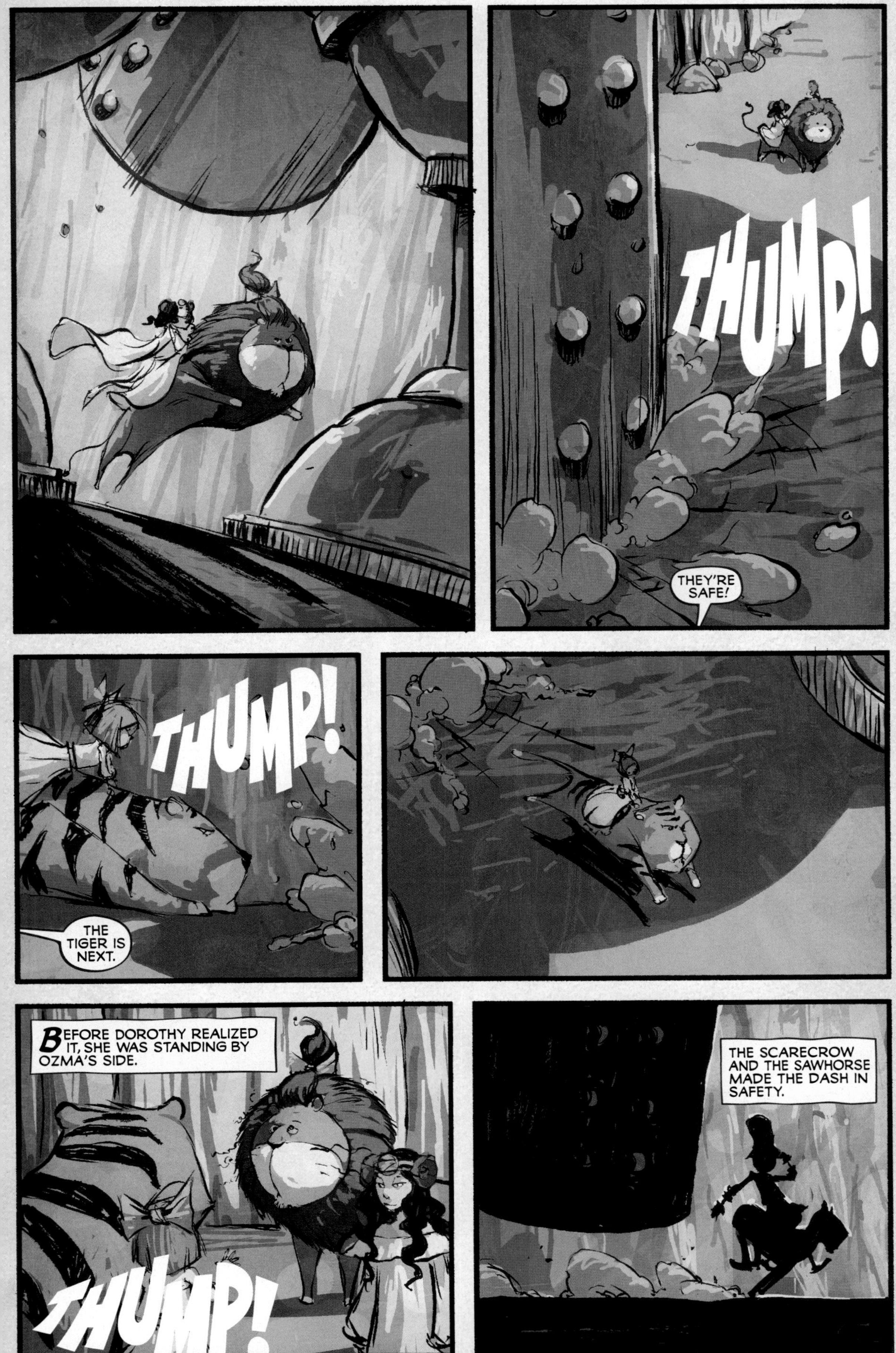
THUMP!
THEY'RE SAFE!
THUMP!
THE TIGER IS NEXT.
BEFORE DOROTHY REALIZED IT, SHE WAS STANDING BY OZMA'S SIDE.
THUMP!
THE SCARECROW AND THE SAWHORSE MADE THE DASH IN SAFETY.

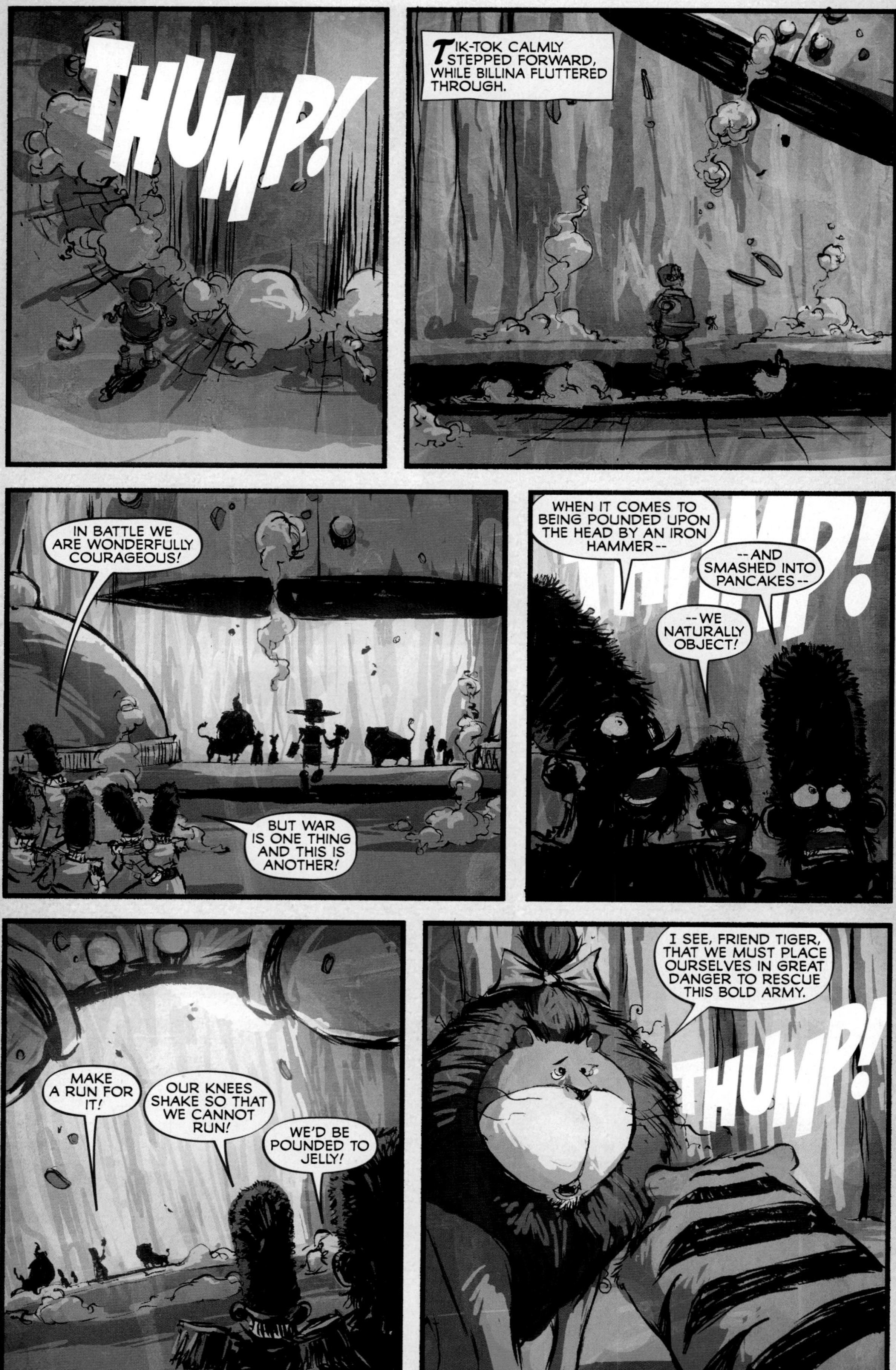
THUMP!
TIK-TOK CALMLY STEPPED FORWARD, WHILE BILLINA FLUTTERED THROUGH.
IN BATTLE WE ARE WONDERFULLY COURAGEOUS!
BUT WAR IS ONE THING AND THIS IS ANOTHER!
WHEN IT COMES TO BEING POUNDED UPON THE HEAD BY AN IRON HAMMER--
--AND SMASHED INTO PANCAKES--
--WE NATURALLY OBJECT!
MAKE A RUN FOR IT!
OUR KNEES SHAKE SO THAT WE CANNOT RUN!
WE'D BE POUNDED TO JELLY!
I SEE, FRIEND TIGER, THAT WE MUST PLACE OURSELVES IN GREAT DANGER TO RESCUE THIS BOLD ARMY.
THUMP!

THE LION AND THE TIGER REPEATED THEIR DARING PASSAGE MANY TIMES.

WHAT IS TO BECOME OF THE PRIVATE?

OH, LEAVE HIM THERE. I'M TIRED OUT, AND WON'T PASS UNDER THAT MALLET AGAIN.

WE MUST HAVE THE PRIVATE!

YES, YES!

OR ELSE THERE WOULD BE NO ONE FOR US TO COMMAND!

SO THE SCARECROW SENT THE SAWHORSE.

THUMP!

BUT--

THUMP!

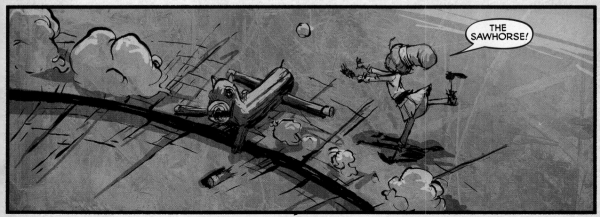

THE SAWHORSE!

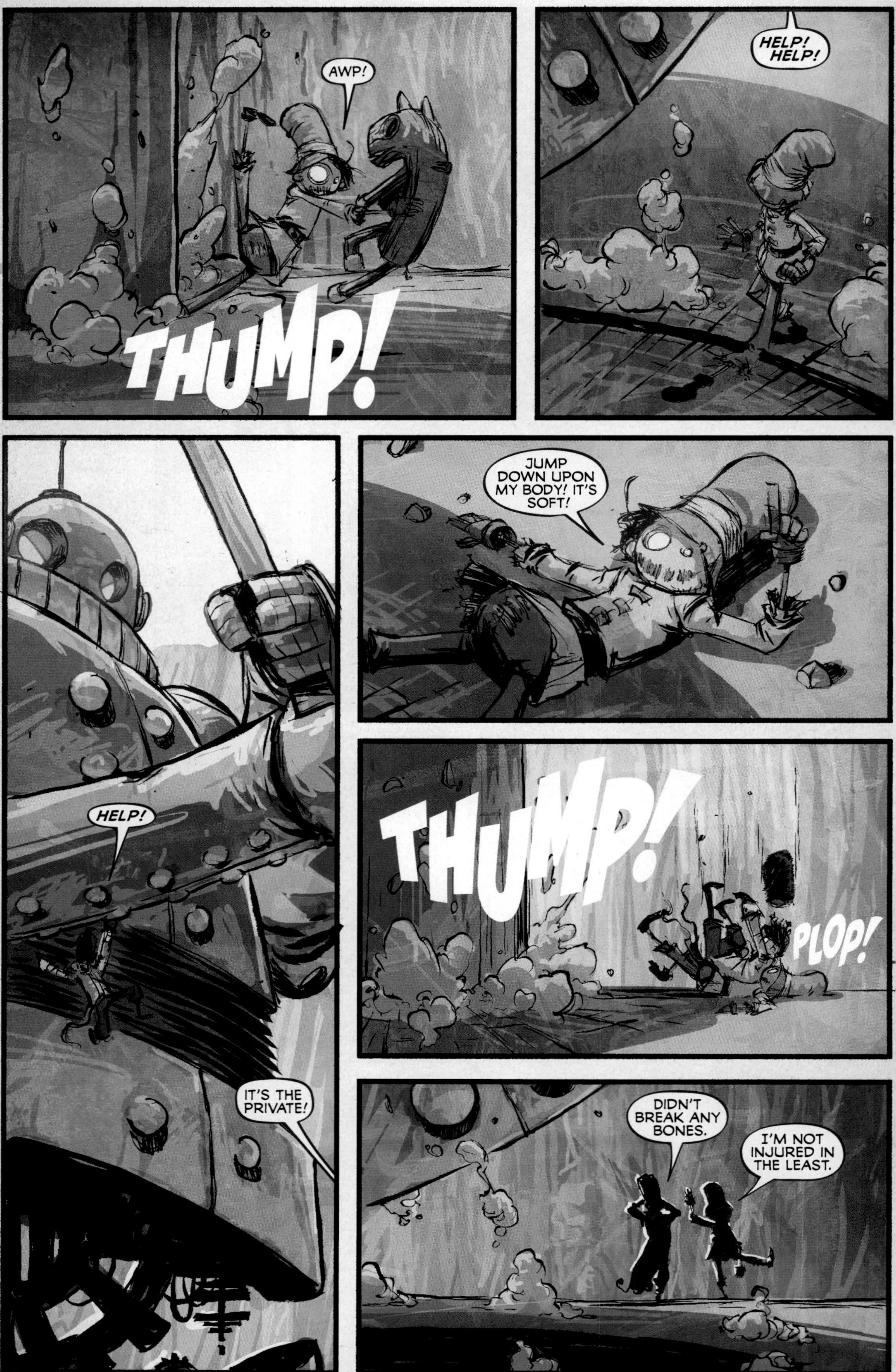
AWP!
THUMP!
HELP! HELP!
HELP!
IT'S THE PRIVATE!
JUMP DOWN UPON MY BODY! IT'S SOFT!
THUMP!
PLOP!
DIDN'T BREAK ANY BONES.
I'M NOT INJURED IN THE LEAST.

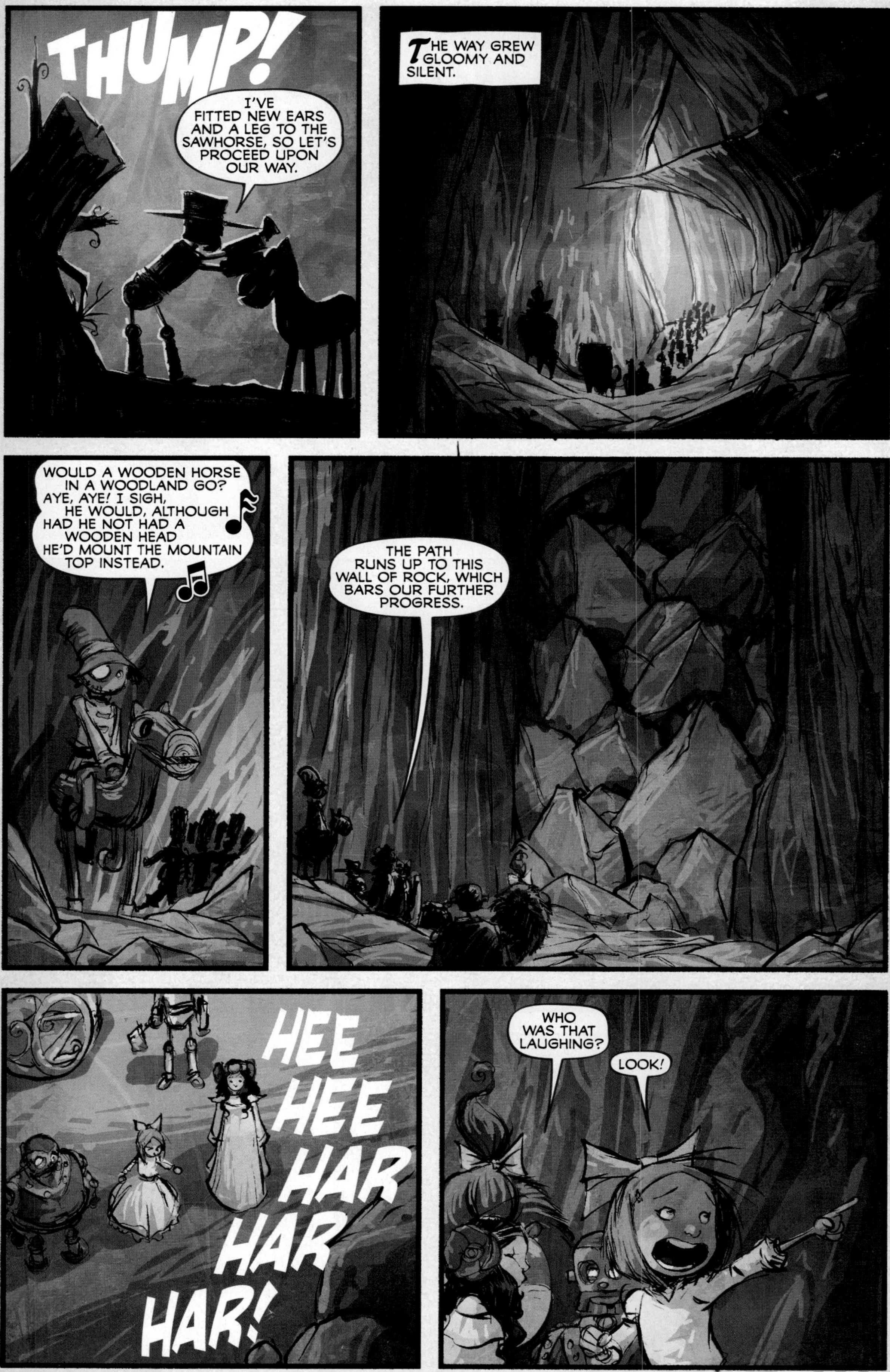
THUMP!
I'VE FITTED NEW EARS AND A LEG TO THE SAWHORSE, SO LET'S PROCEED UPON OUR WAY.
THE WAY GREW GLOOMY AND SILENT.
WOULD A WOODEN HORSE IN A WOODLAND GO? AYE, AYE! I SIGH, HE WOULD, ALTHOUGH HAD HE NOT HAD A WOODEN HEAD HE'D MOUNT THE MOUNTAIN TOP INSTEAD.
THE PATH RUNS UP TO THIS WALL OF ROCK, WHICH BARS OUR FURTHER PROGRESS.
HEE HEE HAR HAR HAR!
WHO WAS THAT LAUGHING?
LOOK!

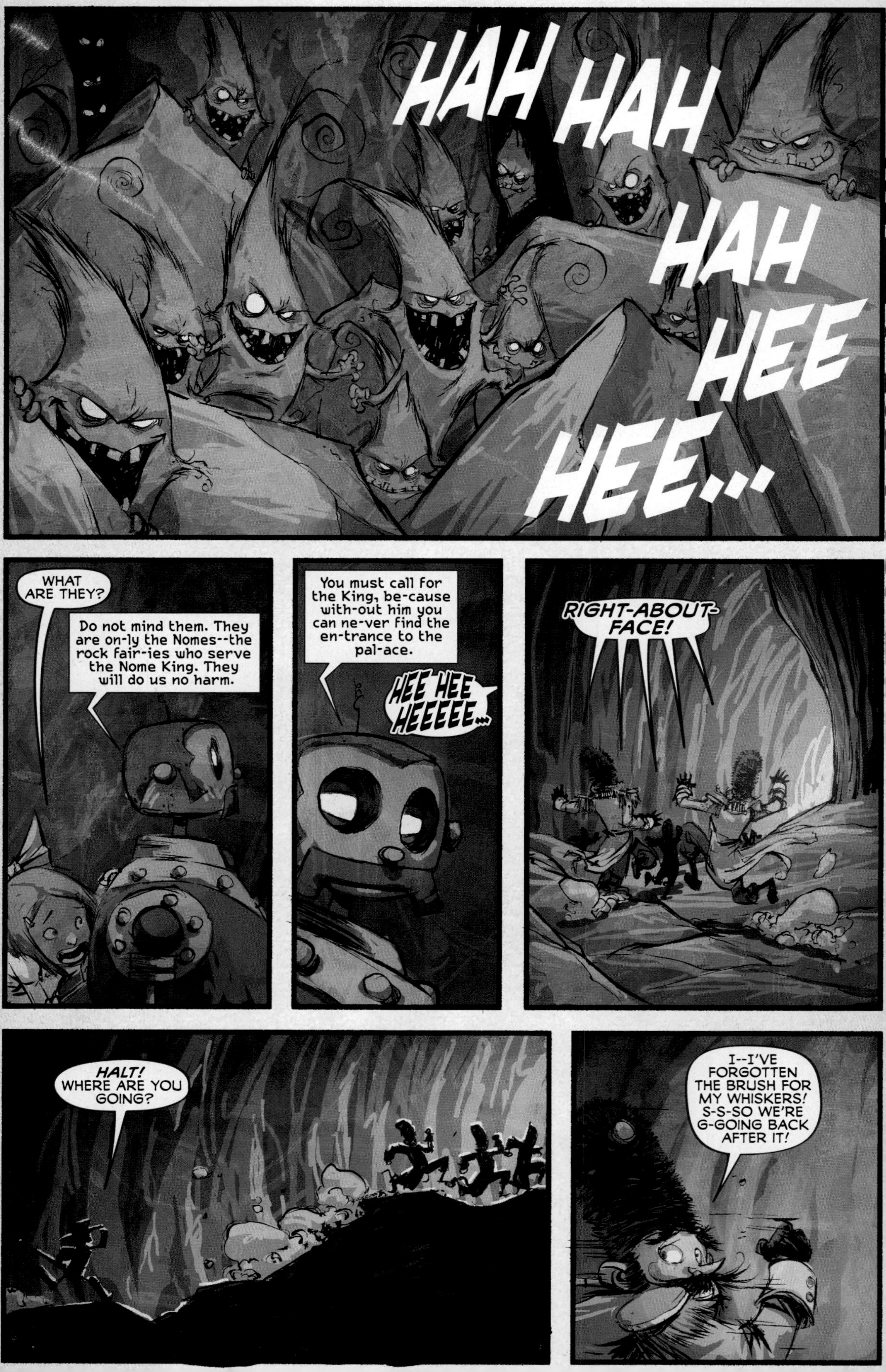
HAH HAH HAH HEE HEE...
WHAT ARE THEY?
Do not mind them. They are on-ly the Nomes--the rock fair-ies who serve the Nome King. They will do us no harm.
You must call for the King, be-cause with-out him you can ne-ver find the en-trance to the pal-ace.
HEE HEE HEEEEE...
RIGHT-ABOUT-FACE!
HALT! WHERE ARE YOU GOING?
I--I'VE FORGOTTEN THE BRUSH FOR MY WHISKERS! S-S-SO WE'RE G-GOING BACK AFTER IT!

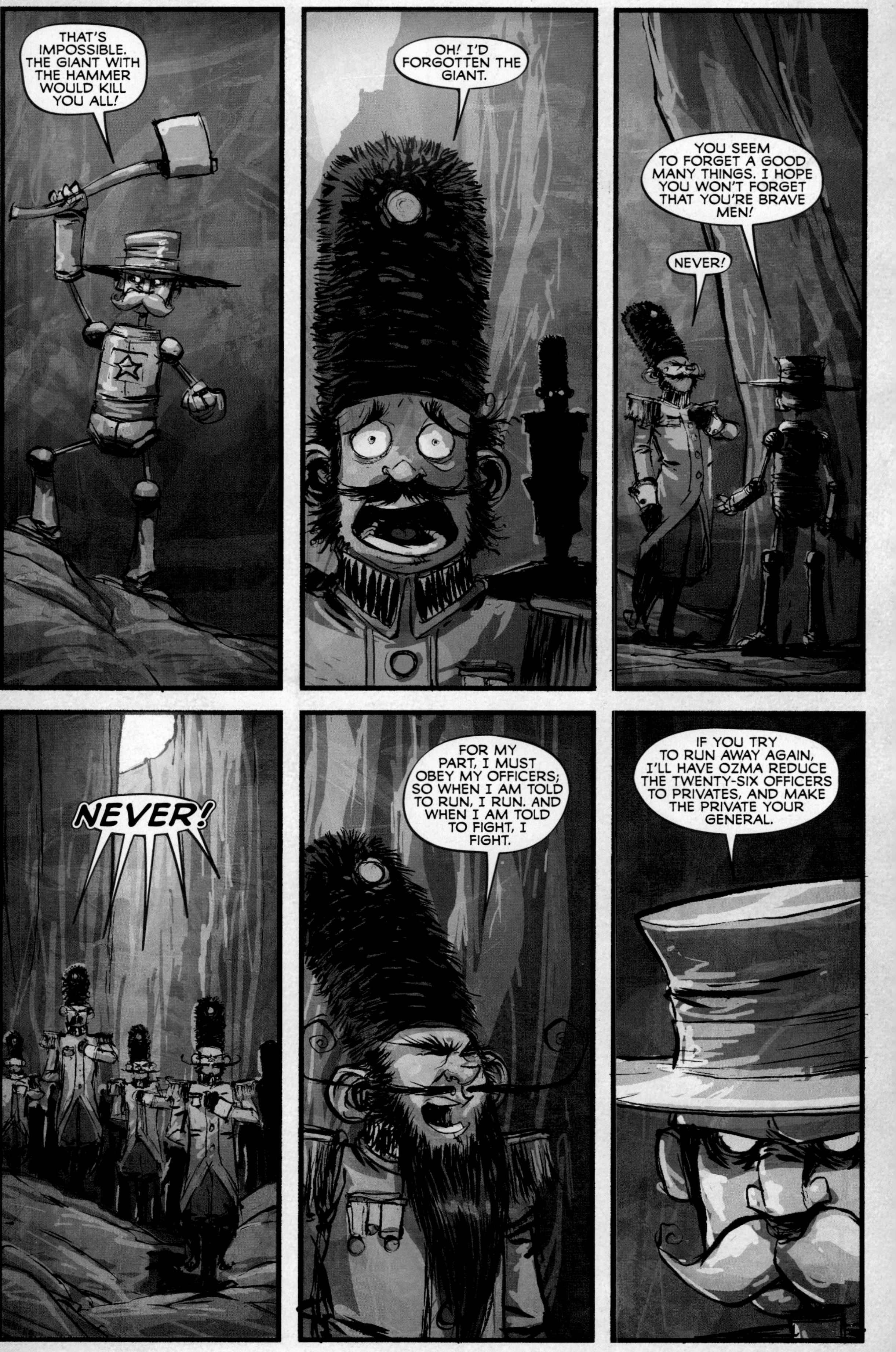
THAT'S IMPOSSIBLE. THE GIANT WITH THE HAMMER WOULD KILL YOU ALL!
OH! I'D FORGOTTEN THE GIANT.
YOU SEEM TO FORGET A GOOD MANY THINGS. I HOPE YOU WON'T FORGET THAT YOU'RE BRAVE MEN!
NEVER!
NEVER!
FOR MY PART, I MUST OBEY MY OFFICERS; SO WHEN I AM TOLD TO RUN, I RUN. AND WHEN I AM TOLD TO FIGHT, I FIGHT.
IF YOU TRY TO RUN AWAY AGAIN, I'LL HAVE OZMA REDUCE THE TWENTY-SIX OFFICERS TO PRIVATES, AND MAKE THE PRIVATE YOUR GENERAL.

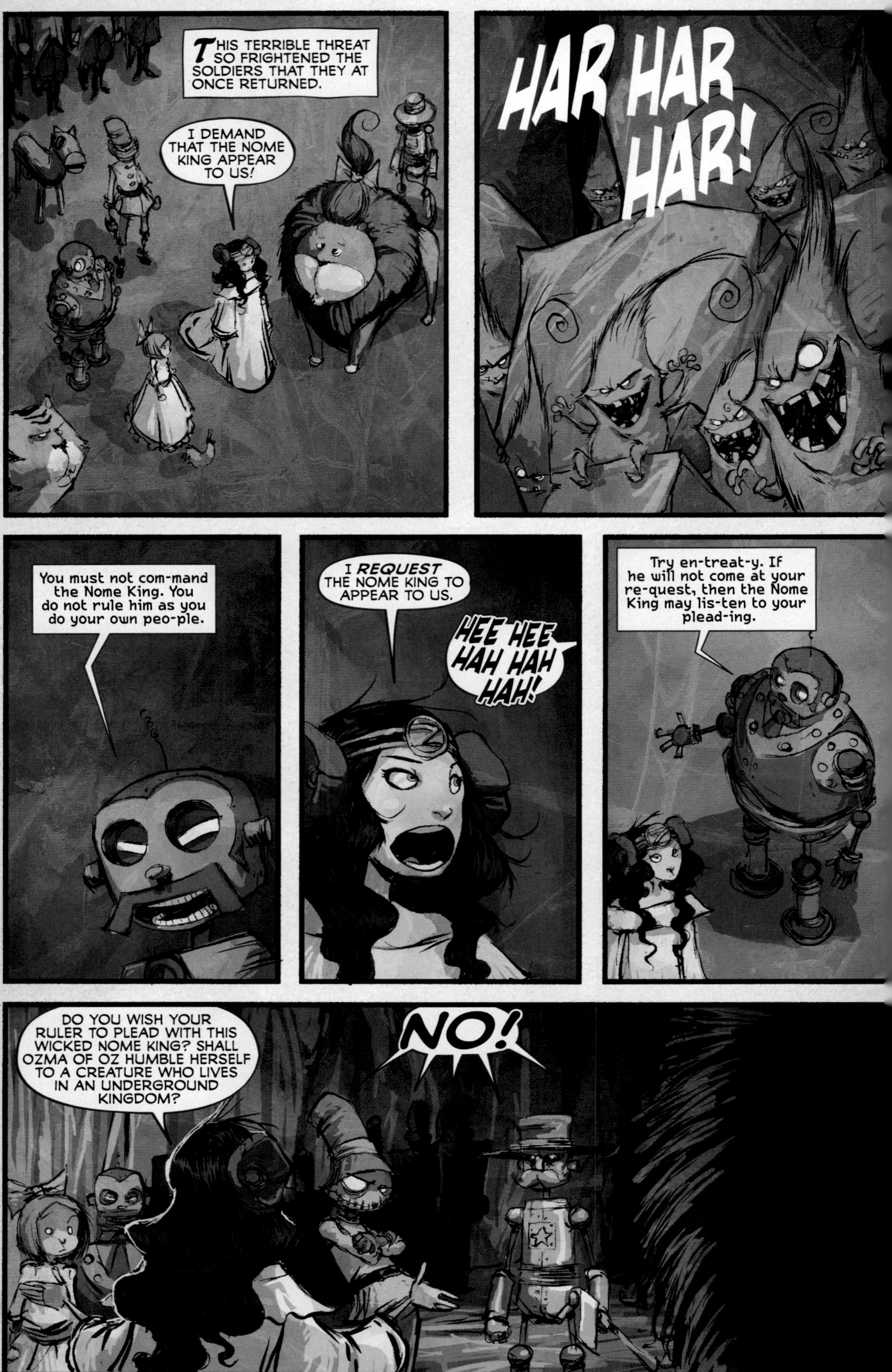
THIS TERRIBLE THREAT SO FRIGHTENED THE SOLDIERS THAT THEY AT ONCE RETURNED.
I DEMAND THAT THE NOME KING APPEAR TO US!
HAR HAR HAR!
You must not com-mand the Nome King. You do not rule him as you do your own peo-ple.
I REQUEST THE NOME KING TO APPEAR TO US.
HEE HEE HAH HAH HAH!
Try en-treat-y. If he will not come at your re-quest, then the Nome King may lis-ten to your plead-ing.
DO YOU WISH YOUR RULER TO PLEAD WITH THIS WICKED NOME KING? SHALL OZMA OF OZ HUMBLE HERSELF TO A CREATURE WHO LIVES IN AN UNDERGROUND KINGDOM?
NO!

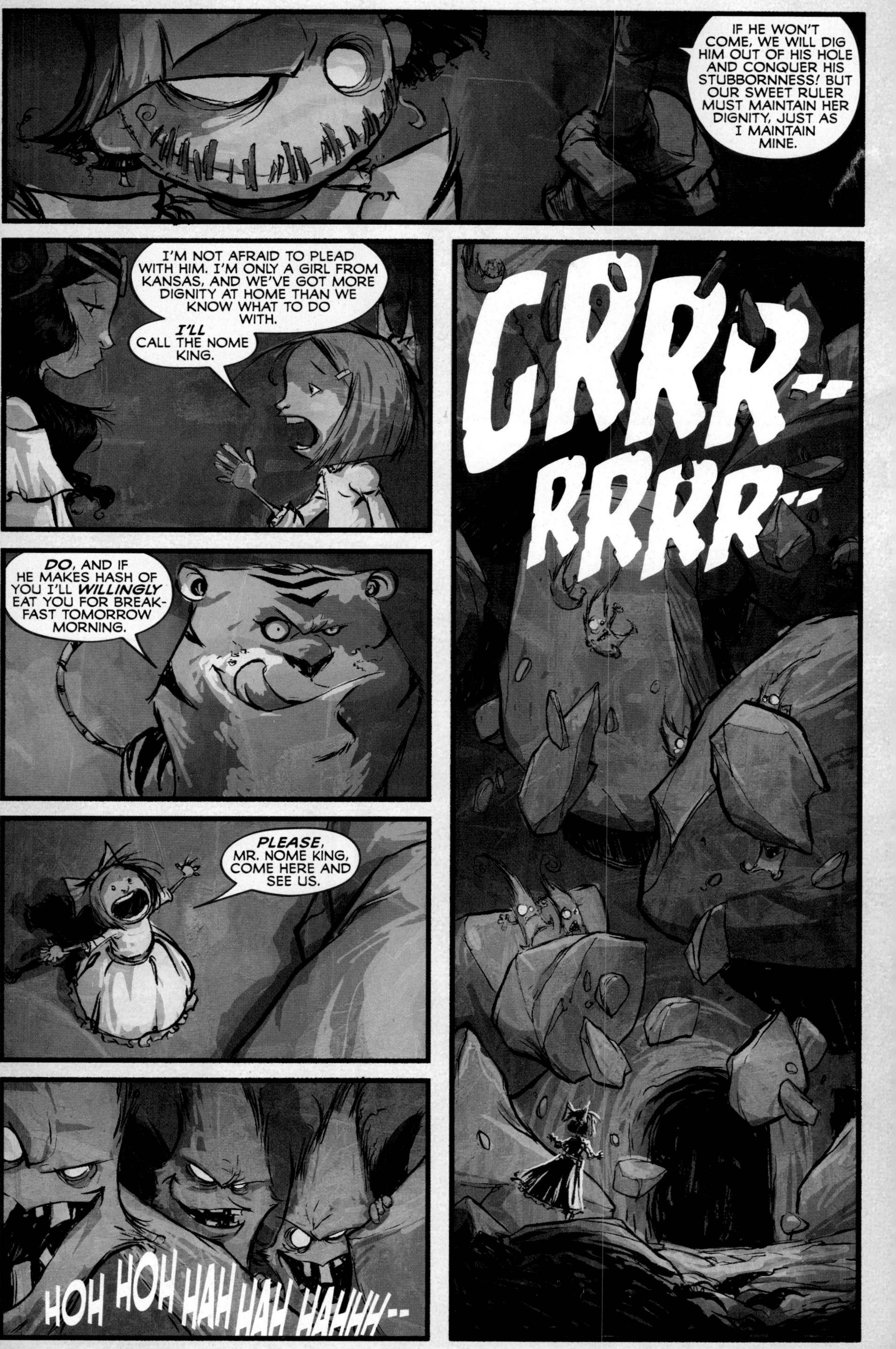
IF HE WON'T COME, WE WILL DIG HIM OUT OF HIS HOLE AND CONQUER HIS STUBBORNNESS! BUT OUR SWEET RULER MUST MAINTAIN HER DIGNITY, JUST AS I MAINTAIN MINE.
I'M NOT AFRAID TO PLEAD WITH HIM. I'M ONLY A GIRL FROM KANSAS, AND WE'VE GOT MORE DIGNITY AT HOME THAN WE KNOW WHAT TO DO WITH.
I'LL CALL THE NOME KING.
DO, AND IF HE MAKES HASH OF YOU I'LL WILLINGLY EAT YOU FOR BREAKFAST TOMORROW MORNING.
PLEASE, MR. NOME KING, COME HERE AND SEE US.
HOH HOH HAH HAH HAHHH--
GRRR-RRRR--

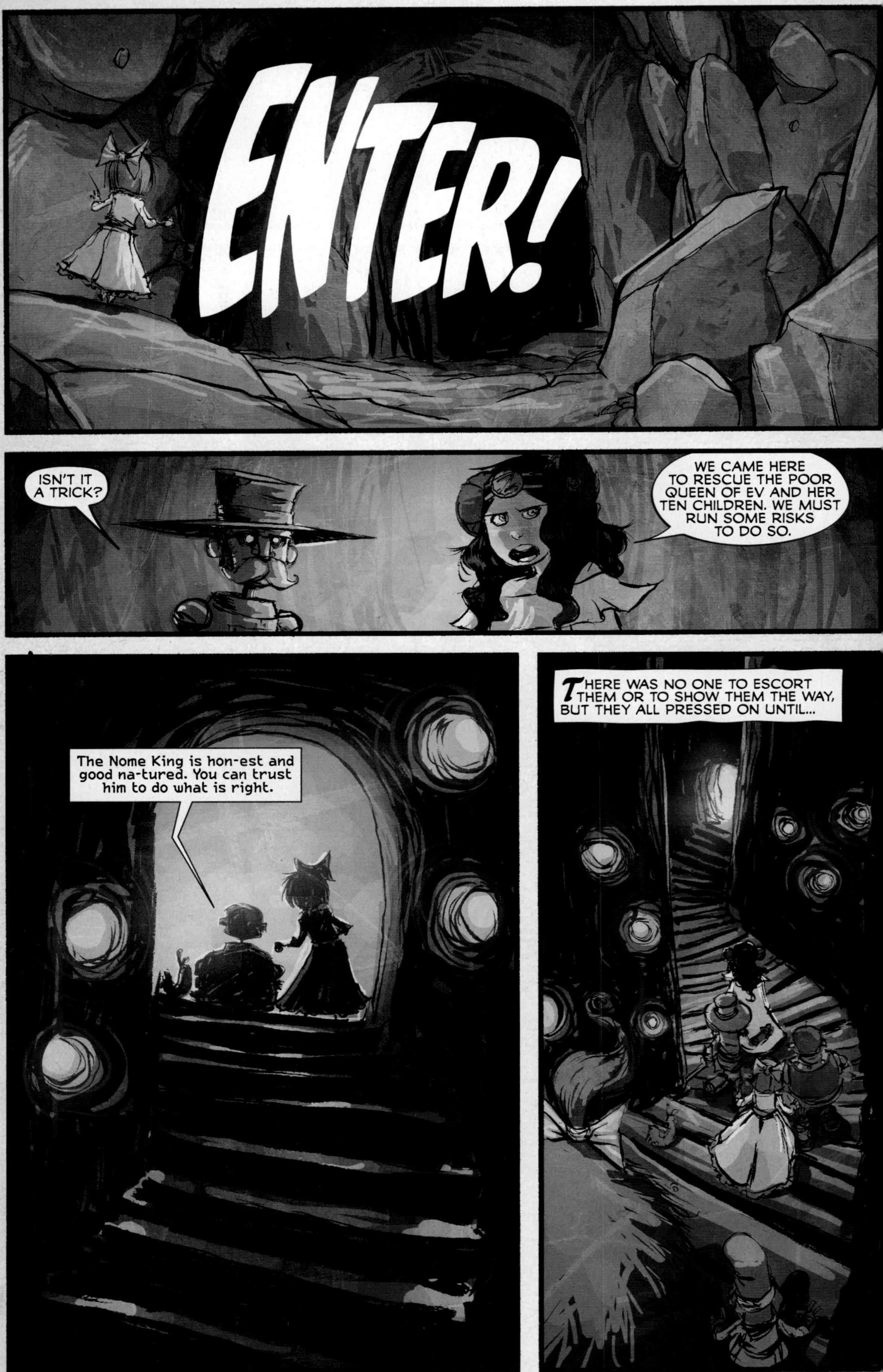
ENTER!
ISN'T IT A TRICK?
WE CAME HERE TO RESCUE THE POOR QUEEN OF EV AND HER TEN CHILDREN. WE MUST RUN SOME RISKS TO DO SO.
The Nome King is hon-est and good na-tured. You can trust him to do what is right.
THERE WAS NO ONE TO ESCORT THEM OR TO SHOW THEM THE WAY, BUT THEY ALL PRESSED ON UNTIL...

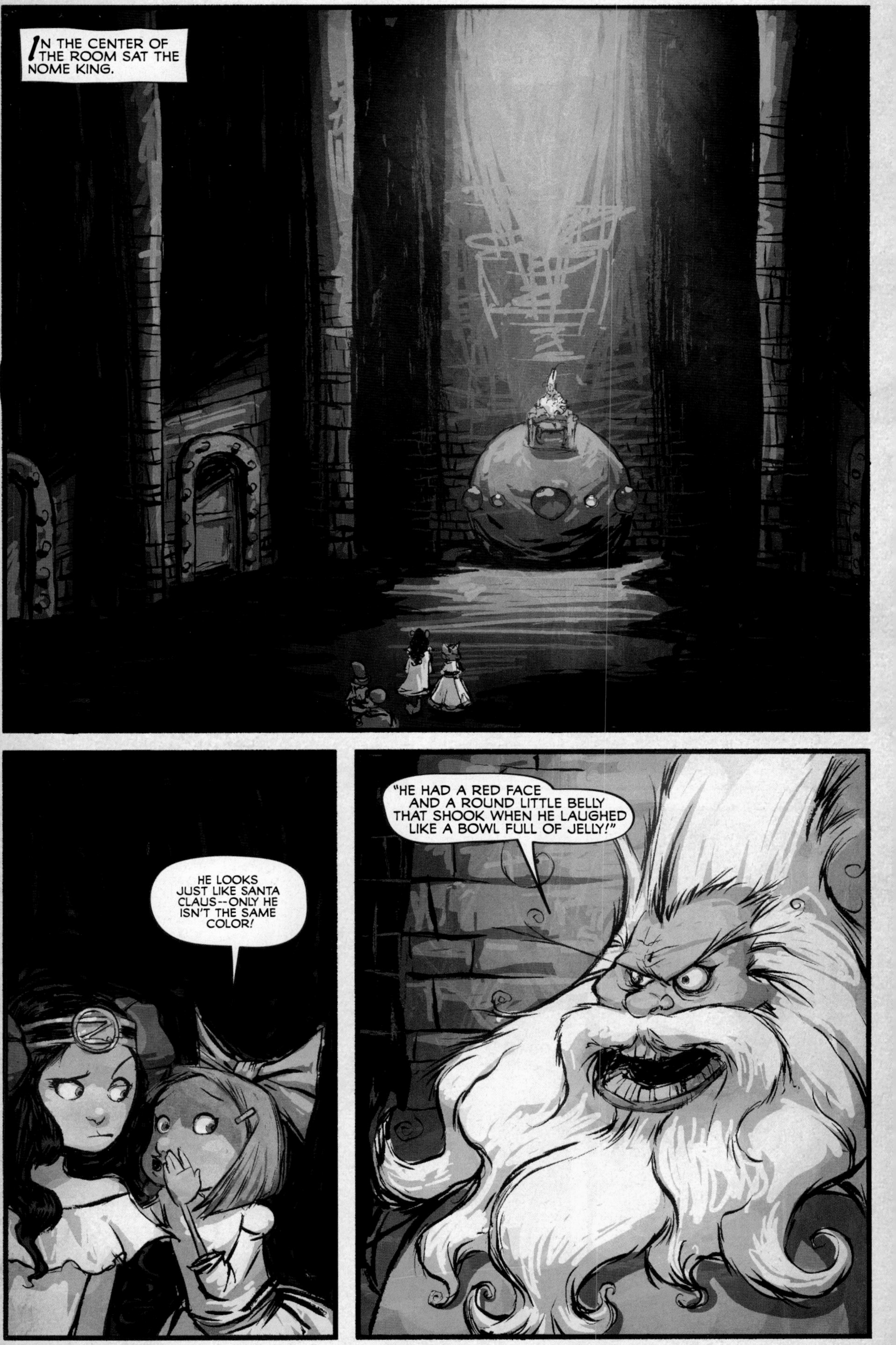
IN THE CENTER OF THE ROOM SAT THE NOME KING.
HE LOOKS JUST LIKE SANTA CLAUS--ONLY HE ISN'T THE SAME COLOR!
"HE HAD A RED FACE AND A ROUND LITTLE BELLY THAT SHOOK WHEN HE LAUGHED LIKE A BOWL FULL OF JELLY!"

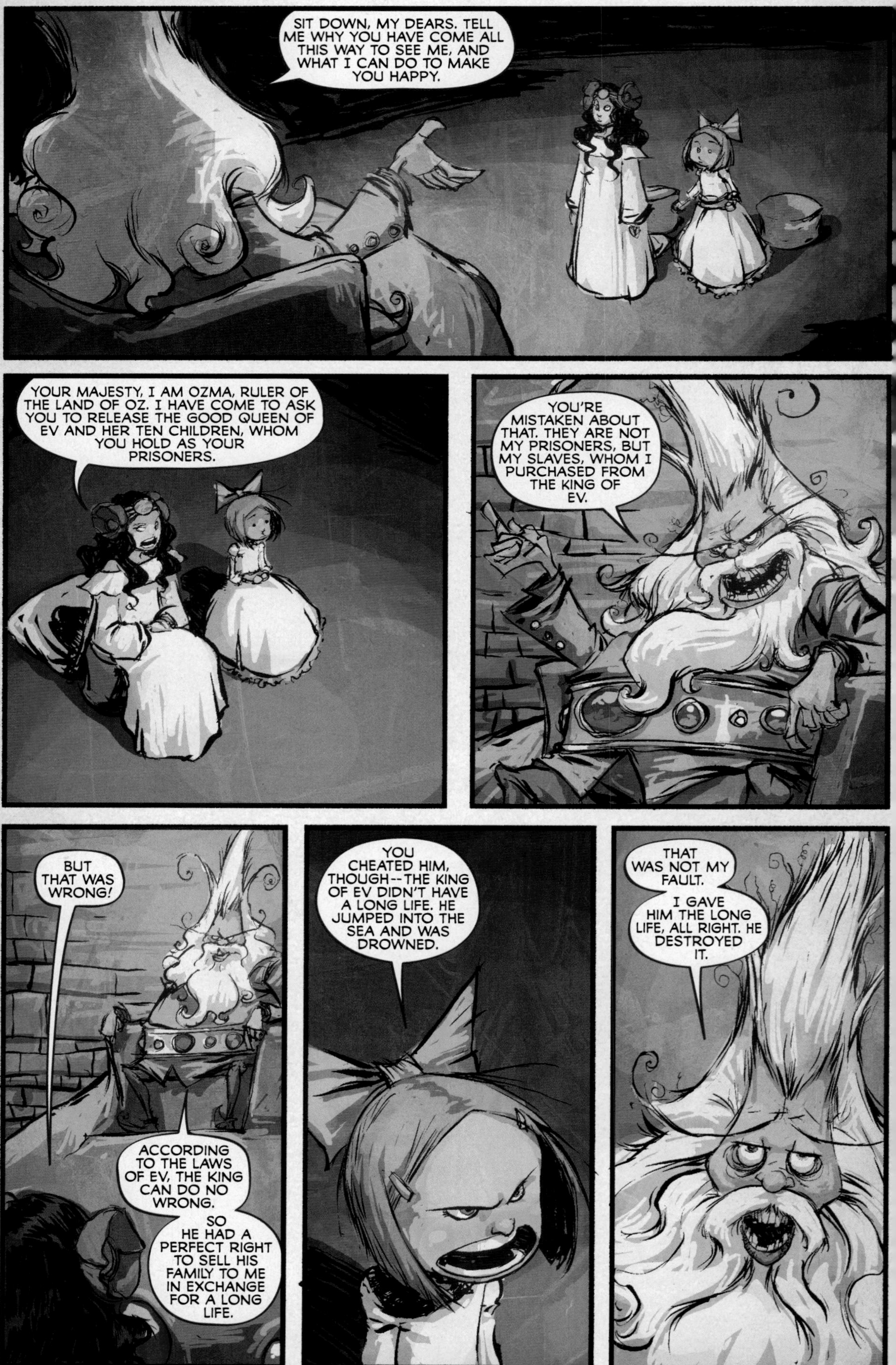
SIT DOWN, MY DEARS. TELL ME WHY YOU HAVE COME ALL THIS WAY TO SEE ME, AND WHAT I CAN DO TO MAKE YOU HAPPY.
YOUR MAJESTY, I AM OZMA, RULER OF THE LAND OF OZ. I HAVE COME TO ASK YOU TO RELEASE THE GOOD QUEEN OF EV AND HER TEN CHILDREN, WHOM YOU HOLD AS YOUR PRISONERS.
YOU'RE MISTAKEN ABOUT THAT. THEY ARE NOT MY PRISONERS, BUT MY SLAVES, WHOM I PURCHASED FROM THE KING OF EV.
BUT THAT WAS WRONG!
ACCORDING TO THE LAWS OF EV, THE KING CAN DO NO WRONG.
SO HE HAD A PERFECT RIGHT TO SELL HIS FAMILY TO ME IN EXCHANGE FOR A LONG LIFE.
YOU CHEATED HIM, THOUGH--THE KING OF EV DIDN'T HAVE A LONG LIFE. HE JUMPED INTO THE SEA AND WAS DROWNED.
THAT WAS NOT MY FAULT.
I GAVE HIM THE LONG LIFE, ALL RIGHT. HE DESTROYED IT.

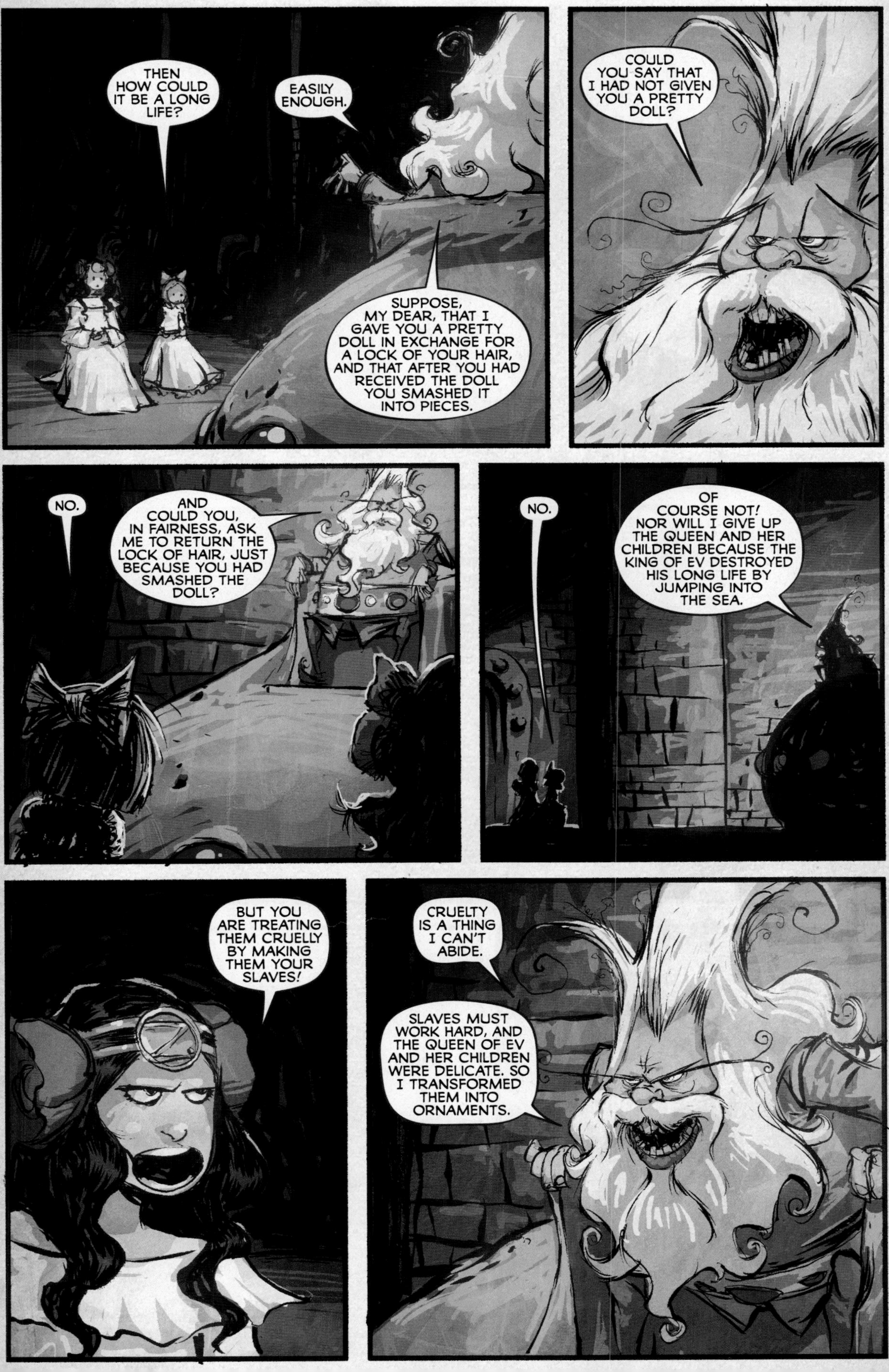
THEN HOW COULD IT BE A LONG LIFE?
EASILY ENOUGH.
SUPPOSE, MY DEAR, THAT I GAVE YOU A PRETTY DOLL IN EXCHANGE FOR A LOCK OF YOUR HAIR, AND THAT AFTER YOU HAD RECEIVED THE DOLL YOU SMASHED IT INTO PIECES.
COULD YOU SAY THAT I HAD NOT GIVEN YOU A PRETTY DOLL?
NO.
AND COULD YOU, IN FAIRNESS, ASK ME TO RETURN THE LOCK OF HAIR, JUST BECAUSE YOU HAD SMASHED THE DOLL?
NO.
OF COURSE NOT! NOR WILL I GIVE UP THE QUEEN AND HER CHILDREN BECAUSE THE KING OF EV DESTROYED HIS LONG LIFE BY JUMPING INTO THE SEA.
BUT YOU ARE TREATING THEM CRUELLY BY MAKING THEM YOUR SLAVES!
CRUELTY IS A THING I CAN'T ABIDE.
SLAVES MUST WORK HARD, AND THE QUEEN OF EV AND HER CHILDREN WERE DELICATE. SO I TRANSFORMED THEM INTO ORNAMENTS.

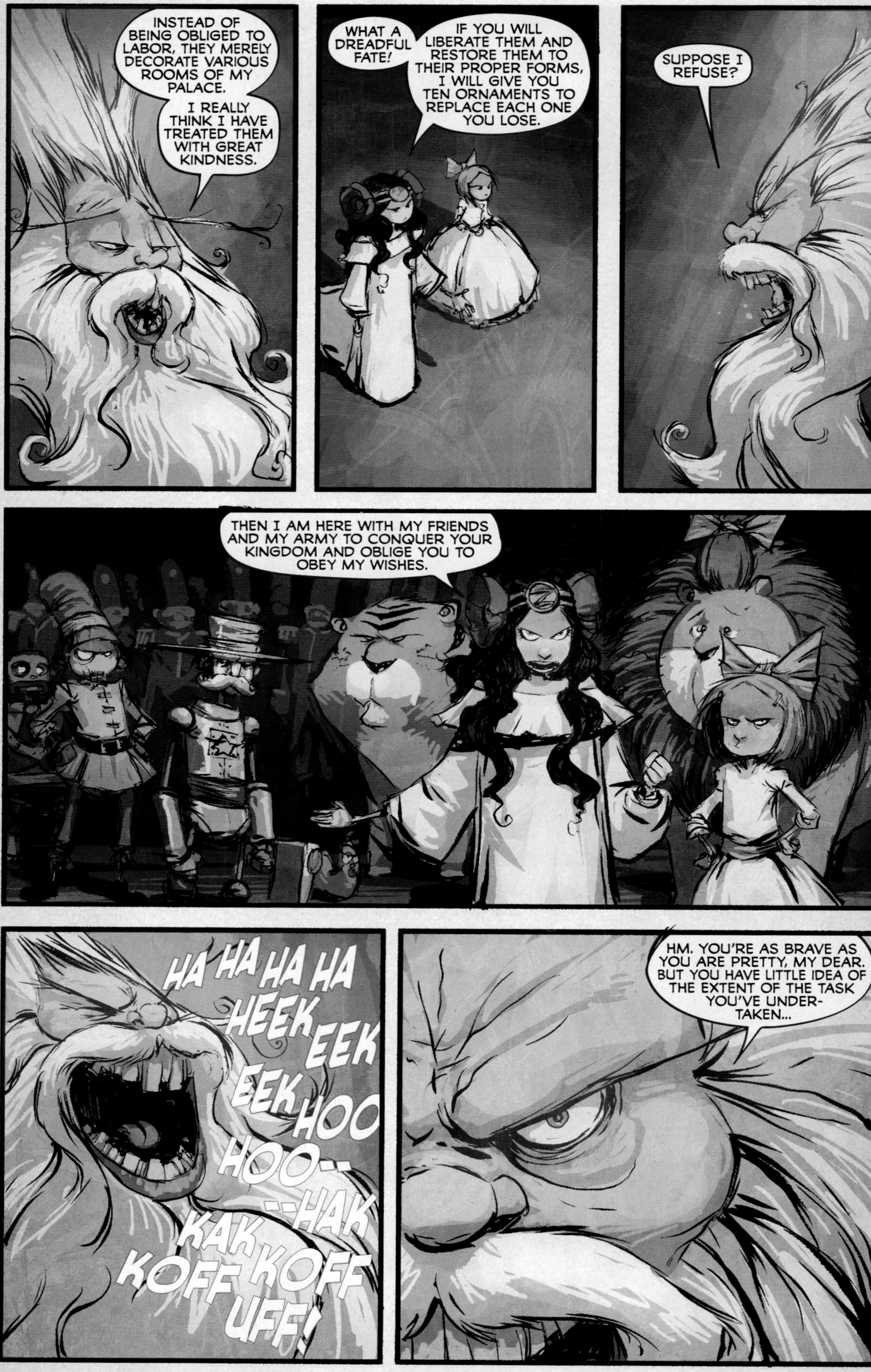
INSTEAD OF BEING OBLIGED TO LABOR, THEY MERELY DECORATE VARIOUS ROOMS OF MY PALACE.
I REALLY THINK I HAVE TREATED THEM WITH GREAT KINDNESS.
WHAT A DREADFUL FATE!
IF YOU WILL LIBERATE THEM AND RESTORE THEM TO THEIR PROPER FORMS, I WILL GIVE YOU TEN ORNAMENTS TO REPLACE EACH ONE YOU LOSE.
SUPPOSE I REFUSE?
THEN I AM HERE WITH MY FRIENDS AND MY ARMY TO CONQUER YOUR KINGDOM AND OBLIGE YOU TO OBEY MY WISHES.
HA HA HA HA HEEK EEK EEK HOO HOO-- --HAK KAK KOFF KOFF UFF!
HM. YOU'RE AS BRAVE AS YOU ARE PRETTY, MY DEAR. BUT YOU HAVE LITTLE IDEA OF THE EXTENT OF THE TASK YOU'VE UNDER-TAKEN...

COME WITH ME FOR A MOMENT, MY DEAR OZMA.

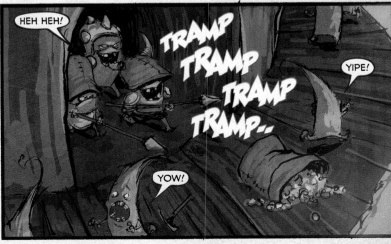

HEH HEH!

TRAMP TRAMP TRAMP TRAMP--

YIPE!

YOW!

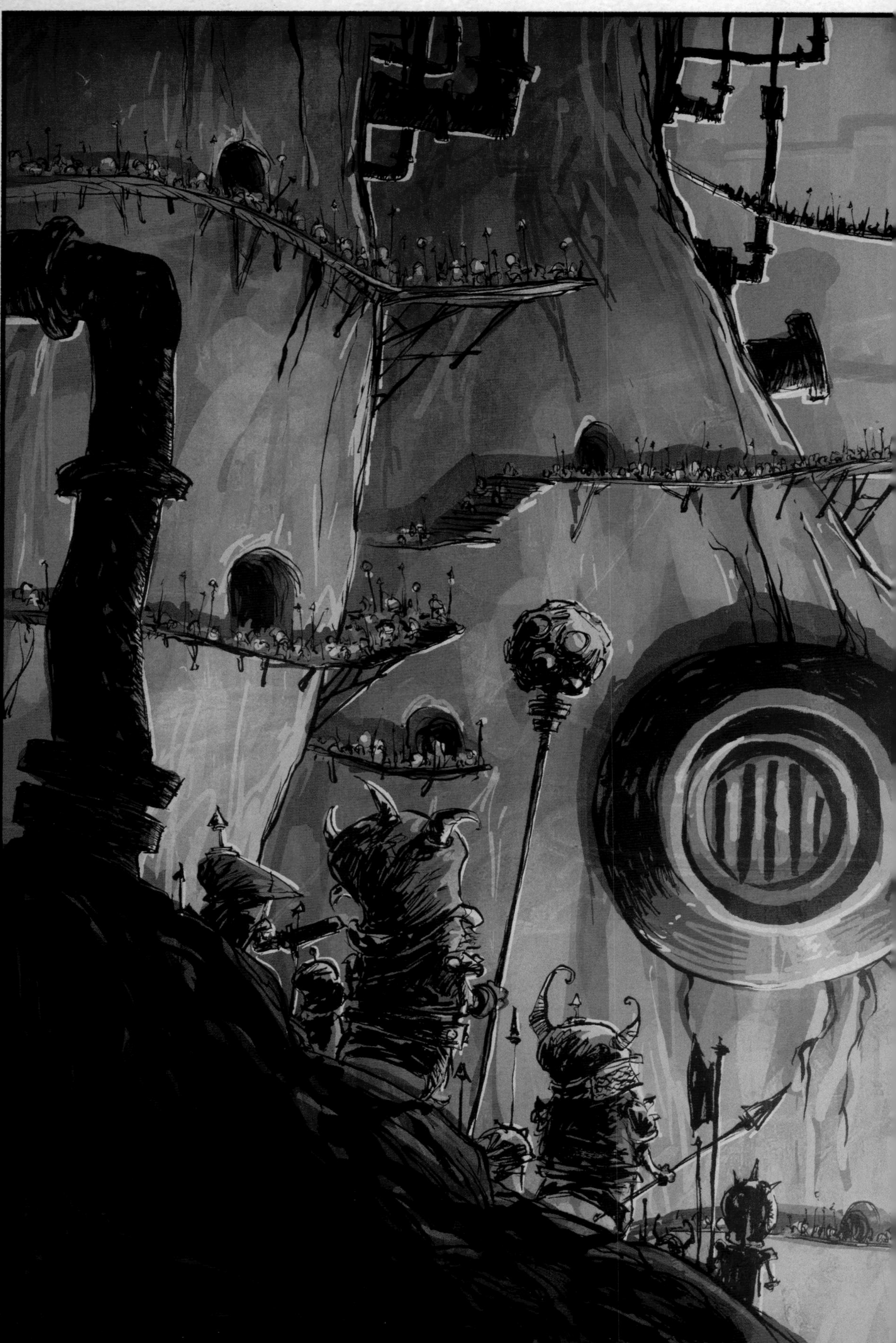

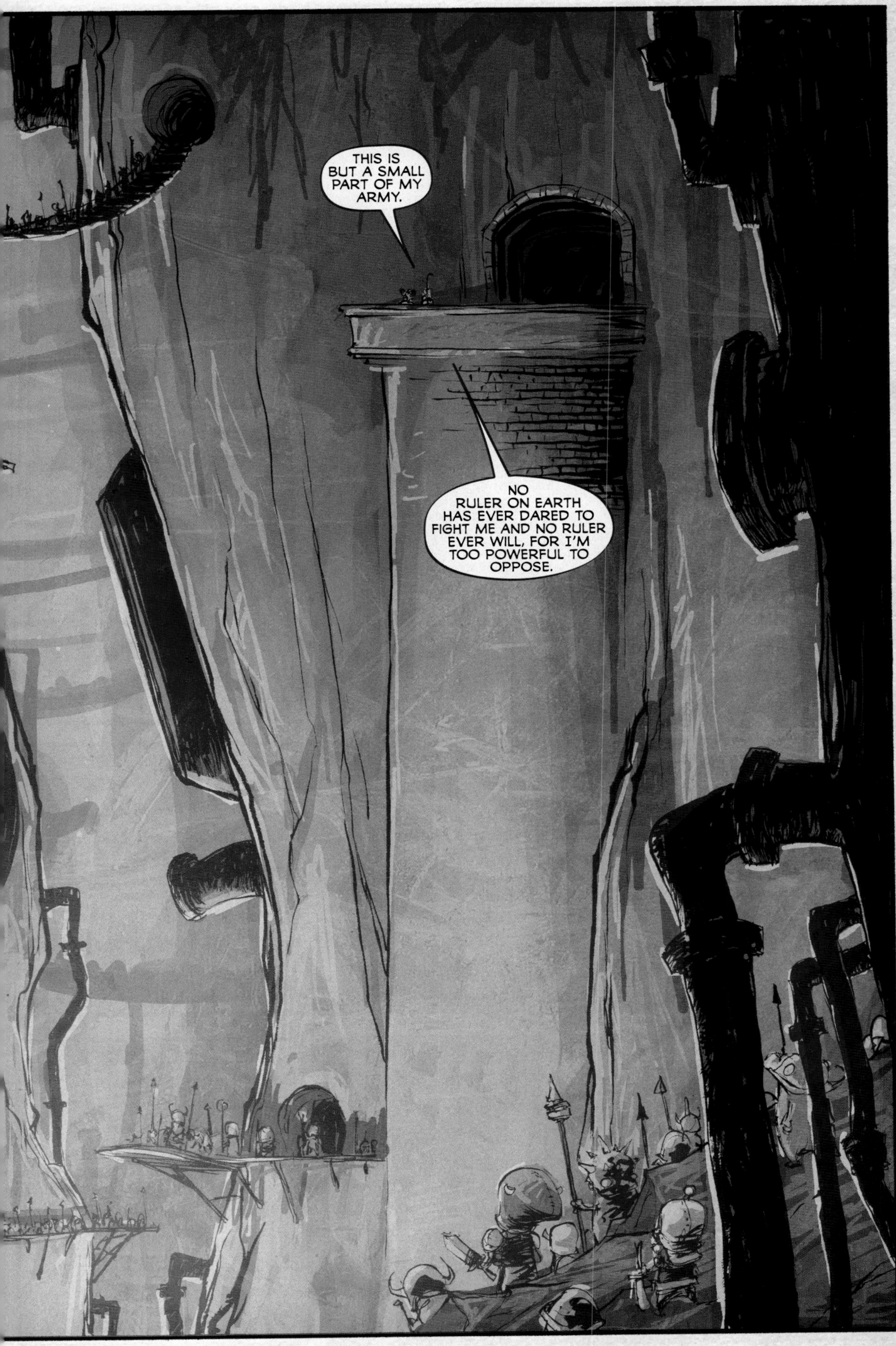
THIS IS BUT A SMALL PART OF MY ARMY.
NO RULER ON EARTH HAS EVER DARED TO FIGHT ME AND NO RULER EVER WILL, FOR I'M TOO POWERFUL TO OPPOSE.

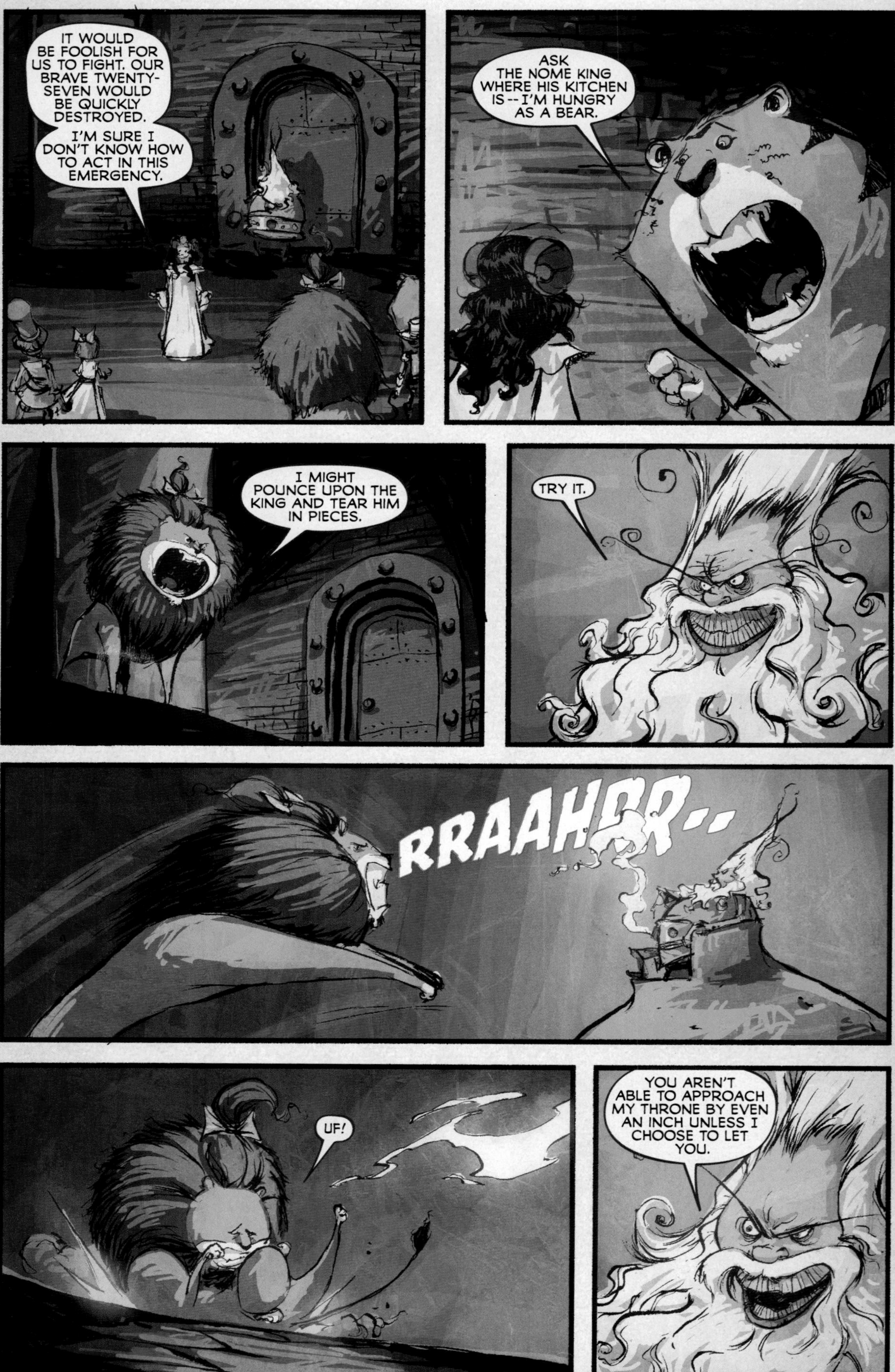
IT WOULD BE FOOLISH FOR US TO FIGHT. OUR BRAVE TWENTY-SEVEN WOULD BE QUICKLY DESTROYED.
I'M SURE I DON'T KNOW HOW TO ACT IN THIS EMERGENCY.
ASK THE NOME KING WHERE HIS KITCHEN IS--I'M HUNGRY AS A BEAR.
I MIGHT POUNCE UPON THE KING AND TEAR HIM IN PIECES.
TRY IT.
RRAAHRR..
UF!
YOU AREN'T ABLE TO APPROACH MY THRONE BY EVEN AN INCH UNLESS I CHOOSE TO LET YOU.

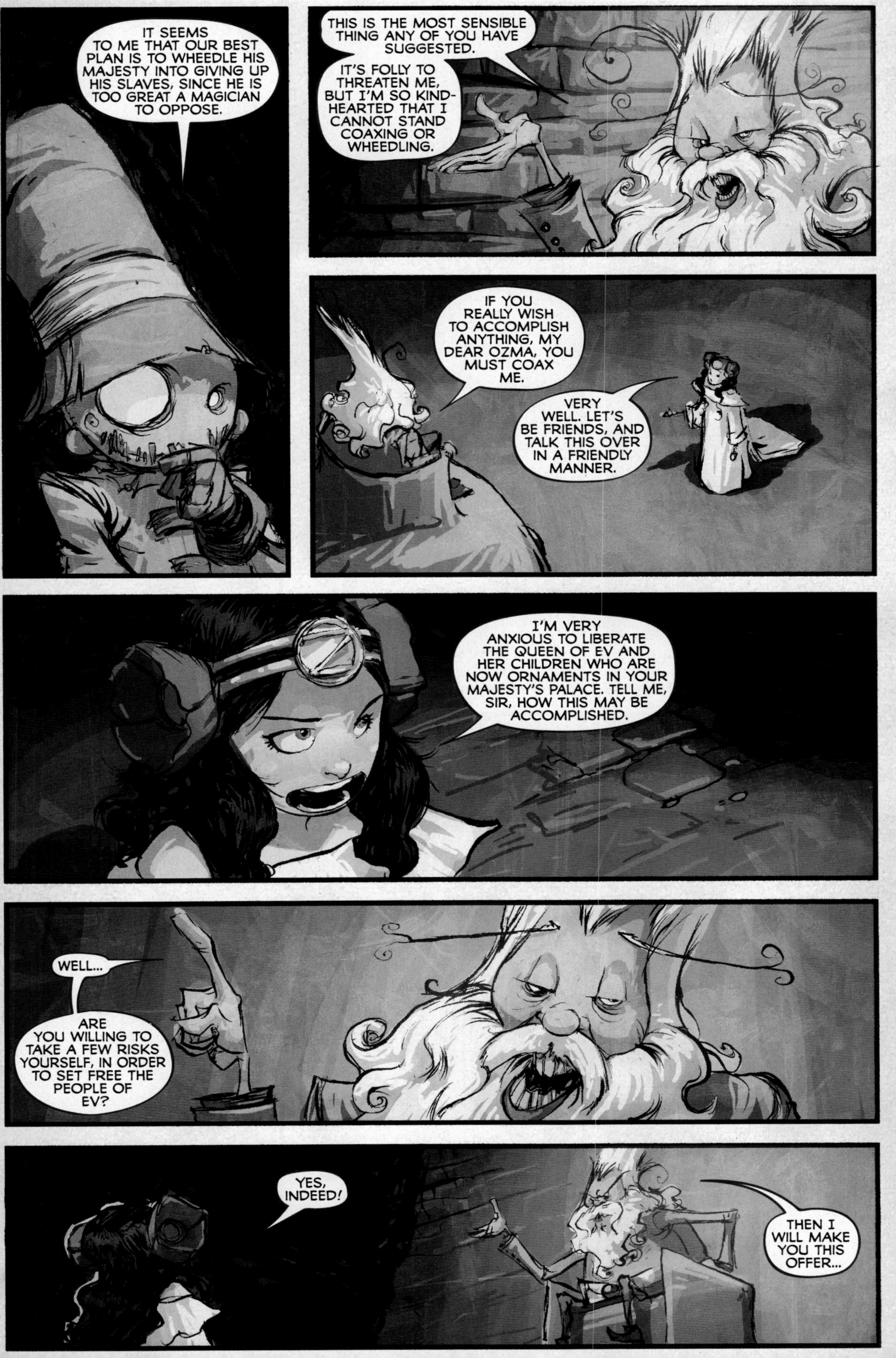
IT SEEMS TO ME THAT OUR BEST PLAN IS TO WHEEDLE HIS MAJESTY INTO GIVING UP HIS SLAVES, SINCE HE IS TOO GREAT A MAGICIAN TO OPPOSE.
THIS IS THE MOST SENSIBLE THING ANY OF YOU HAVE SUGGESTED.
IT'S FOLLY TO THREATEN ME, BUT I'M SO KIND-HEARTED THAT I CANNOT STAND COAXING OR WHEEDLING.
IF YOU REALLY WISH TO ACCOMPLISH ANYTHING, MY DEAR OZMA, YOU MUST COAX ME.
VERY WELL. LET'S BE FRIENDS, AND TALK THIS OVER IN A FRIENDLY MANNER.
I'M VERY ANXIOUS TO LIBERATE THE QUEEN OF EV AND HER CHILDREN WHO ARE NOW ORNAMENTS IN YOUR MAJESTY'S PALACE. TELL ME, SIR, HOW THIS MAY BE ACCOMPLISHED.
WELL...
ARE YOU WILLING TO TAKE A FEW RISKS YOURSELF, IN ORDER TO SET FREE THE PEOPLE OF EV?
YES, INDEED!
THEN I WILL MAKE YOU THIS OFFER...

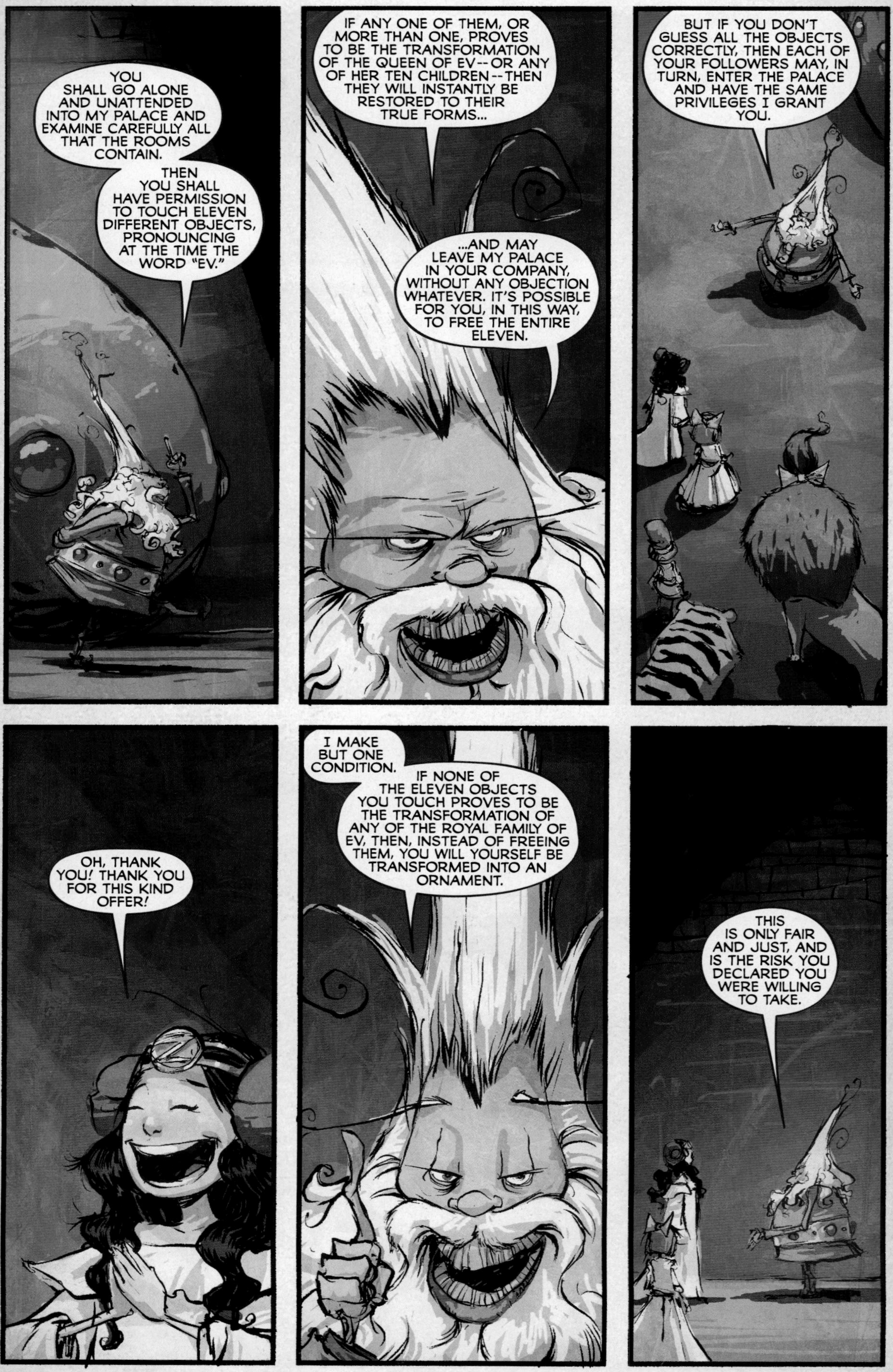
YOU SHALL GO ALONE AND UNATTENDED INTO MY PALACE AND EXAMINE CAREFULLY ALL THAT THE ROOMS CONTAIN.
THEN YOU SHALL HAVE PERMISSION TO TOUCH ELEVEN DIFFERENT OBJECTS, PRONOUNCING AT THE TIME THE WORD "EV."
IF ANY ONE OF THEM, OR MORE THAN ONE, PROVES TO BE THE TRANSFORMATION OF THE QUEEN OF EV--OR ANY OF HER TEN CHILDREN--THEN THEY WILL INSTANTLY BE RESTORED TO THEIR TRUE FORMS...
...AND MAY LEAVE MY PALACE IN YOUR COMPANY, WITHOUT ANY OBJECTION WHATEVER. IT'S POSSIBLE FOR YOU, IN THIS WAY, TO FREE THE ENTIRE ELEVEN.
BUT IF YOU DON'T GUESS ALL THE OBJECTS CORRECTLY, THEN EACH OF YOUR FOLLOWERS MAY, IN TURN, ENTER THE PALACE AND HAVE THE SAME PRIVILEGES I GRANT YOU.
OH, THANK YOU! THANK YOU FOR THIS KIND OFFER!
I MAKE BUT ONE CONDITION.
IF NONE OF THE ELEVEN OBJECTS YOU TOUCH PROVES TO BE THE TRANSFORMATION OF ANY OF THE ROYAL FAMILY OF EV, THEN, INSTEAD OF FREEING THEM, YOU WILL YOURSELF BE TRANSFORMED INTO AN ORNAMENT.
THIS IS ONLY FAIR AND JUST, AND IS THE RISK YOU DECLARED YOU WERE WILLING TO TAKE.

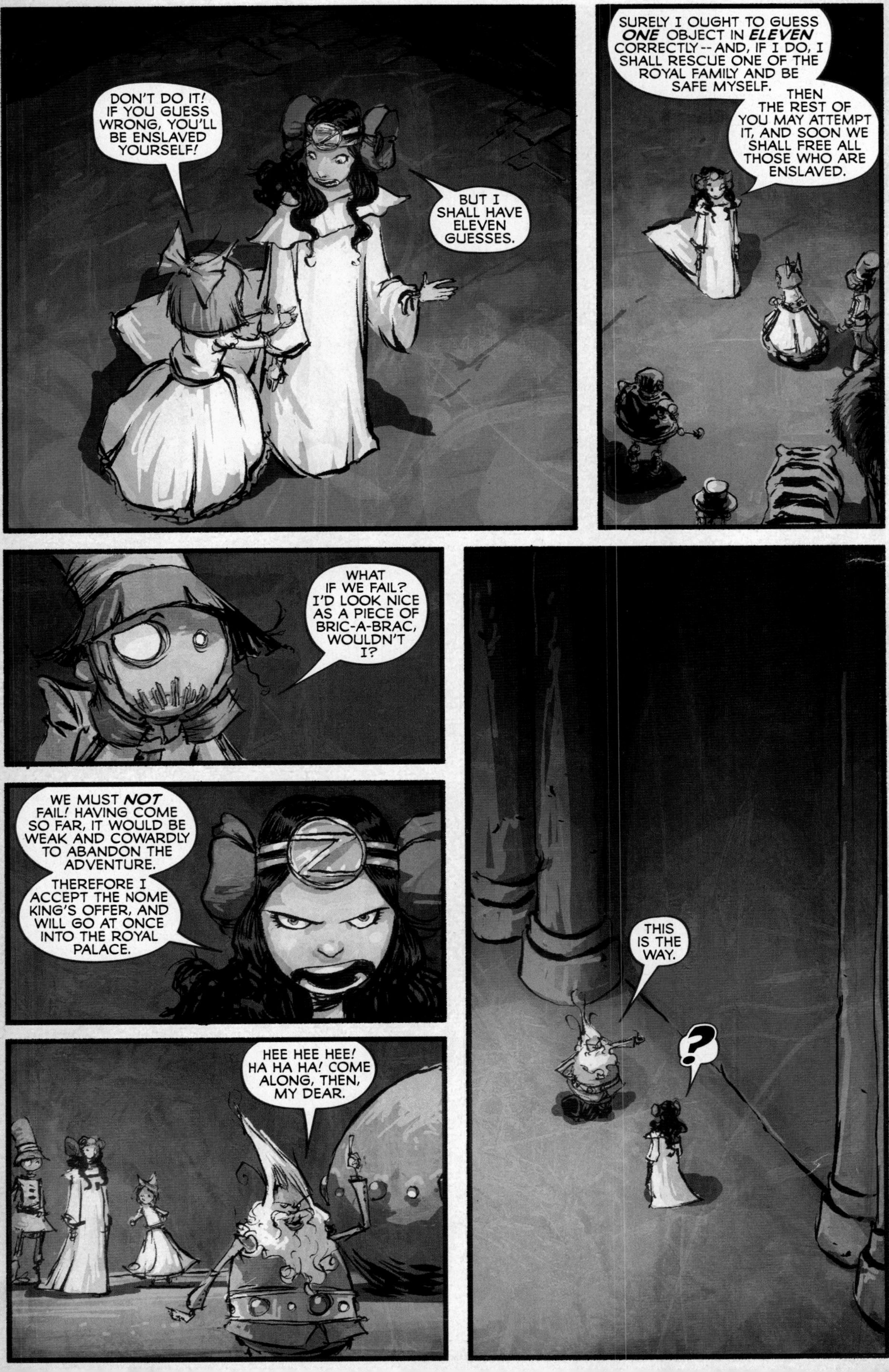

DON'T DO IT! IF YOU GUESS WRONG, YOU'LL BE ENSLAVED YOURSELF!
BUT I SHALL HAVE ELEVEN GUESSES.
SURELY I OUGHT TO GUESS ONE OBJECT IN ELEVEN CORRECTLY -- AND, IF I DO, I SHALL RESCUE ONE OF THE ROYAL FAMILY AND BE SAFE MYSELF.
THEN THE REST OF YOU MAY ATTEMPT IT, AND SOON WE SHALL FREE ALL THOSE WHO ARE ENSLAVED.
WHAT IF WE FAIL? I'D LOOK NICE AS A PIECE OF BRIC-A-BRAC, WOULDN'T I?
WE MUST NOT FAIL! HAVING COME SO FAR, IT WOULD BE WEAK AND COWARDLY TO ABANDON THE ADVENTURE.
THEREFORE I ACCEPT THE NOME KING'S OFFER, AND WILL GO AT ONCE INTO THE ROYAL PALACE.
HEE HEE HEE! HA HA HA! COME ALONG, THEN, MY DEAR.
THIS IS THE WAY.
?

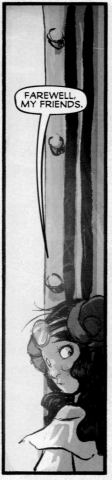

FAREWELL, MY FRIENDS.

SLAM-M-M

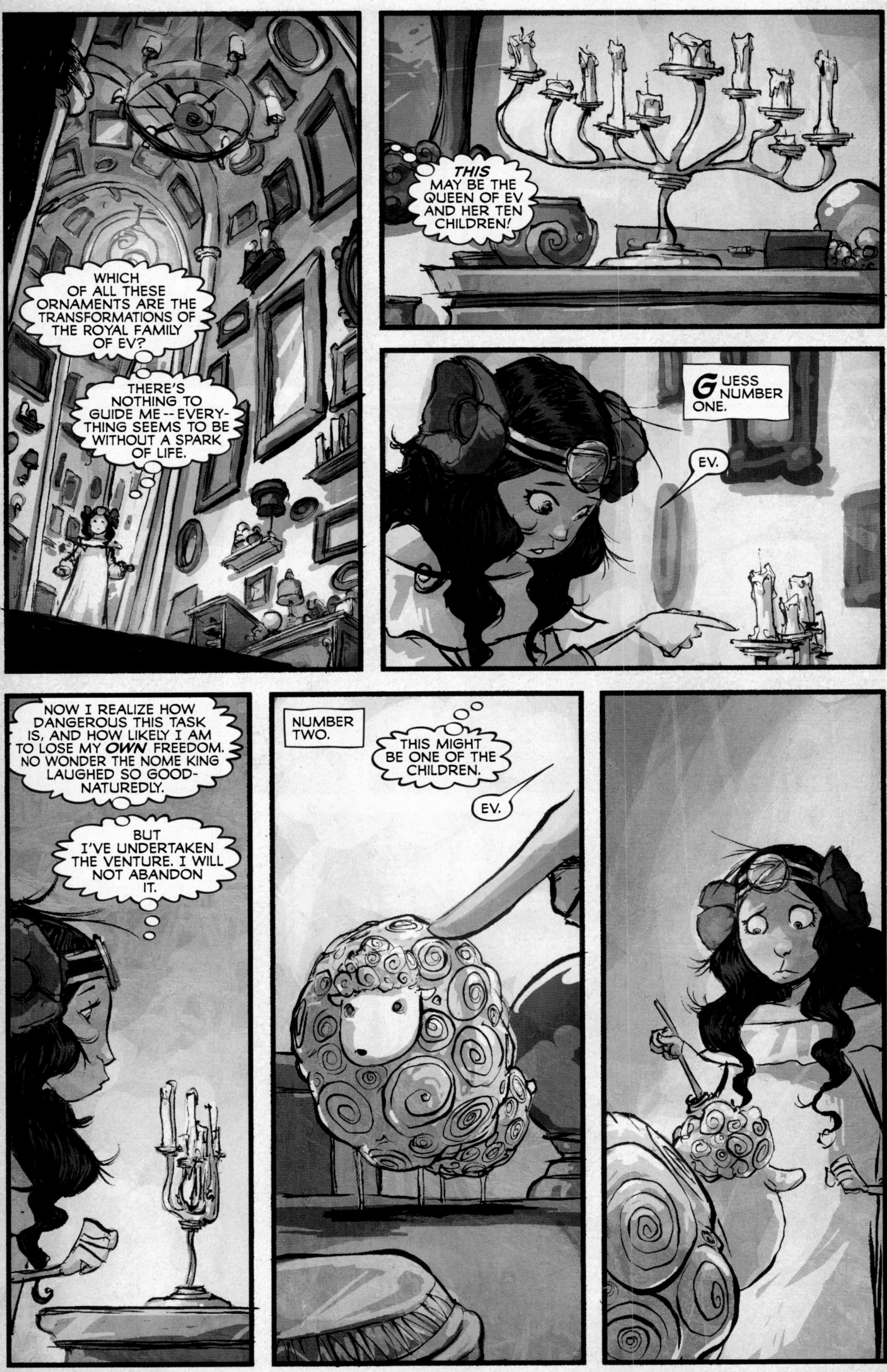
WHICH OF ALL THESE ORNAMENTS ARE THE TRANSFORMATIONS OF THE ROYAL FAMILY OF EV?
THERE'S NOTHING TO GUIDE ME -- EVERYTHING SEEMS TO BE WITHOUT A SPARK OF LIFE.
THIS MAY BE THE QUEEN OF EV AND HER TEN CHILDREN!
GUESS NUMBER ONE.
EV.
NOW I REALIZE HOW DANGEROUS THIS TASK IS, AND HOW LIKELY I AM TO LOSE MY OWN FREEDOM. NO WONDER THE NOME KING LAUGHED SO GOOD-NATUREDLY.
BUT I'VE UNDERTAKEN THE VENTURE. I WILL NOT ABANDON IT.
NUMBER TWO.
THIS MIGHT BE ONE OF THE CHILDREN.
EV.

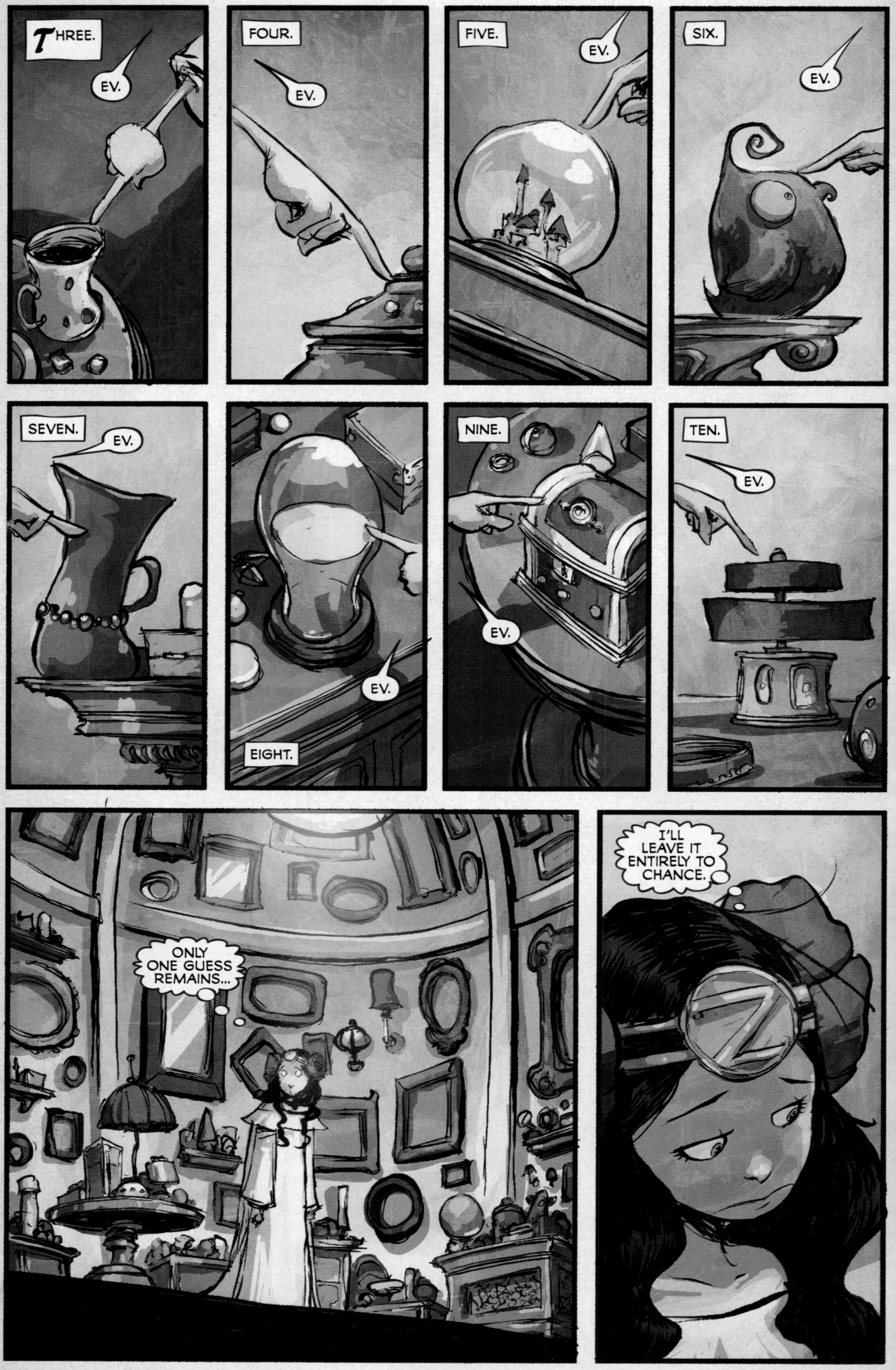
THREE.
EV.
FOUR.
EV.
FIVE.
EV.
SIX.
EV.
SEVEN.
EV.
EV.
EIGHT.
NINE.
EV.
TEN.
EV.
ONLY ONE GUESS REMAINS...
I'LL LEAVE IT ENTIRELY TO CHANCE.

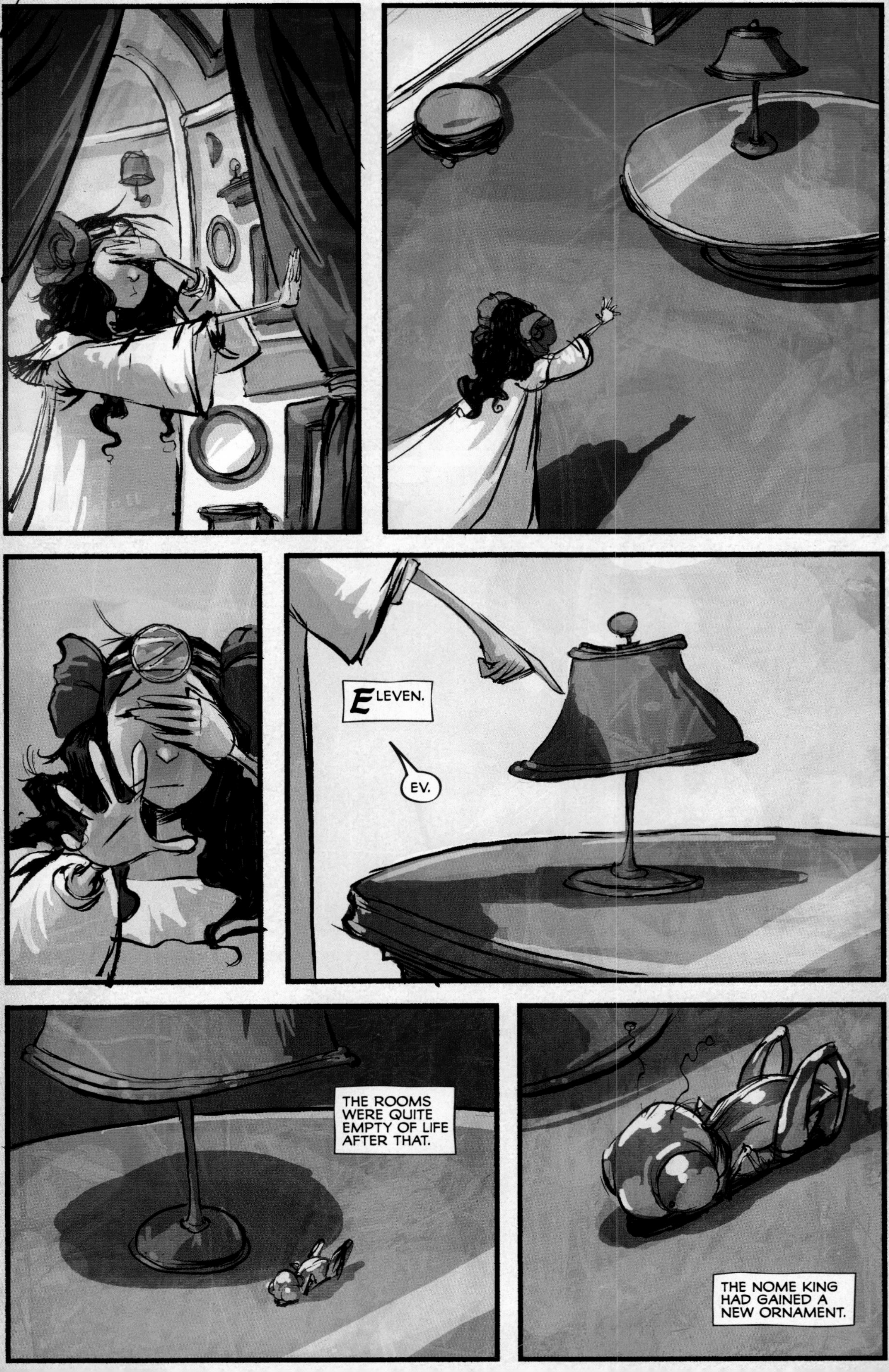
ELEVEN.
EV.
THE ROOMS WERE QUITE EMPTY OF LIFE AFTER THAT.
THE NOME KING HAD GAINED A NEW ORNAMENT.

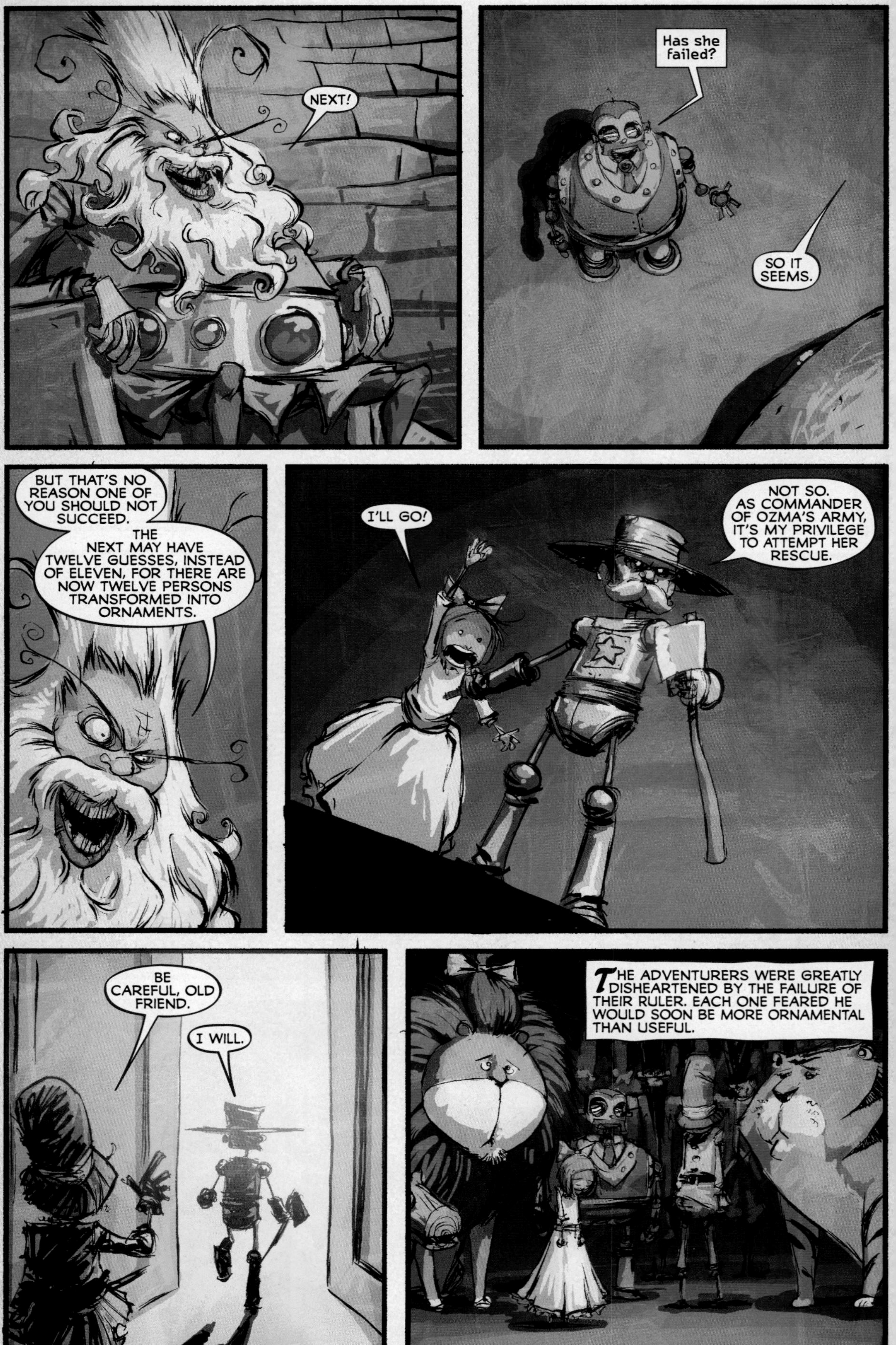
NEXT!
Has she failed?
SO IT SEEMS.
BUT THAT'S NO REASON ONE OF YOU SHOULD NOT SUCCEED.
THE NEXT MAY HAVE TWELVE GUESSES, INSTEAD OF ELEVEN, FOR THERE ARE NOW TWELVE PERSONS TRANSFORMED INTO ORNAMENTS.
I'LL GO!
NOT SO. AS COMMANDER OF OZMA'S ARMY, IT'S MY PRIVILEGE TO ATTEMPT HER RESCUE.
BE CAREFUL, OLD FRIEND.
I WILL.
THE ADVENTURERS WERE GREATLY DISHEARTENED BY THE FAILURE OF THEIR RULER. EACH ONE FEARED HE WOULD SOON BE MORE ORNAMENTAL THAN USEFUL.

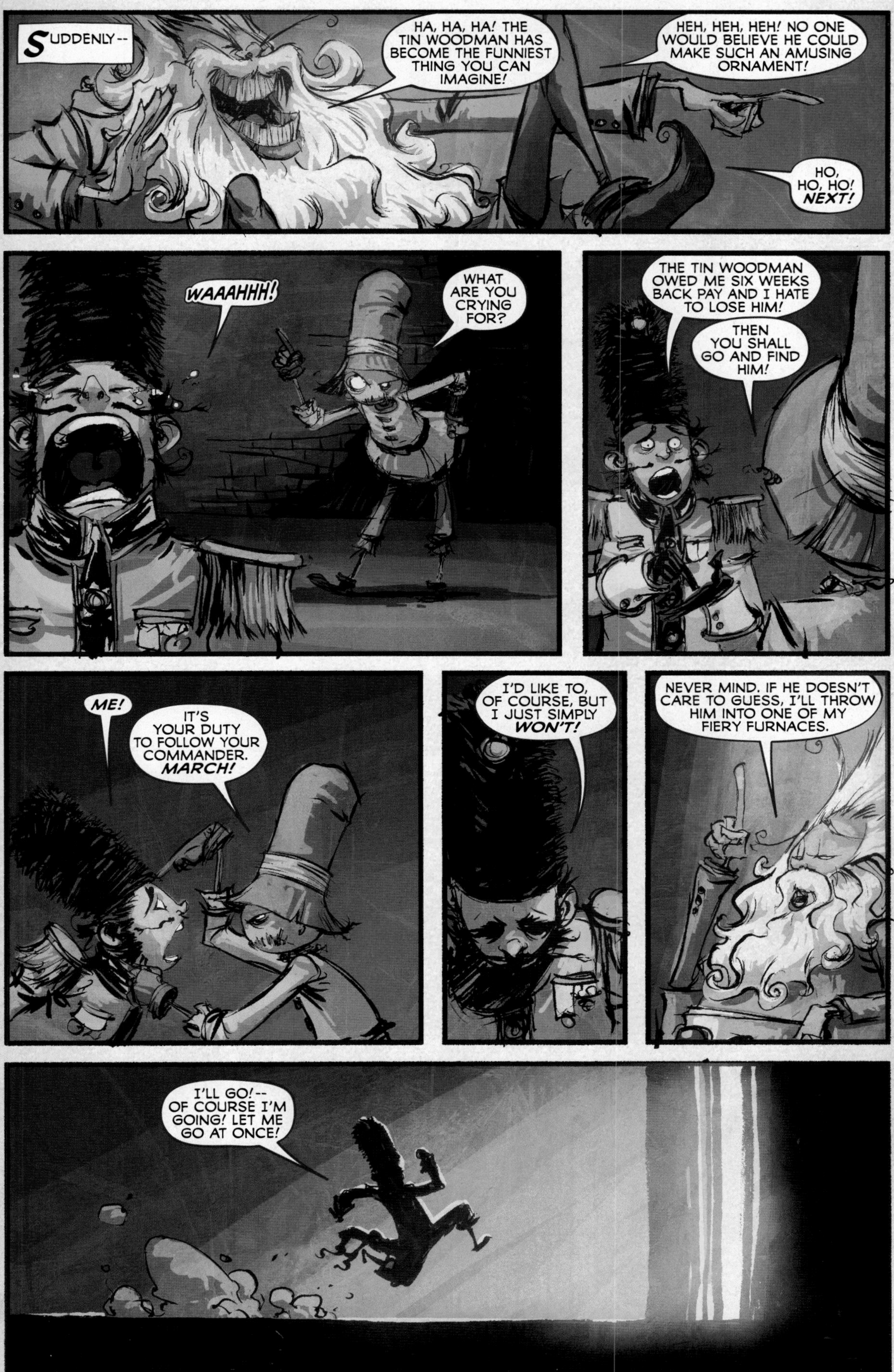
SUDDENLY--
HA, HA, HA! THE TIN WOODMAN HAS BECOME THE FUNNIEST THING YOU CAN IMAGINE!
HEH, HEH, HEH! NO ONE WOULD BELIEVE HE COULD MAKE SUCH AN AMUSING ORNAMENT!
HO, HO, HO! NEXT!
WAAAHHH!
WHAT ARE YOU CRYING FOR?
THE TIN WOODMAN OWED ME SIX WEEKS BACK PAY AND I HATE TO LOSE HIM!
THEN YOU SHALL GO AND FIND HIM!
ME!
IT'S YOUR DUTY TO FOLLOW YOUR COMMANDER. MARCH!
I'D LIKE TO, OF COURSE, BUT I JUST SIMPLY WON'T!
NEVER MIND. IF HE DOESN'T CARE TO GUESS, I'LL THROW HIM INTO ONE OF MY FIERY FURNACES.
I'LL GO!-- OF COURSE I'M GOING! LET ME GO AT ONCE!

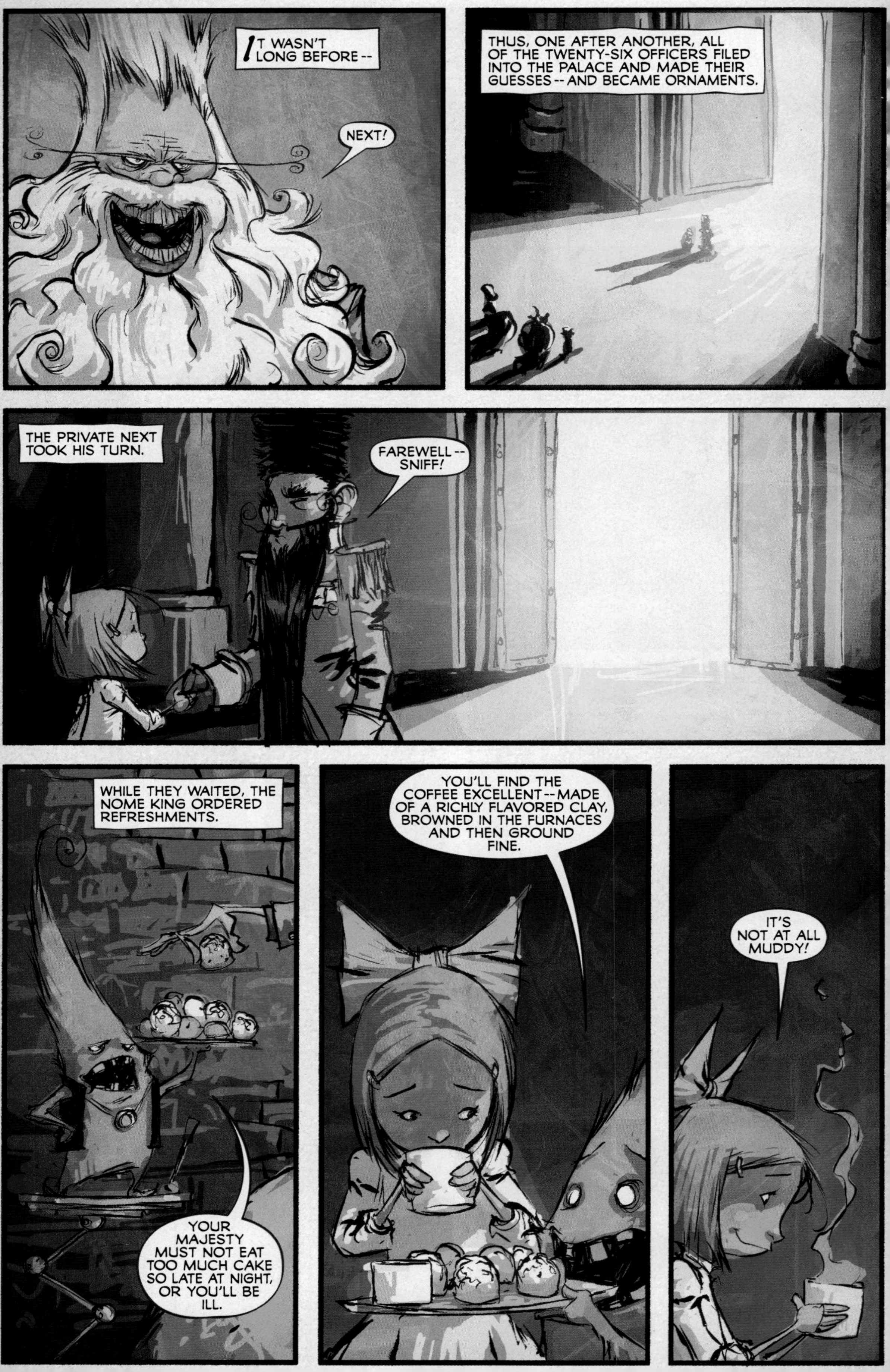
IT WASN'T LONG BEFORE --
NEXT!
THUS, ONE AFTER ANOTHER, ALL OF THE TWENTY-SIX OFFICERS FILED INTO THE PALACE AND MADE THEIR GUESSES -- AND BECAME ORNAMENTS.
THE PRIVATE NEXT TOOK HIS TURN.
FAREWELL -- SNIFF!
WHILE THEY WAITED, THE NOME KING ORDERED REFRESHMENTS.
YOUR MAJESTY MUST NOT EAT TOO MUCH CAKE SO LATE AT NIGHT, OR YOU'LL BE ILL.
YOU'LL FIND THE COFFEE EXCELLENT -- MADE OF A RICHLY FLAVORED CLAY, BROWNED IN THE FURNACES AND THEN GROUND FINE.
IT'S NOT AT ALL MUDDY!

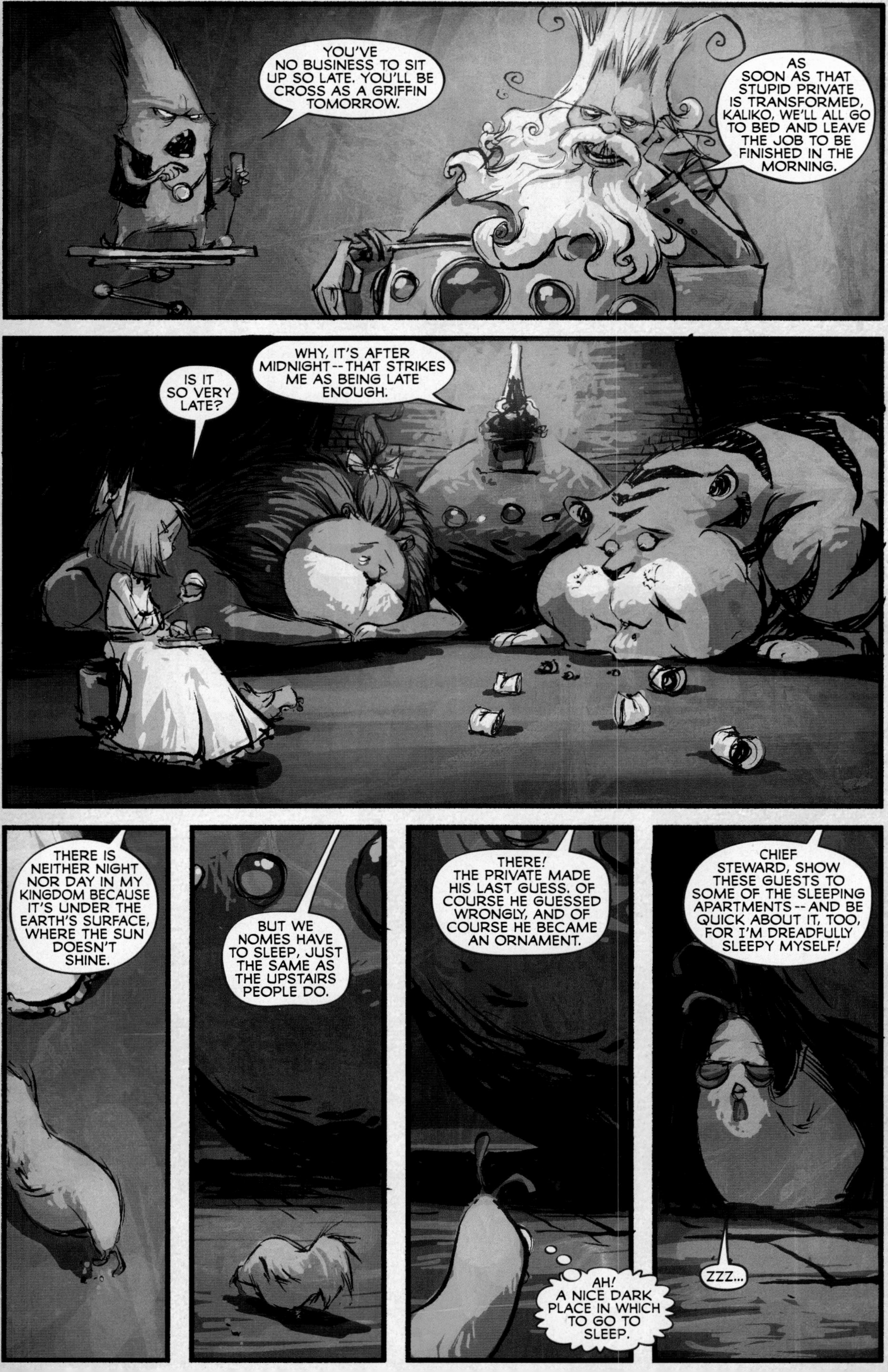
YOU'VE NO BUSINESS TO SIT UP SO LATE. YOU'LL BE CROSS AS A GRIFFIN TOMORROW.
AS SOON AS THAT STUPID PRIVATE IS TRANSFORMED, KALIKO, WE'LL ALL GO TO BED AND LEAVE THE JOB TO BE FINISHED IN THE MORNING.
IS IT SO VERY LATE?
WHY, IT'S AFTER MIDNIGHT--THAT STRIKES ME AS BEING LATE ENOUGH.
THERE IS NEITHER NIGHT NOR DAY IN MY KINGDOM BECAUSE IT'S UNDER THE EARTH'S SURFACE, WHERE THE SUN DOESN'T SHINE.
BUT WE NOMES HAVE TO SLEEP, JUST THE SAME AS THE UPSTAIRS PEOPLE DO.
THERE! THE PRIVATE MADE HIS LAST GUESS. OF COURSE HE GUESSED WRONGLY, AND OF COURSE HE BECAME AN ORNAMENT.
AH! A NICE DARK PLACE IN WHICH TO GO TO SLEEP.
CHIEF STEWARD, SHOW THESE GUESTS TO SOME OF THE SLEEPING APARTMENTS--AND BE QUICK ABOUT IT, TOO, FOR I'M DREADFULLY SLEEPY MYSELF!
ZZZ...

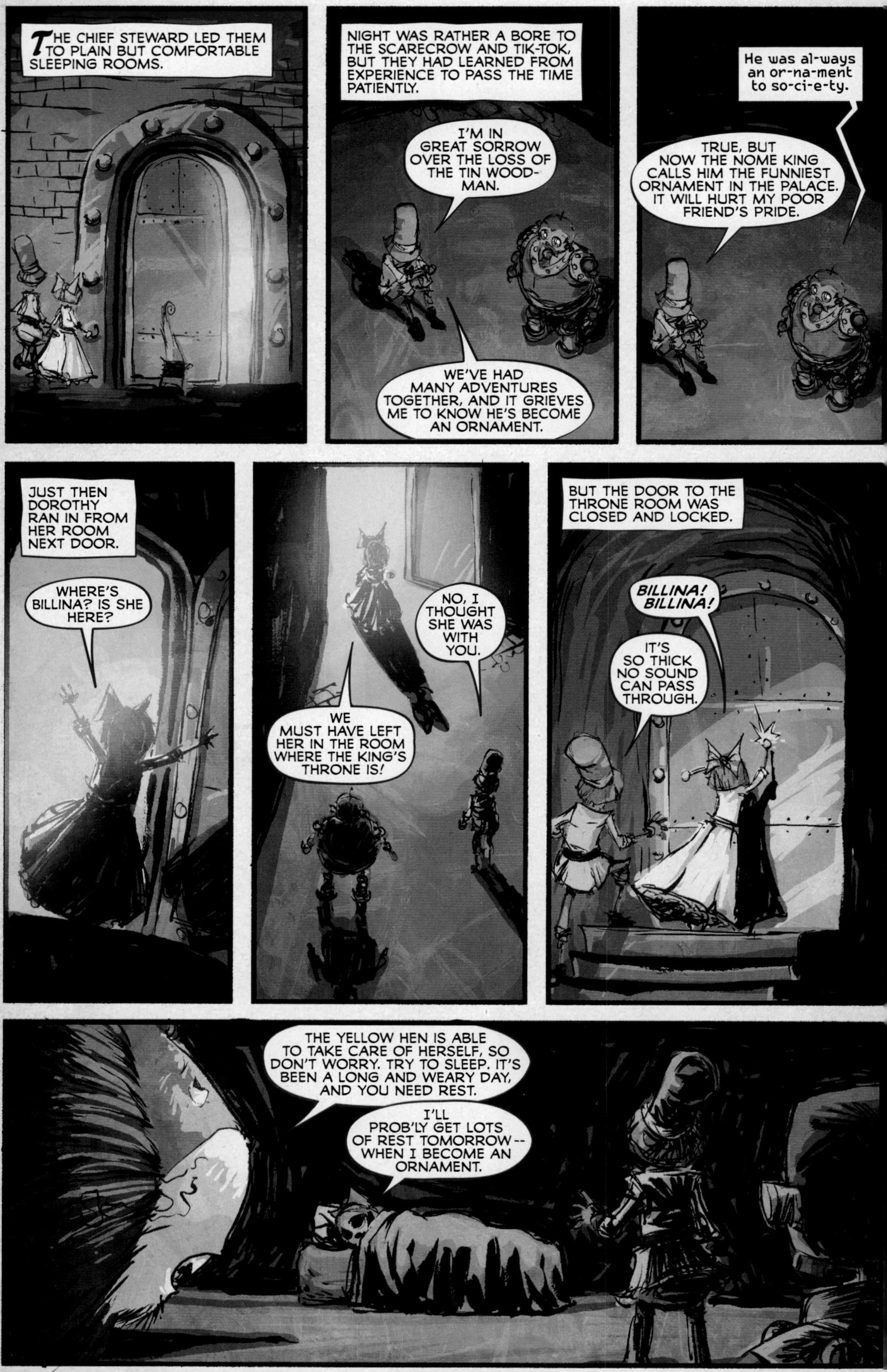
THE CHIEF STEWARD LED THEM TO PLAIN BUT COMFORTABLE SLEEPING ROOMS.
NIGHT WAS RATHER A BORE TO THE SCARECROW AND TIK-TOK, BUT THEY HAD LEARNED FROM EXPERIENCE TO PASS THE TIME PATIENTLY.
I'M IN GREAT SORROW OVER THE LOSS OF THE TIN WOOD-MAN.
WE'VE HAD MANY ADVENTURES TOGETHER, AND IT GRIEVES ME TO KNOW HE'S BECOME AN ORNAMENT.
He was al-ways an or-na-ment to so-ci-e-ty.
TRUE, BUT NOW THE NOME KING CALLS HIM THE FUNNIEST ORNAMENT IN THE PALACE. IT WILL HURT MY POOR FRIEND'S PRIDE.
JUST THEN DOROTHY RAN IN FROM HER ROOM NEXT DOOR.
WHERE'S BILLINA? IS SHE HERE?
NO, I THOUGHT SHE WAS WITH YOU.
WE MUST HAVE LEFT HER IN THE ROOM WHERE THE KING'S THRONE IS!
BUT THE DOOR TO THE THRONE ROOM WAS CLOSED AND LOCKED.
BILLINA! BILLINA!
IT'S SO THICK NO SOUND CAN PASS THROUGH.
THE YELLOW HEN IS ABLE TO TAKE CARE OF HERSELF, SO DON'T WORRY. TRY TO SLEEP. IT'S BEEN A LONG AND WEARY DAY, AND YOU NEED REST.
I'LL PROB'LY GET LOTS OF REST TOMORROW -- WHEN I BECOME AN ORNAMENT.

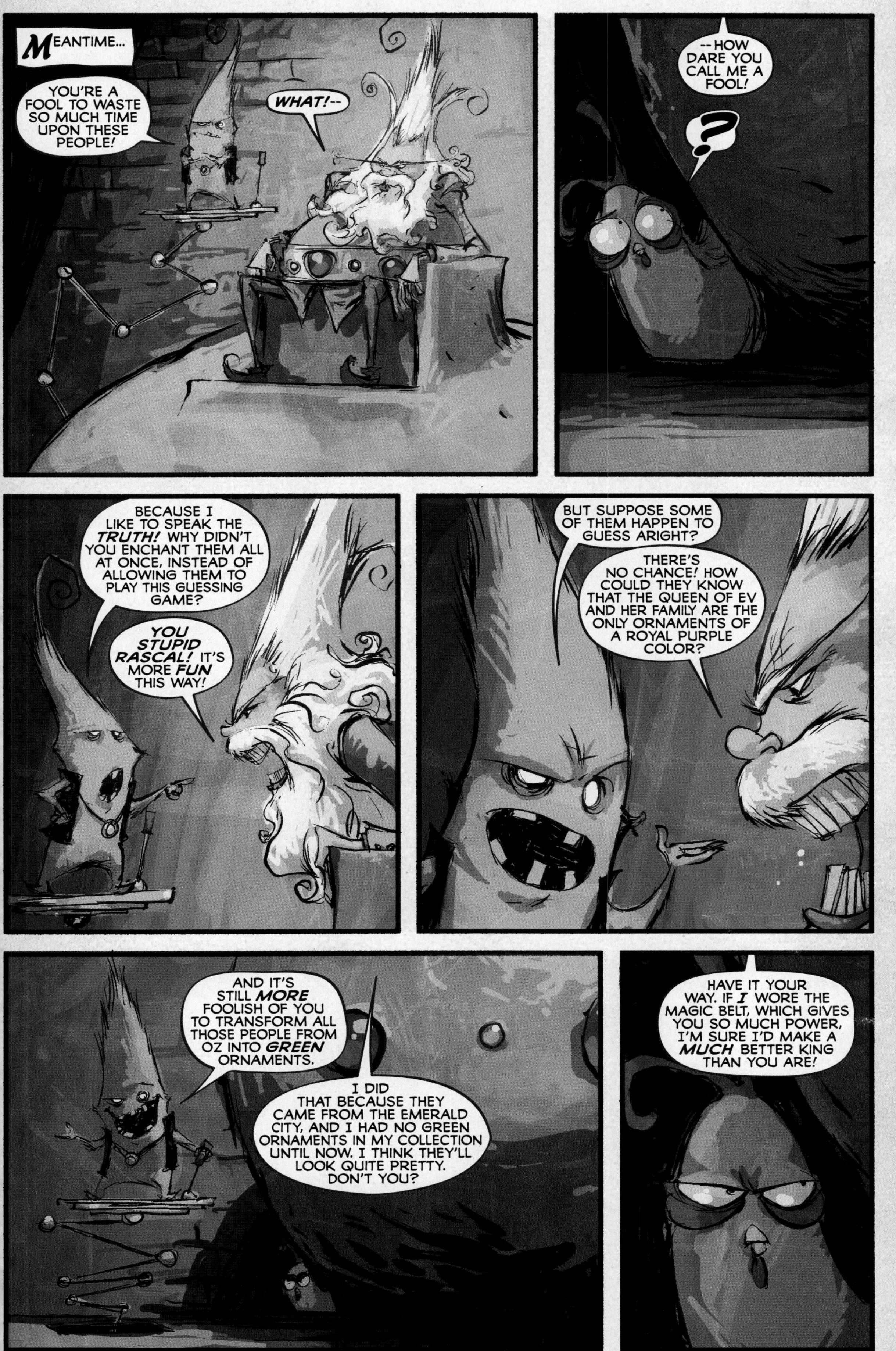
MEANTIME...
YOU'RE A FOOL TO WASTE SO MUCH TIME UPON THESE PEOPLE!
WHAT!--
--HOW DARE YOU CALL ME A FOOL!
?
BECAUSE I LIKE TO SPEAK THE TRUTH! WHY DIDN'T YOU ENCHANT THEM ALL AT ONCE, INSTEAD OF ALLOWING THEM TO PLAY THIS GUESSING GAME?
YOU STUPID RASCAL! IT'S MORE FUN THIS WAY!
BUT SUPPOSE SOME OF THEM HAPPEN TO GUESS ARIGHT?
THERE'S NO CHANCE! HOW COULD THEY KNOW THAT THE QUEEN OF EV AND HER FAMILY ARE THE ONLY ORNAMENTS OF A ROYAL PURPLE COLOR?
AND IT'S STILL MORE FOOLISH OF YOU TO TRANSFORM ALL THOSE PEOPLE FROM OZ INTO GREEN ORNAMENTS.
I DID THAT BECAUSE THEY CAME FROM THE EMERALD CITY, AND I HAD NO GREEN ORNAMENTS IN MY COLLECTION UNTIL NOW. I THINK THEY'LL LOOK QUITE PRETTY. DON'T YOU?
HAVE IT YOUR WAY. IF I WORE THE MAGIC BELT, WHICH GIVES YOU SO MUCH POWER, I'M SURE I'D MAKE A MUCH BETTER KING THAN YOU ARE!

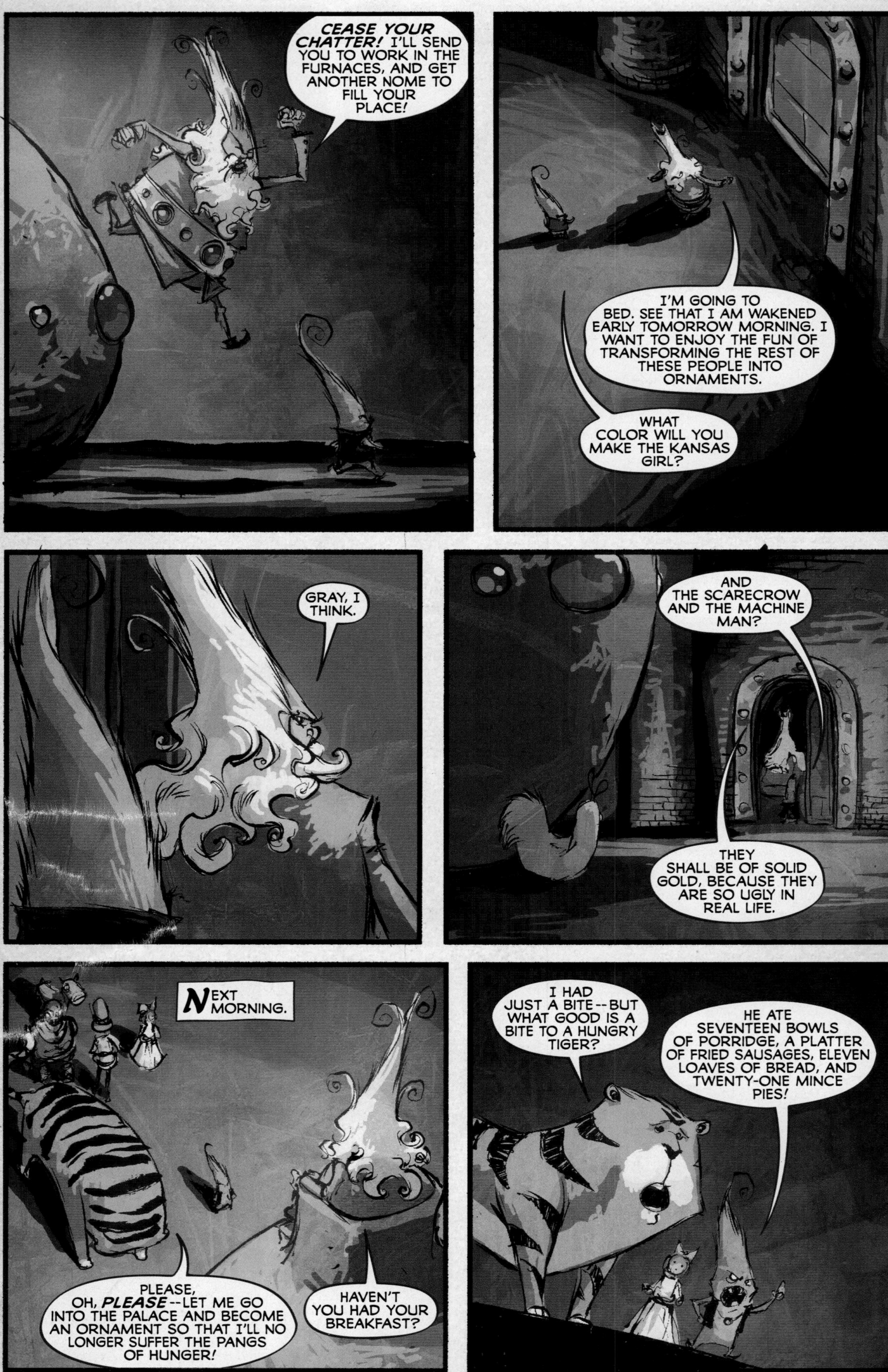

CEASE YOUR CHATTER! I'LL SEND YOU TO WORK IN THE FURNACES, AND GET ANOTHER NOME TO FILL YOUR PLACE!
I'M GOING TO BED. SEE THAT I AM WAKENED EARLY TOMORROW MORNING. I WANT TO ENJOY THE FUN OF TRANSFORMING THE REST OF THESE PEOPLE INTO ORNAMENTS.
WHAT COLOR WILL YOU MAKE THE KANSAS GIRL?
GRAY, I THINK.
AND THE SCARECROW AND THE MACHINE MAN?
THEY SHALL BE OF SOLID GOLD, BECAUSE THEY ARE SO UGLY IN REAL LIFE.
NEXT MORNING.
PLEASE, OH, PLEASE--LET ME GO INTO THE PALACE AND BECOME AN ORNAMENT SO THAT I'LL NO LONGER SUFFER THE PANGS OF HUNGER!
HAVEN'T YOU HAD YOUR BREAKFAST?
I HAD JUST A BITE--BUT WHAT GOOD IS A BITE TO A HUNGRY TIGER?
HE ATE SEVENTEEN BOWLS OF PORRIDGE, A PLATTER OF FRIED SAUSAGES, ELEVEN LOAVES OF BREAD, AND TWENTY-ONE MINCE PIES!

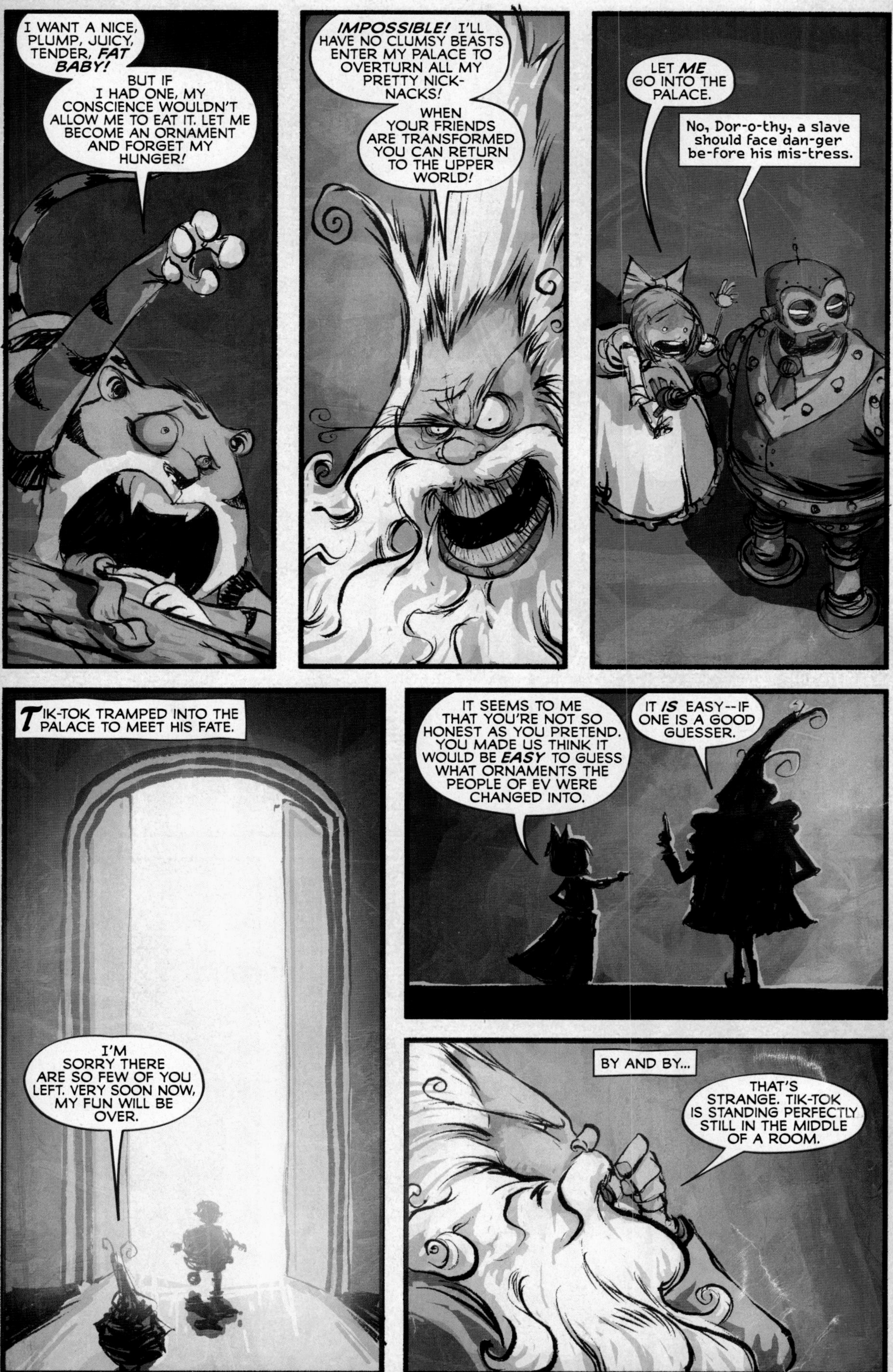
I WANT A NICE, PLUMP, JUICY, TENDER, *FAT BABY!*
BUT IF I HAD ONE, MY CONSCIENCE WOULDN'T ALLOW ME TO EAT IT. LET ME BECOME AN ORNAMENT AND FORGET MY HUNGER!
IMPOSSIBLE! I'LL HAVE NO CLUMSY BEASTS ENTER MY PALACE TO OVERTURN ALL MY PRETTY NICK-NACKS!
WHEN YOUR FRIENDS ARE TRANSFORMED YOU CAN RETURN TO THE UPPER WORLD!
LET *ME* GO INTO THE PALACE.
No, Dor-o-thy, a slave should face dan-ger be-fore his mis-tress.
TIK-TOK TRAMPED INTO THE PALACE TO MEET HIS FATE.
I'M SORRY THERE ARE SO FEW OF YOU LEFT. VERY SOON NOW, MY FUN WILL BE OVER.
IT SEEMS TO ME THAT YOU'RE NOT SO HONEST AS YOU PRETEND. YOU MADE US THINK IT WOULD BE *EASY* TO GUESS WHAT ORNAMENTS THE PEOPLE OF EV WERE CHANGED INTO.
IT *IS* EASY--IF ONE IS A GOOD GUESSER.
BY AND BY...
THAT'S STRANGE. TIK-TOK IS STANDING PERFECTLY STILL IN THE MIDDLE OF A ROOM.

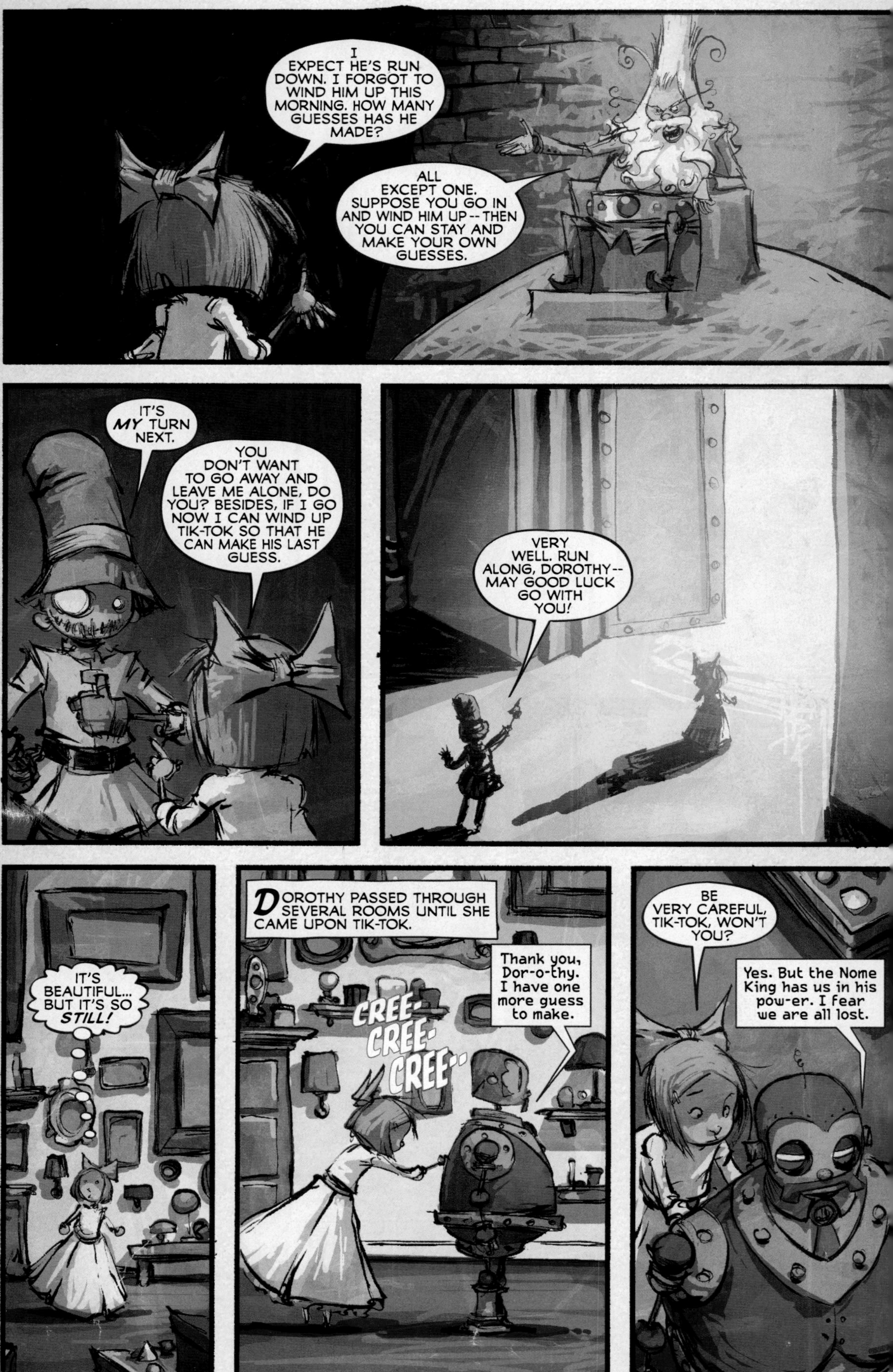
I EXPECT HE'S RUN DOWN. I FORGOT TO WIND HIM UP THIS MORNING. HOW MANY GUESSES HAS HE MADE?
ALL EXCEPT ONE. SUPPOSE YOU GO IN AND WIND HIM UP -- THEN YOU CAN STAY AND MAKE YOUR OWN GUESSES.
IT'S *MY* TURN NEXT.
YOU DON'T WANT TO GO AWAY AND LEAVE ME ALONE, DO YOU? BESIDES, IF I GO NOW I CAN WIND UP TIK-TOK SO THAT HE CAN MAKE HIS LAST GUESS.
VERY WELL. RUN ALONG, DOROTHY -- MAY GOOD LUCK GO WITH YOU!
IT'S BEAUTIFUL... BUT IT'S SO *STILL!*
DOROTHY PASSED THROUGH SEVERAL ROOMS UNTIL SHE CAME UPON TIK-TOK.
CREE- CREE- CREE--
Thank you, Dor-o-thy. I have one more guess to make.
BE VERY CAREFUL, TIK-TOK, WON'T YOU?
Yes. But the Nome King has us in his pow-er. I fear we are all lost.

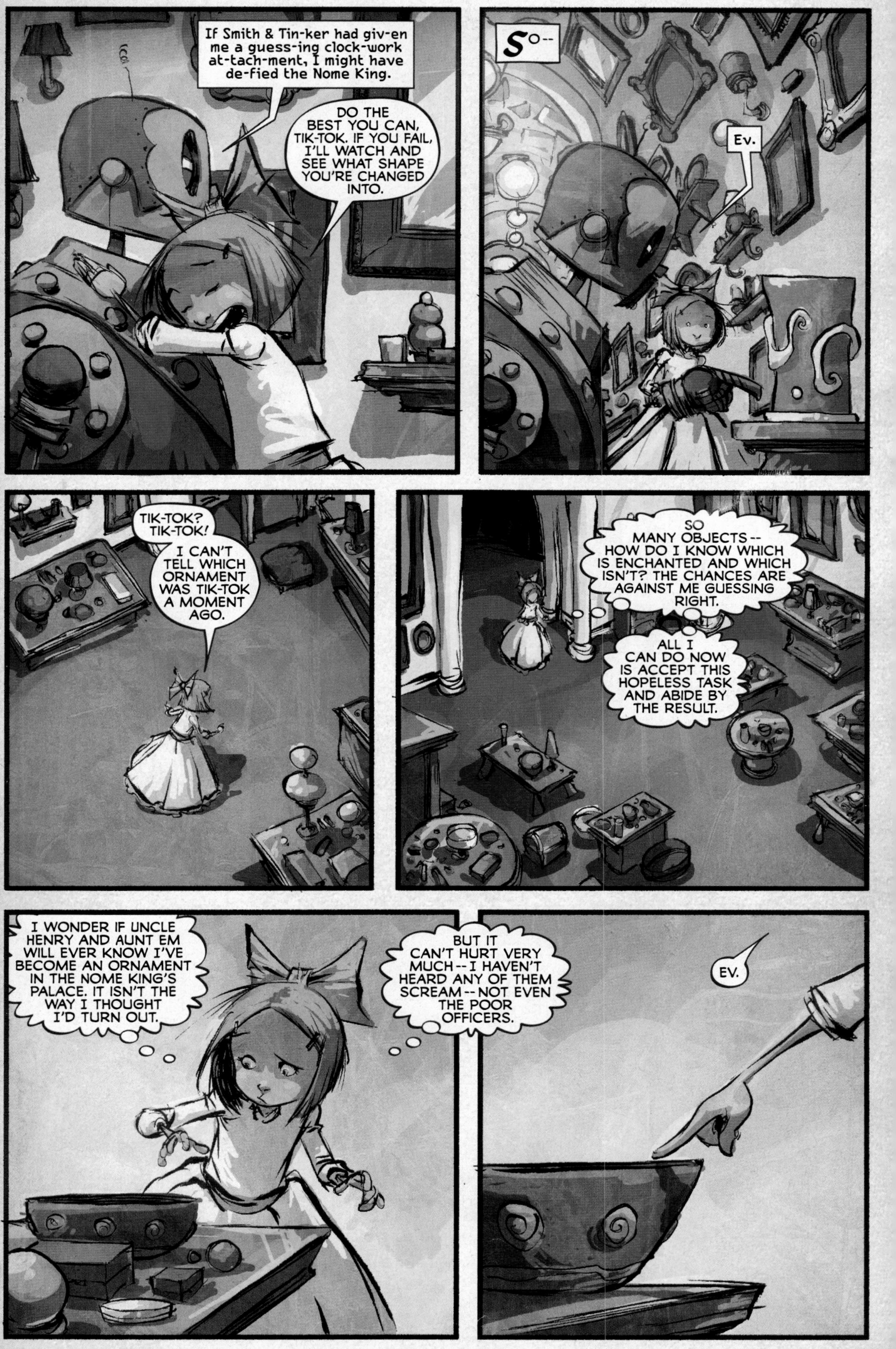
If Smith & Tin-ker had giv-en me a guess-ing clock-work at-tach-ment, I might have de-fied the Nome King.
DO THE BEST YOU CAN, TIK-TOK. IF YOU FAIL, I'LL WATCH AND SEE WHAT SHAPE YOU'RE CHANGED INTO.
So--
Ev.
TIK-TOK? TIK-TOK!
I CAN'T TELL WHICH ORNAMENT WAS TIK-TOK A MOMENT AGO.
SO MANY OBJECTS -- HOW DO I KNOW WHICH IS ENCHANTED AND WHICH ISN'T? THE CHANCES ARE AGAINST ME GUESSING RIGHT.
ALL I CAN DO NOW IS ACCEPT THIS HOPELESS TASK AND ABIDE BY THE RESULT.
I WONDER IF UNCLE HENRY AND AUNT EM WILL EVER KNOW I'VE BECOME AN ORNAMENT IN THE NOME KING'S PALACE. IT ISN'T THE WAY I THOUGHT I'D TURN OUT.
BUT IT CAN'T HURT VERY MUCH -- I HAVEN'T HEARD ANY OF THEM SCREAM -- NOT EVEN THE POOR OFFICERS.
EV.

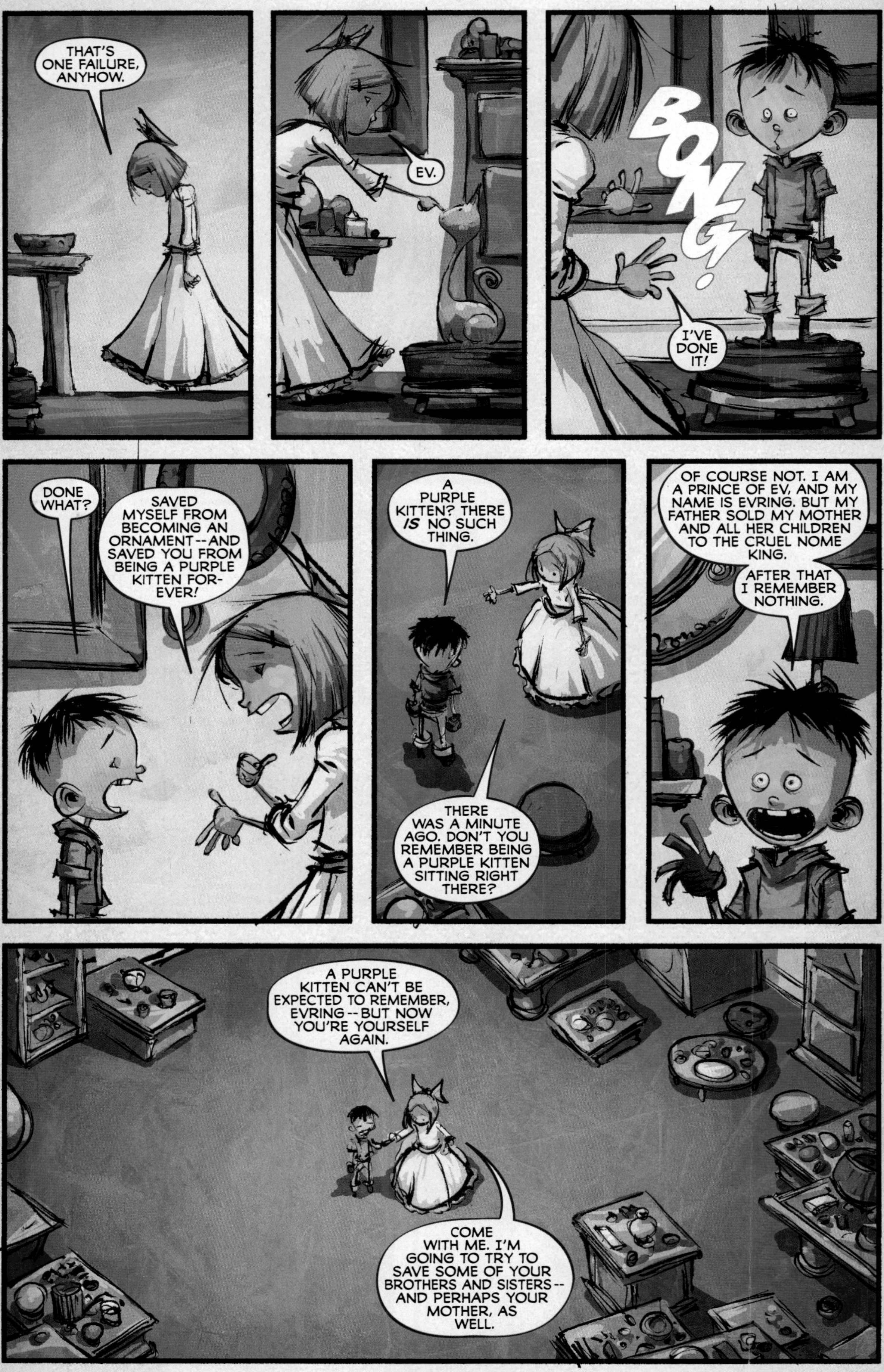
THAT'S ONE FAILURE, ANYHOW.
EV.
BONG!
I'VE DONE IT!
DONE WHAT?
SAVED MYSELF FROM BECOMING AN ORNAMENT--AND SAVED YOU FROM BEING A PURPLE KITTEN FOR-EVER!
A PURPLE KITTEN? THERE *IS* NO SUCH THING.
THERE WAS A MINUTE AGO. DON'T YOU REMEMBER BEING A PURPLE KITTEN SITTING RIGHT THERE?
OF COURSE NOT. I AM A PRINCE OF EV, AND MY NAME IS EVRING. BUT MY FATHER SOLD MY MOTHER AND ALL HER CHILDREN TO THE CRUEL NOME KING.
AFTER THAT I REMEMBER NOTHING.
A PURPLE KITTEN CAN'T BE EXPECTED TO REMEMBER, EVRING--BUT NOW YOU'RE YOURSELF AGAIN.
COME WITH ME. I'M GOING TO TRY TO SAVE SOME OF YOUR BROTHERS AND SISTERS--AND PERHAPS YOUR MOTHER, AS WELL.

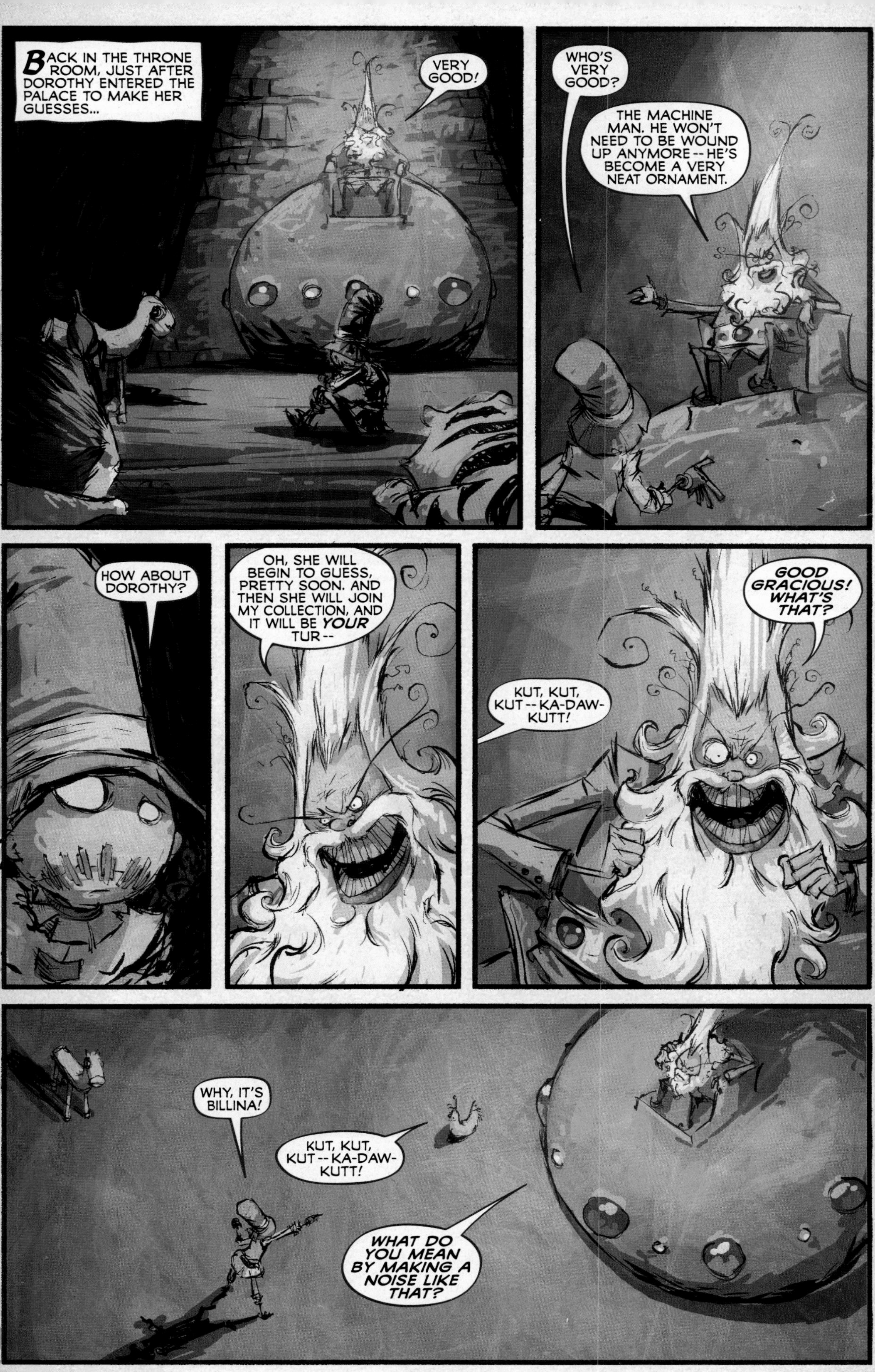
BACK IN THE THRONE ROOM, JUST AFTER DOROTHY ENTERED THE PALACE TO MAKE HER GUESSES...
VERY GOOD!
WHO'S VERY GOOD?
THE MACHINE MAN. HE WON'T NEED TO BE WOUND UP ANYMORE -- HE'S BECOME A VERY NEAT ORNAMENT.
HOW ABOUT DOROTHY?
OH, SHE WILL BEGIN TO GUESS, PRETTY SOON. AND THEN SHE WILL JOIN MY COLLECTION, AND IT WILL BE *YOUR* TUR --
KUT, KUT, KUT -- KA-DAW-KUTT!
GOOD GRACIOUS! WHAT'S THAT?
WHY, IT'S BILLINA!
KUT, KUT, KUT -- KA-DAW-KUTT!
WHAT DO YOU MEAN BY MAKING A NOISE LIKE THAT?

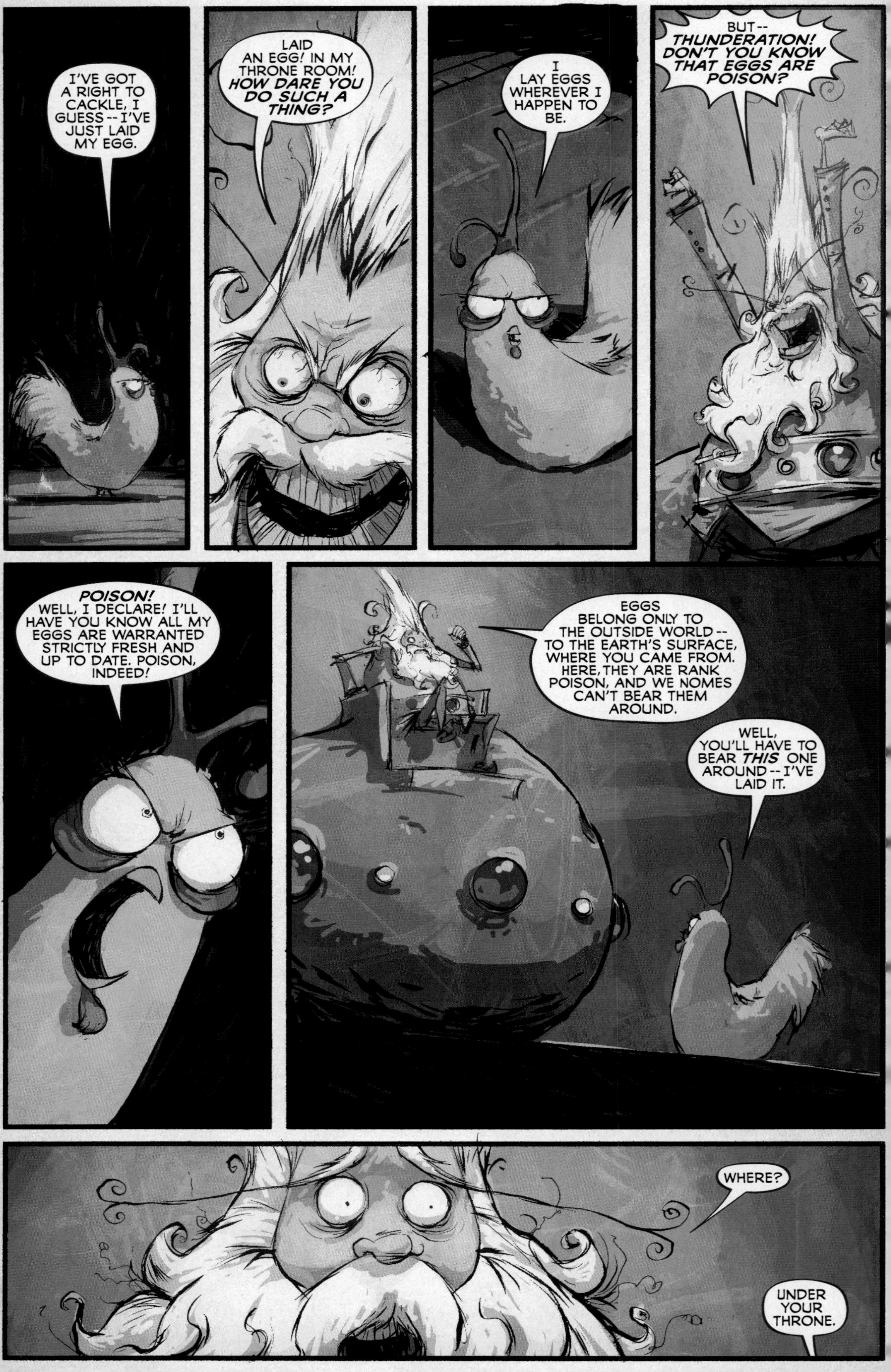
I'VE GOT A RIGHT TO CACKLE, I GUESS -- I'VE JUST LAID MY EGG.
LAID AN EGG! IN MY THRONE ROOM! *HOW DARE YOU DO SUCH A THING?*
I LAY EGGS WHEREVER I HAPPEN TO BE.
BUT -- *THUNDERATION! DON'T YOU KNOW THAT EGGS ARE POISON?*
POISON! WELL, I DECLARE! I'LL HAVE YOU KNOW ALL MY EGGS ARE WARRANTED STRICTLY FRESH AND UP TO DATE. POISON, *INDEED!*
EGGS BELONG ONLY TO THE OUTSIDE WORLD -- TO THE EARTH'S SURFACE, WHERE YOU CAME FROM. HERE, THEY ARE RANK POISON, AND WE NOMES CAN'T BEAR THEM AROUND.
WELL, YOU'LL HAVE TO BEAR *THIS* ONE AROUND -- I'VE LAID IT.
WHERE?
UNDER YOUR THRONE.

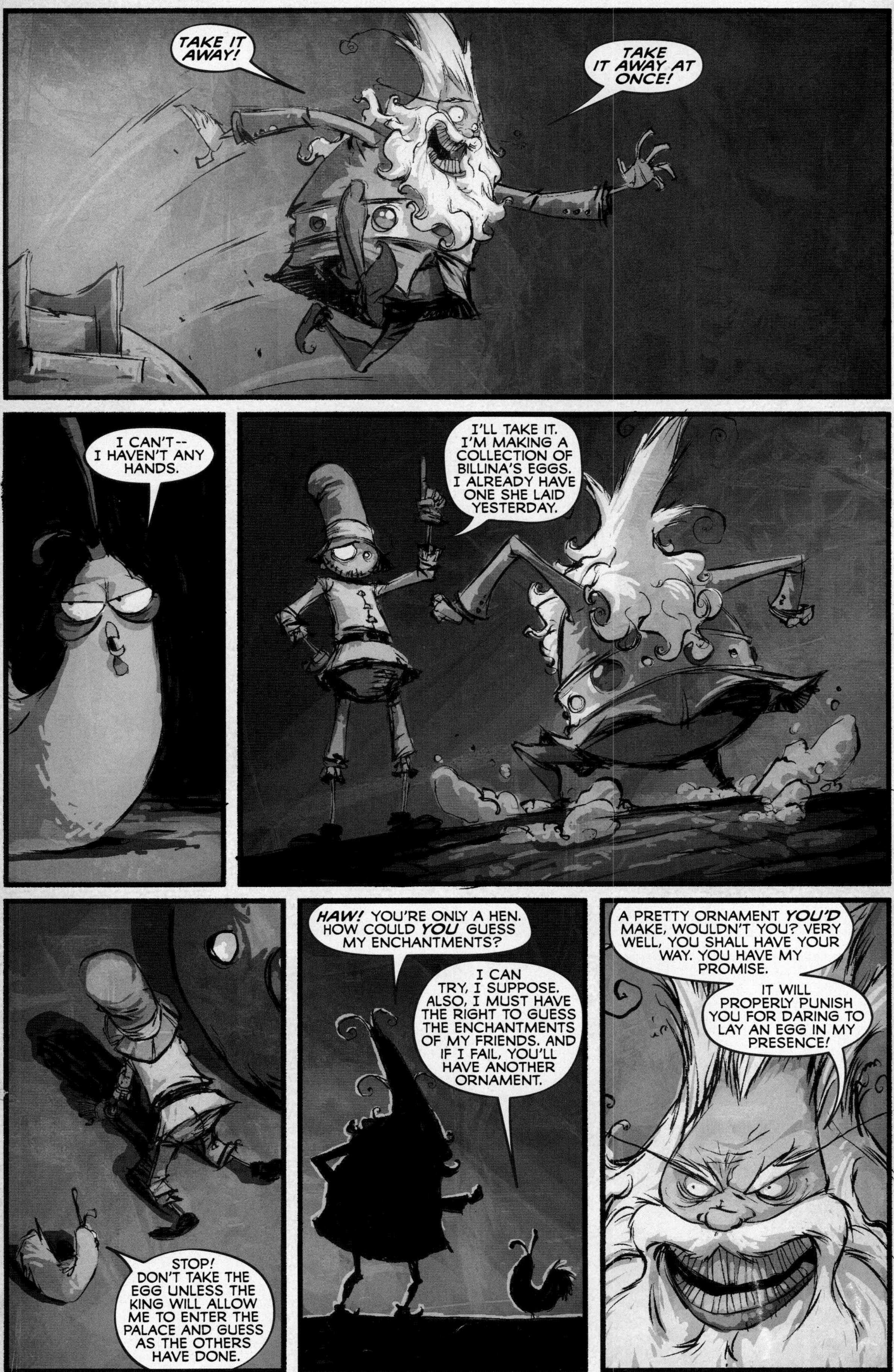

TAKE IT AWAY!
TAKE IT AWAY AT ONCE!
I CAN'T-- I HAVEN'T ANY HANDS.
I'LL TAKE IT. I'M MAKING A COLLECTION OF BILLINA'S EGGS. I ALREADY HAVE ONE SHE LAID YESTERDAY.
STOP! DON'T TAKE THE EGG UNLESS THE KING WILL ALLOW ME TO ENTER THE PALACE AND GUESS AS THE OTHERS HAVE DONE.
HAW! YOU'RE ONLY A HEN. HOW COULD YOU GUESS MY ENCHANTMENTS?
I CAN TRY, I SUPPOSE. ALSO, I MUST HAVE THE RIGHT TO GUESS THE ENCHANTMENTS OF MY FRIENDS. AND IF I FAIL, YOU'LL HAVE ANOTHER ORNAMENT.
A PRETTY ORNAMENT YOU'D MAKE, WOULDN'T YOU? VERY WELL, YOU SHALL HAVE YOUR WAY. YOU HAVE MY PROMISE.
IT WILL PROPERLY PUNISH YOU FOR DARING TO LAY AN EGG IN MY PRESENCE!

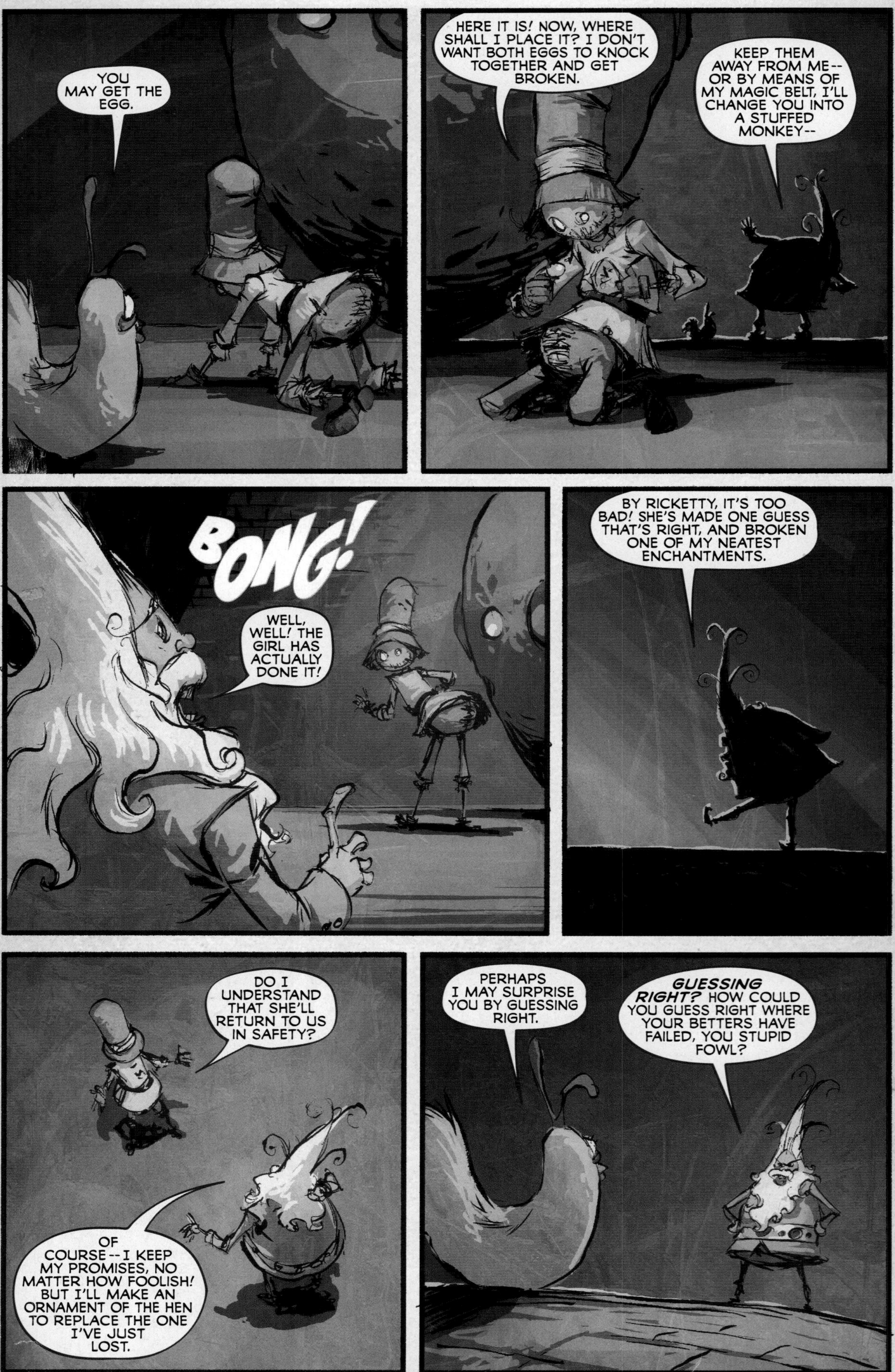
YOU MAY GET THE EGG.
HERE IT IS! NOW, WHERE SHALL I PLACE IT? I DON'T WANT BOTH EGGS TO KNOCK TOGETHER AND GET BROKEN.
KEEP THEM AWAY FROM ME-- OR BY MEANS OF MY MAGIC BELT, I'LL CHANGE YOU INTO A STUFFED MONKEY--
BONG!
WELL, WELL! THE GIRL HAS ACTUALLY DONE IT!
BY RICKETTY, IT'S TOO BAD! SHE'S MADE ONE GUESS THAT'S RIGHT, AND BROKEN ONE OF MY NEATEST ENCHANTMENTS.
DO I UNDERSTAND THAT SHE'LL RETURN TO US IN SAFETY?
OF COURSE--I KEEP MY PROMISES, NO MATTER HOW FOOLISH! BUT I'LL MAKE AN ORNAMENT OF THE HEN TO REPLACE THE ONE I'VE JUST LOST.
PERHAPS I MAY SURPRISE YOU BY GUESSING RIGHT.
GUESSING RIGHT? HOW COULD YOU GUESS RIGHT WHERE YOUR BETTERS HAVE FAILED, YOU STUPID FOWL?

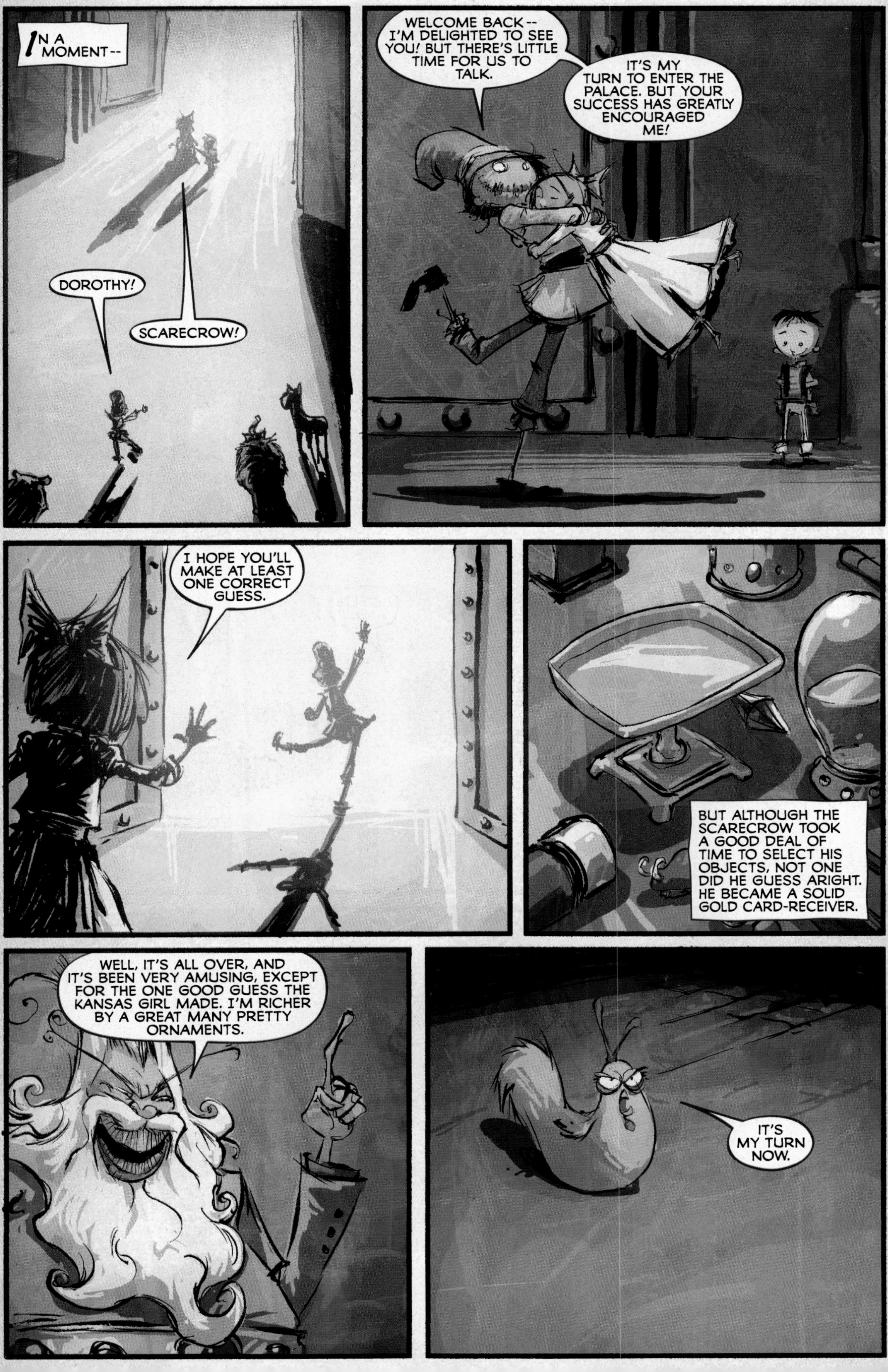
IN A MOMENT--
DOROTHY!
SCARECROW!
WELCOME BACK-- I'M DELIGHTED TO SEE YOU! BUT THERE'S LITTLE TIME FOR US TO TALK.
IT'S MY TURN TO ENTER THE PALACE. BUT YOUR SUCCESS HAS GREATLY ENCOURAGED ME!
I HOPE YOU'LL MAKE AT LEAST ONE CORRECT GUESS.
BUT ALTHOUGH THE SCARECROW TOOK A GOOD DEAL OF TIME TO SELECT HIS OBJECTS, NOT ONE DID HE GUESS ARIGHT. HE BECAME A SOLID GOLD CARD-RECEIVER.
WELL, IT'S ALL OVER, AND IT'S BEEN VERY AMUSING, EXCEPT FOR THE ONE GOOD GUESS THE KANSAS GIRL MADE. I'M RICHER BY A GREAT MANY PRETTY ORNAMENTS.
IT'S MY TURN NOW.

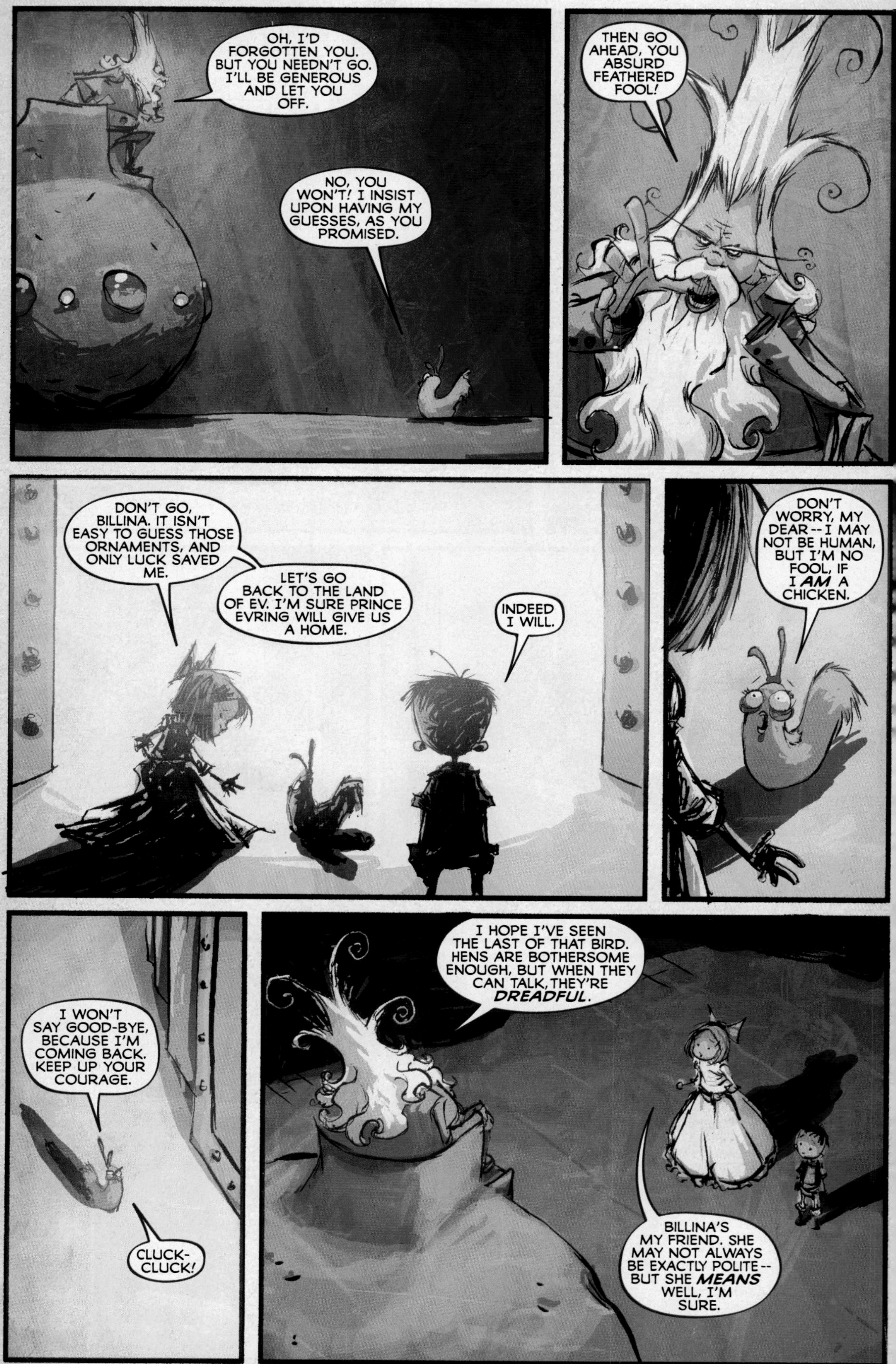
OH, I'D FORGOTTEN YOU. BUT YOU NEEDN'T GO. I'LL BE GENEROUS AND LET YOU OFF.
NO, YOU WON'T! I INSIST UPON HAVING MY GUESSES, AS YOU PROMISED.
THEN GO AHEAD, YOU ABSURD FEATHERED FOOL!
DON'T GO, BILLINA. IT ISN'T EASY TO GUESS THOSE ORNAMENTS, AND ONLY LUCK SAVED ME.
LET'S GO BACK TO THE LAND OF EV. I'M SURE PRINCE EVRING WILL GIVE US A HOME.
INDEED I WILL.
DON'T WORRY, MY DEAR -- I MAY NOT BE HUMAN, BUT I'M NO FOOL, IF I AM A CHICKEN.
I WON'T SAY GOOD-BYE, BECAUSE I'M COMING BACK. KEEP UP YOUR COURAGE.
CLUCK-CLUCK!
I HOPE I'VE SEEN THE LAST OF THAT BIRD. HENS ARE BOTHERSOME ENOUGH, BUT WHEN THEY CAN TALK, THEY'RE DREADFUL.
BILLINA'S MY FRIEND. SHE MAY NOT ALWAYS BE EXACTLY POLITE -- BUT SHE MEANS WELL, I'M SURE.

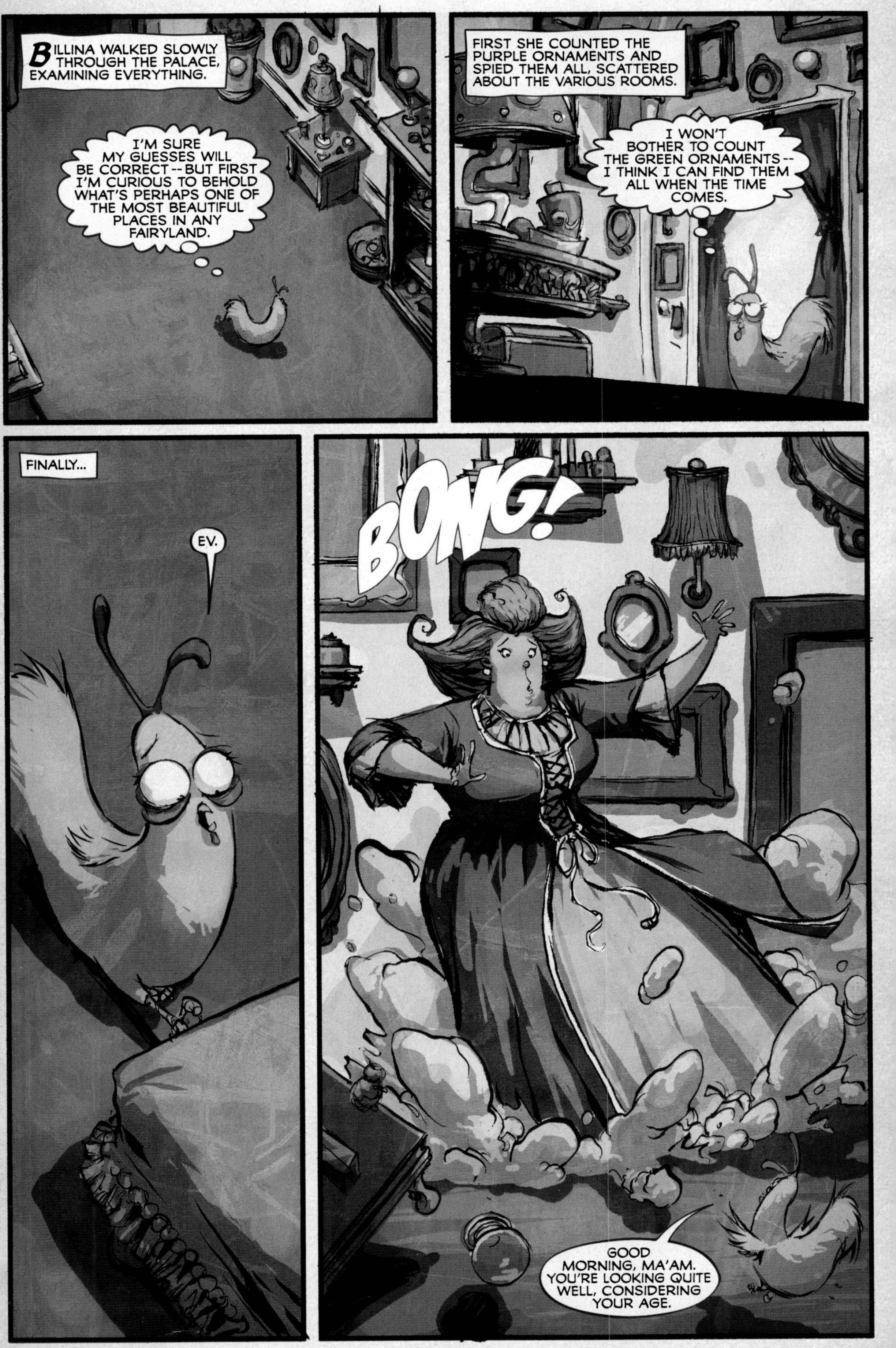
BILLINA WALKED SLOWLY THROUGH THE PALACE, EXAMINING EVERYTHING.
I'M SURE MY GUESSES WILL BE CORRECT--BUT FIRST I'M CURIOUS TO BEHOLD WHAT'S PERHAPS ONE OF THE MOST BEAUTIFUL PLACES IN ANY FAIRYLAND.
FIRST SHE COUNTED THE PURPLE ORNAMENTS AND SPIED THEM ALL, SCATTERED ABOUT THE VARIOUS ROOMS.
I WON'T BOTHER TO COUNT THE GREEN ORNAMENTS--I THINK I CAN FIND THEM ALL WHEN THE TIME COMES.
FINALLY...
EV.
BONG!
GOOD MORNING, MA'AM. YOU'RE LOOKING QUITE WELL, CONSIDERING YOUR AGE.

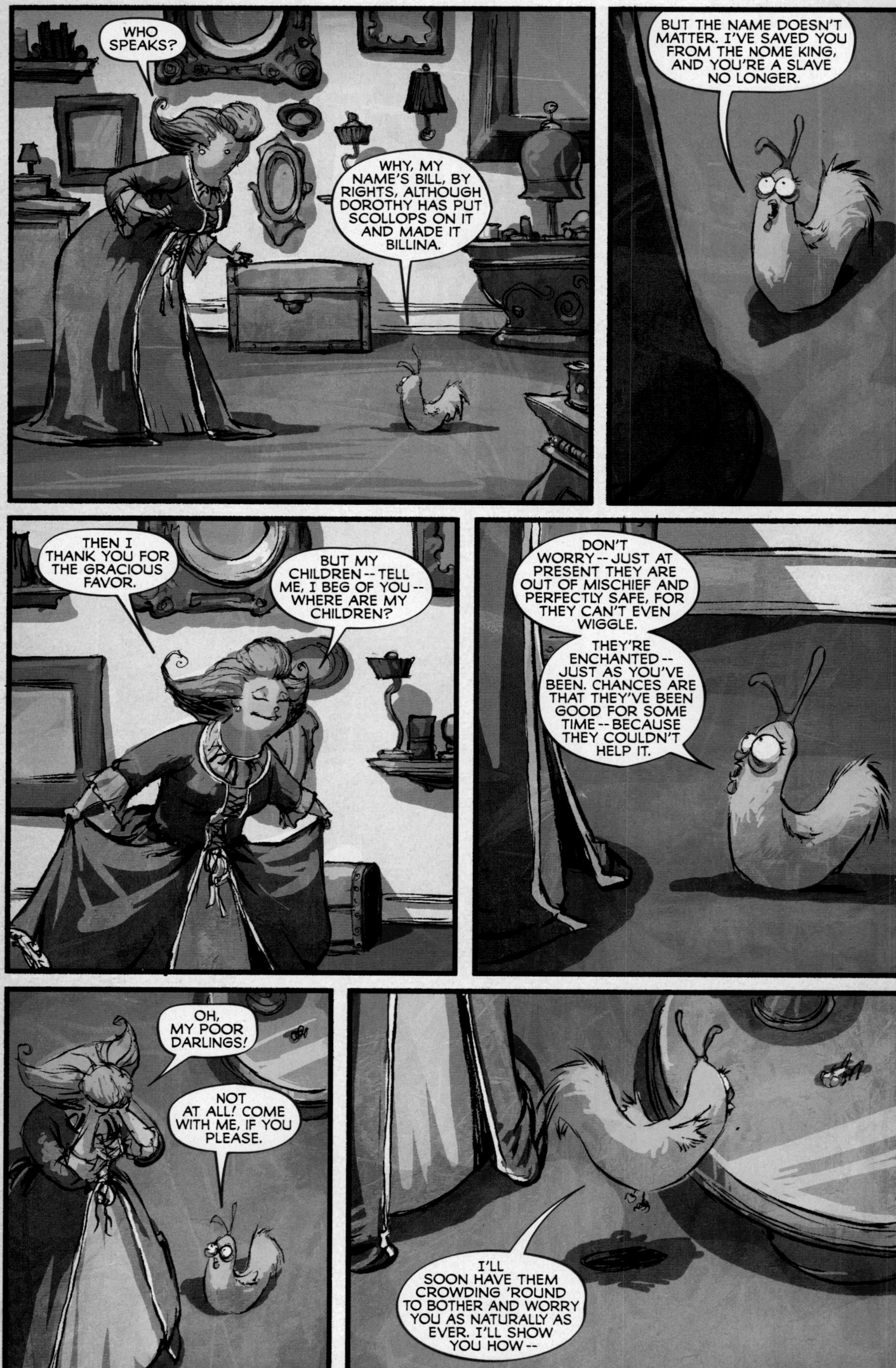
WHO SPEAKS?
WHY, MY NAME'S BILL, BY RIGHTS, ALTHOUGH DOROTHY HAS PUT SCOLLOPS ON IT AND MADE IT BILLINA.
BUT THE NAME DOESN'T MATTER. I'VE SAVED YOU FROM THE NOME KING, AND YOU'RE A SLAVE NO LONGER.
THEN I THANK YOU FOR THE GRACIOUS FAVOR.
BUT MY CHILDREN -- TELL ME, I BEG OF YOU -- WHERE ARE MY CHILDREN?
DON'T WORRY -- JUST AT PRESENT THEY ARE OUT OF MISCHIEF AND PERFECTLY SAFE, FOR THEY CAN'T EVEN WIGGLE.
THEY'RE ENCHANTED -- JUST AS YOU'VE BEEN. CHANCES ARE THAT THEY'VE BEEN GOOD FOR SOME TIME -- BECAUSE THEY COULDN'T HELP IT.
OH, MY POOR DARLINGS!
NOT AT ALL! COME WITH ME, IF YOU PLEASE.
I'LL SOON HAVE THEM CROWDING 'ROUND TO BOTHER AND WORRY YOU AS NATURALLY AS EVER. I'LL SHOW YOU HOW --

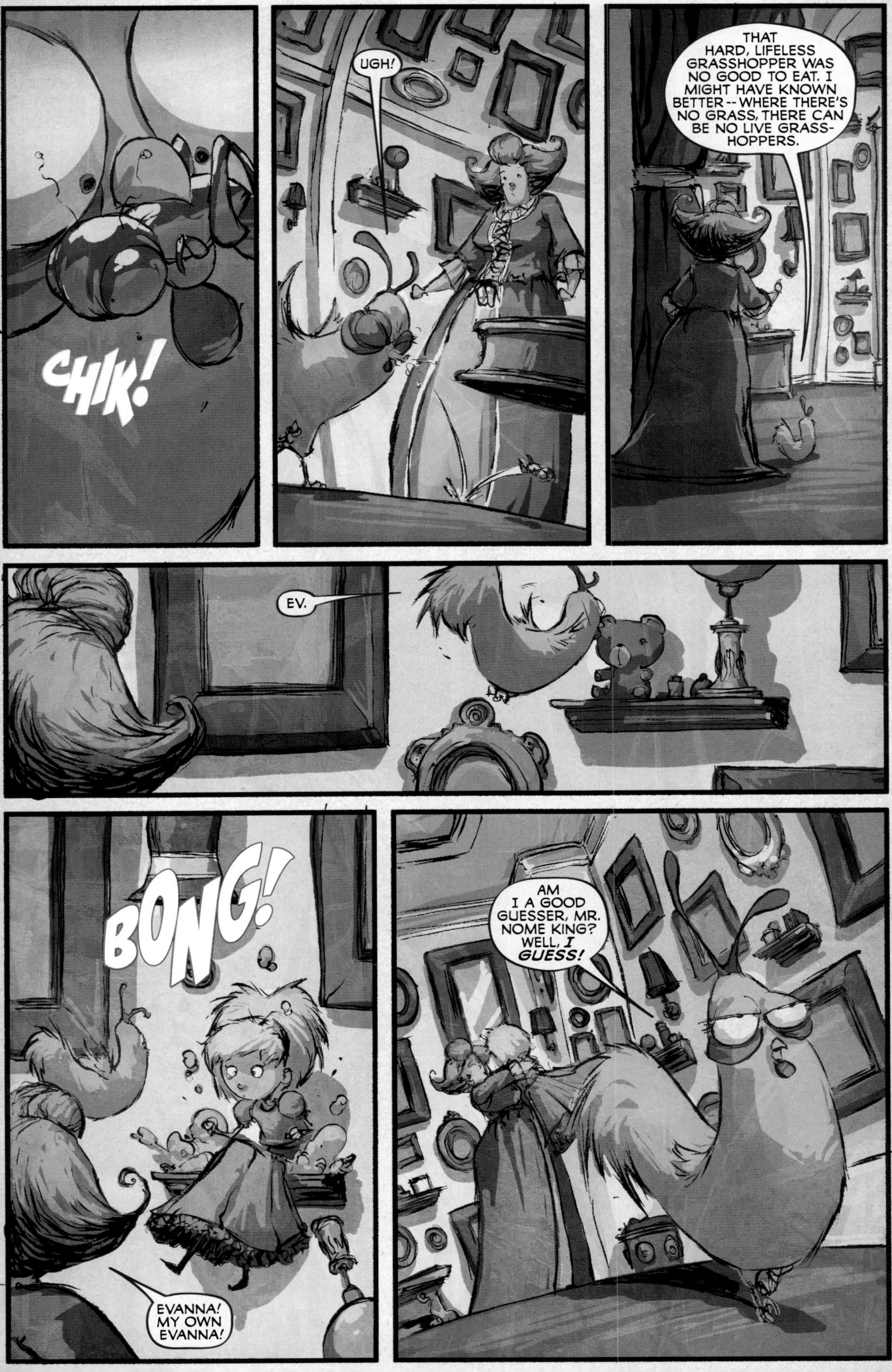
CHIK!
UGH!
THAT HARD, LIFELESS GRASSHOPPER WAS NO GOOD TO EAT. I MIGHT HAVE KNOWN BETTER -- WHERE THERE'S NO GRASS, THERE CAN BE NO LIVE GRASS-HOPPERS.
EV.
BONG!
EVANNA! MY OWN EVANNA!
AM I A GOOD GUESSER, MR. NOME KING? WELL, *I GUESS!*

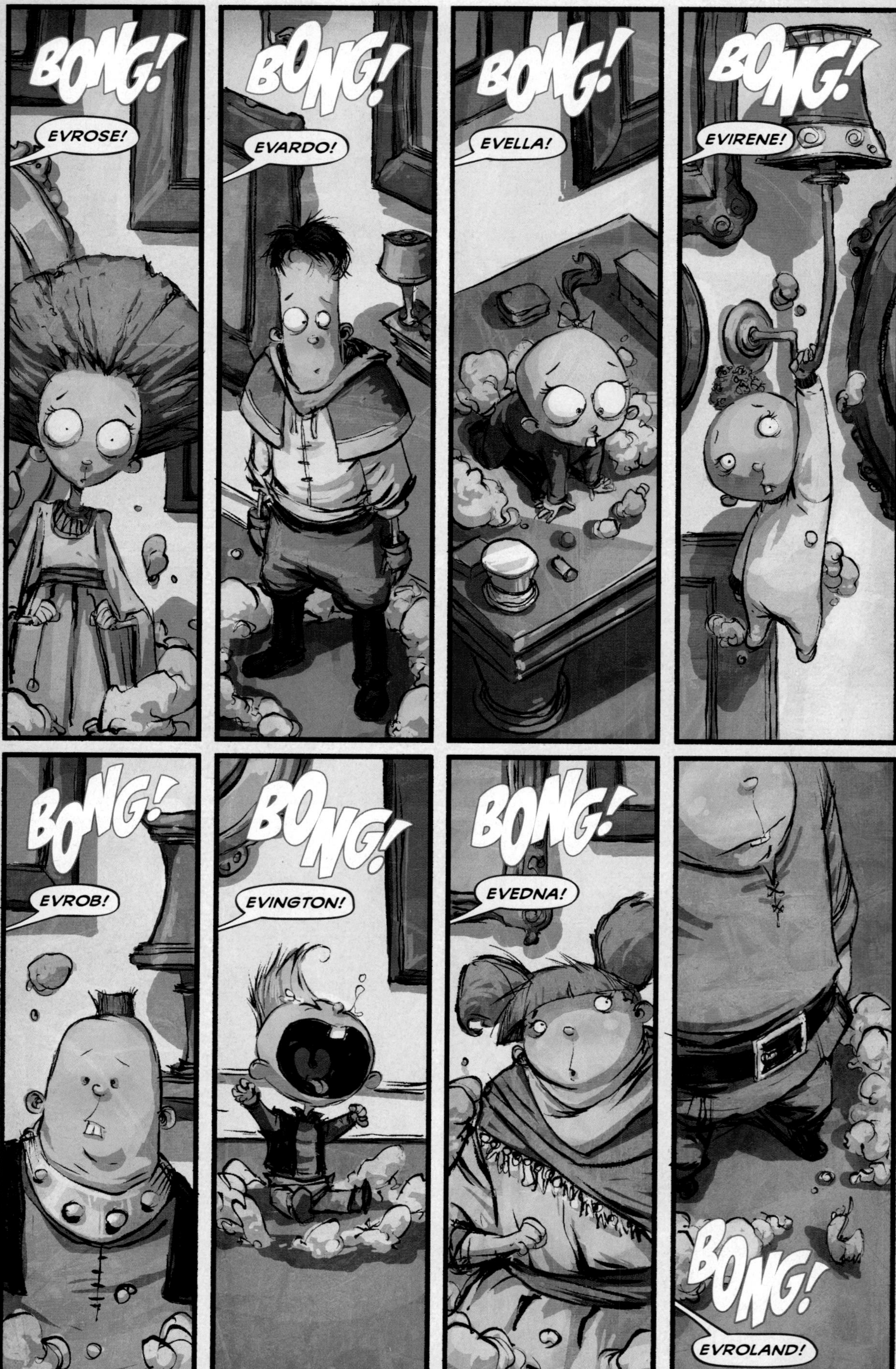
BONG!
EVROSE!
BONG!
EVARDO!
BONG!
EVELLA!
BONG!
EVIRENE!
BONG!
EVROB!
BONG!
EVINGTON!
BONG!
EVEDNA!
BONG!
EVROLAND!

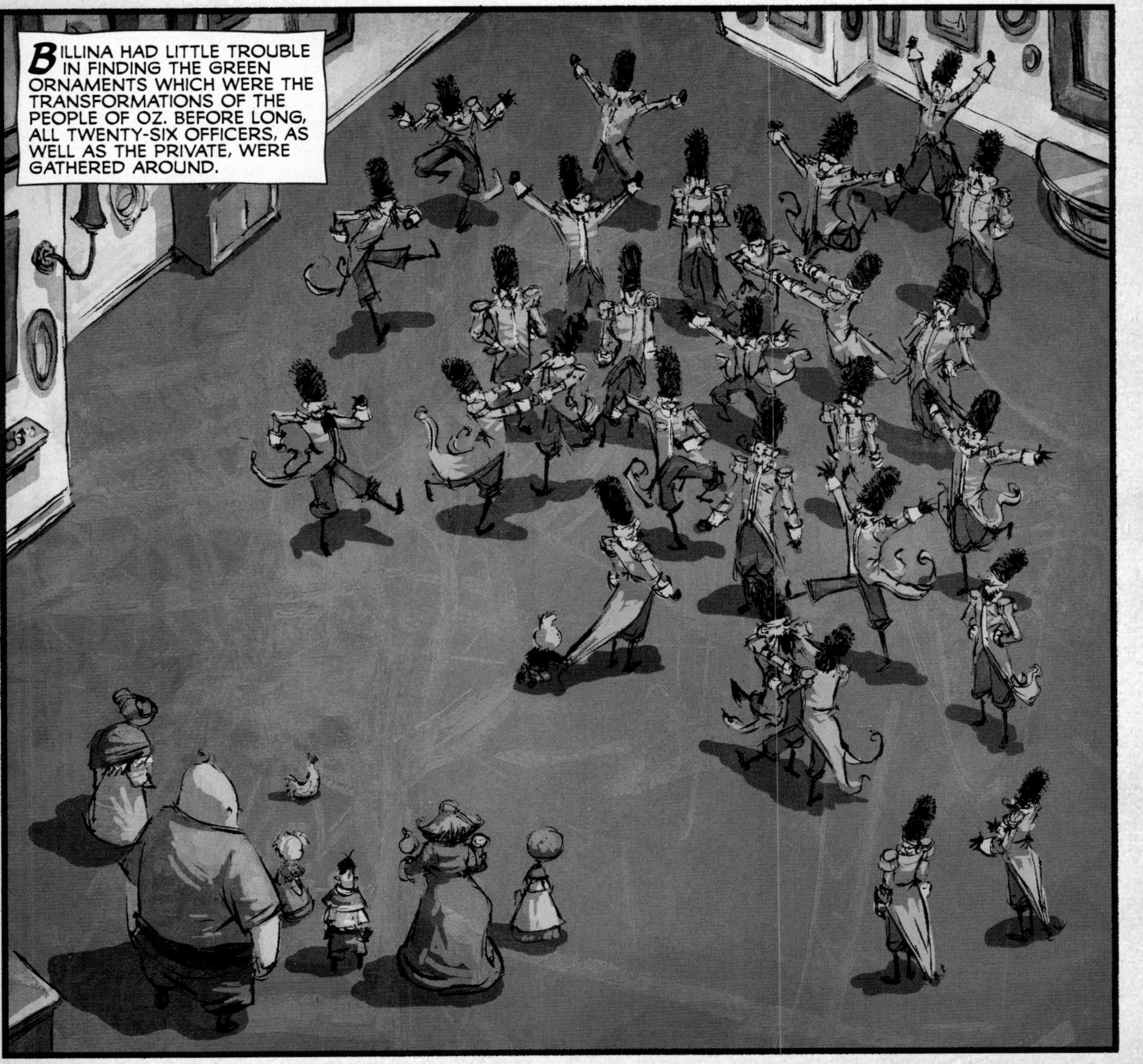
BILLINA HAD LITTLE TROUBLE IN FINDING THE GREEN ORNAMENTS WHICH WERE THE TRANSFORMATIONS OF THE PEOPLE OF OZ. BEFORE LONG, ALL TWENTY-SIX OFFICERS, AS WELL AS THE PRIVATE, WERE GATHERED AROUND.

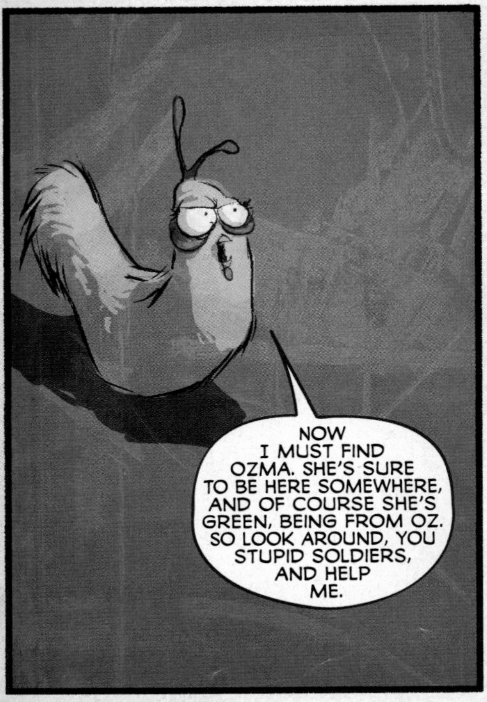
NOW I MUST FIND OZMA. SHE'S SURE TO BE HERE SOMEWHERE, AND OF COURSE SHE'S GREEN, BEING FROM OZ. SO LOOK AROUND, YOU STUPID SOLDIERS, AND HELP ME.

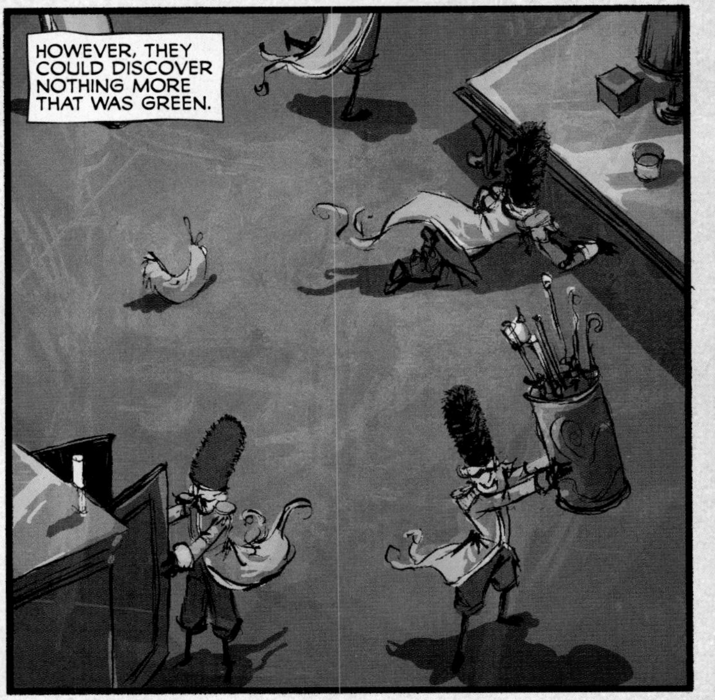
HOWEVER, THEY COULD DISCOVER NOTHING MORE THAT WAS GREEN.

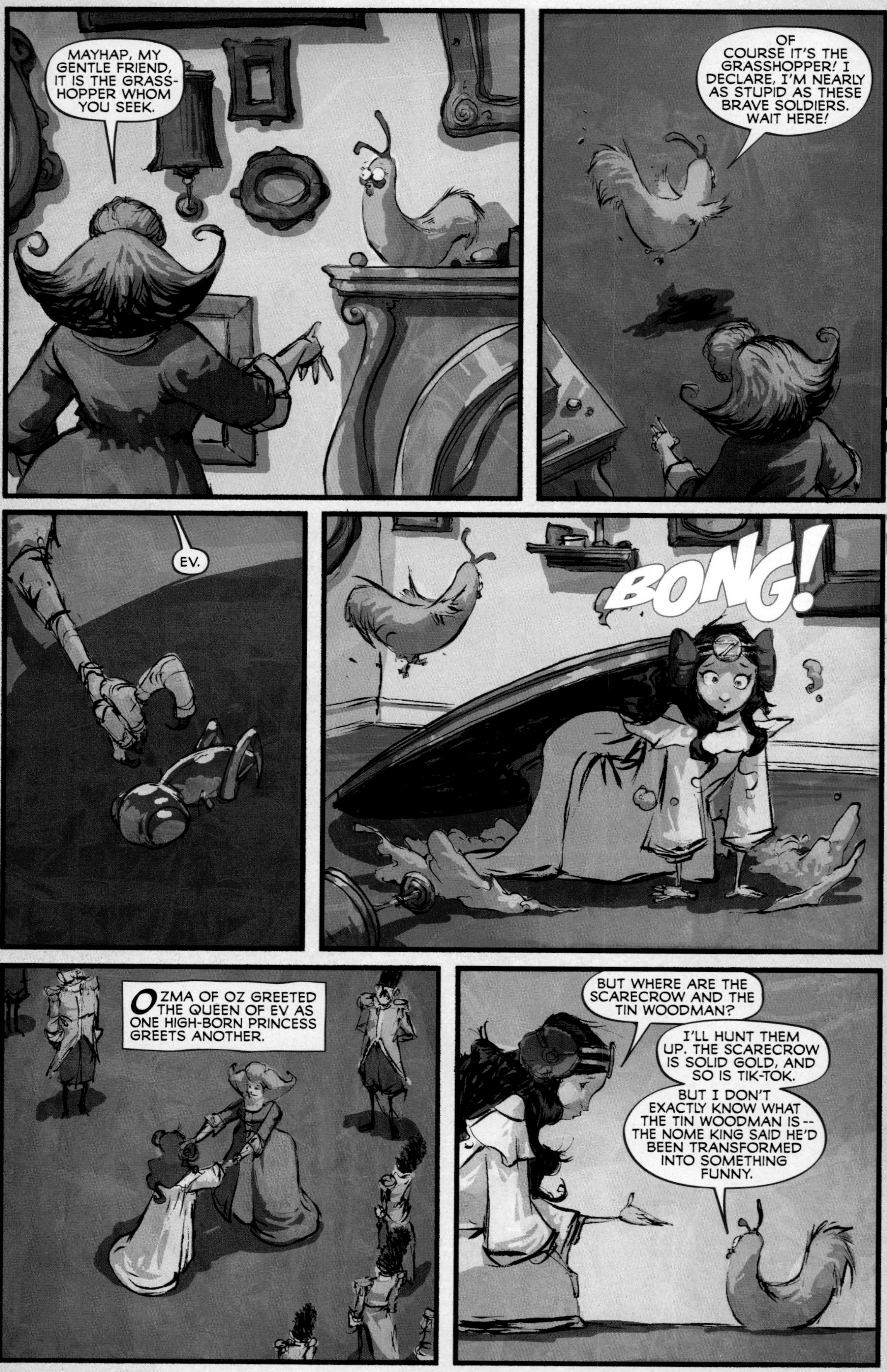
MAYHAP, MY GENTLE FRIEND, IT IS THE GRASS-HOPPER WHOM YOU SEEK.
OF COURSE IT'S THE GRASSHOPPER! I DECLARE, I'M NEARLY AS STUPID AS THESE BRAVE SOLDIERS. WAIT HERE!
EV.
BONG!
OZMA OF OZ GREETED THE QUEEN OF EV AS ONE HIGH-BORN PRINCESS GREETS ANOTHER.
BUT WHERE ARE THE SCARECROW AND THE TIN WOODMAN?
I'LL HUNT THEM UP. THE SCARECROW IS SOLID GOLD, AND SO IS TIK-TOK.
BUT I DON'T EXACTLY KNOW WHAT THE TIN WOODMAN IS -- THE NOME KING SAID HE'D BEEN TRANSFORMED INTO SOMETHING FUNNY.

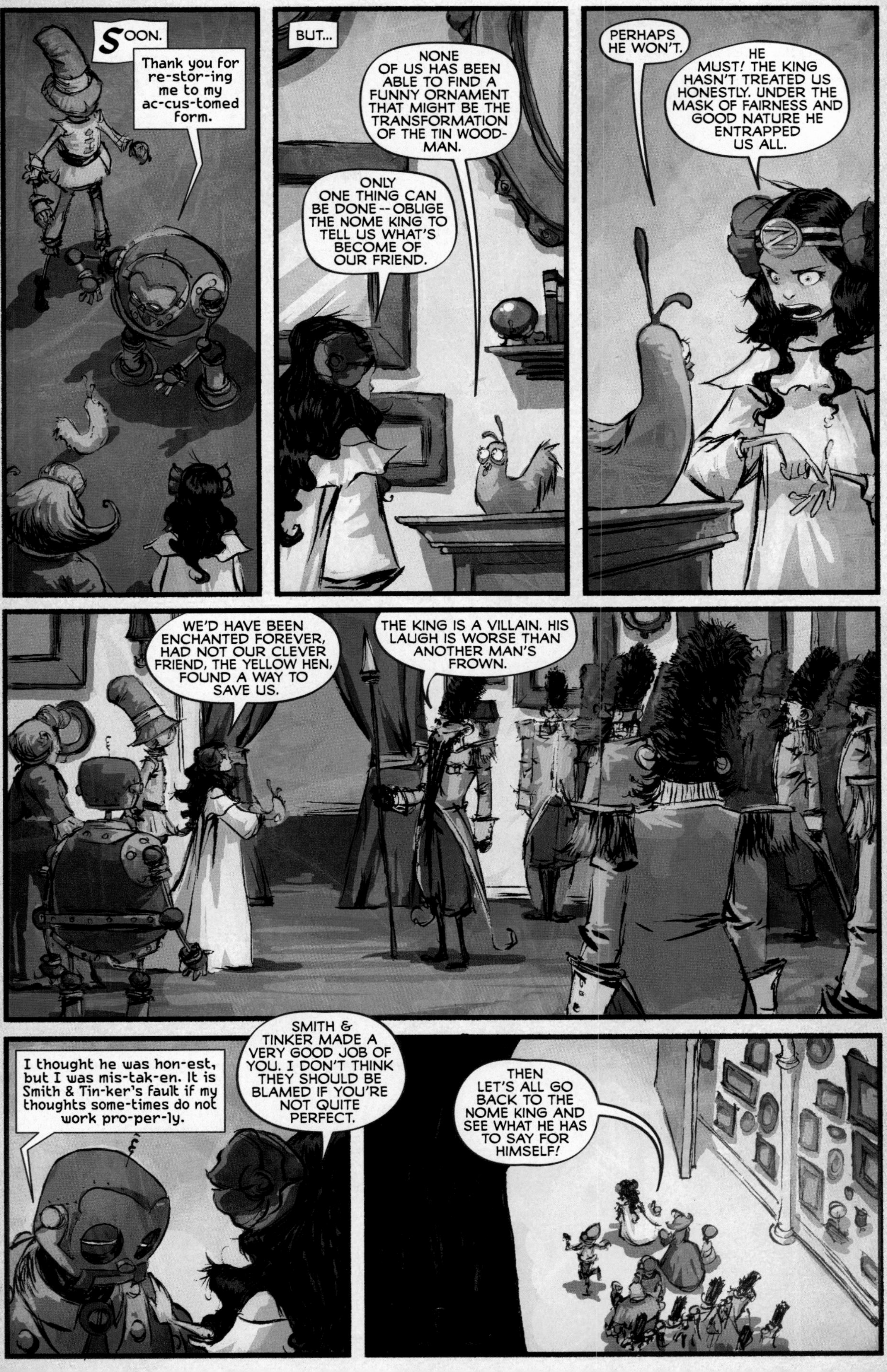
SOON.
Thank you for re-stor-ing me to my ac-cus-tomed form.
BUT...
NONE OF US HAS BEEN ABLE TO FIND A FUNNY ORNAMENT THAT MIGHT BE THE TRANSFORMATION OF THE TIN WOOD-MAN.
ONLY ONE THING CAN BE DONE -- OBLIGE THE NOME KING TO TELL US WHAT'S BECOME OF OUR FRIEND.
PERHAPS HE WON'T.
HE MUST! THE KING HASN'T TREATED US HONESTLY. UNDER THE MASK OF FAIRNESS AND GOOD NATURE HE ENTRAPPED US ALL.
WE'D HAVE BEEN ENCHANTED FOREVER, HAD NOT OUR CLEVER FRIEND, THE YELLOW HEN, FOUND A WAY TO SAVE US.
THE KING IS A VILLAIN. HIS LAUGH IS WORSE THAN ANOTHER MAN'S FROWN.
I thought he was hon-est, but I was mis-tak-en. It is Smith & Tin-ker's fault if my thoughts some-times do not work pro-per-ly.
SMITH & TINKER MADE A VERY GOOD JOB OF YOU. I DON'T THINK THEY SHOULD BE BLAMED IF YOU'RE NOT QUITE PERFECT.
THEN LET'S ALL GO BACK TO THE NOME KING AND SEE WHAT HE HAS TO SAY FOR HIMSELF!

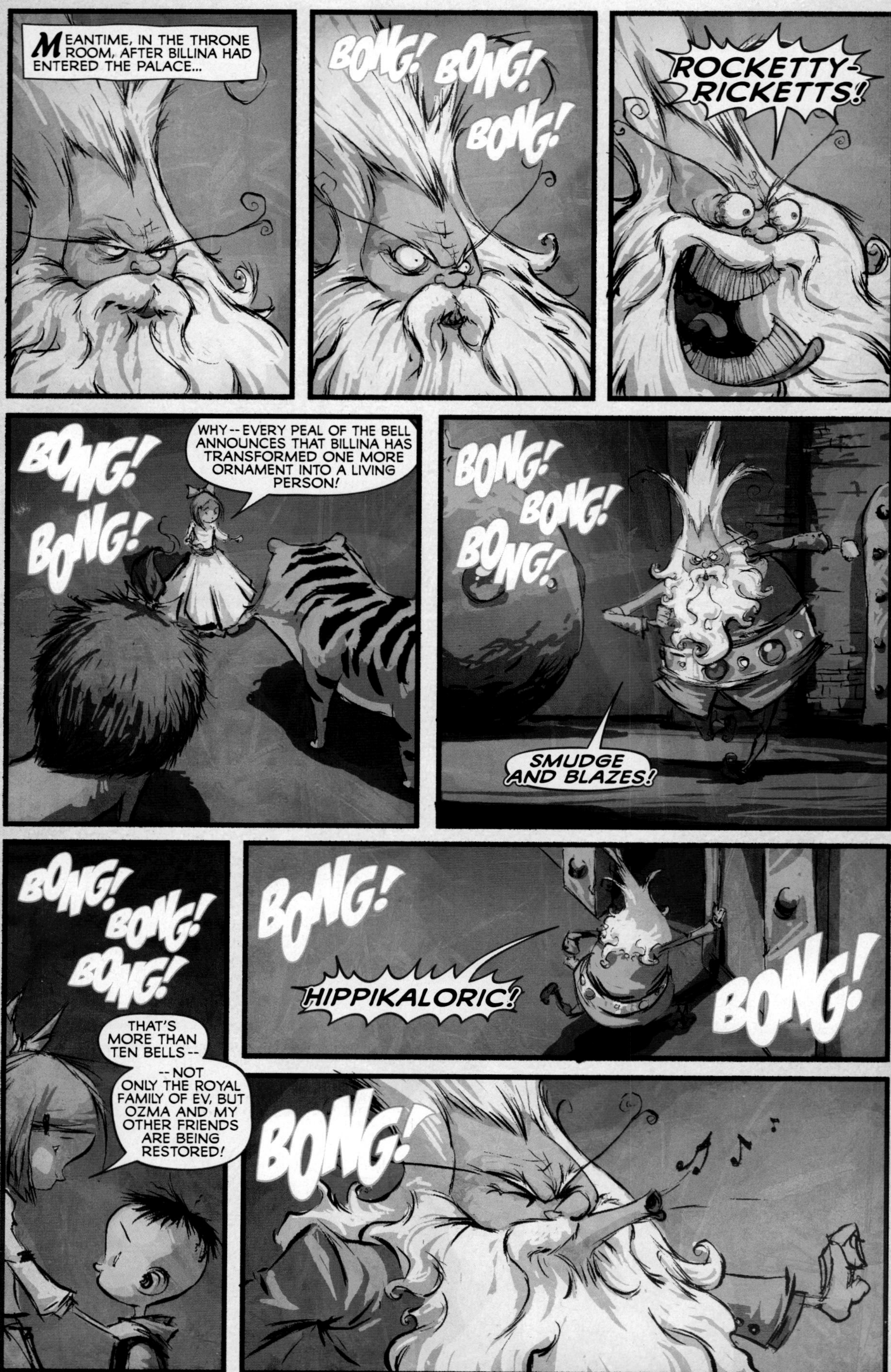
MEANTIME, IN THE THRONE ROOM, AFTER BILLINA HAD ENTERED THE PALACE...
BONG! BONG! BONG!
ROCKETTY-RICKETTS!
BONG! BONG!
WHY--EVERY PEAL OF THE BELL ANNOUNCES THAT BILLINA HAS TRANSFORMED ONE MORE ORNAMENT INTO A LIVING PERSON!
BONG! BONG! BONG!
SMUDGE AND BLAZES!
BONG! BONG! BONG!
THAT'S MORE THAN TEN BELLS--
--NOT ONLY THE ROYAL FAMILY OF EV, BUT OZMA AND MY OTHER FRIENDS ARE BEING RESTORED!
BONG!
HIPPIKALORIC!
BONG!
BONG!

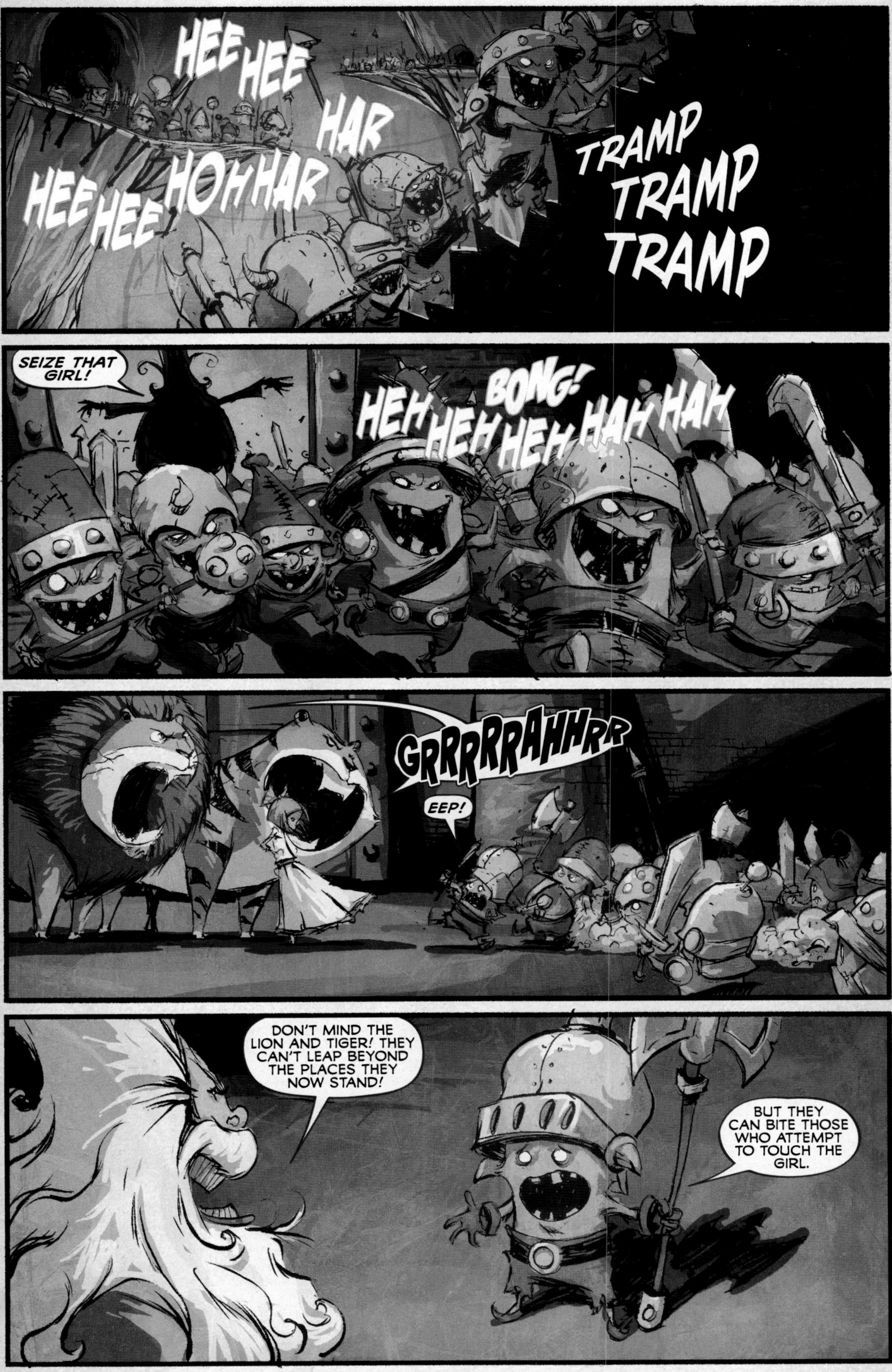
HEE HEE
HAR
HEE HEE HOH HAR
TRAMP
TRAMP
TRAMP
SEIZE THAT GIRL!
HEH HEH HEH HAH HAH
BONG!
GRRRRRAHHRR
EEP!
DON'T MIND THE LION AND TIGER! THEY CAN'T LEAP BEYOND THE PLACES THEY NOW STAND!
BUT THEY CAN BITE THOSE WHO ATTEMPT TO TOUCH THE GIRL.

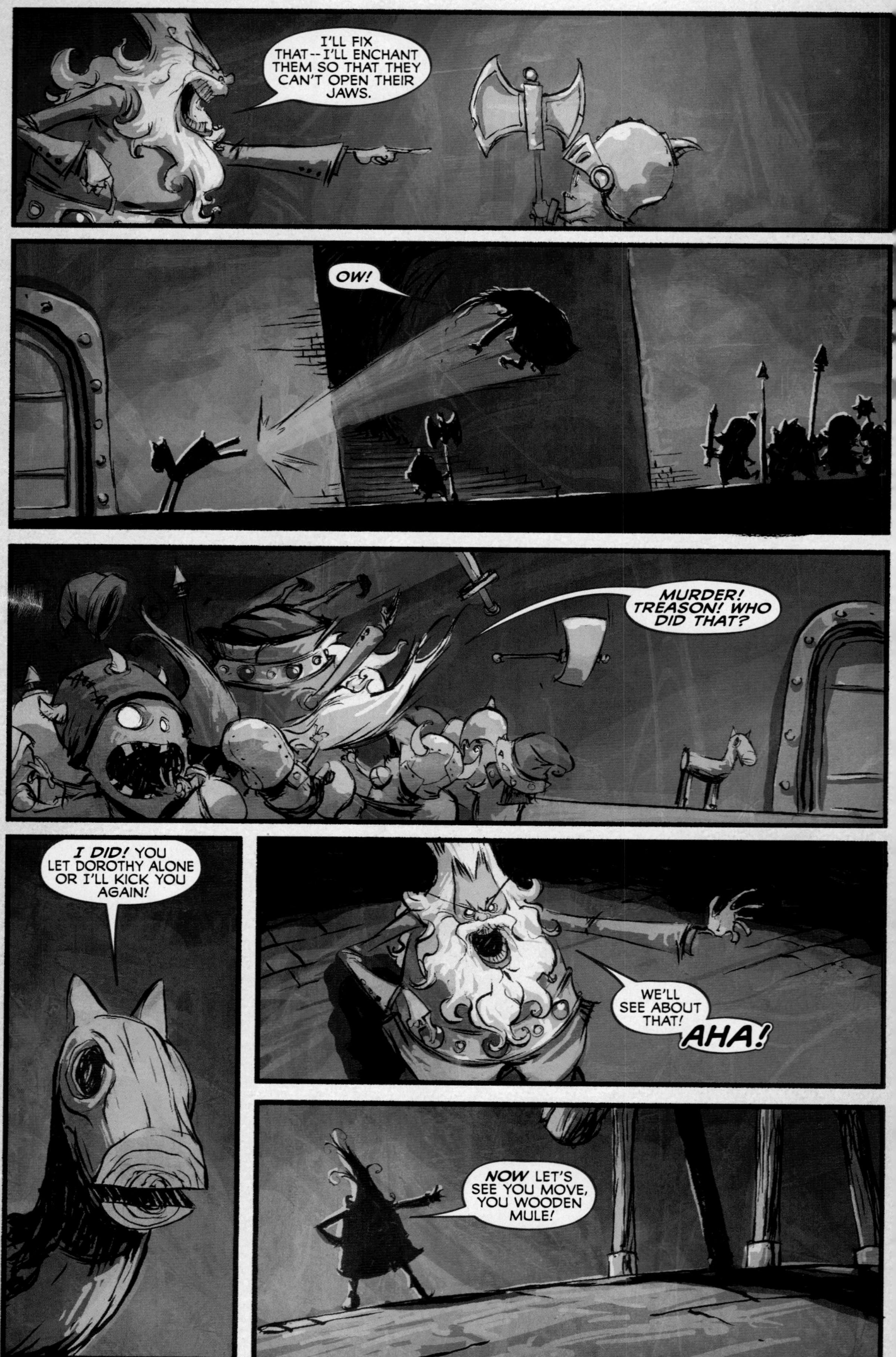

I'LL FIX THAT--I'LL ENCHANT THEM SO THAT THEY CAN'T OPEN THEIR JAWS.
OW!
MURDER! TREASON! WHO DID THAT?
I DID! YOU LET DOROTHY ALONE OR I'LL KICK YOU AGAIN!
WE'LL SEE ABOUT THAT!
AHA!
NOW LET'S SEE YOU MOVE, YOU WOODEN MULE!

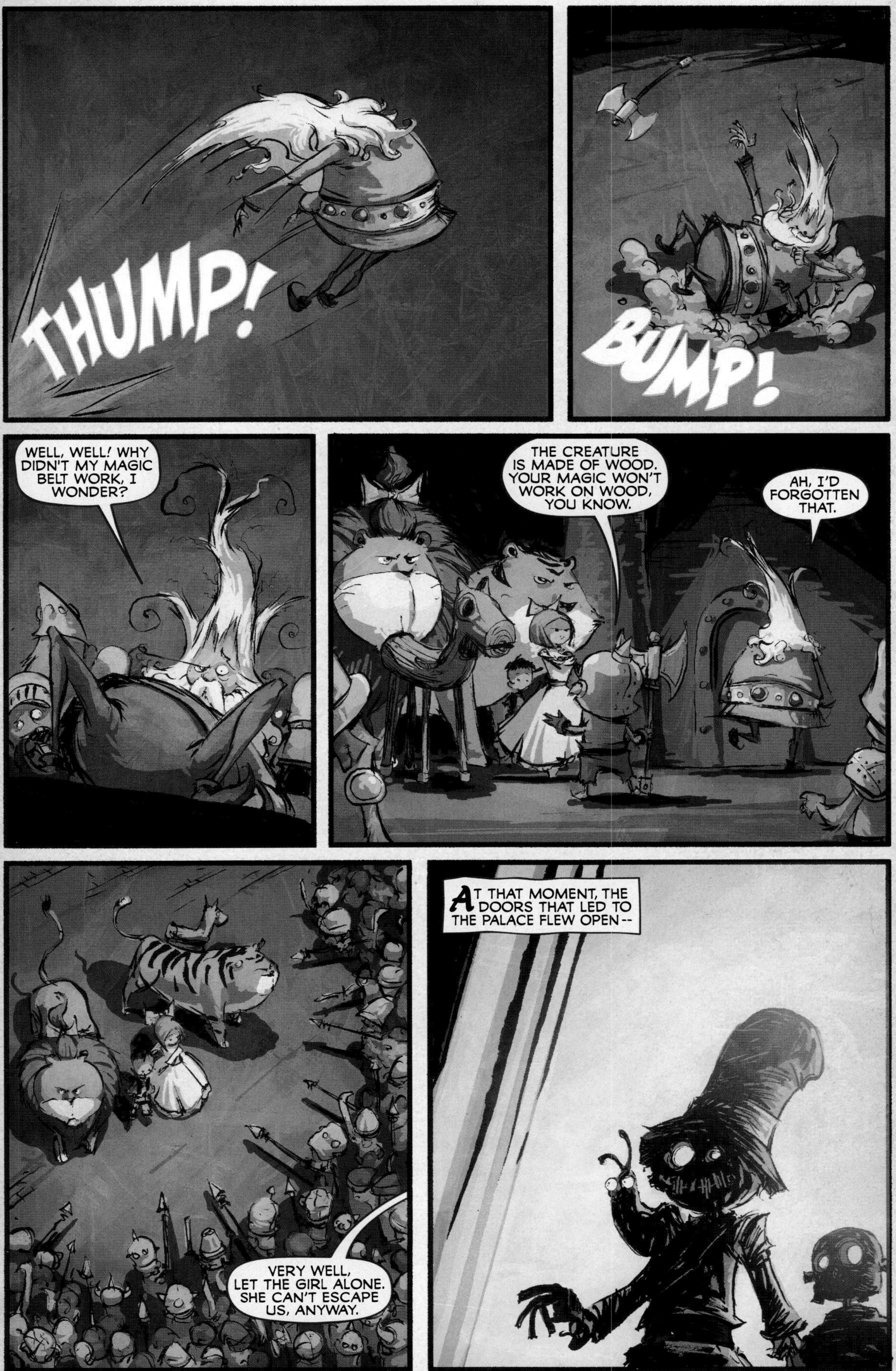
THUMP!
BUMP!
WELL, WELL! WHY DIDN'T MY MAGIC BELT WORK, I WONDER?
THE CREATURE IS MADE OF WOOD. YOUR MAGIC WON'T WORK ON WOOD, YOU KNOW.
AH, I'D FORGOTTEN THAT.
VERY WELL, LET THE GIRL ALONE. SHE CAN'T ESCAPE US, ANYWAY.
AT THAT MOMENT, THE DOORS THAT LED TO THE PALACE FLEW OPEN--

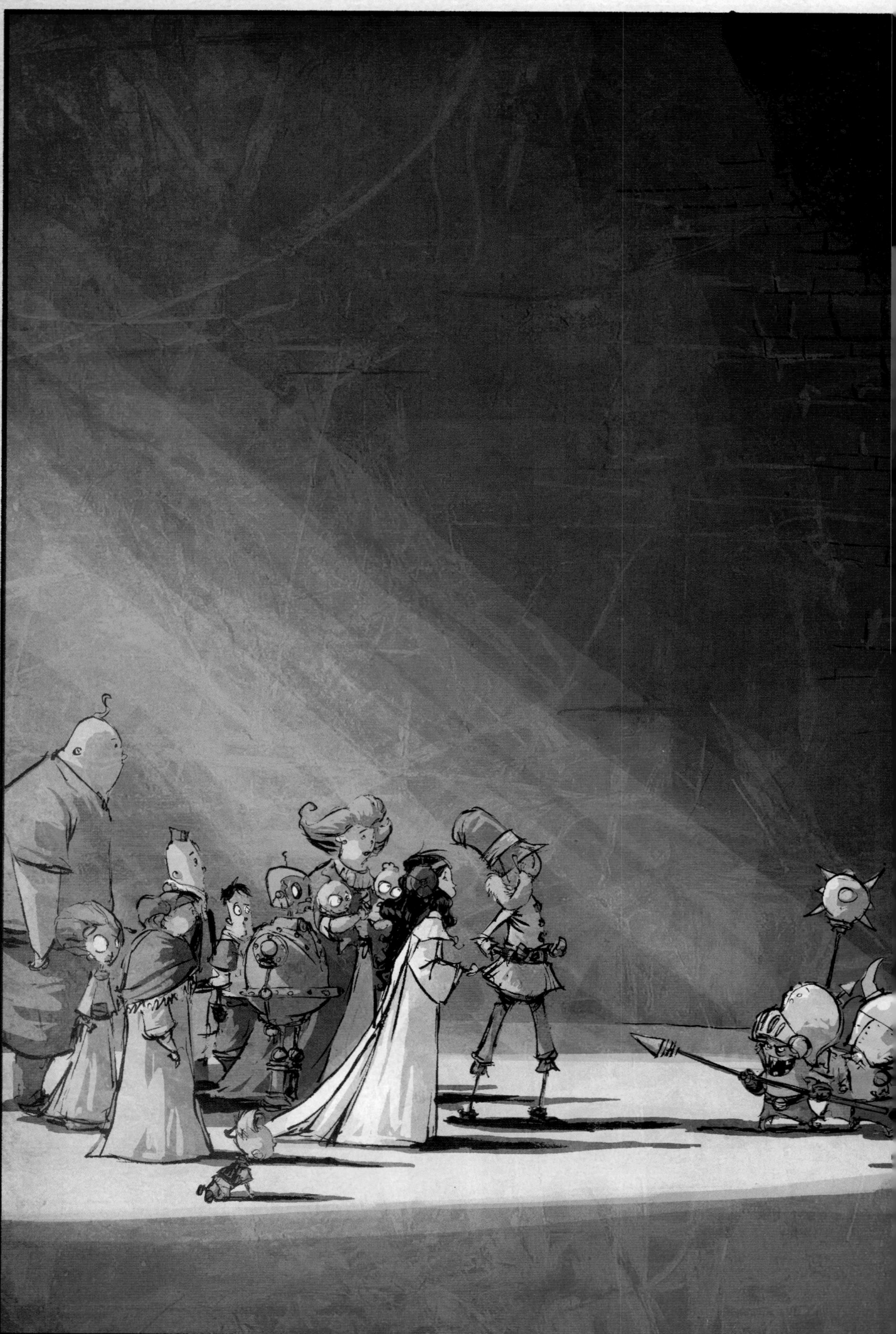

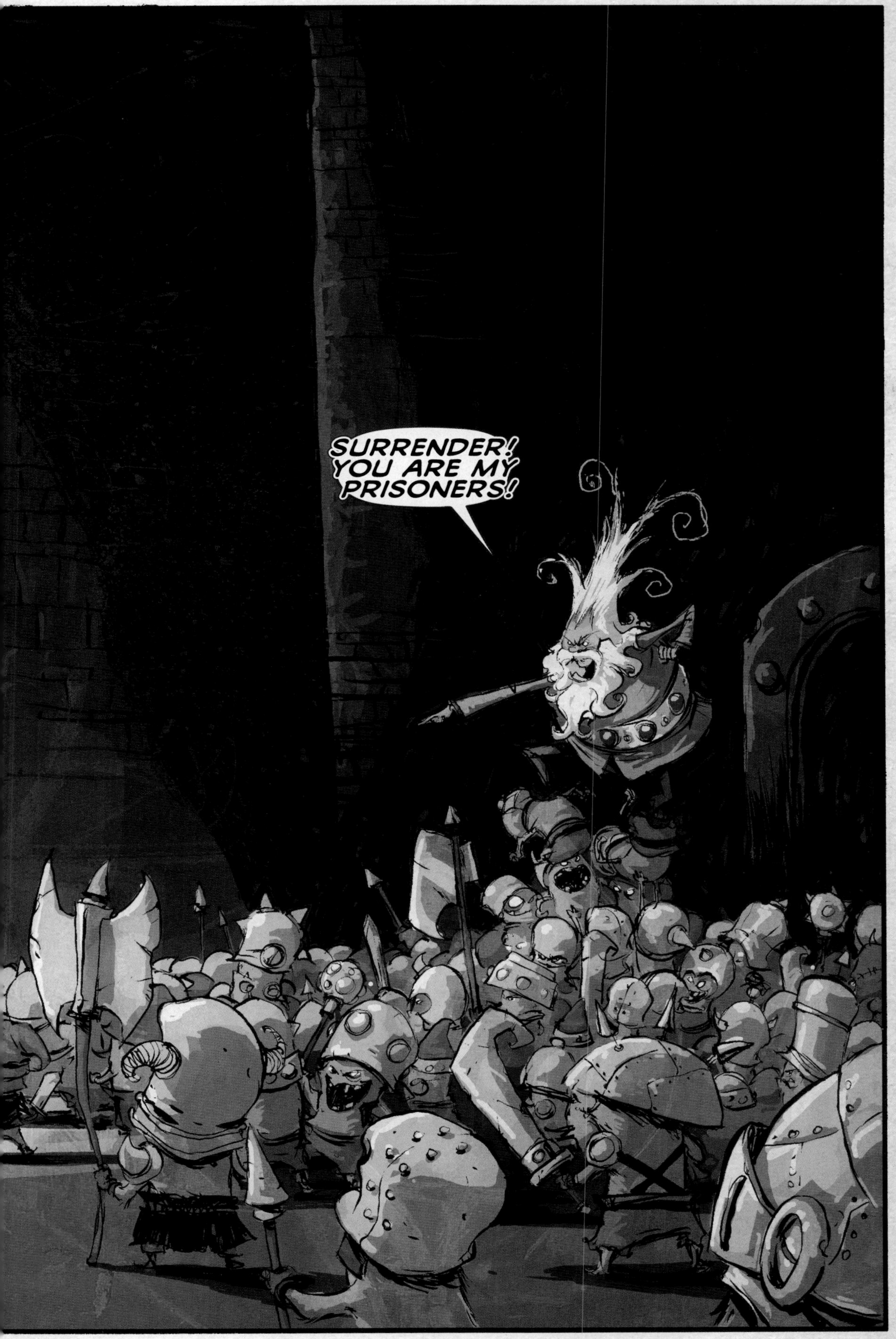
SURRENDER! YOU ARE MY PRISONERS!

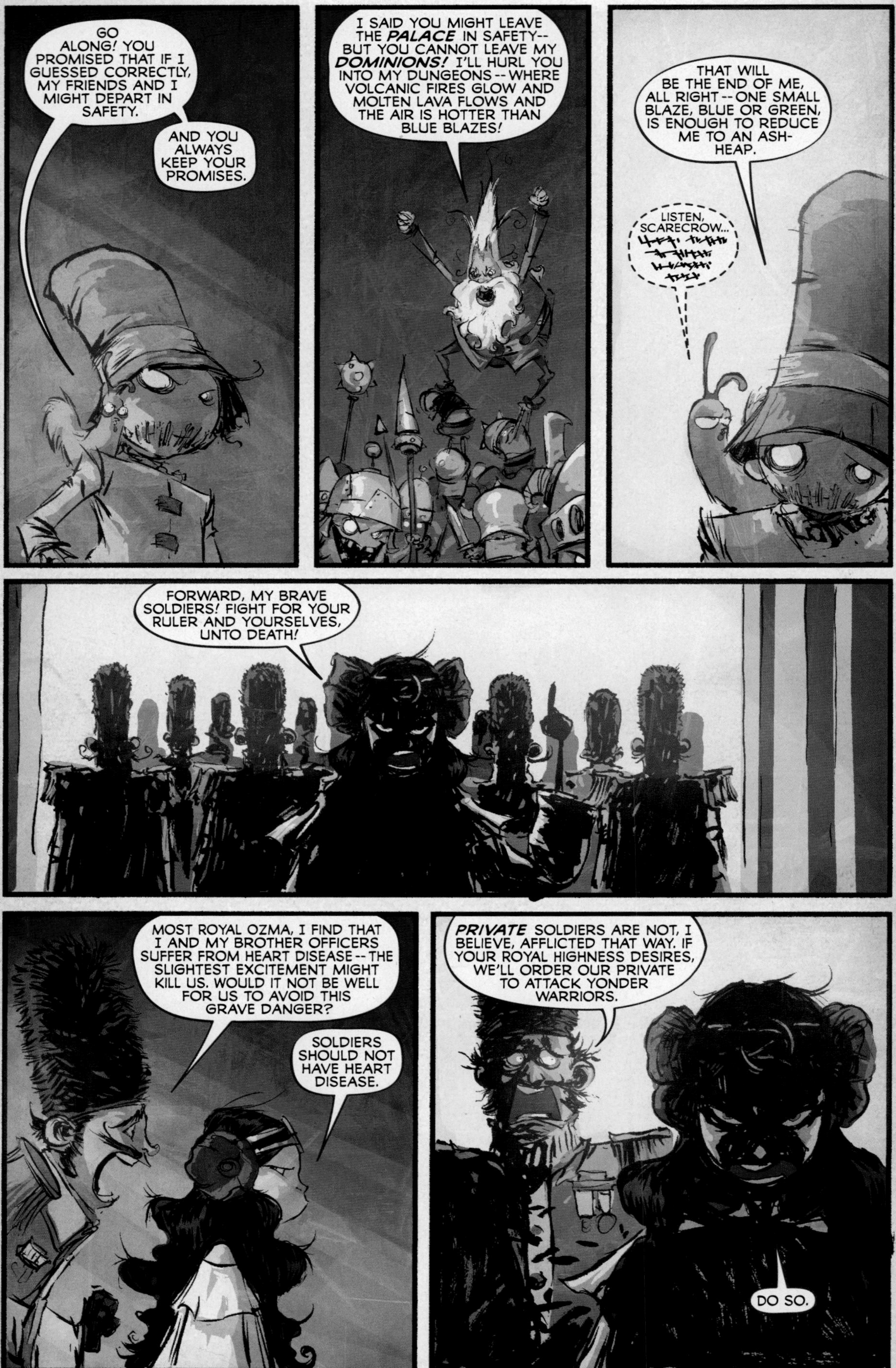
GO ALONG! YOU PROMISED THAT IF I GUESSED CORRECTLY, MY FRIENDS AND I MIGHT DEPART IN SAFETY.
AND YOU ALWAYS KEEP YOUR PROMISES.
I SAID YOU MIGHT LEAVE THE PALACE IN SAFETY-- BUT YOU CANNOT LEAVE MY DOMINIONS! I'LL HURL YOU INTO MY DUNGEONS--WHERE VOLCANIC FIRES GLOW AND MOLTEN LAVA FLOWS AND THE AIR IS HOTTER THAN BLUE BLAZES!
THAT WILL BE THE END OF ME, ALL RIGHT--ONE SMALL BLAZE, BLUE OR GREEN, IS ENOUGH TO REDUCE ME TO AN ASH-HEAP.
LISTEN, SCARECROW...
FORWARD, MY BRAVE SOLDIERS! FIGHT FOR YOUR RULER AND YOURSELVES, UNTO DEATH!
MOST ROYAL OZMA, I FIND THAT I AND MY BROTHER OFFICERS SUFFER FROM HEART DISEASE--THE SLIGHTEST EXCITEMENT MIGHT KILL US. WOULD IT NOT BE WELL FOR US TO AVOID THIS GRAVE DANGER?
SOLDIERS SHOULD NOT HAVE HEART DISEASE.
PRIVATE SOLDIERS ARE NOT, I BELIEVE, AFFLICTED THAT WAY. IF YOUR ROYAL HIGHNESS DESIRES, WE'LL ORDER OUR PRIVATE TO ATTACK YONDER WARRIORS.
DO SO.

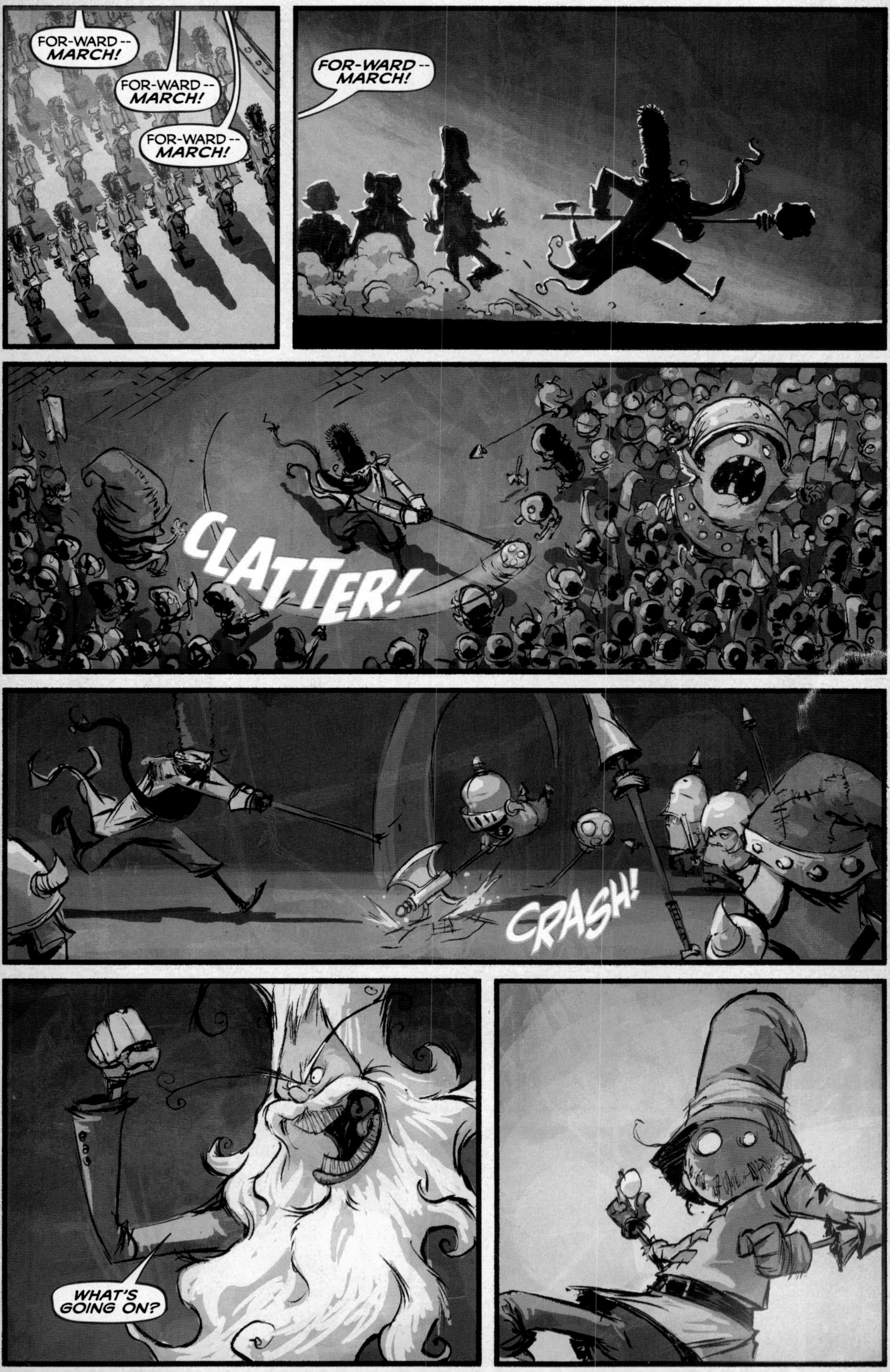
FOR-WARD -- MARCH!
FOR-WARD -- MARCH!
FOR-WARD -- MARCH!
FOR-WARD -- MARCH!
CLATTER!
CRASH!
WHAT'S GOING ON?

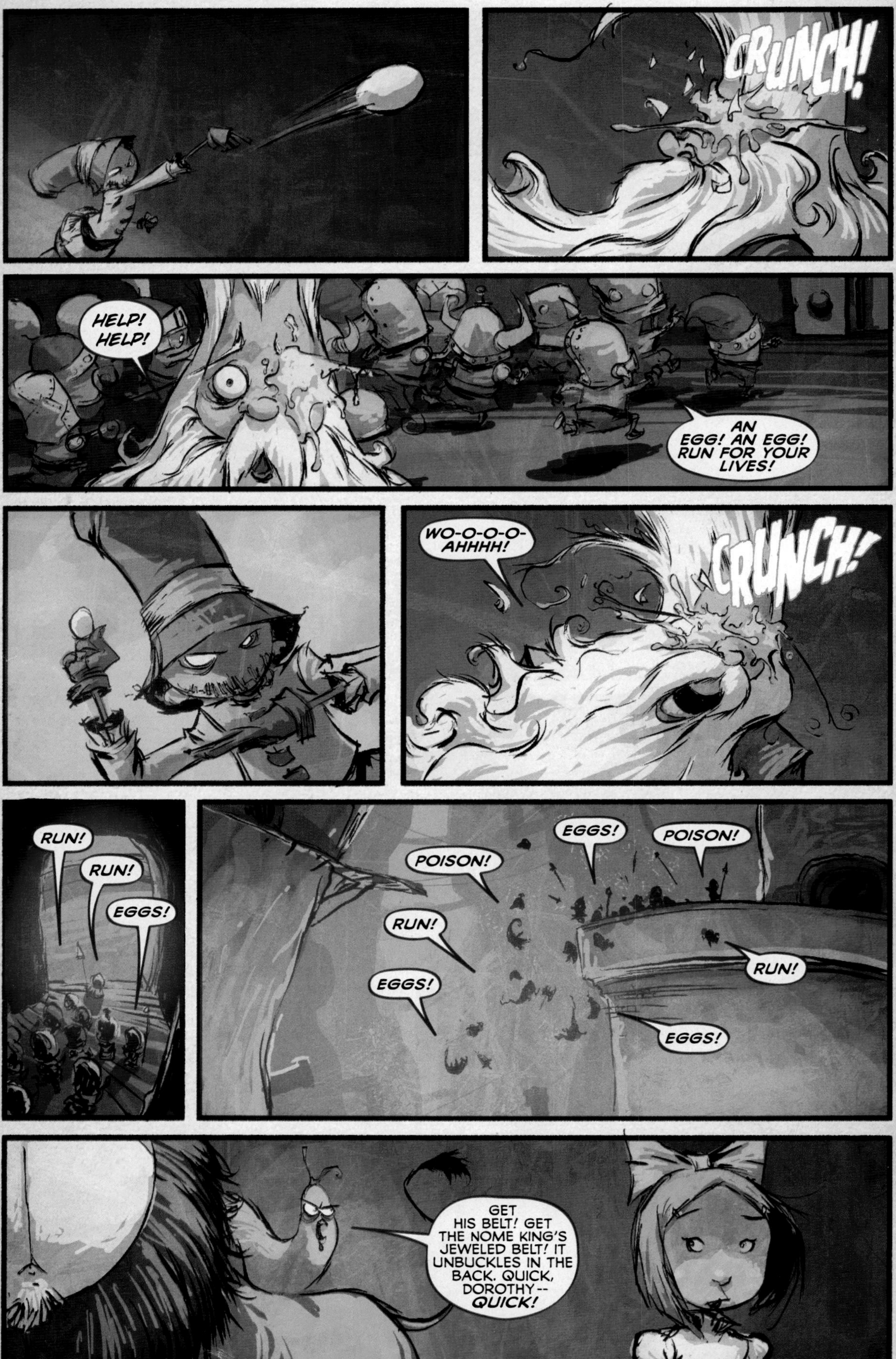
CRUNCH!
HELP! HELP!
AN EGG! AN EGG! RUN FOR YOUR LIVES!
WO-O-O-O-AHHHH!
CRUNCH!
RUN!
RUN!
EGGS!
POISON!
EGGS!
POISON!
RUN!
EGGS!
RUN!
EGGS!
GET HIS BELT! GET THE NOME KING'S JEWELED BELT! IT UNBUCKLES IN THE BACK. QUICK, DOROTHY-- QUICK!

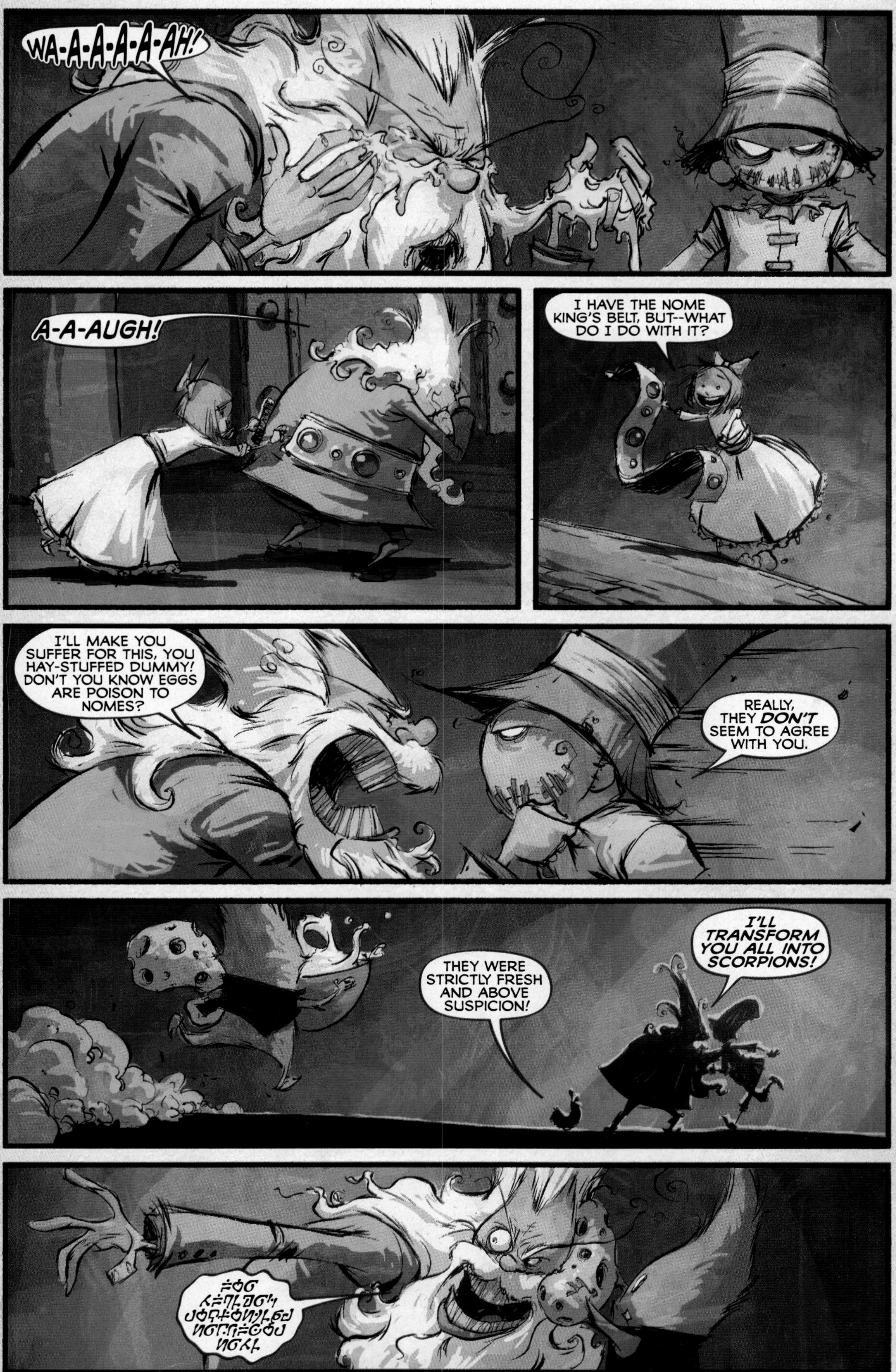
WA-A-A-A-A-AH!
A-A-AUGH!
I HAVE THE NOME KING'S BELT, BUT--WHAT DO I DO WITH IT?
I'LL MAKE YOU SUFFER FOR THIS, YOU HAY-STUFFED DUMMY! DON'T YOU KNOW EGGS ARE POISON TO NOMES?
REALLY, THEY *DON'T* SEEM TO AGREE WITH YOU.
THEY WERE STRICTLY FRESH AND ABOVE SUSPICION!
I'LL TRANSFORM YOU ALL INTO SCORPIONS!

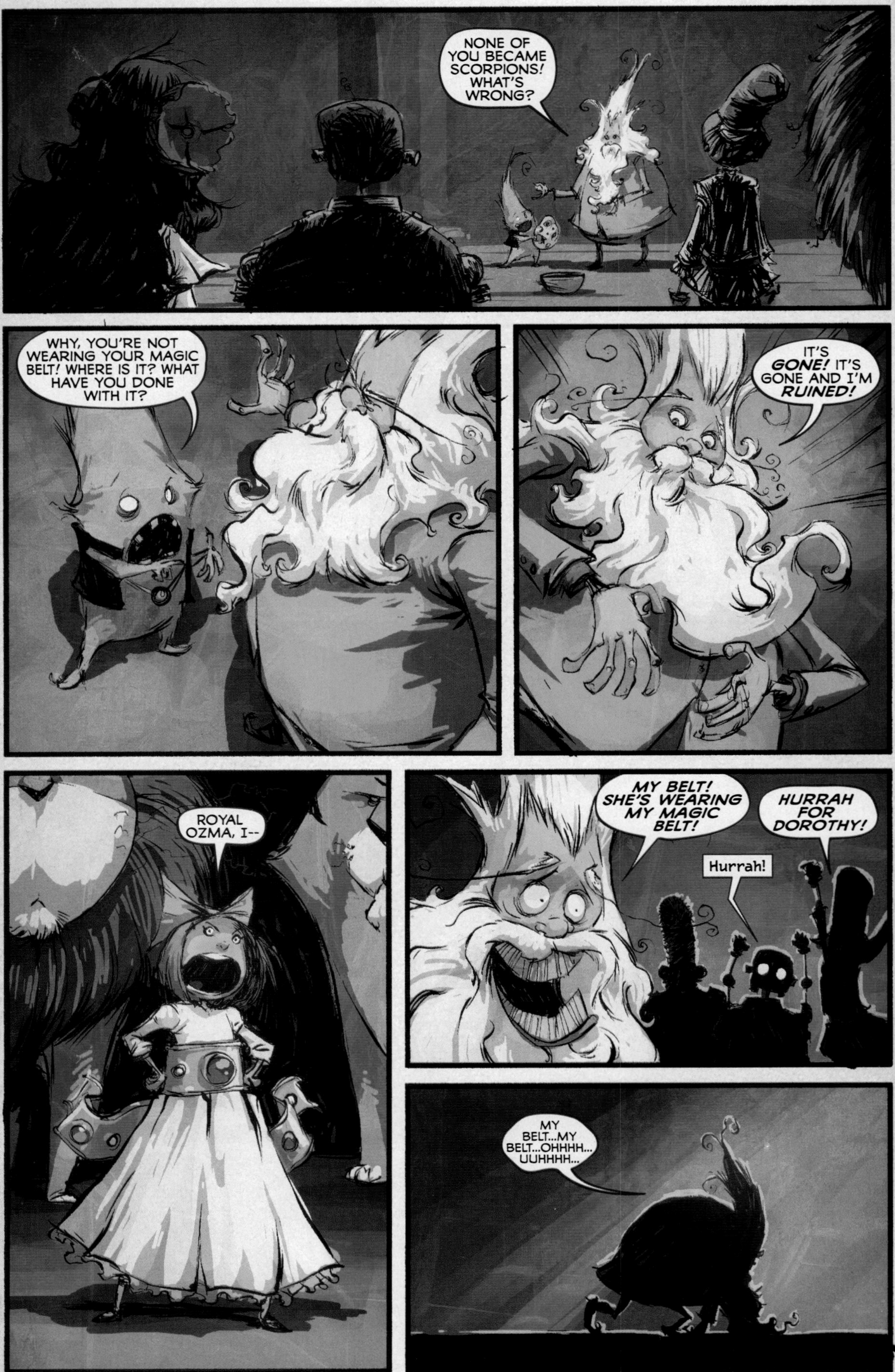
NONE OF YOU BECAME SCORPIONS! WHAT'S WRONG?
WHY, YOU'RE NOT WEARING YOUR MAGIC BELT! WHERE IS IT? WHAT HAVE YOU DONE WITH IT?
IT'S GONE! IT'S GONE AND I'M RUINED!
ROYAL OZMA, I--
MY BELT! SHE'S WEARING MY MAGIC BELT!
HURRAH FOR DOROTHY!
Hurrah!
MY BELT...MY BELT...OHHHH... UUHHHH...

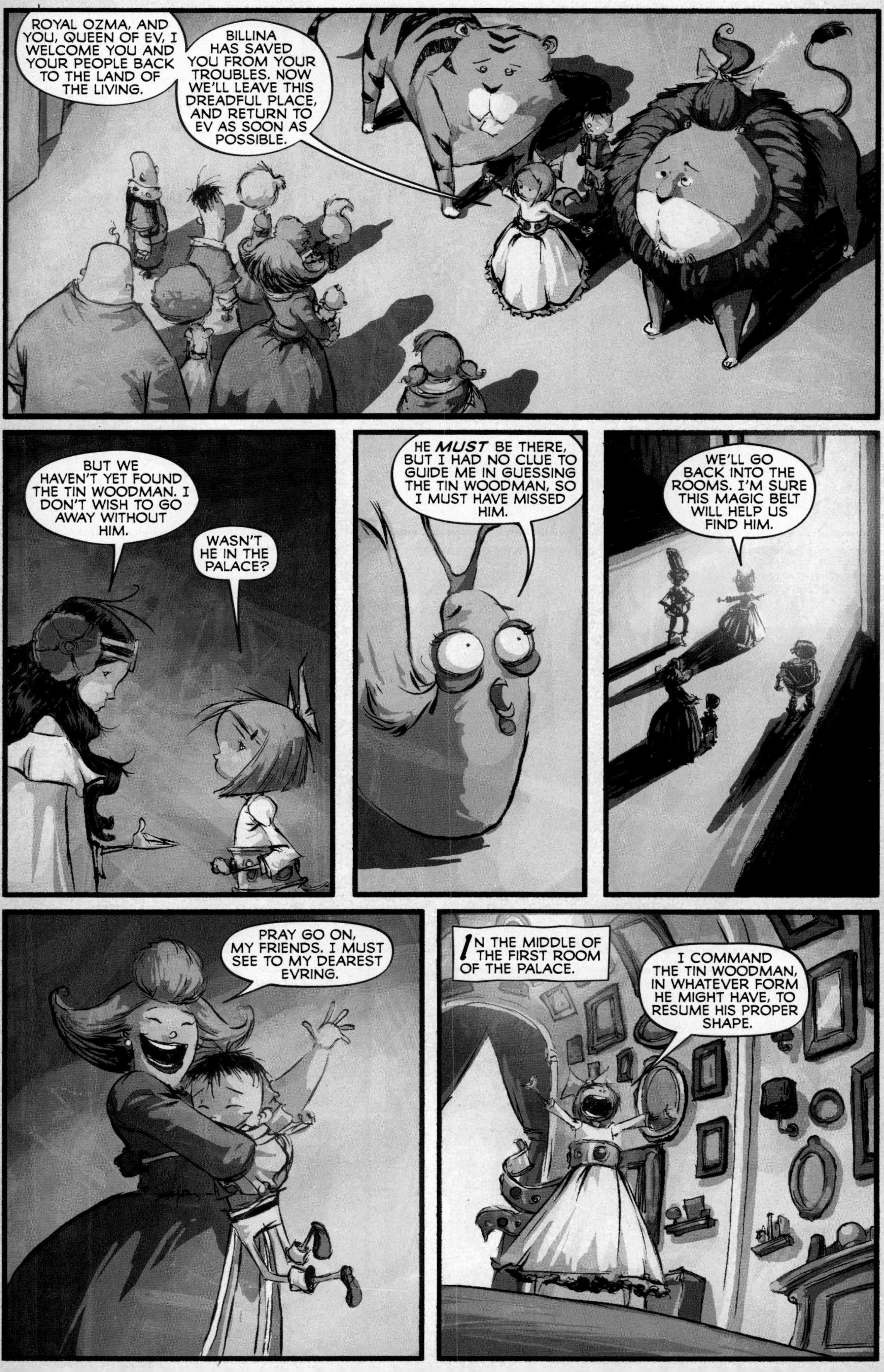
ROYAL OZMA, AND YOU, QUEEN OF EV, I WELCOME YOU AND YOUR PEOPLE BACK TO THE LAND OF THE LIVING.
BILLINA HAS SAVED YOU FROM YOUR TROUBLES. NOW WE'LL LEAVE THIS DREADFUL PLACE, AND RETURN TO EV AS SOON AS POSSIBLE.
BUT WE HAVEN'T YET FOUND THE TIN WOODMAN. I DON'T WISH TO GO AWAY WITHOUT HIM.
WASN'T HE IN THE PALACE?
HE *MUST* BE THERE, BUT I HAD NO CLUE TO GUIDE ME IN GUESSING THE TIN WOODMAN, SO I MUST HAVE MISSED HIM.
WE'LL GO BACK INTO THE ROOMS. I'M SURE THIS MAGIC BELT WILL HELP US FIND HIM.
PRAY GO ON, MY FRIENDS. I MUST SEE TO MY DEAREST EVRING.
IN THE MIDDLE OF THE FIRST ROOM OF THE PALACE.
I COMMAND THE TIN WOODMAN, IN WHATEVER FORM HE MIGHT HAVE, TO RESUME HIS PROPER SHAPE.

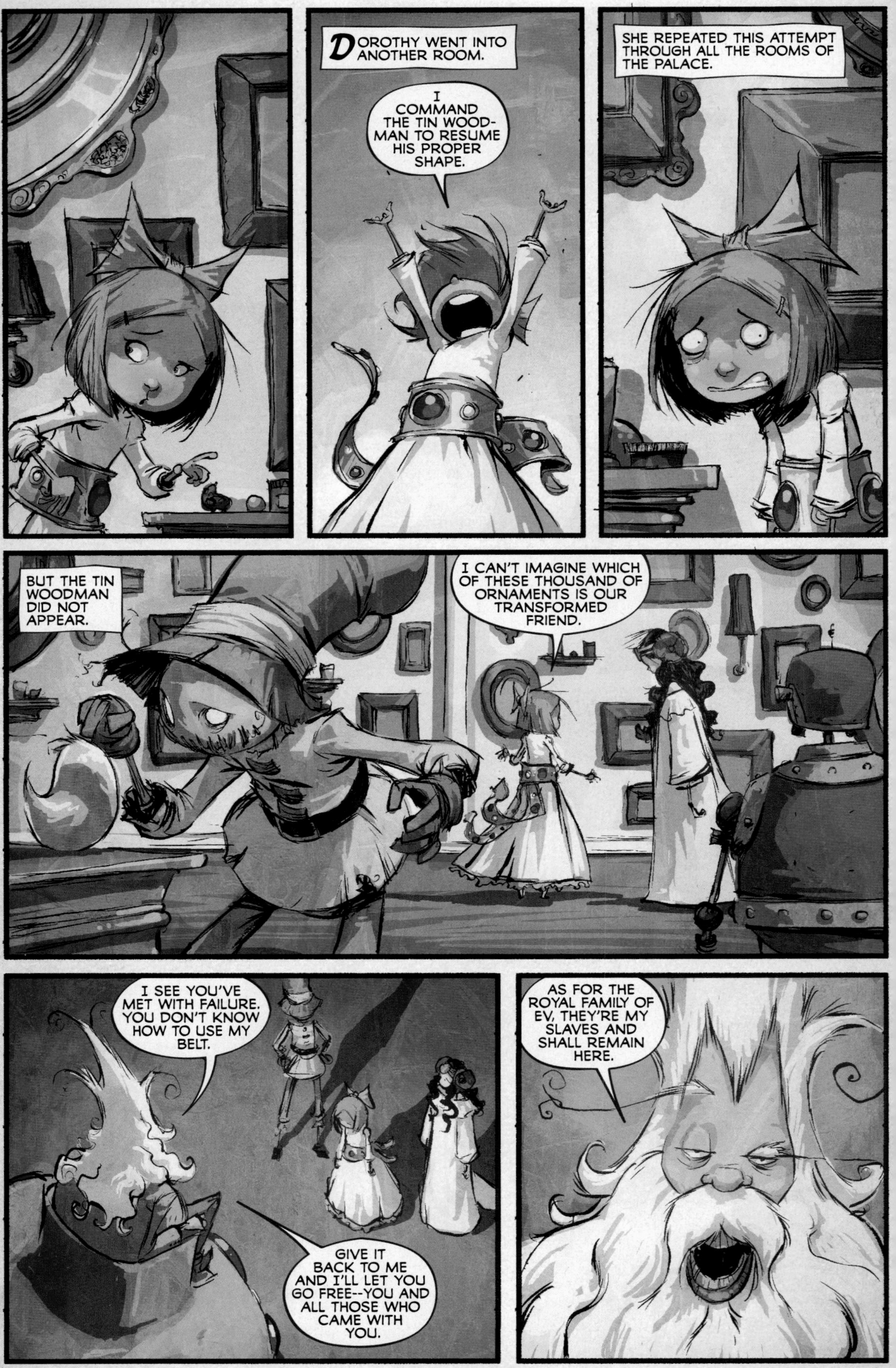
DOROTHY WENT INTO ANOTHER ROOM.
I COMMAND THE TIN WOODMAN TO RESUME HIS PROPER SHAPE.
SHE REPEATED THIS ATTEMPT THROUGH ALL THE ROOMS OF THE PALACE.
BUT THE TIN WOODMAN DID NOT APPEAR.
I CAN'T IMAGINE WHICH OF THESE THOUSAND OF ORNAMENTS IS OUR TRANSFORMED FRIEND.
I SEE YOU'VE MET WITH FAILURE. YOU DON'T KNOW HOW TO USE MY BELT.
GIVE IT BACK TO ME AND I'LL LET YOU GO FREE--YOU AND ALL THOSE WHO CAME WITH YOU.
AS FOR THE ROYAL FAMILY OF EV, THEY'RE MY SLAVES AND SHALL REMAIN HERE.

I'LL KEEP THE BELT. ALL WE NEED TO DO IS TO WALK OUT THE WAY THAT WE CAME IN.

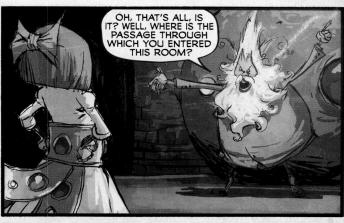

OH, THAT'S ALL, IS IT? WELL, WHERE IS THE PASSAGE THROUGH WHICH YOU ENTERED THIS ROOM?

IT'S--IT'S...

IT'S LONG SINCE CLOSED! HOW CAN YOU ESCAPE WITHOUT MY CONSENT?

I COMMAND THE PASSAGE TO OPEN!

IF THE BELT OBEYS YOU, WHY, THEN, WERE WE UNABLE TO DISCOVER THE TIN WOOD-MAN?

I CAN'T IMAGINE.

SEE HERE, GIRL--

--GIVE ME THE BELT, AND I'LL TELL YOU WHAT SHAPE THE TIN WOOD-MAN WAS CHANGED INTO.

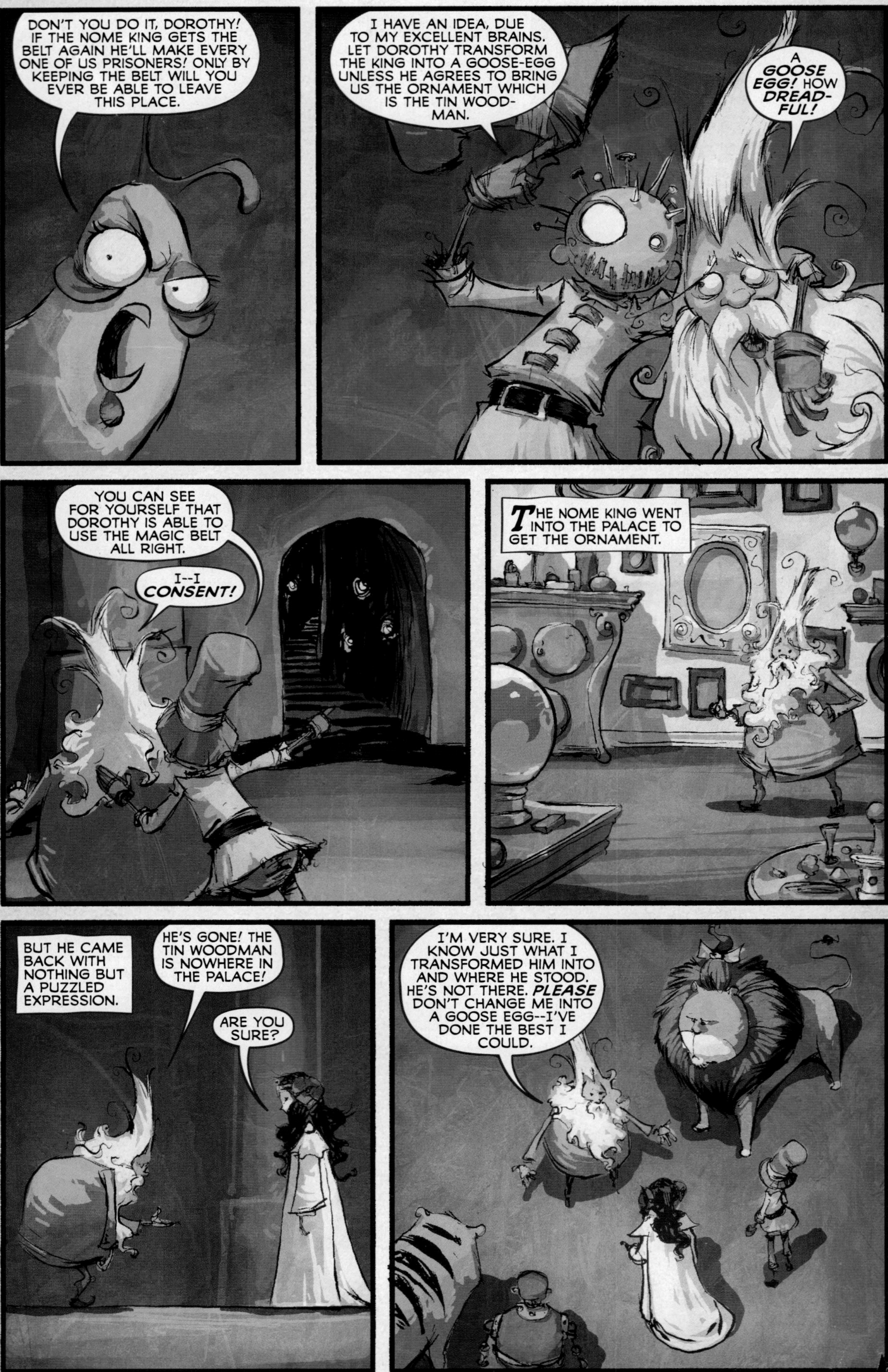
DON'T YOU DO IT, DOROTHY! IF THE NOME KING GETS THE BELT AGAIN HE'LL MAKE EVERY ONE OF US PRISONERS! ONLY BY KEEPING THE BELT WILL YOU EVER BE ABLE TO LEAVE THIS PLACE.
I HAVE AN IDEA, DUE TO MY EXCELLENT BRAINS. LET DOROTHY TRANSFORM THE KING INTO A GOOSE-EGG UNLESS HE AGREES TO BRING US THE ORNAMENT WHICH IS THE TIN WOOD-MAN.
A GOOSE EGG! HOW DREAD-FUL!
YOU CAN SEE FOR YOURSELF THAT DOROTHY IS ABLE TO USE THE MAGIC BELT ALL RIGHT.
I--I CONSENT!
THE NOME KING WENT INTO THE PALACE TO GET THE ORNAMENT.
BUT HE CAME BACK WITH NOTHING BUT A PUZZLED EXPRESSION.
HE'S GONE! THE TIN WOODMAN IS NOWHERE IN THE PALACE!
ARE YOU SURE?
I'M VERY SURE. I KNOW JUST WHAT I TRANSFORMED HIM INTO AND WHERE HE STOOD. HE'S NOT THERE. PLEASE DON'T CHANGE ME INTO A GOOSE EGG--I'VE DONE THE BEST I COULD.

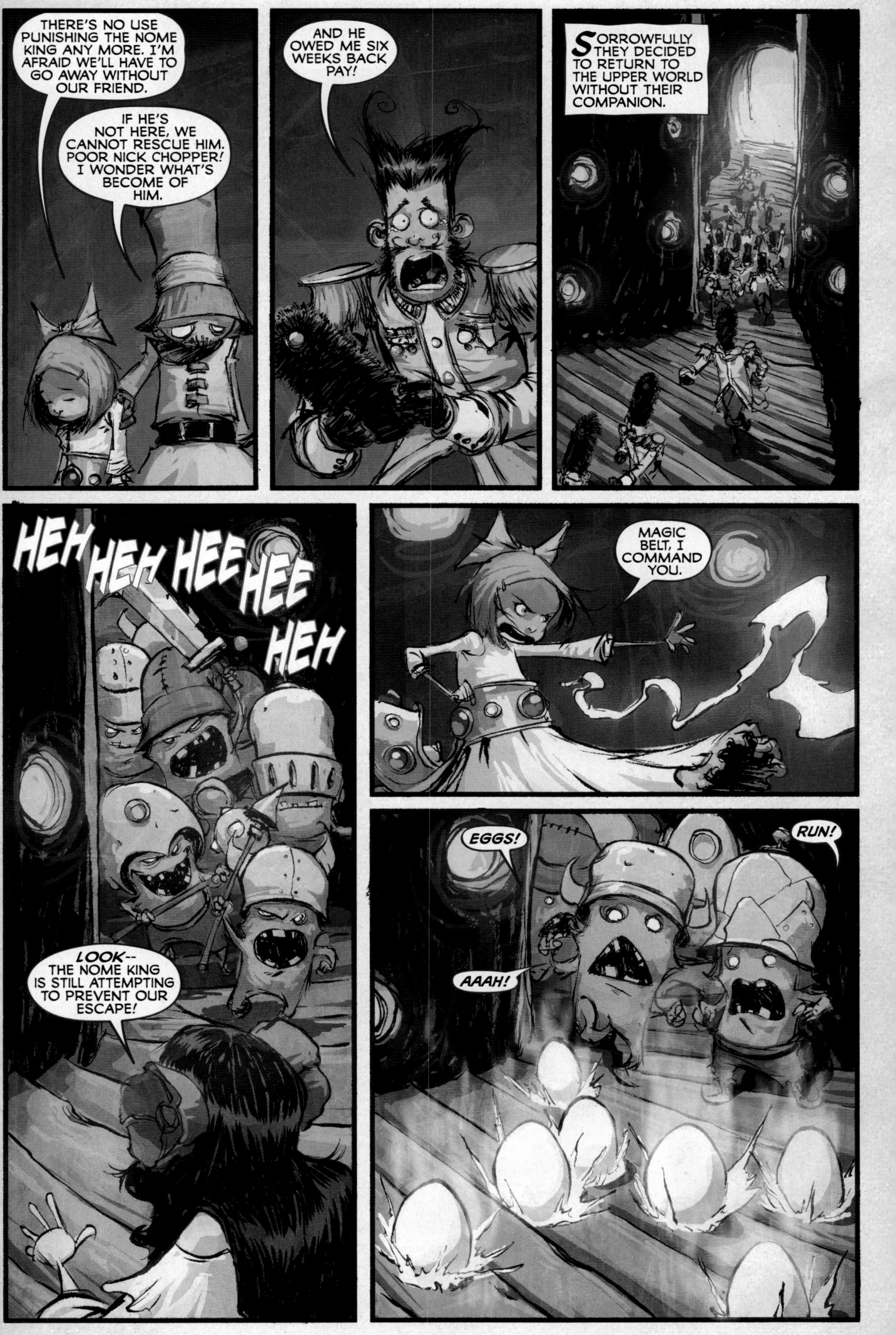
THERE'S NO USE PUNISHING THE NOME KING ANY MORE. I'M AFRAID WE'LL HAVE TO GO AWAY WITHOUT OUR FRIEND.
IF HE'S NOT HERE, WE CANNOT RESCUE HIM. POOR NICK CHOPPER! I WONDER WHAT'S BECOME OF HIM.
AND HE OWED ME SIX WEEKS BACK PAY!
SORROWFULLY THEY DECIDED TO RETURN TO THE UPPER WORLD WITHOUT THEIR COMPANION.
HEH HEH HEE HEE HEH
LOOK-- THE NOME KING IS STILL ATTEMPTING TO PREVENT OUR ESCAPE!
MAGIC BELT, I COMMAND YOU.
EGGS!
RUN!
AAAH!

POISON!

RETREAT!

EGGS!

I REFUSE TO ADVANCE AGAIN!

OUR FRIENDS HAD NO FURTHER TROUBLE IN REACHING THE OUTER AIR.

I FERVENTLY HOPE WE'VE SEEN THE LAST OF THE NOME KING AND HIS DREADFUL PALACE.

DOROTHY WHISPERED A WORD TO THE MAGIC BELT, AND THE GIANT WITH THE HAMMER PAUSED, ALLOWING THEM TO PASS IN SAFETY.

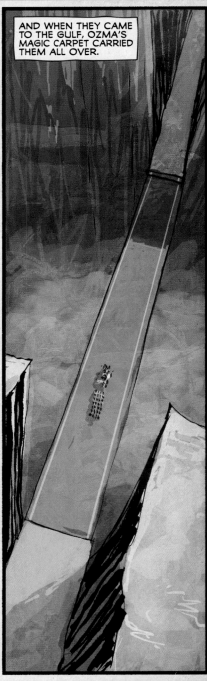

AND WHEN THEY CAME TO THE GULF, OZMA'S MAGIC CARPET CARRIED THEM ALL OVER.

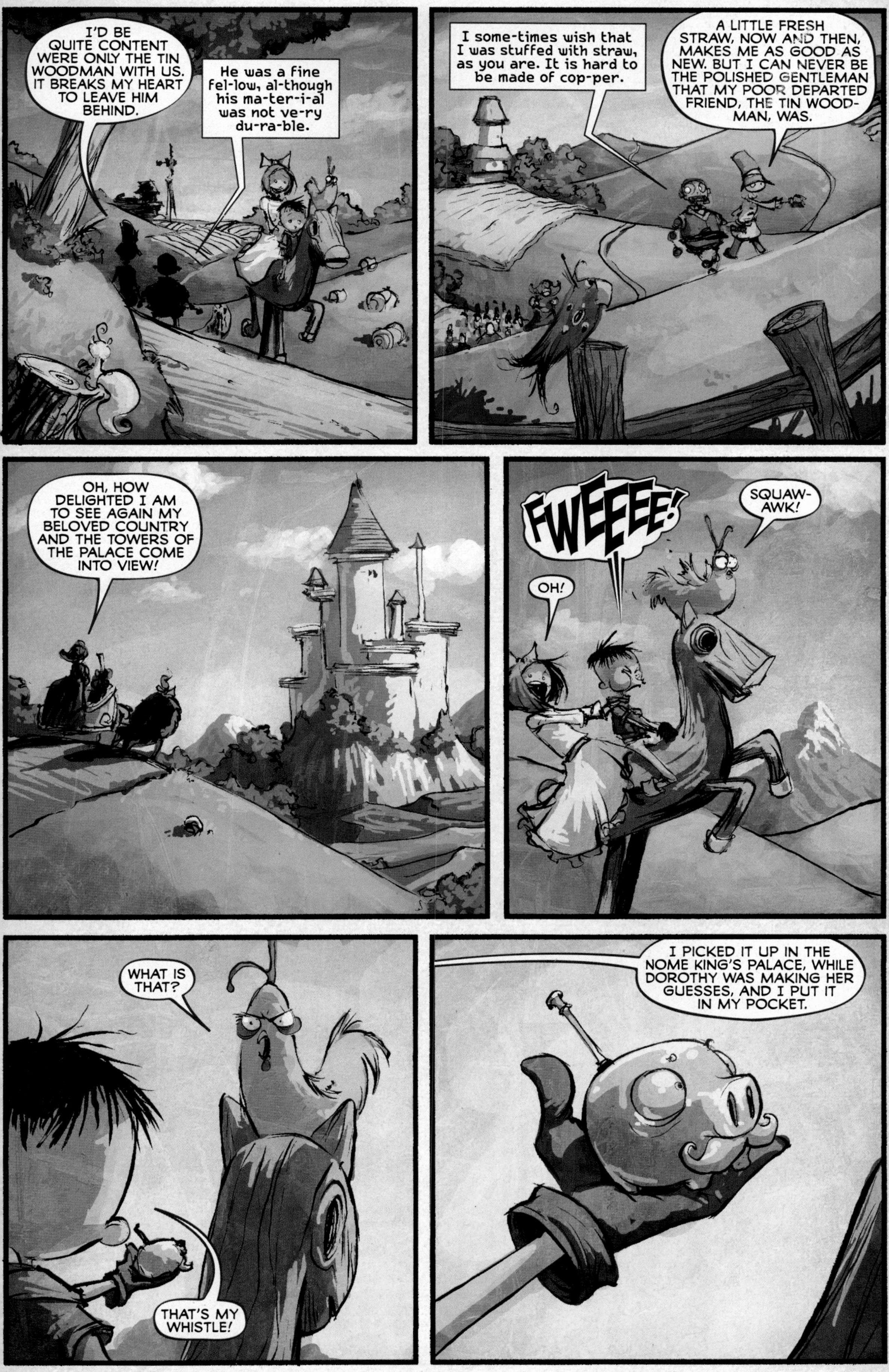
I'D BE QUITE CONTENT WERE ONLY THE TIN WOODMAN WITH US. IT BREAKS MY HEART TO LEAVE HIM BEHIND.
He was a fine fel-low, al-though his ma-ter-i-al was not ve-ry du-ra-ble.
I some-times wish that I was stuffed with straw, as you are. It is hard to be made of cop-per.
A LITTLE FRESH STRAW, NOW AND THEN, MAKES ME AS GOOD AS NEW. BUT I CAN NEVER BE THE POLISHED GENTLEMAN THAT MY POOR DEPARTED FRIEND, THE TIN WOODMAN, WAS.
OH, HOW DELIGHTED I AM TO SEE AGAIN MY BELOVED COUNTRY AND THE TOWERS OF THE PALACE COME INTO VIEW!
FWEEEE!
SQUAW-AWK!
OH!
WHAT IS THAT?
THAT'S MY WHISTLE!
I PICKED IT UP IN THE NOME KING'S PALACE, WHILE DOROTHY WAS MAKING HER GUESSES, AND I PUT IT IN MY POCKET.

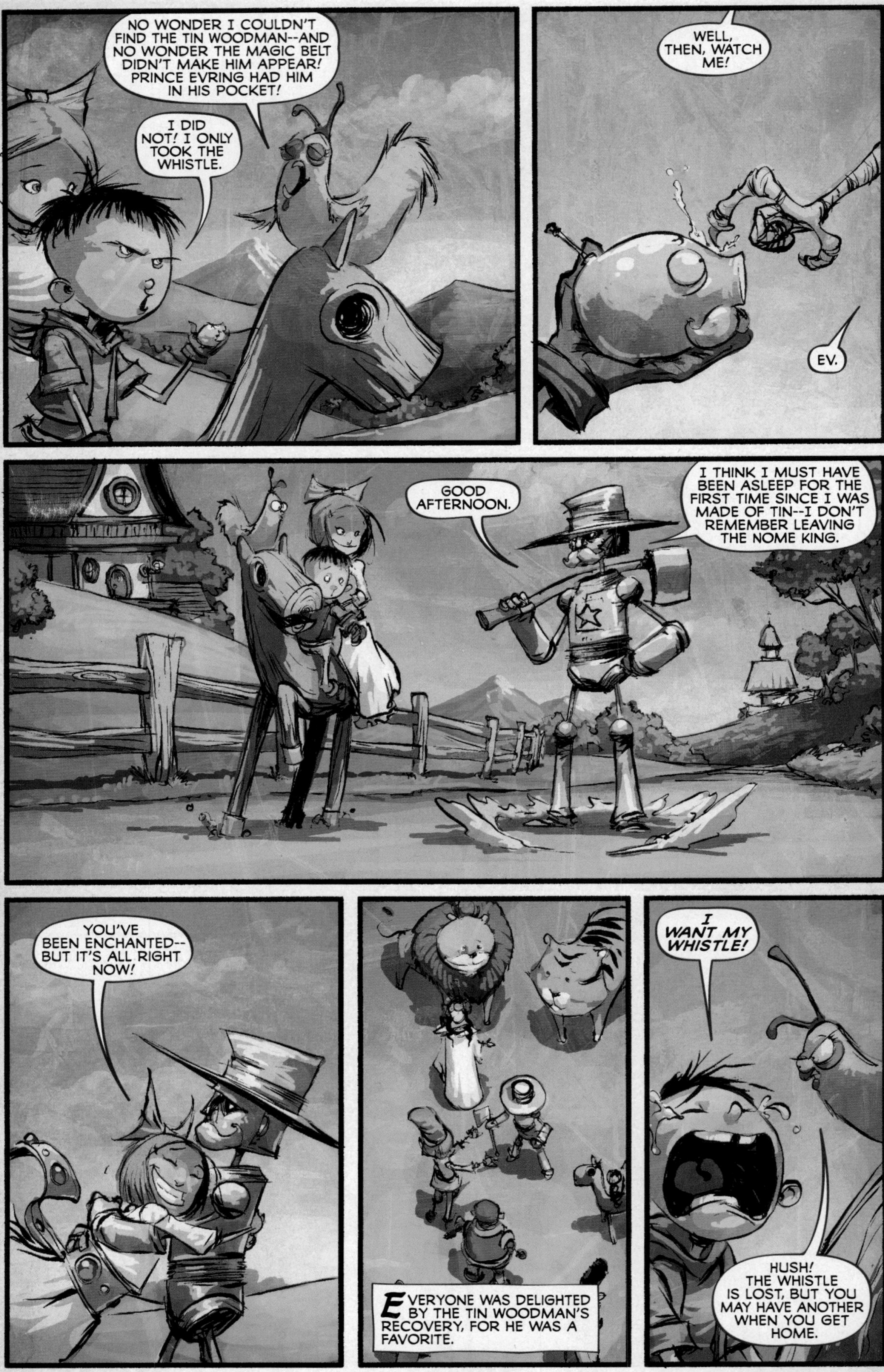
NO WONDER I COULDN'T FIND THE TIN WOODMAN--AND NO WONDER THE MAGIC BELT DIDN'T MAKE HIM APPEAR! PRINCE EVRING HAD HIM IN HIS POCKET!
I DID NOT! I ONLY TOOK THE WHISTLE.
WELL, THEN, WATCH ME!
EV.
GOOD AFTERNOON.
I THINK I MUST HAVE BEEN ASLEEP FOR THE FIRST TIME SINCE I WAS MADE OF TIN--I DON'T REMEMBER LEAVING THE NOME KING.
YOU'VE BEEN ENCHANTED-- BUT IT'S ALL RIGHT NOW!
EVERYONE WAS DELIGHTED BY THE TIN WOODMAN'S RECOVERY, FOR HE WAS A FAVORITE.
I WANT MY WHISTLE!
HUSH! THE WHISTLE IS LOST, BUT YOU MAY HAVE ANOTHER WHEN YOU GET HOME.

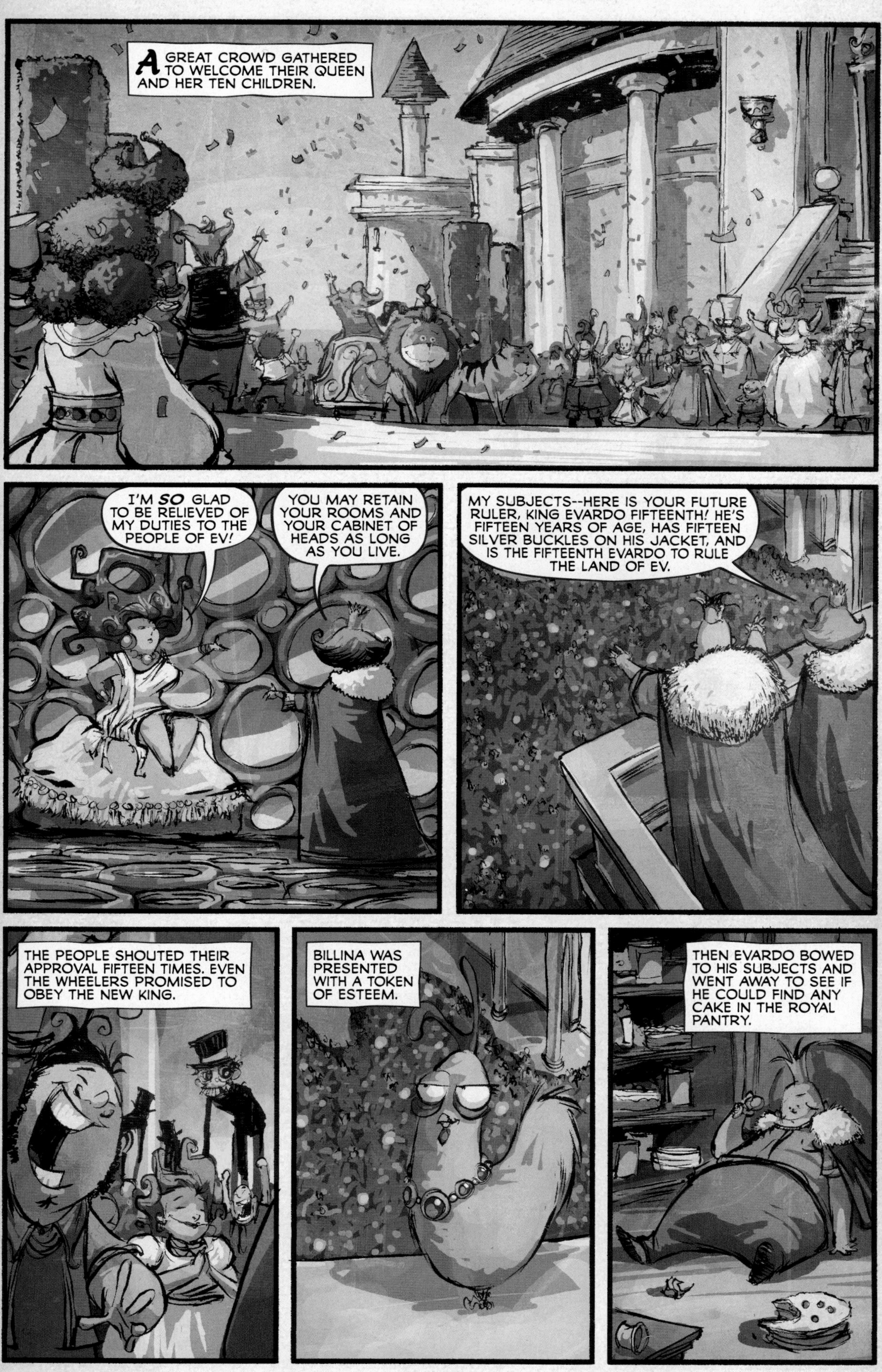
A GREAT CROWD GATHERED TO WELCOME THEIR QUEEN AND HER TEN CHILDREN.
I'M SO GLAD TO BE RELIEVED OF MY DUTIES TO THE PEOPLE OF EV!
YOU MAY RETAIN YOUR ROOMS AND YOUR CABINET OF HEADS AS LONG AS YOU LIVE.
MY SUBJECTS--HERE IS YOUR FUTURE RULER, KING EVARDO FIFTEENTH! HE'S FIFTEEN YEARS OF AGE, HAS FIFTEEN SILVER BUCKLES ON HIS JACKET, AND IS THE FIFTEENTH EVARDO TO RULE THE LAND OF EV.
THE PEOPLE SHOUTED THEIR APPROVAL FIFTEEN TIMES. EVEN THE WHEELERS PROMISED TO OBEY THE NEW KING.
BILLINA WAS PRESENTED WITH A TOKEN OF ESTEEM.
THEN EVARDO BOWED TO HIS SUBJECTS AND WENT AWAY TO SEE IF HE COULD FIND ANY CAKE IN THE ROYAL PANTRY.

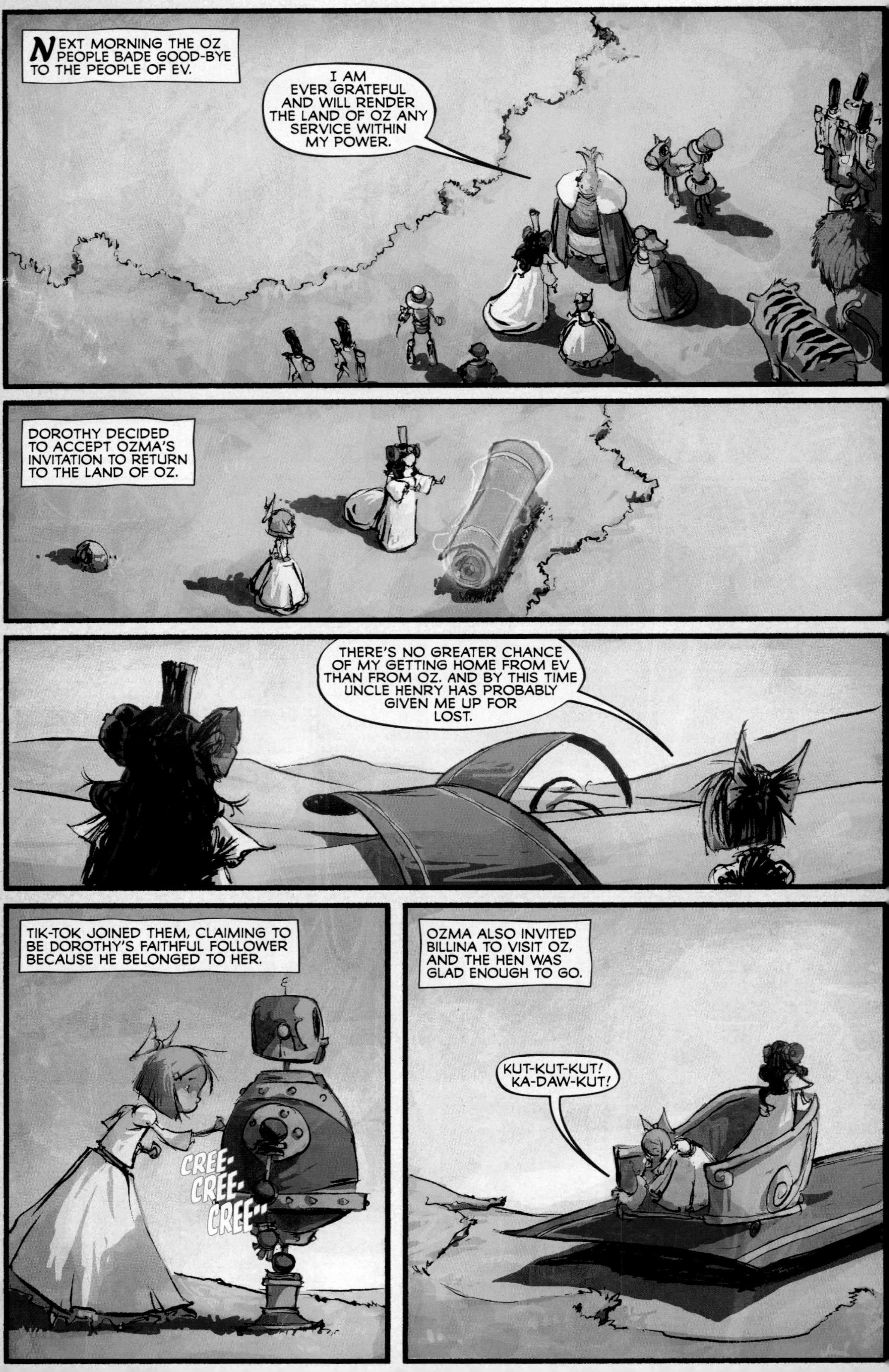
NEXT MORNING THE OZ PEOPLE BADE GOOD-BYE TO THE PEOPLE OF EV.
I AM EVER GRATEFUL AND WILL RENDER THE LAND OF OZ ANY SERVICE WITHIN MY POWER.
DOROTHY DECIDED TO ACCEPT OZMA'S INVITATION TO RETURN TO THE LAND OF OZ.
THERE'S NO GREATER CHANCE OF MY GETTING HOME FROM EV THAN FROM OZ. AND BY THIS TIME UNCLE HENRY HAS PROBABLY GIVEN ME UP FOR LOST.
TIK-TOK JOINED THEM, CLAIMING TO BE DOROTHY'S FAITHFUL FOLLOWER BECAUSE HE BELONGED TO HER.
CREE- CREE- CREE--
OZMA ALSO INVITED BILLINA TO VISIT OZ, AND THE HEN WAS GLAD ENOUGH TO GO.
KUT-KUT-KUT! KA-DAW-KUT!

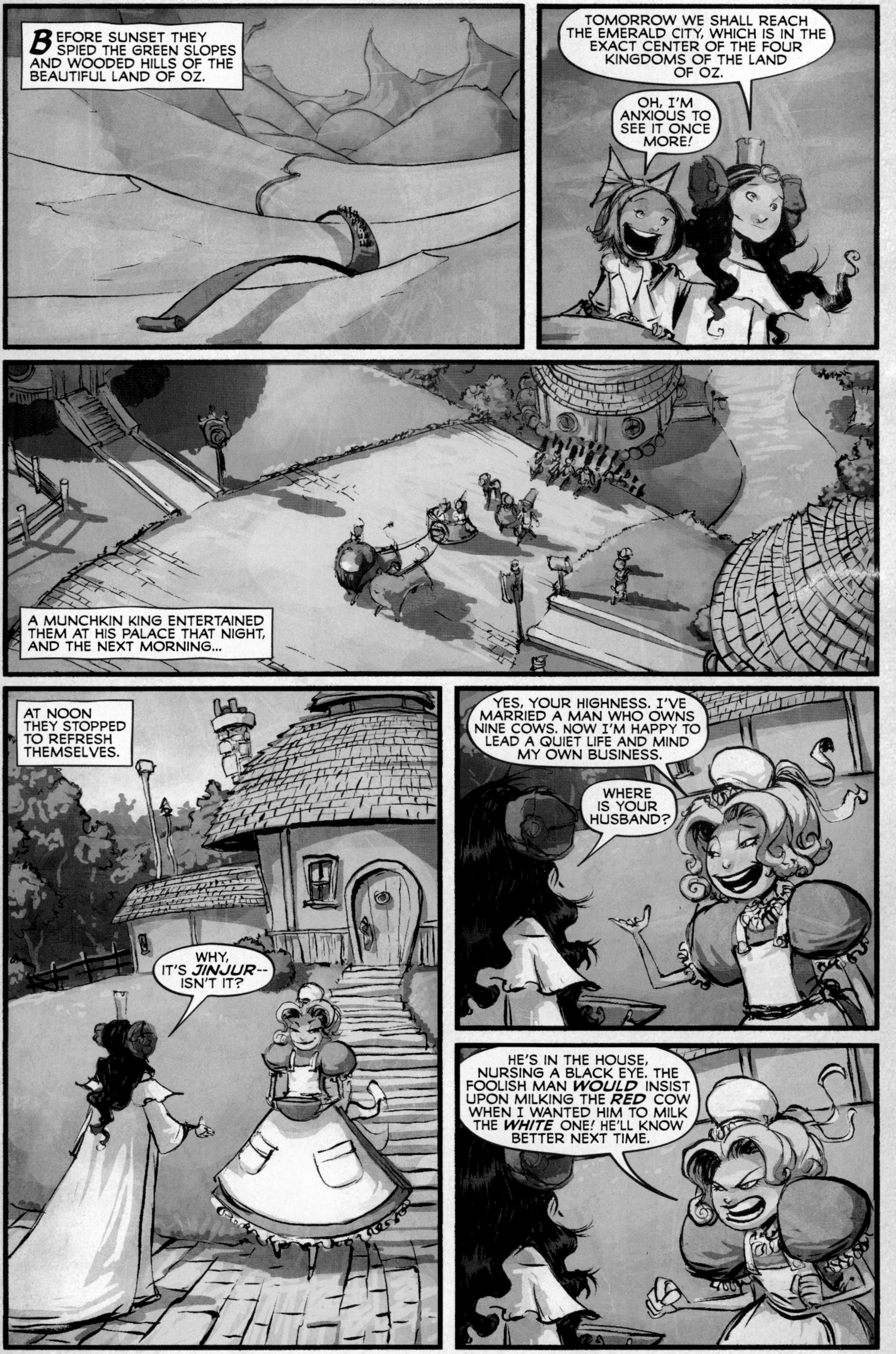

BEFORE SUNSET THEY SPIED THE GREEN SLOPES AND WOODED HILLS OF THE BEAUTIFUL LAND OF OZ.
TOMORROW WE SHALL REACH THE EMERALD CITY, WHICH IS IN THE EXACT CENTER OF THE FOUR KINGDOMS OF THE LAND OF OZ.
OH, I'M ANXIOUS TO SEE IT ONCE MORE!
A MUNCHKIN KING ENTERTAINED THEM AT HIS PALACE THAT NIGHT, AND THE NEXT MORNING...
AT NOON THEY STOPPED TO REFRESH THEMSELVES.
WHY, IT'S JINJUR-- ISN'T IT?
YES, YOUR HIGHNESS. I'VE MARRIED A MAN WHO OWNS NINE COWS. NOW I'M HAPPY TO LEAD A QUIET LIFE AND MIND MY OWN BUSINESS.
WHERE IS YOUR HUSBAND?
HE'S IN THE HOUSE, NURSING A BLACK EYE. THE FOOLISH MAN WOULD INSIST UPON MILKING THE RED COW WHEN I WANTED HIM TO MILK THE WHITE ONE! HE'LL KNOW BETTER NEXT TIME.

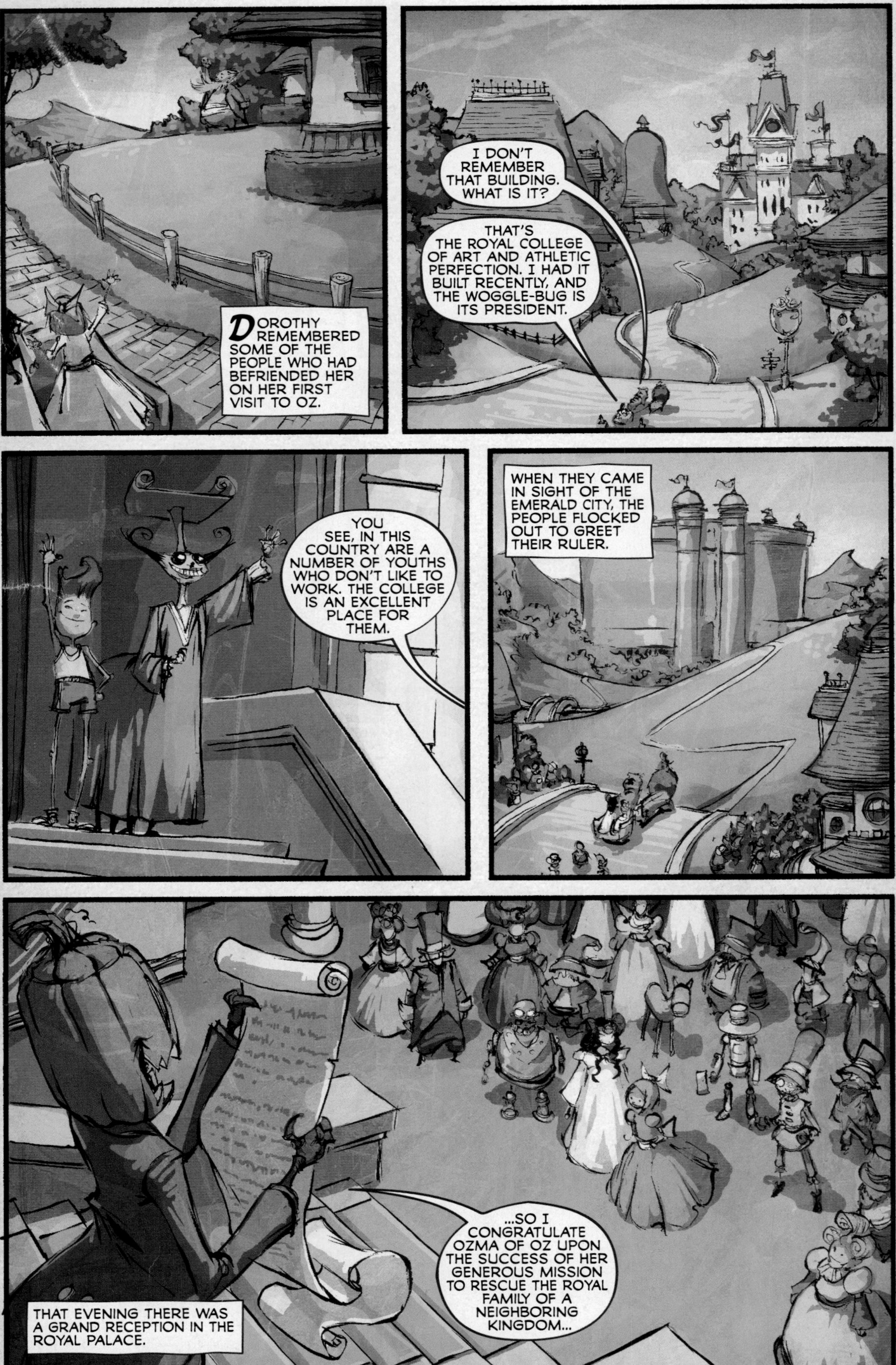
DOROTHY REMEMBERED SOME OF THE PEOPLE WHO HAD BEFRIENDED HER ON HER FIRST VISIT TO OZ.
I DON'T REMEMBER THAT BUILDING. WHAT IS IT?
THAT'S THE ROYAL COLLEGE OF ART AND ATHLETIC PERFECTION. I HAD IT BUILT RECENTLY, AND THE WOGGLE-BUG IS ITS PRESIDENT.
YOU SEE, IN THIS COUNTRY ARE A NUMBER OF YOUTHS WHO DON'T LIKE TO WORK. THE COLLEGE IS AN EXCELLENT PLACE FOR THEM.
WHEN THEY CAME IN SIGHT OF THE EMERALD CITY, THE PEOPLE FLOCKED OUT TO GREET THEIR RULER.
THAT EVENING THERE WAS A GRAND RECEPTION IN THE ROYAL PALACE.
...SO I CONGRATULATE OZMA OF OZ UPON THE SUCCESS OF HER GENEROUS MISSION TO RESCUE THE ROYAL FAMILY OF A NEIGHBORING KINGDOM...

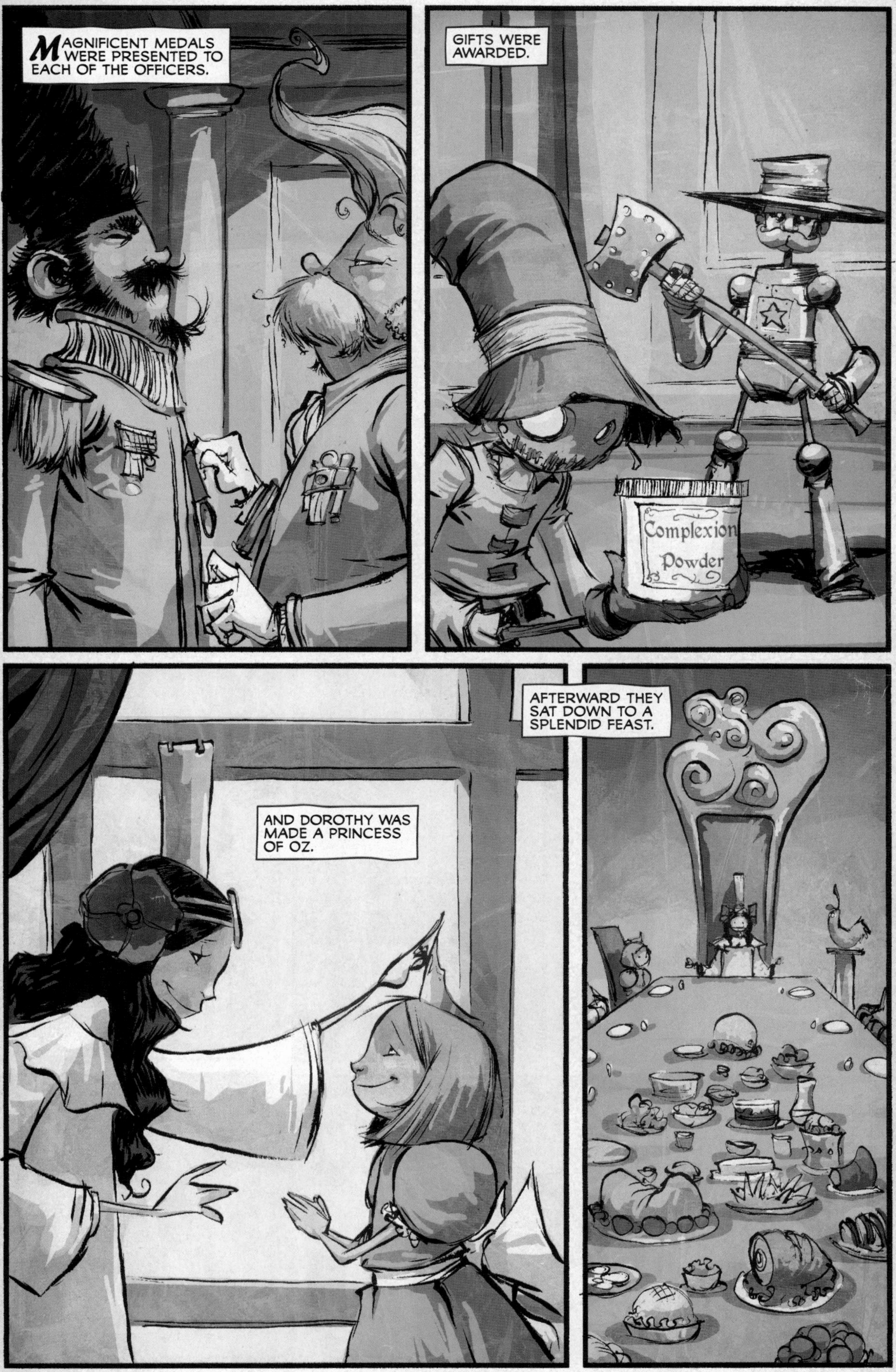
MAGNIFICENT MEDALS WERE PRESENTED TO EACH OF THE OFFICERS.
GIFTS WERE AWARDED.
Complexion Powder
AND DOROTHY WAS MADE A PRINCESS OF OZ.
AFTERWARD THEY SAT DOWN TO A SPLENDID FEAST.

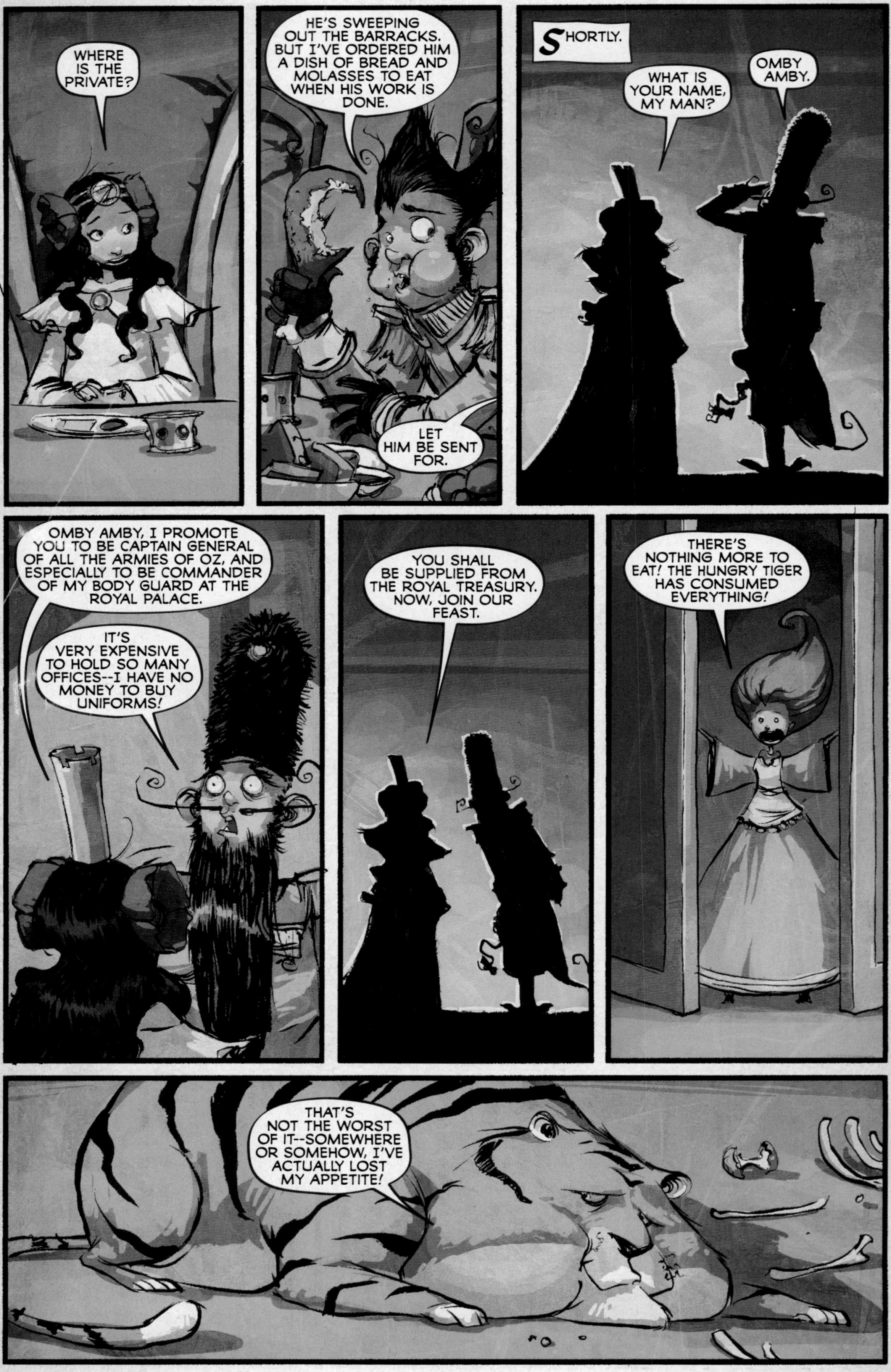
WHERE IS THE PRIVATE?
HE'S SWEEPING OUT THE BARRACKS. BUT I'VE ORDERED HIM A DISH OF BREAD AND MOLASSES TO EAT WHEN HIS WORK IS DONE.
LET HIM BE SENT FOR.
SHORTLY.
WHAT IS YOUR NAME, MY MAN?
OMBY AMBY.
OMBY AMBY, I PROMOTE YOU TO BE CAPTAIN GENERAL OF ALL THE ARMIES OF OZ, AND ESPECIALLY TO BE COMMANDER OF MY BODY GUARD AT THE ROYAL PALACE.
IT'S VERY EXPENSIVE TO HOLD SO MANY OFFICES--I HAVE NO MONEY TO BUY UNIFORMS!
YOU SHALL BE SUPPLIED FROM THE ROYAL TREASURY. NOW, JOIN OUR FEAST.
THERE'S NOTHING MORE TO EAT! THE HUNGRY TIGER HAS CONSUMED EVERYTHING!
THAT'S NOT THE WORST OF IT--SOMEWHERE OR SOMEHOW, I'VE ACTUALLY LOST MY APPETITE!

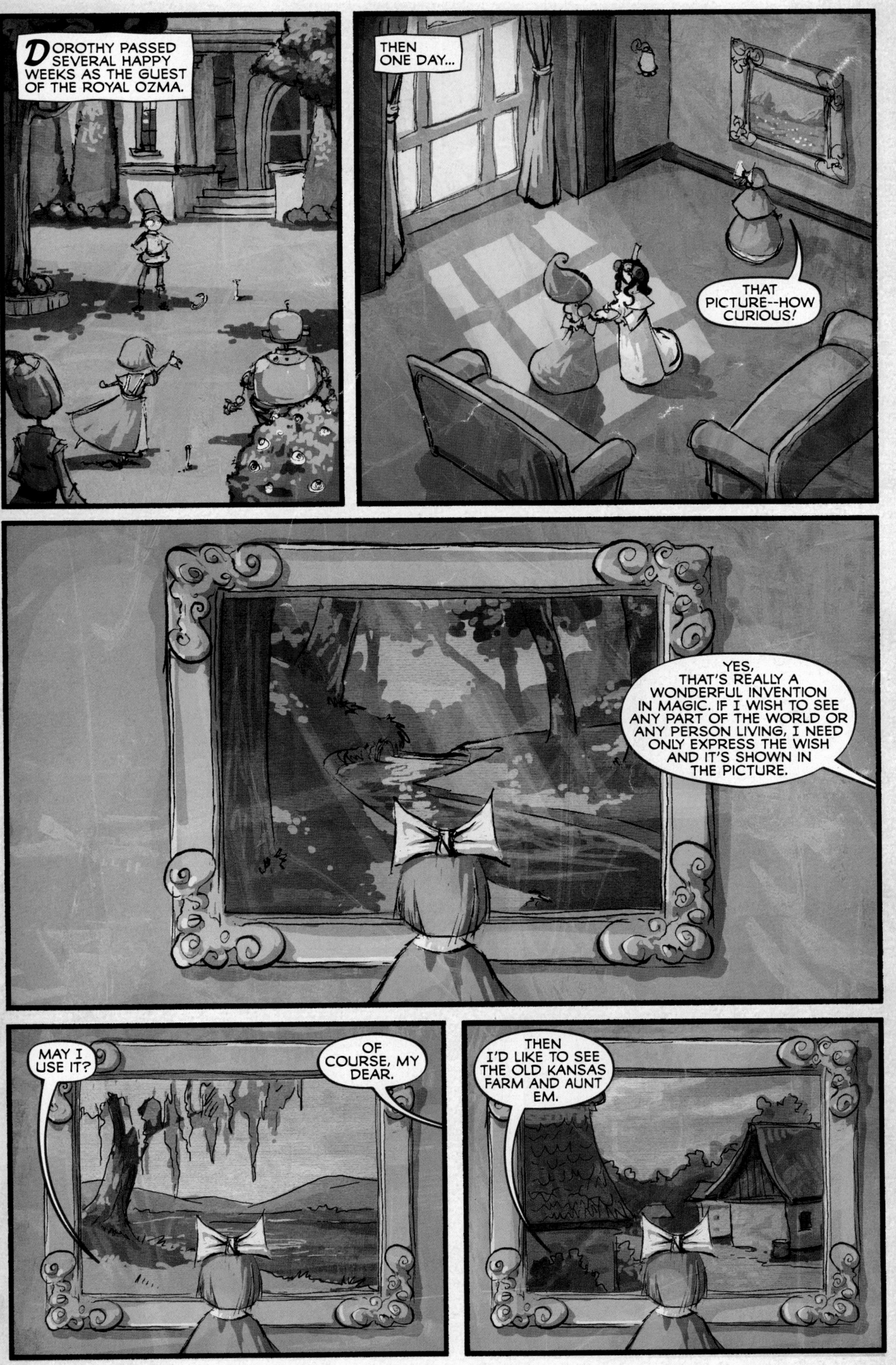
DOROTHY PASSED SEVERAL HAPPY WEEKS AS THE GUEST OF THE ROYAL OZMA.
THEN ONE DAY...
THAT PICTURE--HOW CURIOUS!
YES, THAT'S REALLY A WONDERFUL INVENTION IN MAGIC. IF I WISH TO SEE ANY PART OF THE WORLD OR ANY PERSON LIVING, I NEED ONLY EXPRESS THE WISH AND IT'S SHOWN IN THE PICTURE.
MAY I USE IT?
OF COURSE, MY DEAR.
THEN I'D LIKE TO SEE THE OLD KANSAS FARM AND AUNT EM.

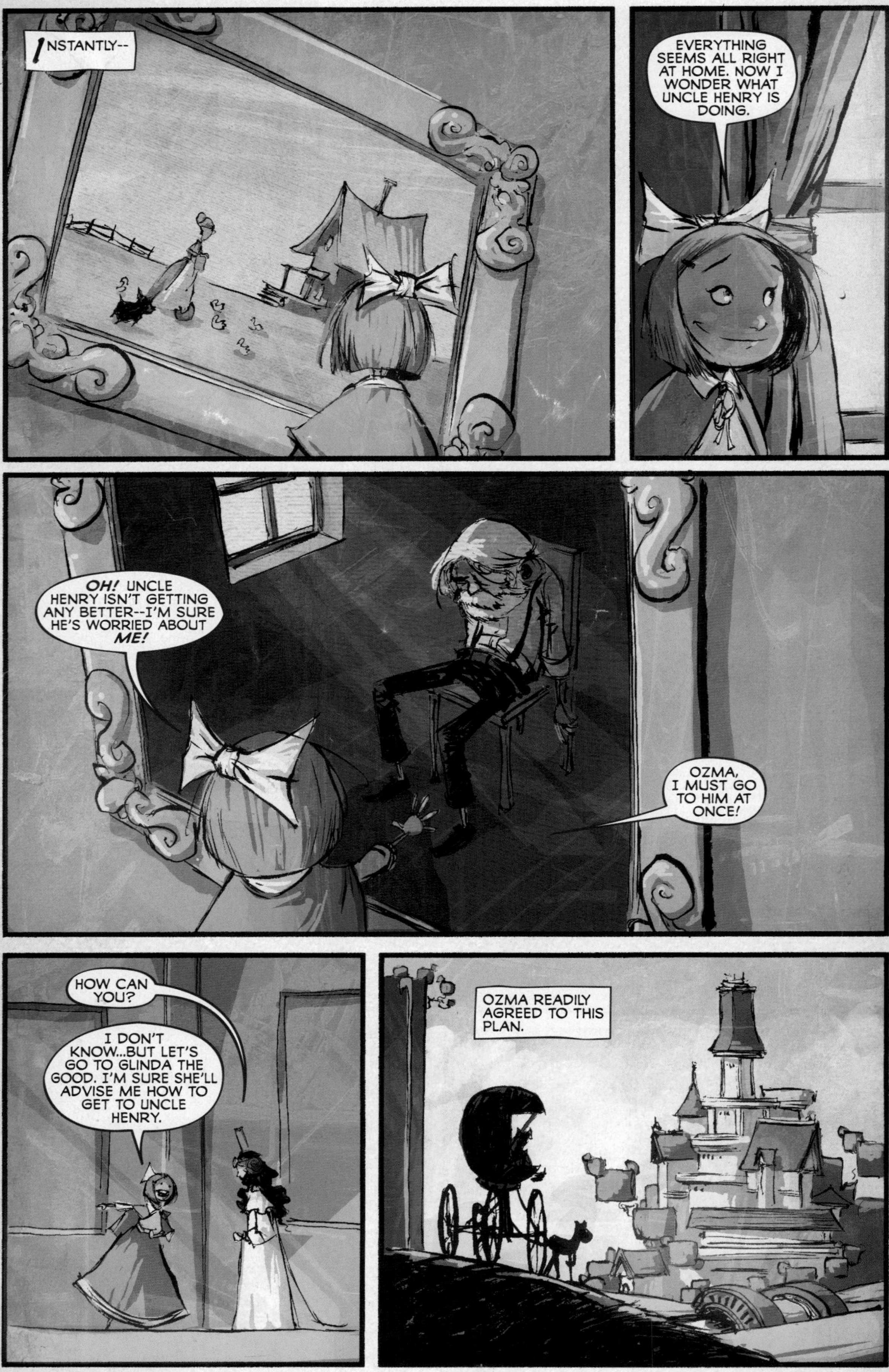
INSTANTLY--
EVERYTHING SEEMS ALL RIGHT AT HOME. NOW I WONDER WHAT UNCLE HENRY IS DOING.
OH! UNCLE HENRY ISN'T GETTING ANY BETTER--I'M SURE HE'S WORRIED ABOUT ME!
OZMA, I MUST GO TO HIM AT ONCE!
HOW CAN YOU?
I DON'T KNOW...BUT LET'S GO TO GLINDA THE GOOD. I'M SURE SHE'LL ADVISE ME HOW TO GET TO UNCLE HENRY.
OZMA READILY AGREED TO THIS PLAN.

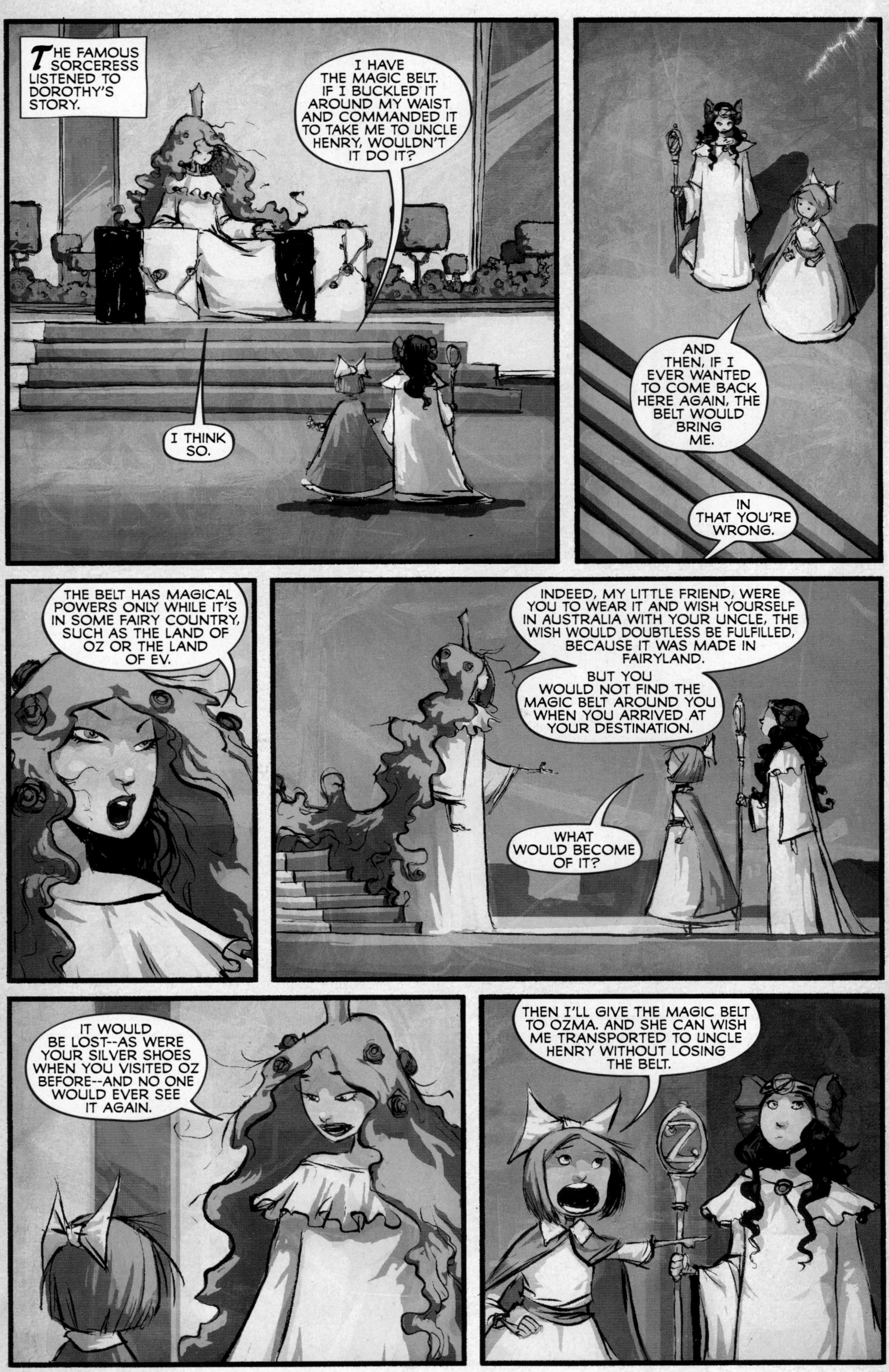
THE FAMOUS SORCERESS LISTENED TO DOROTHY'S STORY.
I HAVE THE MAGIC BELT. IF I BUCKLED IT AROUND MY WAIST AND COMMANDED IT TO TAKE ME TO UNCLE HENRY, WOULDN'T IT DO IT?
I THINK SO.
AND THEN, IF I EVER WANTED TO COME BACK HERE AGAIN, THE BELT WOULD BRING ME.
IN THAT YOU'RE WRONG.
THE BELT HAS MAGICAL POWERS ONLY WHILE IT'S IN SOME FAIRY COUNTRY, SUCH AS THE LAND OF OZ OR THE LAND OF EV.
INDEED, MY LITTLE FRIEND, WERE YOU TO WEAR IT AND WISH YOURSELF IN AUSTRALIA WITH YOUR UNCLE, THE WISH WOULD DOUBTLESS BE FULFILLED, BECAUSE IT WAS MADE IN FAIRYLAND.
BUT YOU WOULD NOT FIND THE MAGIC BELT AROUND YOU WHEN YOU ARRIVED AT YOUR DESTINATION.
WHAT WOULD BECOME OF IT?
IT WOULD BE LOST--AS WERE YOUR SILVER SHOES WHEN YOU VISITED OZ BEFORE--AND NO ONE WOULD EVER SEE IT AGAIN.
THEN I'LL GIVE THE MAGIC BELT TO OZMA. AND SHE CAN WISH ME TRANSPORTED TO UNCLE HENRY WITHOUT LOSING THE BELT.

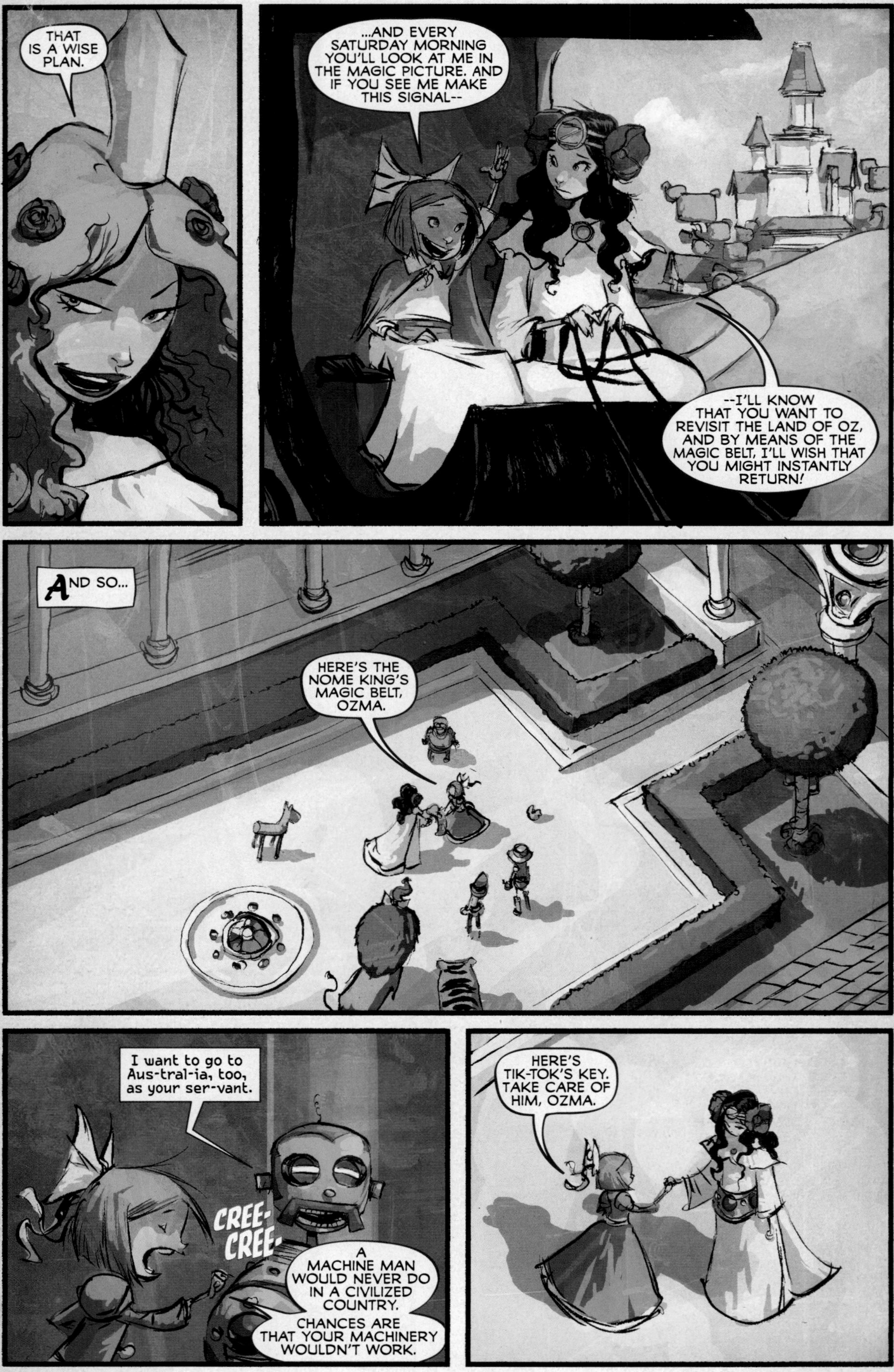
THAT IS A WISE PLAN.
...AND EVERY SATURDAY MORNING YOU'LL LOOK AT ME IN THE MAGIC PICTURE. AND IF YOU SEE ME MAKE THIS SIGNAL--
--I'LL KNOW THAT YOU WANT TO REVISIT THE LAND OF OZ, AND BY MEANS OF THE MAGIC BELT, I'LL WISH THAT YOU MIGHT INSTANTLY RETURN!
AND SO...
HERE'S THE NOME KING'S MAGIC BELT, OZMA.
I want to go to Aus-tral-ia, too, as your ser-vant.
CREE-CREE-
A MACHINE MAN WOULD NEVER DO IN A CIVILIZED COUNTRY.
CHANCES ARE THAT YOUR MACHINERY WOULDN'T WORK.
HERE'S TIK-TOK'S KEY. TAKE CARE OF HIM, OZMA.

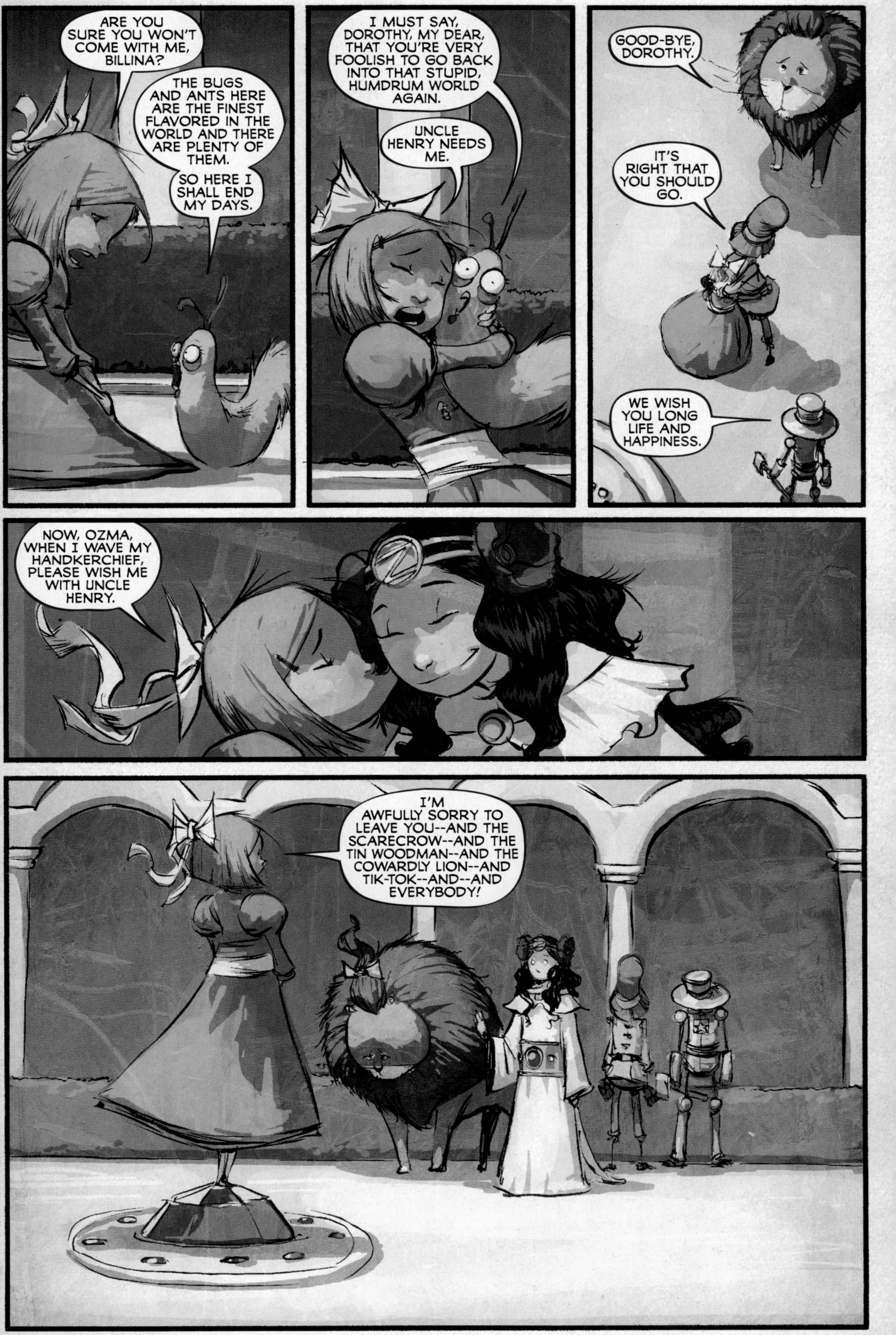
ARE YOU SURE YOU WON'T COME WITH ME, BILLINA?
THE BUGS AND ANTS HERE ARE THE FINEST FLAVORED IN THE WORLD AND THERE ARE PLENTY OF THEM.
SO HERE I SHALL END MY DAYS.
I MUST SAY, DOROTHY, MY DEAR, THAT YOU'RE VERY FOOLISH TO GO BACK INTO THAT STUPID, HUMDRUM WORLD AGAIN.
UNCLE HENRY NEEDS ME.
GOOD-BYE, DOROTHY.
IT'S RIGHT THAT YOU SHOULD GO.
WE WISH YOU LONG LIFE AND HAPPINESS.
NOW, OZMA, WHEN I WAVE MY HANDKERCHIEF, PLEASE WISH ME WITH UNCLE HENRY.
I'M AWFULLY SORRY TO LEAVE YOU--AND THE SCARECROW--AND THE TIN WOODMAN--AND THE COWARDLY LION--AND TIK-TOK--AND--AND EVERYBODY!

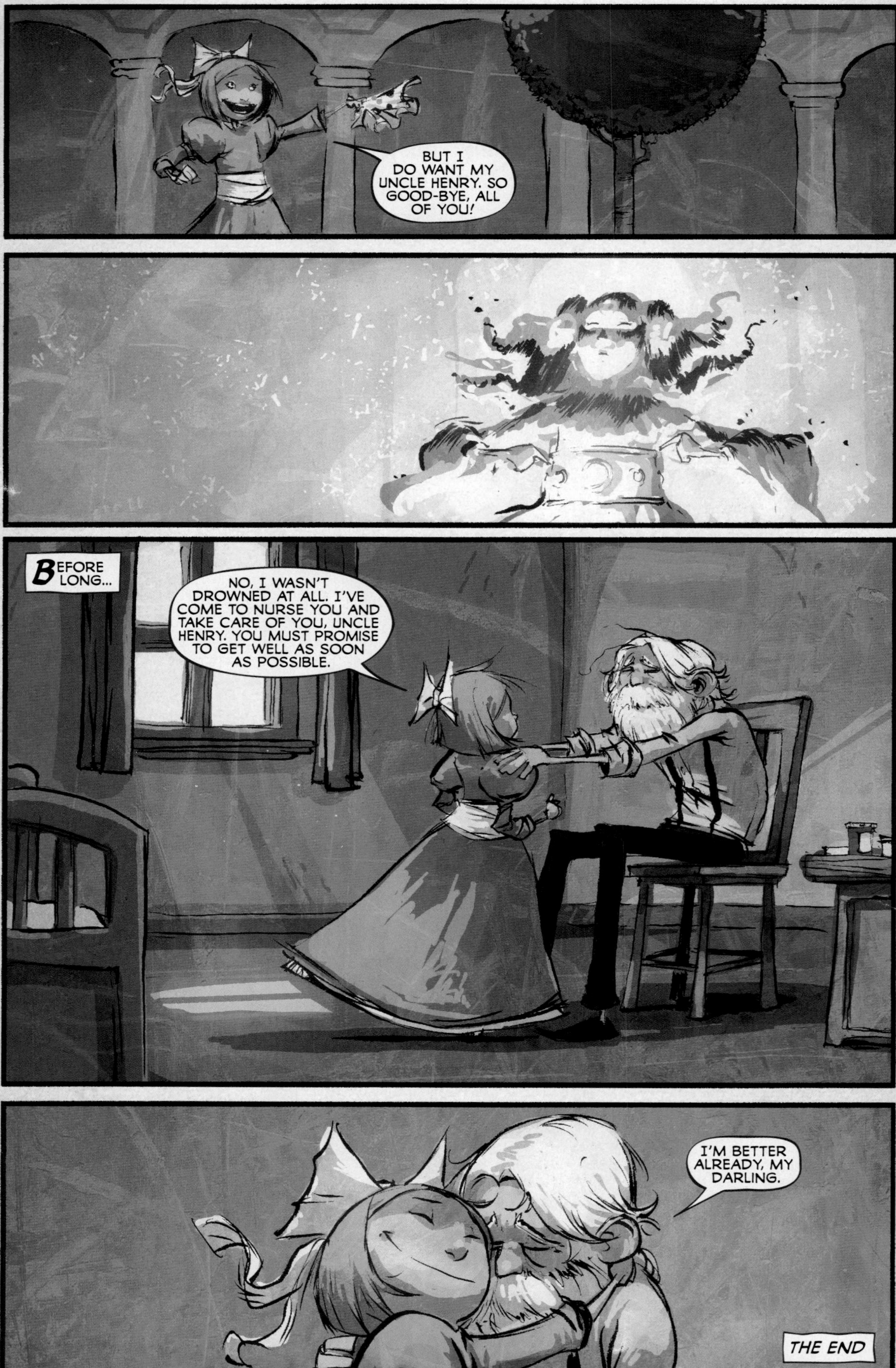
BUT I DO WANT MY UNCLE HENRY. SO GOOD-BYE, ALL OF YOU!
BEFORE LONG...
NO, I WASN'T DROWNED AT ALL. I'VE COME TO NURSE YOU AND TAKE CARE OF YOU, UNCLE HENRY. YOU MUST PROMISE TO GET WELL AS SOON AS POSSIBLE.
I'M BETTER ALREADY, MY DARLING.
THE END

THE STORY CONTINUES IN...

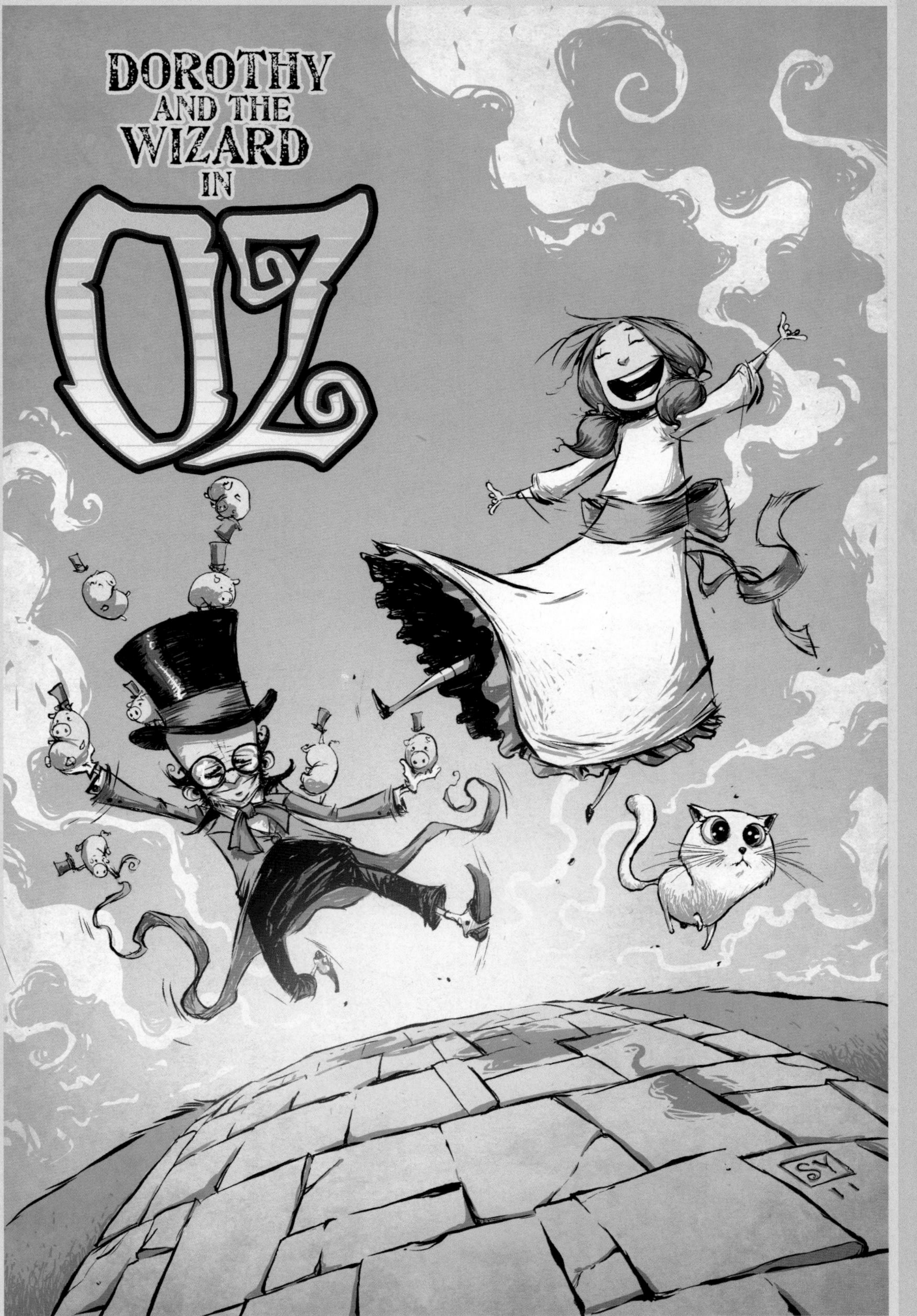
DOROTHY
AND THE
WIZARD
IN
OZ
SY

ONE

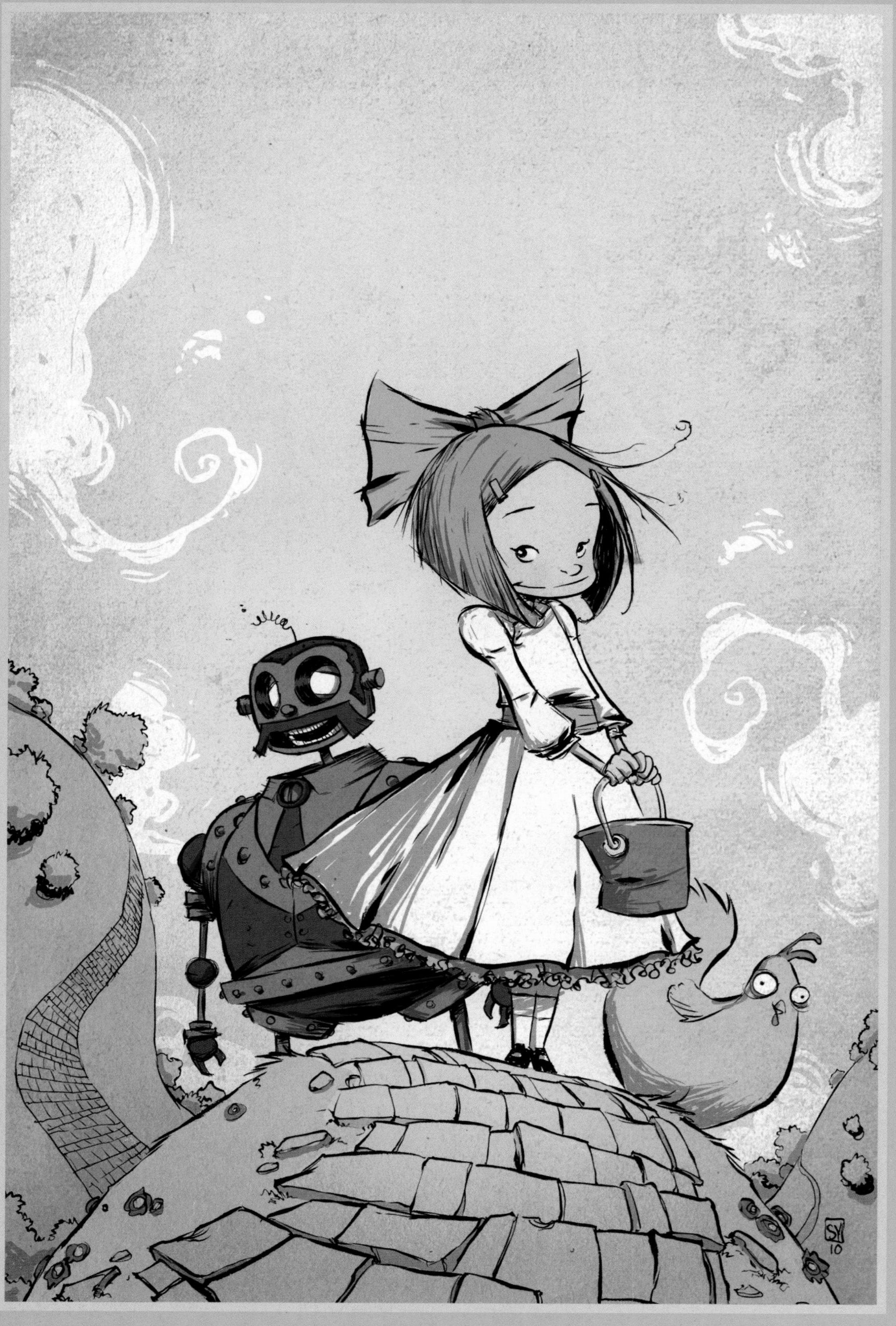
SY
10

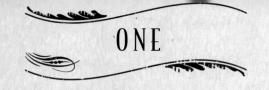

ONE

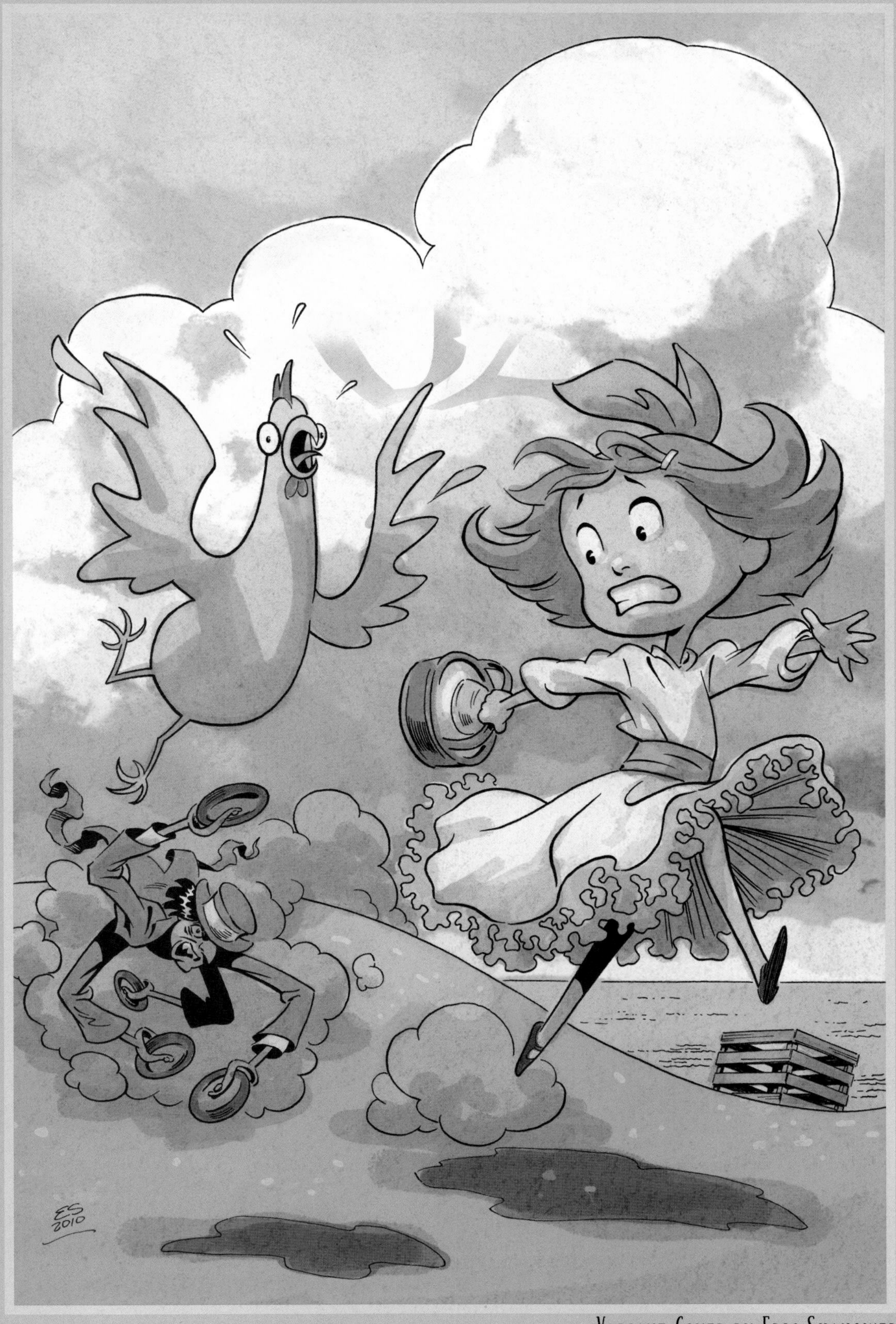
ES
2010

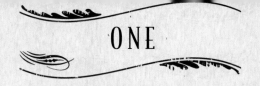

Variant Cover by Eric Shanower

ONE

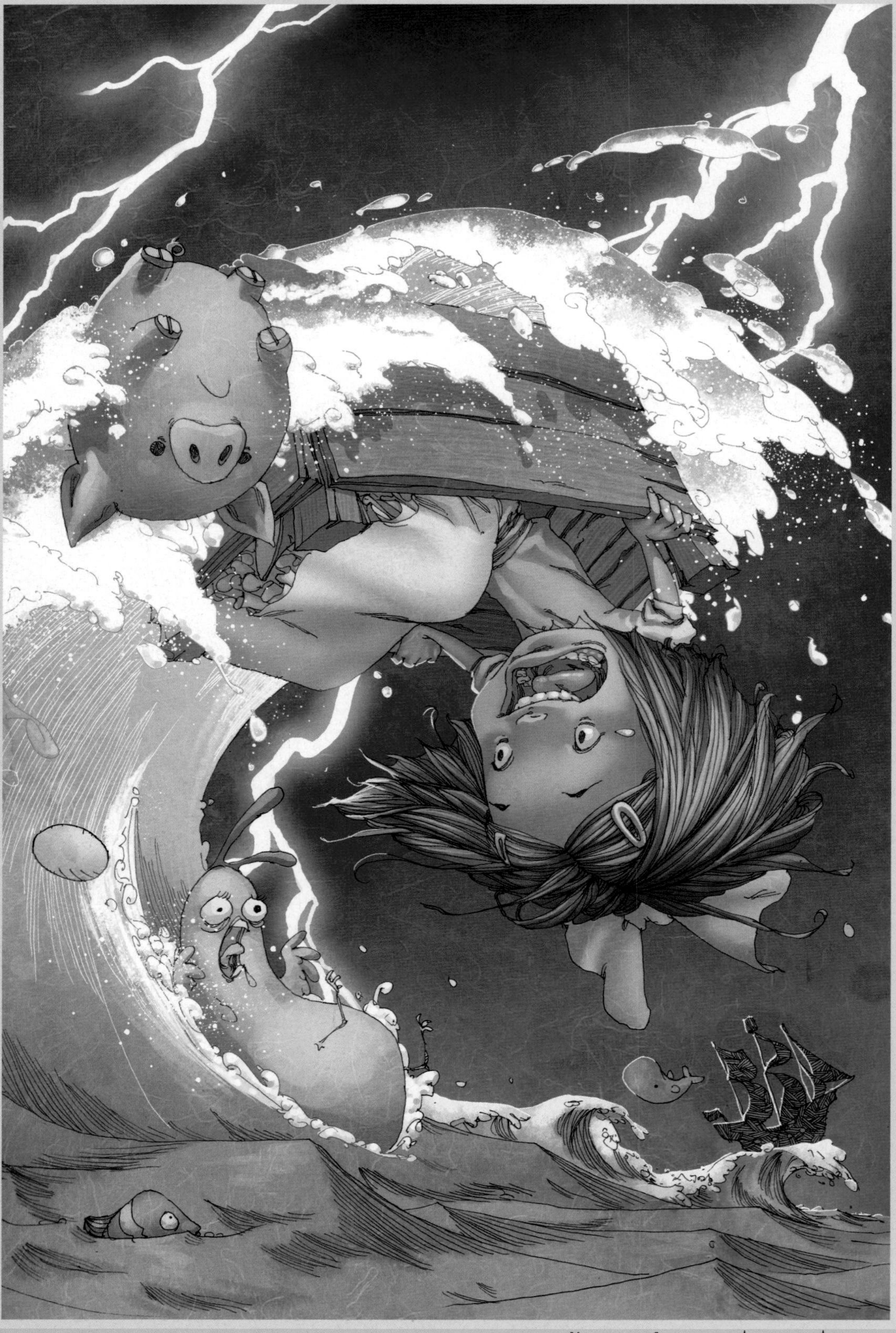

Variant Cover by Adrian Alphona

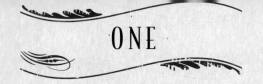

TWO

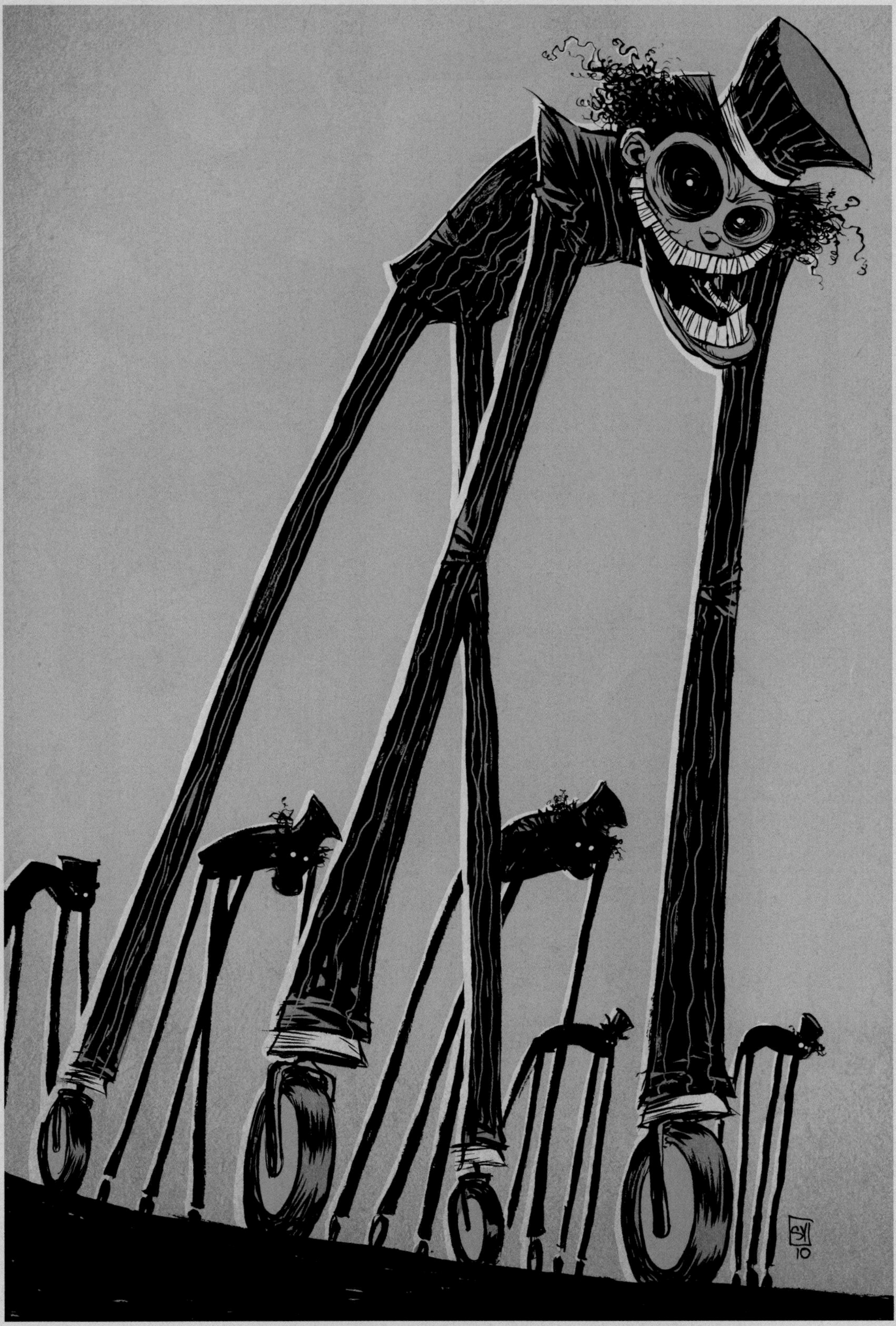

THREE

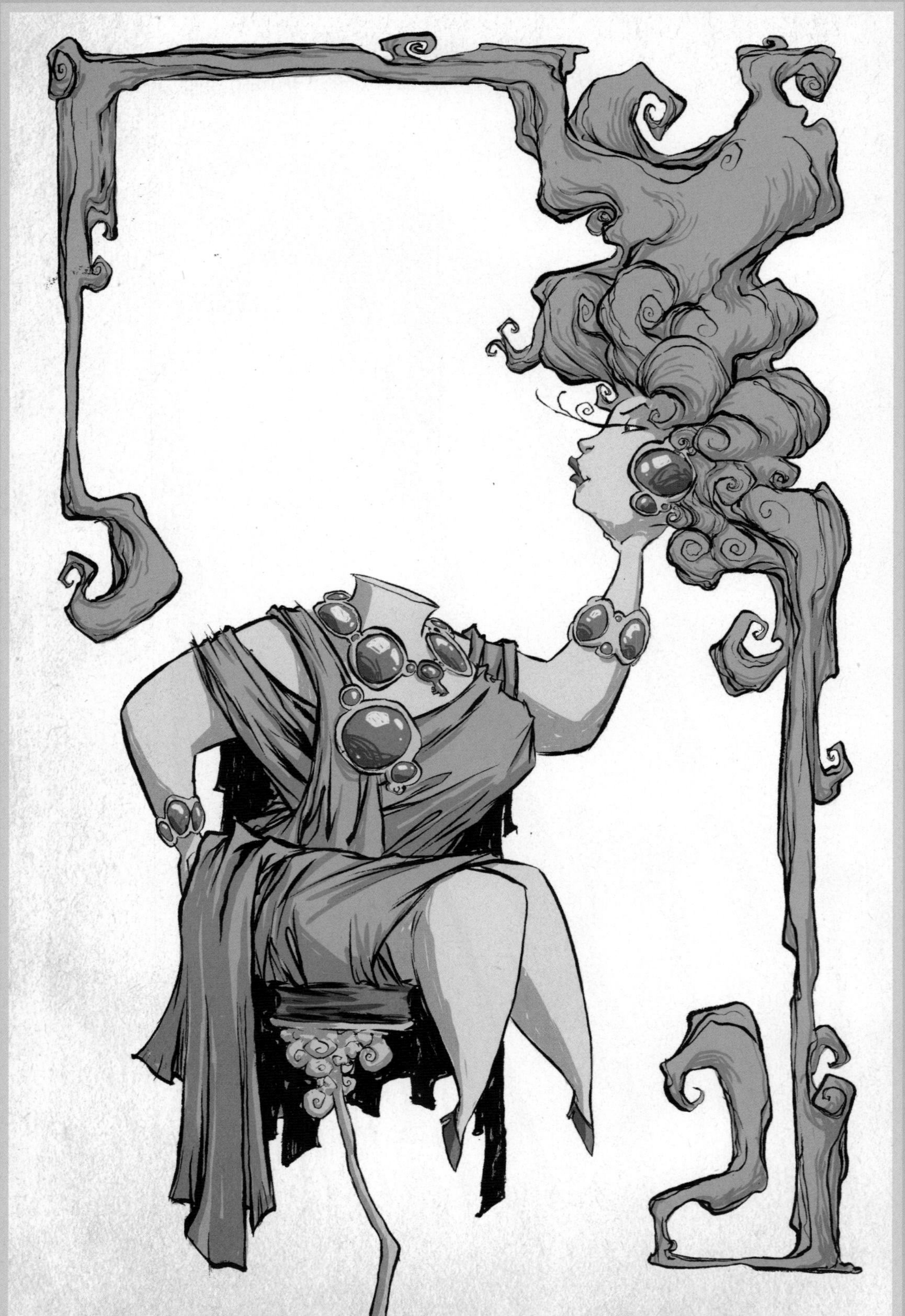

FOUR

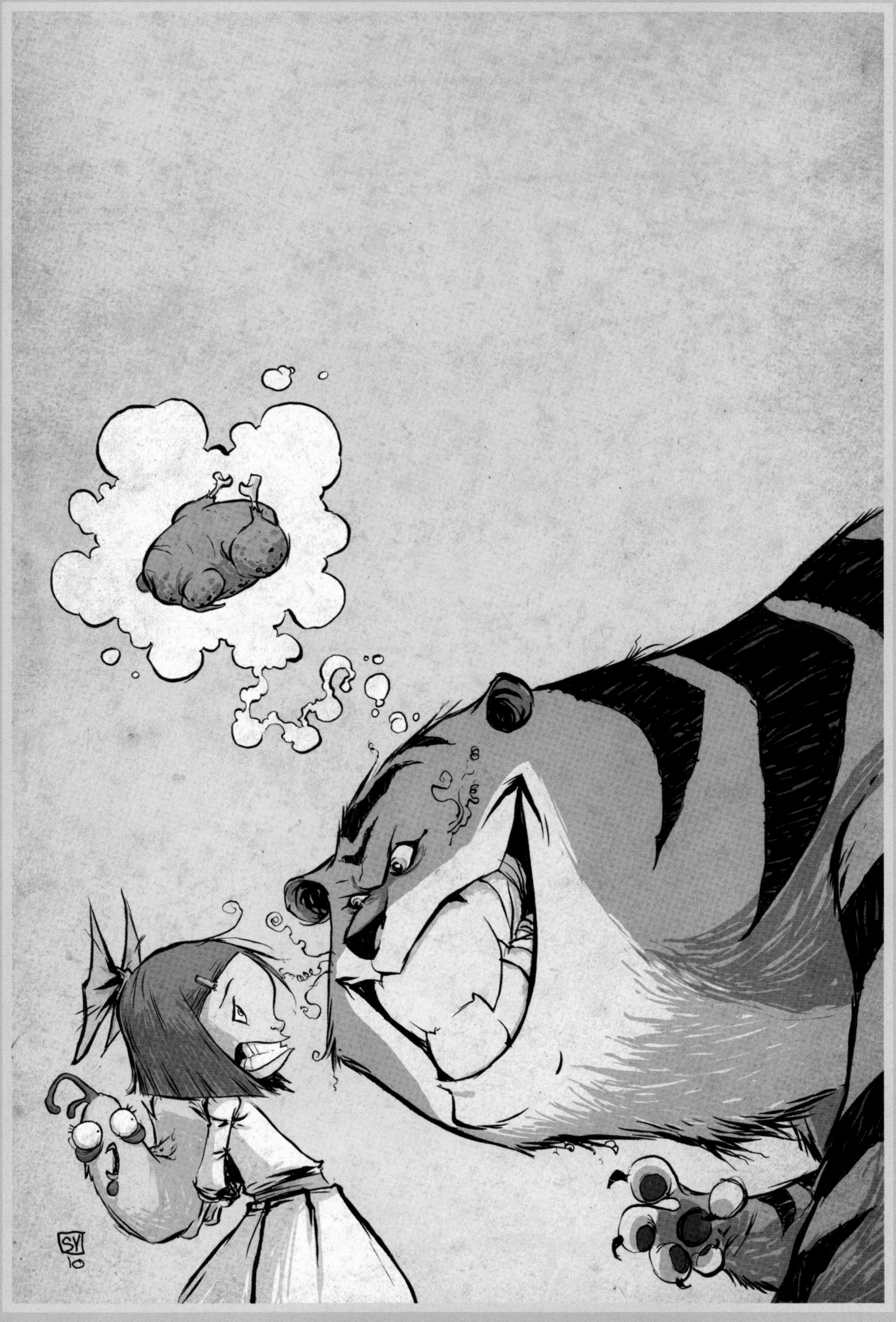

SY
10

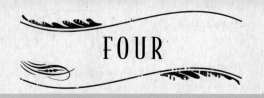

FIVE

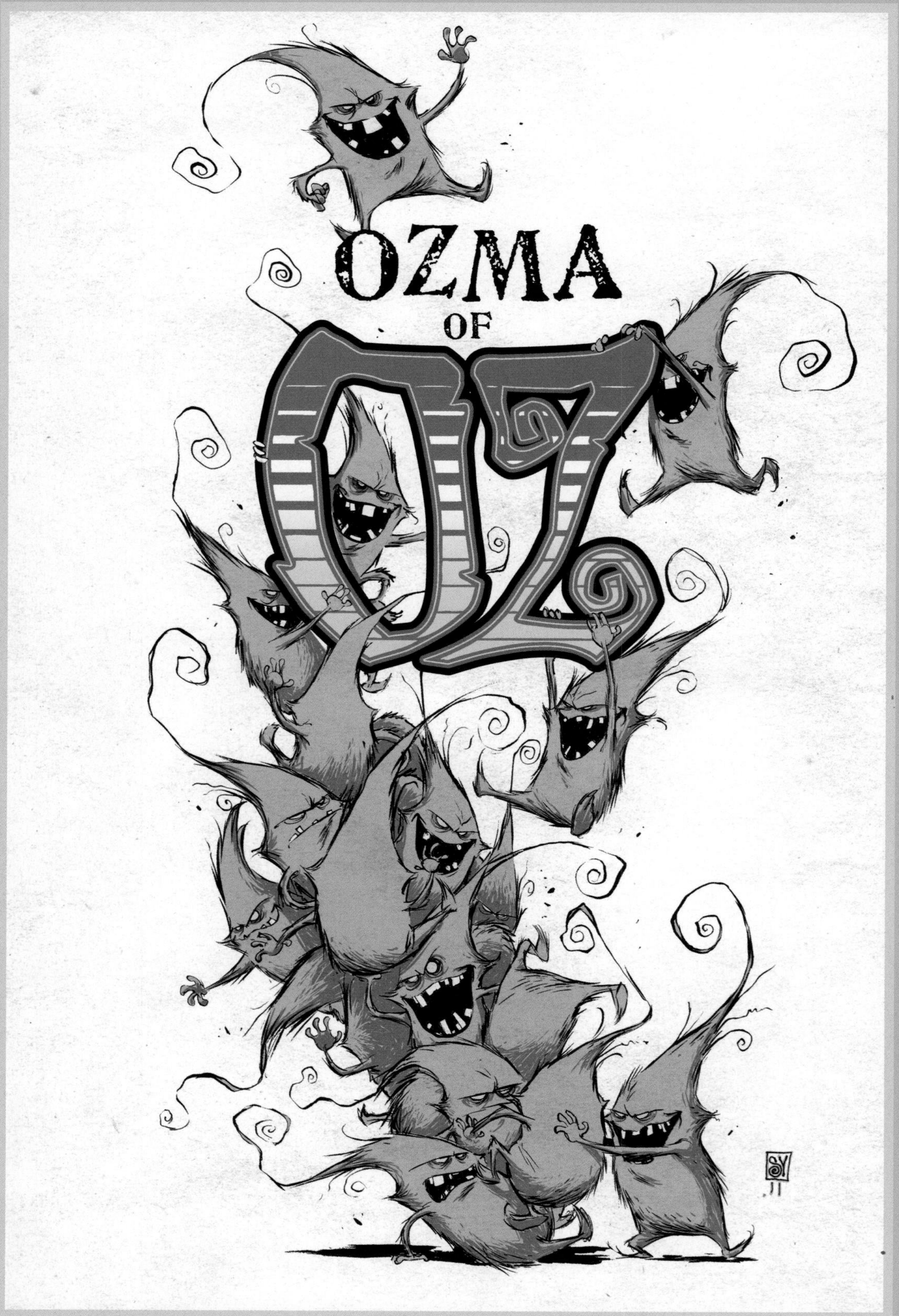
OZMA
OF
OZ

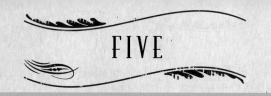

SIX

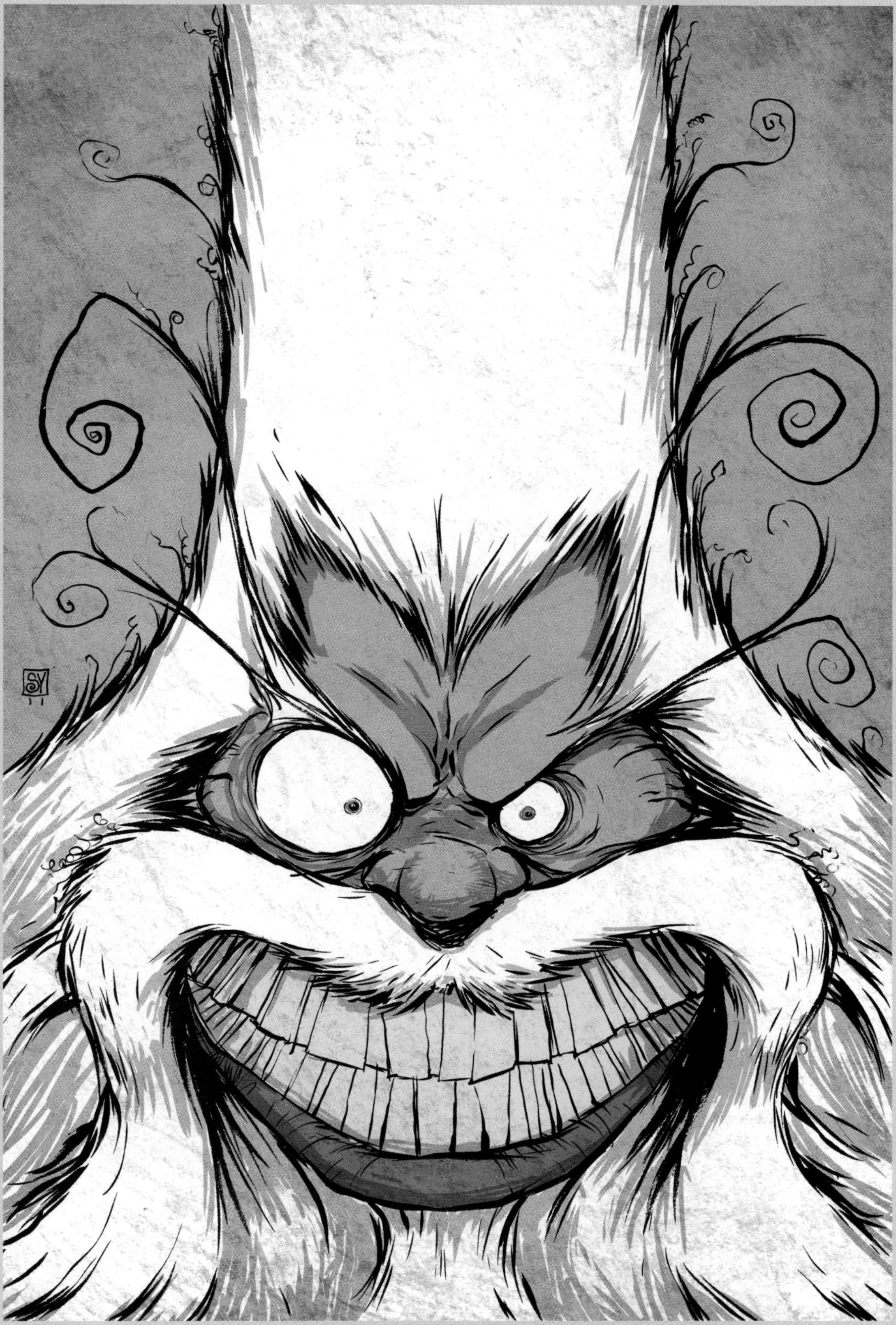

SEVEN

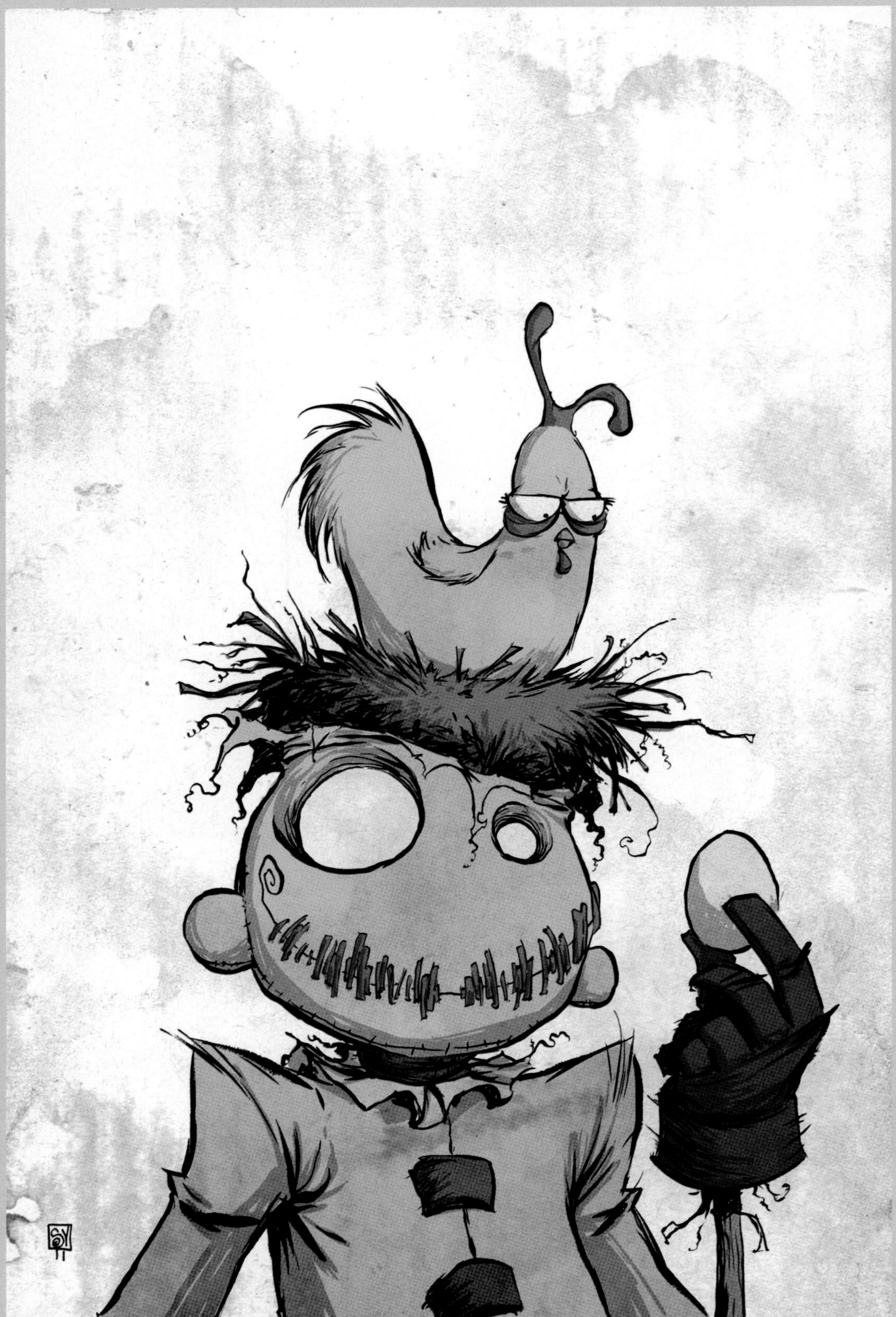

EIGHT

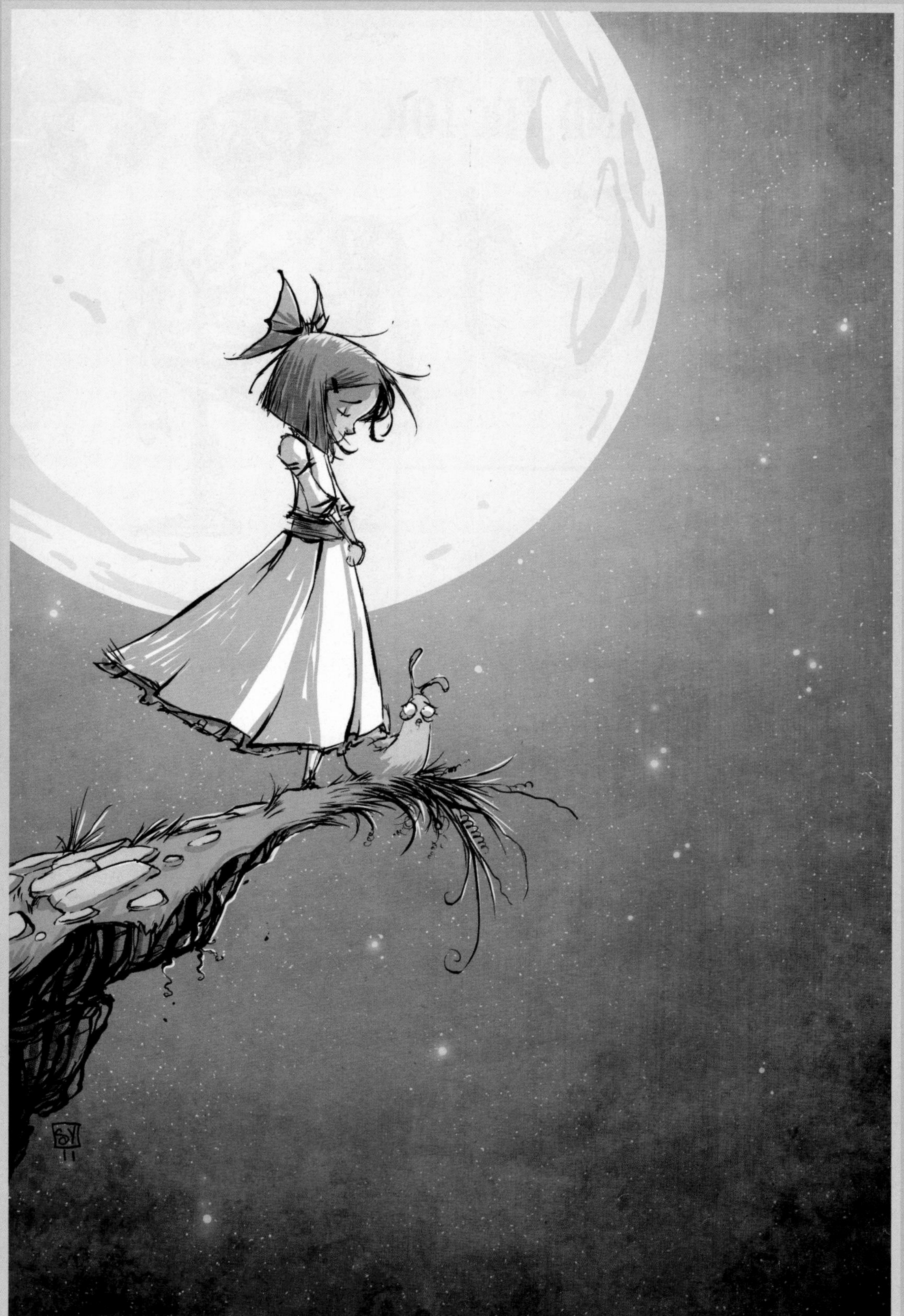

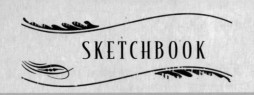

Billina and Tik Tok

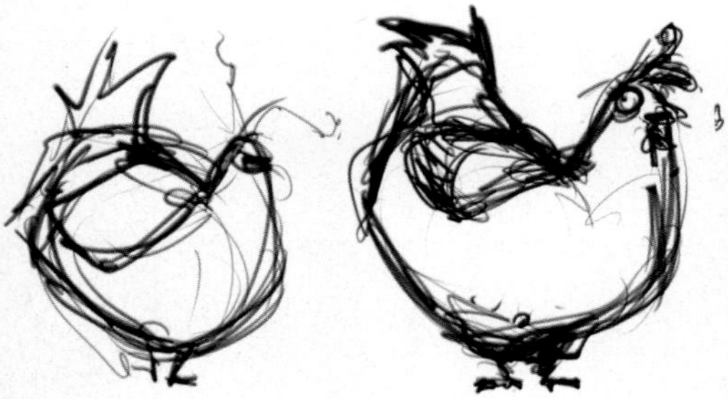

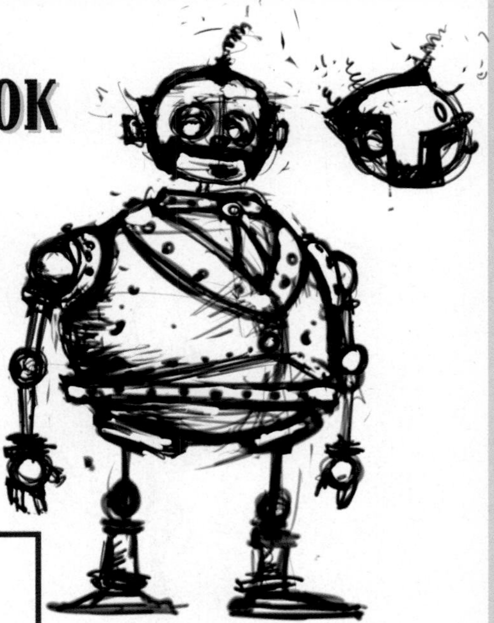

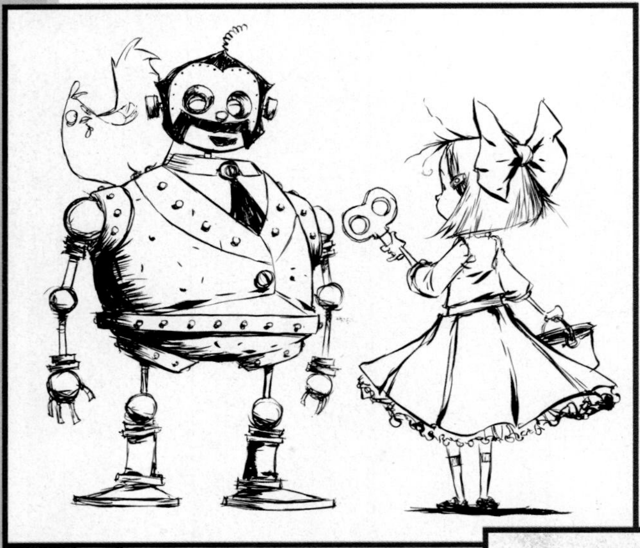

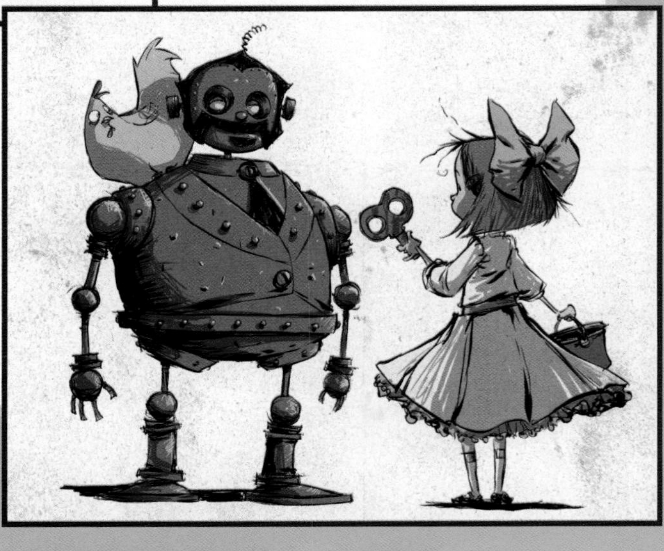

ISSUE ONE COVER PROCESS

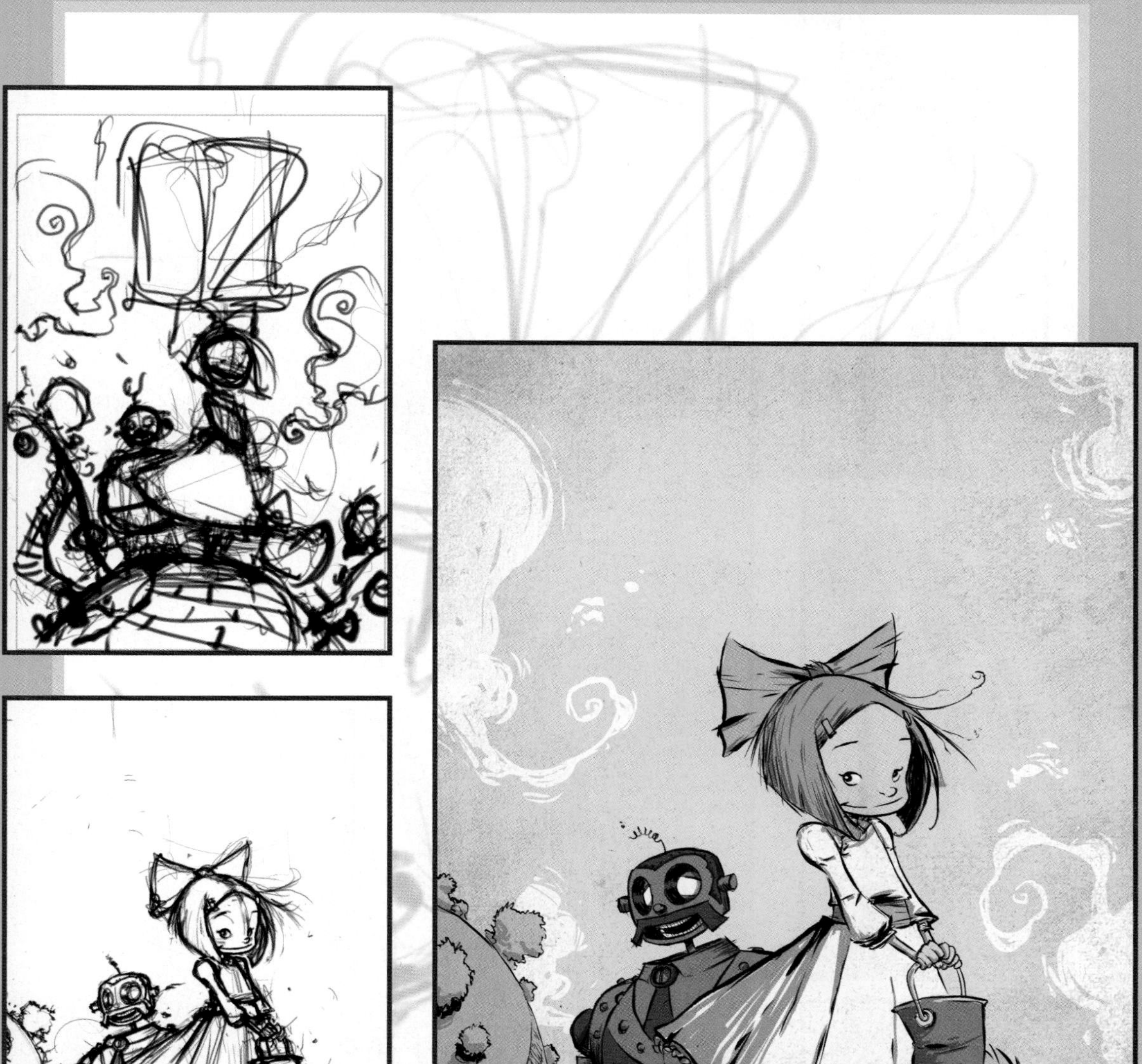

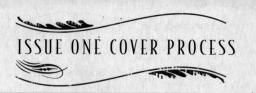

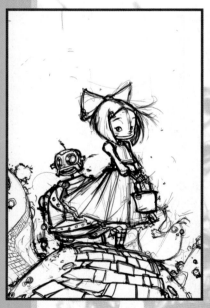

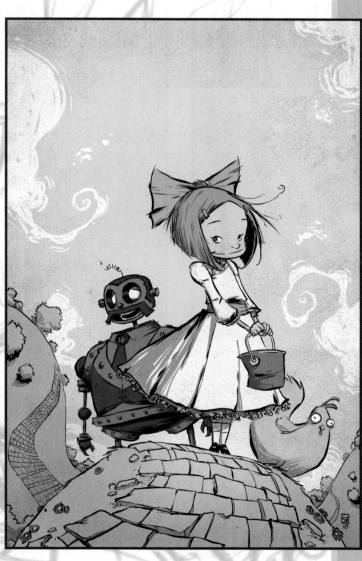

ISSUE TWO COVER PROCESS

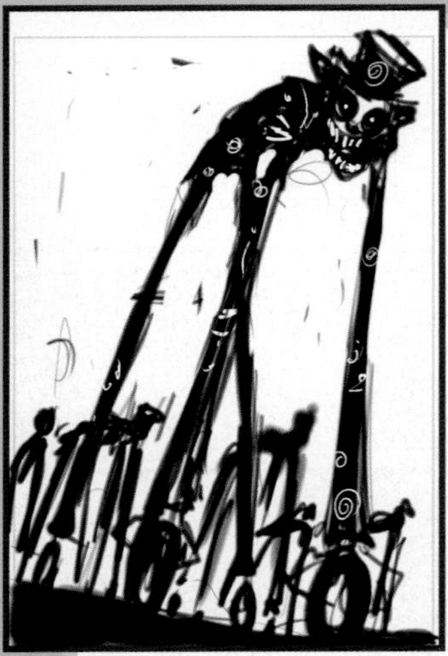

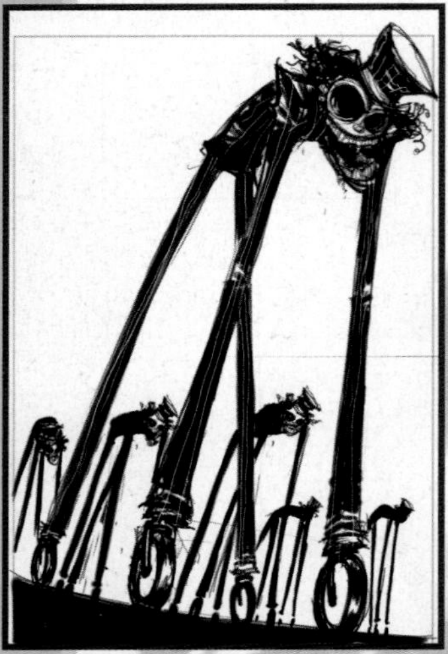

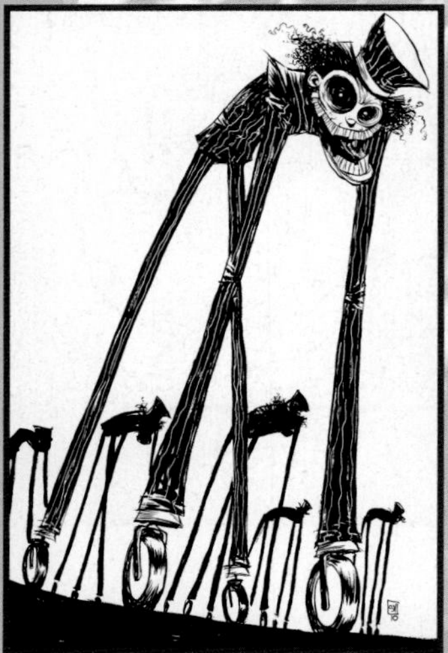

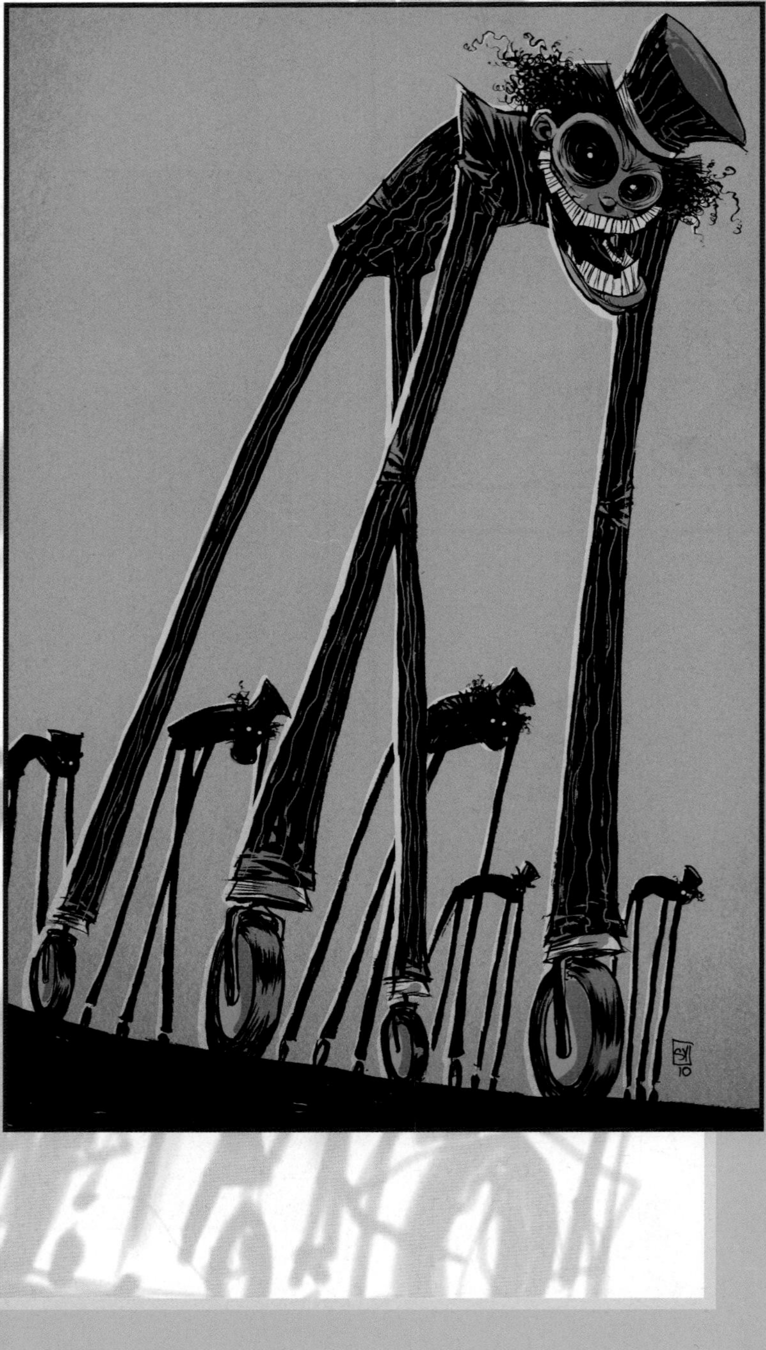

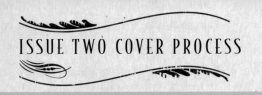

ISSUE ONE, PAGE 6 PROCESS

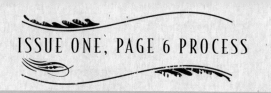

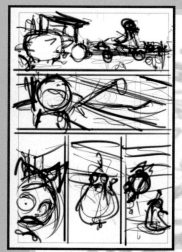

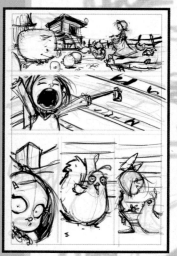

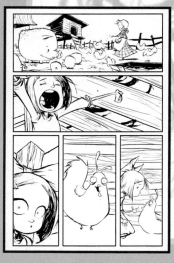

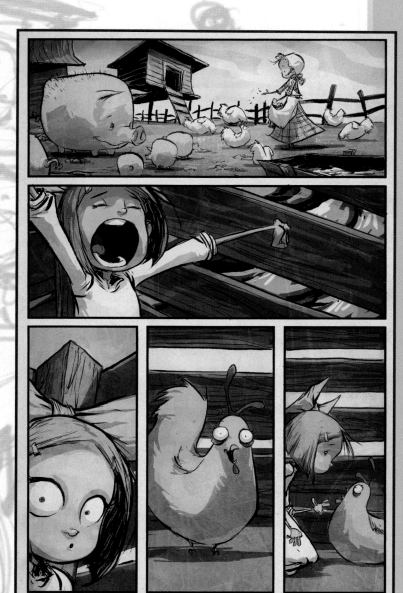

ISSUE THREE, PAGES 10–11 PROCESS

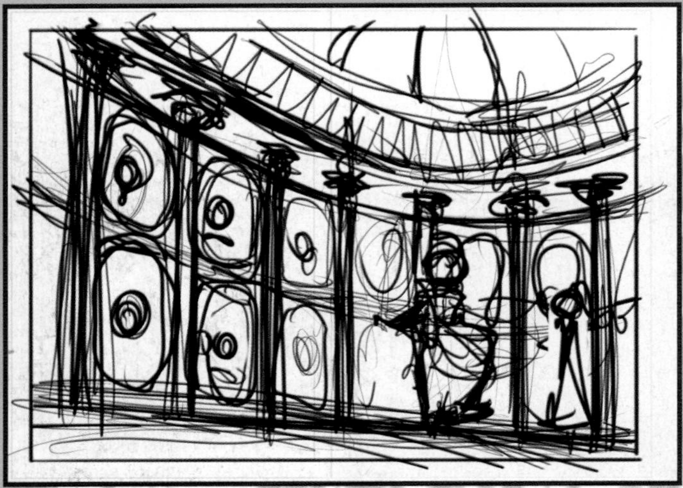

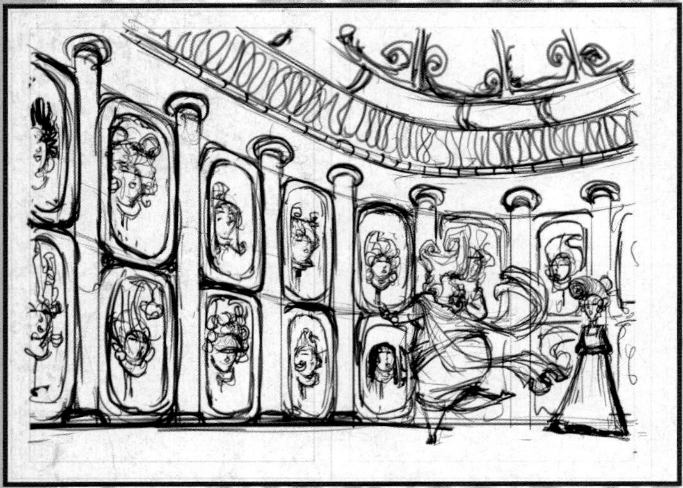

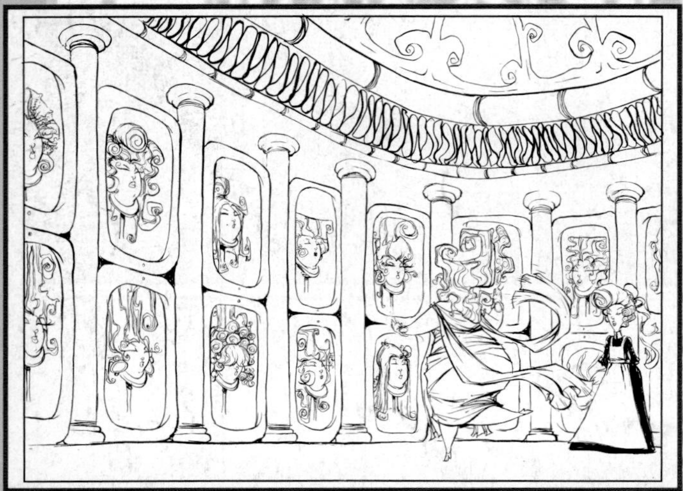

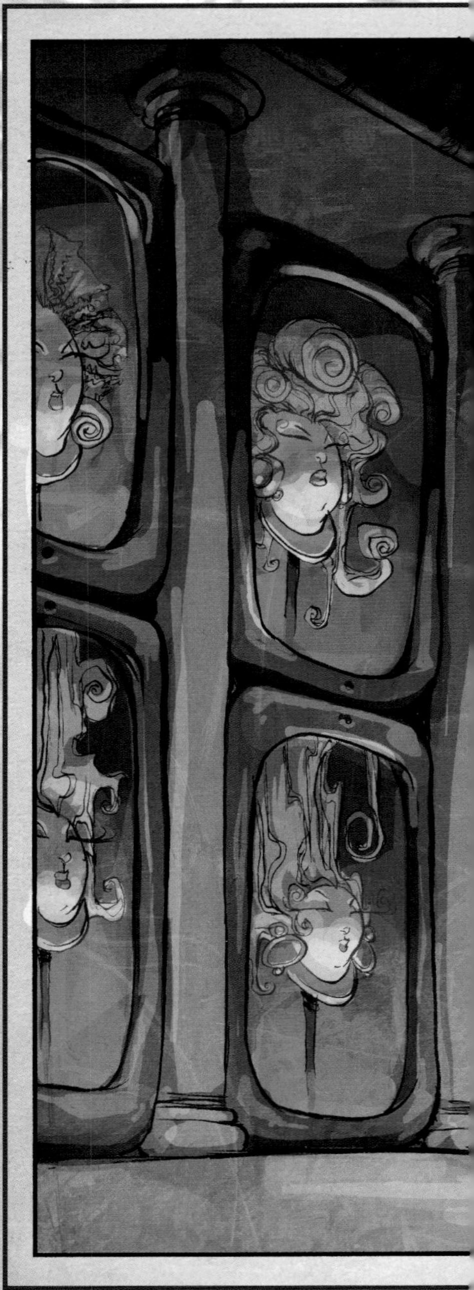

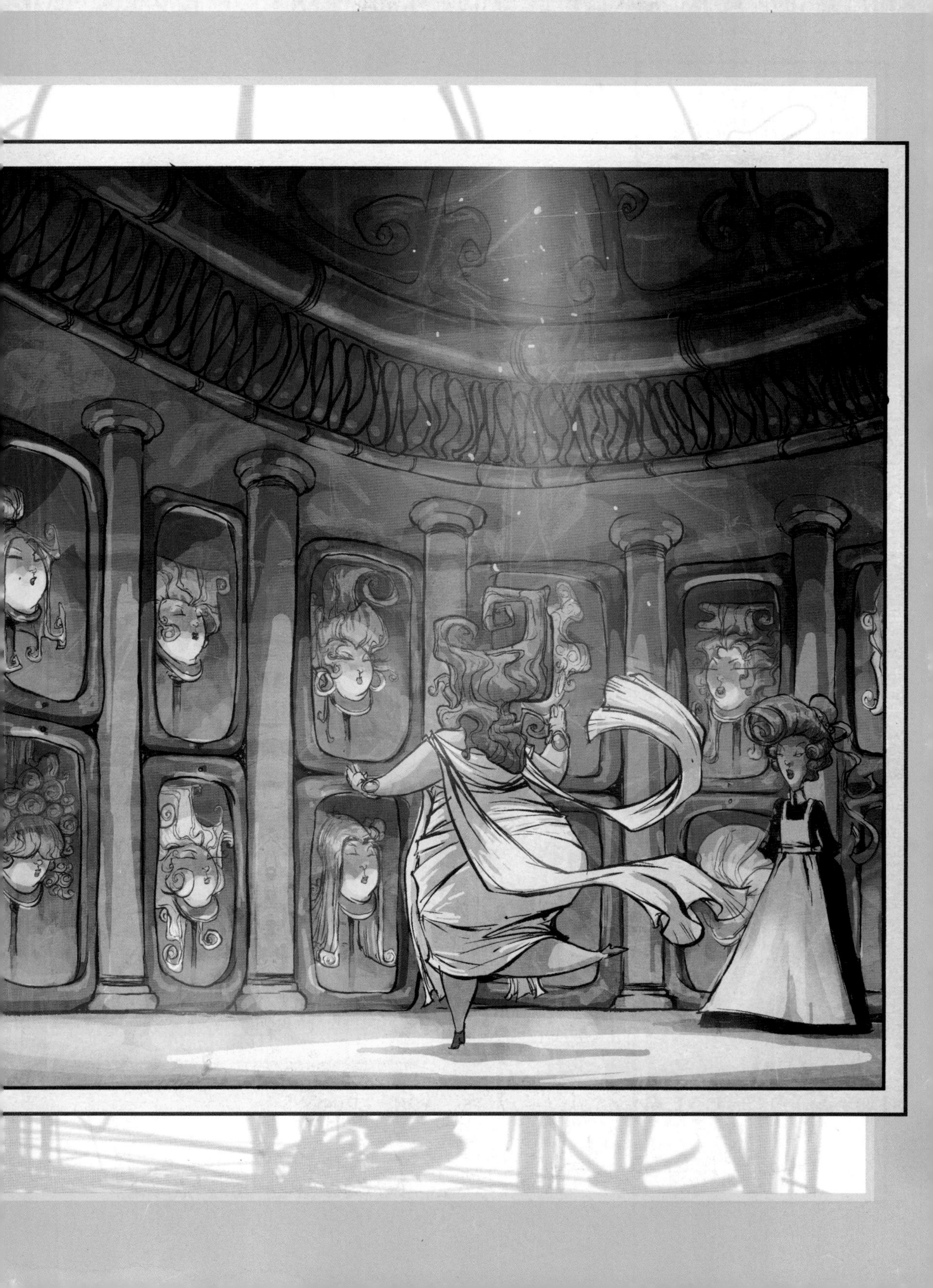

ISSUE SEVEN, PAGE 15 PROCESS

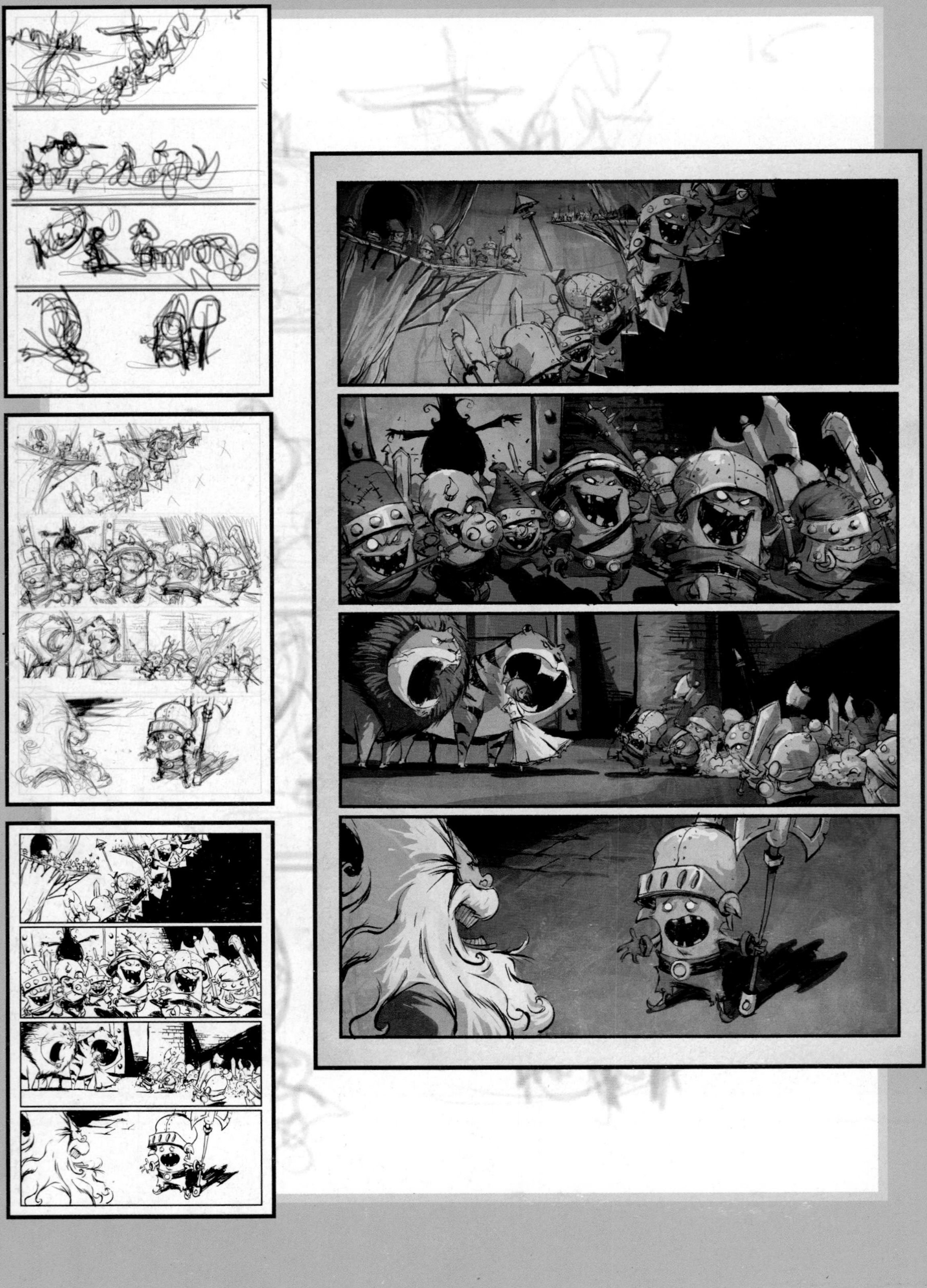